POST-FORDISM

A READER

Edited by Ash Amin

BLACKWELL
Publishers

Introduction and editorial arrangement
copyright © Blackwell Publishers Ltd 1994
Other copyright © as stated as the end of each chapter

First published 1994
Reprinted 1995, 1996, 1997, 2000
Transferred to Digital print 2003

Blackwell Publishers Ltd
108 Cowley Road
Oxford OX4 1JF, UK

Blackwell Publishers Inc
350 Main Street
Malden, Massachusetts 02148, USA

British Library Cataloguing in Publication Data
A CIP catalogue record for this book is available from the British Library

Library of Congress Cataloging in Publication Data
Post-Fordism: a reader/edited by Ash Amin.
  p. cm. — (Studies in urban and social change)
 Includes bibliographical references (p.)and index.
 ISBN 0–631–18856–8 (acid-free paper)
 ISBN 0–631–18857–6 (pbk: acid-free paper)
  1. Technological innovations—Economic aspects. 2. Technological
innovations—Social aspects. 3. Industrial organization.
4. Capitalism. 5. Regional economic disparities. I. Amin, Ash.
II. Series.
HC79.T4P667   1995   94 10761
338'.064—dc20   CIP

Typeset in 10.5 on 12pt Baskerville
by Colset Pte Ltd, Singapore

Printed and bound in Great Britain by
Marston Lindsay Ross International,
Oxfordshire

Contents

Contributors

Ash Amin is Professor of Geography at the University of Newcastle upon Tyne, UK.

Susan Christopherson is Associate Professor in the Department of City and Regional Planning and Cornell University, USA.

Mark Elam is Research Fellow in the Department of Technology and Social Change at Linköping University, Sweden.

Josef Esser is Professor of Political Science at the Goethe University in Frankfurt, Germany.

Mike Featherstone is Professor of Sociology at Teesside University, UK.

David Harvey is Professor of Geography at the Johns Hopkins University in Baltimore, USA.

Joachim Hirsch is Professor of Political Science at the Goethe University in Frankfurt, Germany.

Bob Jessop is Professor of Sociology at Lancaster University, UK.

Alain Lipietz is Director of Research at CEPREMAP in Paris, France.

Anders Malmberg is Lecturer in the Department of Social and Economic Geography at Uppsala University, Sweden.

Margit Mayer is Professor of Politics at the Free University in Berlin, Germany.

Jamie Peck is Lecturer in Geography at Manchester University, UK.

Charles Sabel is Professor of Sociology at the Massachusetts Institute of Technology, USA.

Michael Storper is Professor of Regional and International Development at the University of California, Los Angeles, USA.

John Tomaney is Lecturer in Geography at the University of Newcastle upon Tyne, UK.

Adam Tickell is Lecturer in Geography at Leeds University, UK.

Acknowledgements

The publishers and editor are grateful to the following for permission to reproduce material.

Sage Publications Ltd for chapter 2, reprinted from Mark Elam, Puzzling out the post-Fordist debate, in *Economic and Industrial Debate*, volume 11, © 1990; and for chapter 13, reprinted from Mike Featherstone, *Consumer Culture and Postmodernism*, © 1991.

Charles Sabel and Berg Publishers for chapter 4, reprinted from Charles Sabel, Flexible specialisation and the re-emergence of regional economies, in P. Hirst and J. Zeitlin (eds) *Reversing Industrial Decline?*, pages 17–70, © 1989.

Michael Storper for chapter 6.

Pion Limited for chapter 7, reprinted from A. Amin and A. Malmberg, Competing structural and institutional influences on the geography of production in Europe, in *Environment and Planning A*, volume 24, © 1992.

David Harvey for chapter 12.

1

Post-Fordism: Models, Fantasies and Phantoms cf Transition

Ash Amin

INTRODUCTION

These appear to be times of bewildering transformation and change in the structure and organization of modern Western economy and society. It seems that capitalism is at a crossroads in its historical development signalling the emergence of forces – technological, market, social and institutional – that will be very different from those which dominated the economy after the Second World War. Though not uncontroversial, there is an emerging consensus in the social sciences that the period since the mid-1970s represents a transition from one distinct phase of capitalist development to a new phase. Thus, there is a sense that these are times of epoch-making transformation in the very forces which drive, stabilize and reproduce the capitalist world. Terms such as 'structural crisis', 'transformation' and 'transition' have become common descriptors of the present, while new epithets such as 'post-Fordist', 'post-industrial', 'post-modern', 'fifth Kondratiev' and 'post-collective' have been coined by the academic prophets of our times to describe the emerging new age of capitalism.

One observer, Ernest Sternberg (1993), lists no fewer than eight potential new ages. The first is the information age, which will generate wealth through the exercise of knowledge, trade in information activities and the potentialities for information technology. The second is the age of post-modernity, which will extend the frontier of consumerism into all areas of social and private life, including aesthetics, art, leisure, recreation and pleasure. Third, Sternberg refers to the age of global interdependence, to convey a sense of the pervasive globalization of production, finance, distribution and trade within the contemporary economy, a process which increasingly bestraddles and shapes local and national fortunes. The fourth trend identified is a new mercantilism, which Sternberg describes as an age in which national coalitions (industry–government–labour) will seek to develop strategic technological advantage as a basis for national prosperity. Fifth is a new age of corporate control, in which global corporations and banks will exercise systemic power over markets, firms and states; shaping consumption patterns in every corner of the world and run by a new global class of executives and professionals living in select world cities. The sixth age is the age of 'flexible specialization', characterized by new principles in production, including specialist units of production, decentralized management and versatile technologies and workforces, to satisfy increasingly volatile markets. Seventh is the age of new social movements working to 'humanize' the new capitalism and to negotiate for a 'social economy' which might incorporate the rights of minorities and women as well as guarantee ecological sensitivity, economic security and basic human needs. It will contrast with the social movements of the passing age, said to be organized around lines of class and nationality, and often in the name of anti-capitalist and anti-establishment goals. Finally, Sternberg identifies the rise of an age of fundamentalist rejection in many parts of the world of the technocracy and consumerism of the new information age, in defence of territorial or ethnic identities rooted in pre-enlightenment religious or communitarian traditions and values.

Which of these purported new ages will consolidate or combine into the next millenium remains an open and vexed issue. Equally contested is the issue of whether the emerging new trends represent a radical break with the past or a refinement or modification of old trends. New or not, it seems indisputable that the salience of so many of the icons of the age of mass industrialization and mass consumerism appears to be diminishing. Under threat in the West appears to be the centrality of large industrial complexes, blue-collar work, full employment, centralized bureaucracies of management, mass markets for cheap standardized goods, the welfare state, mass political parties and the centrality of the national state as a unit of organization. While, of course, each individual trend is open to dispute, taken together they make it difficult to avoid a sense that an old way of doing things might be disappearing or becoming reorganized.

The 'post-Fordist' debate concerns the nature and direction of such epoch-making change. It is a debate about the putative transition from one dominant phase of capitalist development in the post-war period to another thirty to fifty year cycle of development based upon very different economic, societal and political norms. It seeks to identify the driving forces in each historical phase and, through this process, to elaborate how these forces constitute a paradigm or system capable of securing relative economic stability over the long term. Different positions within the debate each accept that history can be periodized into distinct phases, guided by a coherent frame of dominant principles, but giving way to a period of uncertainty and transition during which the elements of a new paradigm may develop and mature.

Such a theorization of historical evolution and change is not unchallenged, which is one reason why the literature on post-Fordism must be considered as a debate rather than an achieved or universally accepted theory of transition. Indeed, the entire project of periodizing capitalist history has been criticized in particular from within a Marxist tradition which stresses the dialectical and evolutionary nature of historical change. Critics of the post-Fordist literature, many of them gathered around the Conference of Socialist Economists in Britain and its journal *Capital and Class*, tend to reject the debate for its functionalist or systemic theorization of the historical process, preferring instead an approach which stresses the non path-dependent, contested and open nature of change in class societies (Rustin, 1989; Clarke, 1990; Bonefeld and Holloway, 1991; Pollert, 1991; Psychopedis, 1991). They also criticize the idea of absolute turning points, 'rules of transition' and clear breaks between distinct phases or stages of development, preferring instead a more evolutionary interpretation of change which stresses a mixture of continuity and change from one period to another (Meegan, 1988; Hyman, 1991; Lovering, 1991; Bonefeld, 1993). Reliance on sharp distinctions between phases has been criticized for falling prey, in its worst applications, to a logic of binary contrasts between, say, rigid or collective 'old times' and flexible or individualistic 'new times' (Williams et al., 1987; Sayer, 1989; Thrift, 1989; Sayer and Walker, 1992). It is claimed that such a logic produces overviews based on arbitrarily derived guiding principles and universal claims based on partial truths, thus denying the key aspect of history as a complex and heterogeneous process of many determinations (Gertler, 1988, 1992; Amin and Robins, 1990; Graham, 1992).

But use of the term 'debate' is appropriate in another, 'internal', sense since the meaning and application of the term 'post-Fordism' is disputed among those within the debate. Arguments exist over the nature of the passing age, the origins of its crisis, the bearers of change and the shape of things to come. It would be an error to think of the post-Fordist debate as variants of one position. Yet there is a perception among observers of the debate that the perspectives within it, with the passing of time, are becoming strands of one broad theorization of change (Amin and Robins, 1990; Graham, 1992) or cohabitants within one approach (Dankbaar, 1992; Elam, chapter 2 in this reader; and to a lesser extent, Boyer, 1988a).

Such a perception has been reinforced by the more popular accounts of transition which draw eclectically from a diverse body of thought to synthesize a new age under the banner of 'post-Fordism'. One example is the work of a group of British intellectuals and activists associated with the magazine *Marxism Today*, which ceased to publish in 1991 (Hall and Jacques, 1989). Through its search for an explanation of Thatcherism rooted in irreversible and deep-rooted changes within modern industrial society, this group draws selectively from the literature to articulate a blend of post-Fordist times:

> A shift to the new 'information technologies'; more flexible, decen-tralised forms of labour process and work organisation; decline of the old manufacturing base and the growth of the 'sunrise', computer-based industries; the hiving off or contracting out of functions and services; a greater emphasis on choice and product differentiation, on marketing, packaging and design, on the 'targetting' of consumers by lifestyle, taste, and culture rather than by categories of social class; a decline in the proportion of the skilled, male, manual working class, the rise of the service and white-collar classes and the 'feminization' of the work force; an economy dominated by multinationals, with their new international division of labour and their greater autonomy from nation state control; and the 'globalisation' of the new financial markets, linked by the communications revolution. *(Hall, 1988, p. 24)*

This version of 'new times' does not stop at the economy, but also identifies new cultural patterns: 'Post-Fordism is also associated with broader social and cultural changes. For example, greater fragmenta-tion and pluralism, the weakening of older collective solidarities and block identities and the emergence of new identities associated with greater work flexibility, the maximisation of individual choices through personal consumption' (Hall, 1988, p. 24).

The *Marxism Today* version of post-Fordism is brave enough to prophesize the future, to use the term to encapsulate a totality of change and to discard Fordism as an exhausted age characterized by the opposite of all the post-Fordist features described above. Its audacity has been matched by the depth of criticism it has attracted. Some have attacked its theory and method, dismissing its struc-turalism, lack of conceptual rigour, eclecticism, holism and inescapable futurology (Pollert, 1988; Hirst and Zeitlin, 1991). Others within the Left have criticized it for: reading off political strategies from structural changes; overstressing the subjective, individual and aesthetic nature of the future; painting a romantically rosy picture of society and culture in the new times; and embracing a politics which, in conjuring away existing social and political conflicts, plays into the hands of the New Right and its social constituency (Meiskins Wood, 1989; Rustin, 1989; Sivanandan, 1990).

In many senses, dispute over the politics of the future lies at the heart of the post-Fordist debate. An underlying theme is the search for a political project which is more democratic, more egalitarian and more humane than neo-liberal Conservatism. On this question the debate represents competing political alternatives, ranging from a defence of traditional class, race and gender politics, through to a desire for 'yeoman democracy' (Piore and Sabel, 1984) or new alliances between diverse social forces including ecologists, the labour movement and the voluntary sector.

The perspective taken in this book, therefore, is that the post-Fordist debate is a confrontation of diverse viewpoints, a heterogeneity of positions which draw on different concepts to say different things about past, present and future. These positions offer different explanations and conjure up different fantasies and phantoms. They also operate at different levels of analysis, from production and industrial organization to the macroeconomy, culture and politics.

The aim of this book is to reflect and represent the diversity and difference of perspective within the debate. The next part of the chapter outlines the broad arguments of three theories of transition which have come to dominate the debate, while the second part of the chapter, reflecting the sections of the book, focuses on the major themes covered within the debate (the macroeconomy, industrial organization, policy and politics, culture and lifestyles). In a field of inquiry which has produced a vast literature, no single book can do full justice to the breadth or depth of the debate. This reader has selected some of the seminal contributions of the past decade and new ones in order to provide broad coverage of the debate. In addition, though the book seeks to represent the main areas in social science involved in the debate (political economy, geography, industrial and urban sociology, political science) the focus of the book is inflected towards the uneven geography of post-Fordism (e.g. industrial geography, urban sociology).

THREE TRANSITION MODELS

It is commonly accepted that three theoretical positions lie at the heart of the post-Fordist debate. These are the regulation approach, the flexible specialization approach and the neo-Schumpeterian approach. All three offer a developed theoretical framework to substantiate and explain the claim that an era of mass production (or Fordism) is under challenge, and portends to give way to a new set of organizational principles if a new long wave of economic growth is to be secured and sustained.

Other cognate theorizations of transition also exist, and could be brought more centrally into the debate than they have been thus far. For example, in the United States, a group of radical economists including David Gordon, Sam Bowles and Herb Gintis has developed the concept of 'social structure of accumulation' to offer an analytical framework which is close to regulation theory, but which places a premium on the role of state and class politics in explaining the transition (see Dankbaar, 1992, for a summary and a comparison with other post-Fordist approaches). Another approach, in which the analysis extends into the social and cultural sphere, derives from the work of two British sociologists, Scott Lash and John Urry (1987, 1993), who distinguish between a passing era of 'organized' capitalism and a new, flexible, era of 'disorganized' capitalism (see Hirst and Zeitlin, 1991, who place Lash and Urry squarely into the debate). A third position, inspired by the work of the Marxist geographer David Harvey, refers to the transition from Fordism to 'flexible accumulation', to signal the rise of flexible labour markets and flexible geographies of production (Harvey, 1987, 1989a, 1991; Harvey and Scott, 1988). Yet another approach, but with a narrower focus than the latter two, draws upon the idea of 'new production concepts' (Kern and Schumann, 1987) to argue that in the arena of work, advanced technology is encouraging a new age of worker–employer cooperation and worker involvement; a new industrial democracy reversing the Fordist interpretation of workers as a restraint in production (see Tomaney, chapter 5 in this reader; Hyman, 1991; Dankbaar, 1992).

There is no space here to consider these approaches but they merit further attention, not only for their intrinsic merit, but also because their particular inflections on change confirm that what comes after Fordism may well be an open matter. Like other reviews of post-Fordist theories (Elam, chapter 2 in this reader; Boyer, 1991; Hirst and Zeitlin, 1991; Hyman, 1991; Nielsen, 1991; Webber, 1991; Dankbaar, 1992; Jessop, 1992a), the discussion below focuses on the three approaches most closely associated with the debate.

The regulation approach

The regulation approach was pioneered in France in the 1970s, and refined in the 1980s, by political economists attempting to explain the dynamics of long-term cycles of economic stability and change (Aglietta, 1979; Coriat, 1979; André and Delorme, 1982; Lipietz, 1985, 1987; Boyer, 1986; Mistral, 1986). The approach has had a huge international impact and has emerged as a major theorization of the patterns of post-war economic growth until the mid 1970s and of its crisis thereafter. Its diffusion as an approach, inevitably, has resulted in considerable internal differentiation (Jessop, 1992a, for instance, identifies seven regulationist schools), and a broadening of the base of heterodox economic theories it draws upon (from Marxian value theory to Keynesian macroeconomic ideas). There is a large body of literature on the regulation approach, including summaries and reviews (see, for example, Boyer, 1986; Nöel, 1987; Dunford, 1990; Hirst and Zeitlin, 1991; Nielsen, 1991; Jessop, 1992a). The summary that follows consequently seeks to provide only a crystallized account of core concepts and arguments, in order to make sense of it in relation to the other theories of transition (see chapter 2 by Elam for a fuller critical evaluation).

The aim of the early French regulationists was to develop a theoretical framework which could encapsulate and explain the paradox within capitalism between its inherent tendency towards instability, crisis and change, and its ability to coalesce and stabilize around a set of institutions, rules and norms which serve to secure a relatively long period of economic stability. This conceptual effort was underpinned by the observation that the stagnation of growth in the world economy after the mid-1970s amounted to much more than a cyclical lull, symbolizing a generalized crisis of the institutional forms that had come to guide the post-war world economy.

The project was thus to identify the structures, principles and mechanisms which underpinned the passing regime, to explain its internal contradictions and to speculate on future possibilities for growth. For the regulationists, it was important to think of a phase or regime as a 'partial, temporary and unstable result of embedded social practices rather than the pre-determined outcome of quasi-natural economic laws' (Jessop, 1992b, p. 26). Thus, while it wished to acknowledge that rules drive a system, it rejected the notion that such rules should be pre-given, immutable or pre-figurative of a future development path. Accordingly, its theorization of economic development and change claimed to give as much regard to historical processes as to the basic rules of the capitalist economy.

In order to articulate and explain the systemic coherence of individual phases of capitalist development, regulation theory draws on a number of key concepts which identify the core mechanisms at work. Two key concepts are 'regime of accumulation' and 'mode of regulation'. The regime of accumulation refers to a 'set of regularities at the level of the whole economy, enabling a more or less coherent process of capital accumulation' (Nielsen, 1991, p. 22). It includes norms pertaining to the organization of production and work (the labour process), relationships and forms of exchange between branches of the economy, common rules of industrial and commercial management, principles of income sharing between wages, profits and taxes, norms of consumption and patterns of demand in the marketplace, and other aspects of the macroeconomy. The mode of regulation (or similar terms – see chapters 3, 8 and 9 in this reader) refers to 'the institutional ensemble (laws, agreements, etc.) and the complex of cultural habits and norms which secures capitalist reproduction as such. It consists of a set of 'formal or informal "rules" that codify the main social relationships' (Nielsen, 1991, p. 22). It therefore refers to institutions and conventions which 'regulate' and reproduce a given accumulation regime through application across a wide range of areas, including the law, state policy, political practices, industrial codes, governance philosophies, rules of negotiation and bargaining, cultures of consumption and social expectations.

Nielsen (1991) refers to three other concepts deployed varyingly within the regulation school either to specify further the two main concepts or to identify other forces of 'systemic cohesion'. One is the concept of 'dominant industrial paradigm' or 'labour process' (Coriat, 1979), which refers to patterns of industrial and work organization, and includes the nature of technologies, management rules, division of tasks, industrial relations and wage relations. The second concept is 'mode of development', used by Lipietz (1988) in particular to denote the total pattern of development within an economy, based on the industrial paradigm, regime of accumulation and mode of regulation. The third concept is 'mode of societalization', or 'societal paradigm' adopted by Jessop (1992a) and Lipietz (chapter 11, this volume) as well as the German exponents of the regulation school (e.g. Esser and Hirsch, chapter 3, this volume; Hirsch, 1991). This concept refers to a series of political compromises, social alliances and hegemonic processes of domination which feed into a pattern of mass integration and social cohesion, thus serving to underwrite and stabilize a given development path.

It is with these five major concepts that the regulation approach has sought to periodize capitalist development, explain relative stability and systemic coherence, and interpret structural crisis (as the breakdown of the norms captured by the five concepts). The passing age, with its heyday in the 1950s and 1960s, has been named 'Fordism', a term coined to reflect loosely the pioneering mass production methods and rules of management applied by Henry Ford in his car factories in America during the 1920s and 1930s. Fordism is summarized as the age of 'intensive accumulation' with 'monopolistic regulation' of the economy. Although the term is applied at separate levels of analysis (industrial paradigm, regime of accumulation, mode of regulation, mode of societalization), it is its usage to synthesize a macrosystem which makes the regulation approach most interesting and distinctive from the two other theories of transition.

The driving force of Fordist 'intensive accumulation' is claimed to be the mass production dynamic, pioneered by the United States and reliant upon the intensification of work, the detailed division of tasks and mechanization to raise productivity, and various forms of 'monopolistic' regulation to maintain this dynamic. Jessop (1991, pp. 136–7) succinctly summarizes the central features of this dynamic:

> Fordism itself can be analysed on four levels. As a distinctive type of labour process [or industrial paradigm], it involves mass production based on moving assembly-line techniques operated with the semi-skilled labour of the mass worker. Not all branches nor workers will be directly involved in mass production in a Fordist economy, of course: the important point is that mass production is the main source of its dynamism. As a stable mode of macroeconomic growth [regime of accumulation], Fordism involves a virtuous circle of growth based on mass production, rising productivity based on economies of scale, rising incomes linked to productivity, increased mass demand due to rising wages, increased profits based on full utilisation of capacity, and increased investment in improved mass production equipment and techniques. As a mode of social and economic regulation [mode of regulation], Fordism involves the separation of ownership and control in large corporations with a distinctive multi-divisional, decentralised organisation subject to central controls [Taylorist division of labour]; monopoly pricing; union recognition and collective bargaining; wages indexed to productivity growth and retail price inflation; and monetary emission and credit policies orientated to securing effective aggregate demand. In this context the key wage bargains will be struck in the mass production industries; the going rate will then spread through comparability claims among the employed and through the indexation of welfare benefits financed through progressive taxation for those not economically active. This pattern need not mean the demise of dual labour markets or non-unionised firms or sectors as long as mass demand rises in line with productivity. And, fourthly, Fordism can be seen as a general pattern

of social organisation ('societalisation'). In this context it involves the consumption of standardised, mass commodities in nuclear family households and provision of standardised, collective goods and services by the bureaucratic state. The latter also has a key role in managing the conflicts between capital and labour over both the individual and social wage. These latter features are clearly linked to the rise of Keynesian economic management and the universalist welfare state but neither element is essential for the growth of Fordism.

This is a description of an 'ideal-type' Fordism modelled around the US macroeconomy after the 1950s. The regulation approach is careful to insist, against a criticism it has attracted, that Fordism in different national contexts is not envisaged as a clone of the ideal-type, but as 'different combinations of Fordist and non-Fordist features (Nielsen, 1991, p. 23) leading to specific national growth 'solutions' which none the less were forced to measure up to Fordist 'best practice'.

The slow-down of growth and recurrent recessions since the mid-1970s are seen by the regulation approach as symptoms of the crisis of Fordism, underpinned by mismatches and imbalances between its different levels of organization. Summarizing Boyer's analysis of the structural crisis of Fordism, Nielsen (1991, p. 24) identifies four contributing factors with varying significance in different national contexts:

> Firstly, productivity gains decreased as a result of the social and technical limits of Fordism (worker resistance to the Fordist organisation of work and increasing difficulties in 'balancing' ever longer and more rigid production lines). Secondly, the expansion of mass production led to an increasing globalisation of economic flows which made national economic management increasingly difficult. Thirdly, Fordism led to growing social expenditure (the relative costs of collective consumption increased, because of the inapplicability of mass production methods in this area, leading to inflationary pressures and distributional conflicts). Fourthly, the consumption pattern has gradually changed towards a greater variety of use values (the new demands are at odds with standardization, the basis of economies of scale, and cannot easily be satisfied through mass production methods).

Before we move on to the analysis of what might emerge out of the crisis of Fordism (in the next main section) it has to be noted that the regulation approach, though much admired for the clarity of its synthesis of the recent past, has also attracted criticism. At the simplest level, its description of Fordism has been challenged, through the recognition of the importance in the economy of non-Taylorist forms of work organization, non-Fordist production processes and non-Keynesian state policies (Clarke, 1988; Foster, 1988; Williams and Haslam, 1991). The relationship between the ideal-type or dominant form of Fordism and diverse national Fordisms has also been questioned, with critics arguing that recognition of national diversity undermines the notion of a single, dominant Fordist logic (Hirst and Zeitlin, 1991).

It has also been argued that despite its appeals to historical contingency, the regulation approach ends up ascribing history a systemic, functionalist and logical coherence which it rarely possesses. The argument here is that capitalist development is better seen as permanently crisis-ridden and contradictory, depending, as it does, on conflicting relations within and between social classes, business, government and society. Thus historical outcomes are the result of 'battles and struggles', rather than universalist logics binding economy and society (Clarke, 1988; Bonefeld and Holloway, 1991; Graham, 1992).

Finally, other critics, who accept the idea of an underlying logic of historical development in capitalism, have questioned the status of the conceptual edifice of French regulation theory, arguing that it is an edifice based on a *post hoc* rationalization of history, rather than an *ex ante* explanation of the mechanisms and logic of the motor of capitalist regimes and their limits (Harvey, 1989a; Salvati, 1989). This has led Salvati to conclude, echoing the criticism of Brenner and Glick (1991), that the regulation approach is 'neither theory nor history' (Salvati, 1989, p. 70).

The neo-Schumpeterian approach

Although the neo-Schumpeterian approach cannot claim the breadth of reach of the regulation approach, it shares certain similarities, and one regulationist (Boyer, 1988a) has been quite explicit about building bridges between the two approaches (see also Roobeek, 1987). There is broad agreement between the two approaches over: the systemic and cyclical nature of capitalist development; the periodization and general dynamic of Fordism; the significance of the degree of match between, in neo-Schumpeterian language, the 'techno-economic paradigm' (regime of accumulation) and the 'socio-institutional framework' (mode of regulation); and the stability of a 'long wave' or 'long cycle' of economic development. One major difference, however, is the salience attributed in the neo-Schumpeterian approach to technology and technical standards in initiating, sustaining and separating individual long waves.

This approach is most closely associated with the work on innovation during the mid-1980s by Freeman and Perez and their colleagues based at one time or another at the Science Policy Research Unit (SPRU) at Sussex University (Freeman et al., 1982; Dosi et al., 1988; Freeman and Perez, 1988). Freeman and Perez build on a tradition first initiated by Kondratiev's work in the 1920s on fifty-year long waves of 'boom' and 'bust' in the development of capitalist economies, and then developed further by Schumpeter in the 1930s through his work on the path-breaking role of innovative entrepreneurs in giving birth to a new technical paradigm for future growth. For Freeman and Perez, the successful transition from one long wave to another is dependent, first, on 'quantum leaps' in industrial productivity, which are secured once pioneering advances in technology diffuse across the economy. Second, it is dependent on 'matching' innovations within the framework of socio-institutional norms and regulations, in order to facilitate such diffusion. Once these conditions are achieved, a new long wave of growth can be said to be in full swing, with a distinctive techno-economic paradigm that establishes a universal standard across the economy. The definition of 'innovation' is not confined narrowly to a range of new products or industrial processes. It also includes new forms of work organization and management, new high growth sectors, new transport and communications technologies, new geographies of location, and so on. However, Freeman and Perez are keen to stress the central role, within a paradigm, of 'carrier' products or industrial sectors, which act as system-wide inputs or efficiency-enhancing universal technologies (Perez, 1985).

In neo-Schumpeterian analysis, the passing age of mass production, referred to as the fourth Kondratiev or the fourth long wave, is claimed to have been underpinned by electro-mechanical technologies, the products of the mass consumption industries and oil and petro-chemicals as basic sources of cheap energy. Like the regulation approach, it identifies standardization, massification, scale economies, oligopolistic competition and mass consumption of cheap goods as the distinguishing features of the fourth Kondratiev (organized around vertically integrated and hierarchically governed large corporations). Similarly, the approach broadly agrees with the socio-institutional arrangements identified by the regulation approach, but focuses more on the state policies – from education and welfare to micro- and macroeconomic policy – which, under the banner of Keynesianism, served to sustain the virtuous link between employment, output and productivity growth.

As regards the crisis of the fourth Kondratiev, particular emphasis is placed on the dampening effect on growth of oligopolistic competition in a context of maturing technologies: a process limiting productivity gains as a consequence of increases in wages, prices and the inefficiency of large corporations. But, importantly, the crisis is also related to the mismatch between an emerging techno-economic paradigm which could renew growth, and the enduring socio-institutional framework of the fourth Kondratiev. For Freeman and Perez, the institutional legacy of the preceding paradigm is slow in changing, thus preventing the widespread diffusion of the benefits of innovation across the economy (Perez, 1986). This inertia is traced not only to the failure of contemporary neo-liberal government policies to provide coordinated and directed industrial policy action, but also to the difficulties and time lags involved in radically changing embedded socio-cultural habits and norms across the wide range of institutions which constitute the 'socio-institutional framework' (e.g. management and labour attitudes, industrial relations, working arrangements, industrial expectations, political and legislative priorities, etc.).

Notwithstanding the importance accorded by Freeman and Perez to socio-institutional factors, the neo-Schumpeterian approach has been criticized for being technologically determinist (see Elam, chapter 2 in this reader). Technology-induced changes (in products, processes, communications systems), rather than social, organizational or market changes which might influence economic efficiency and growth, are given prime position in explaining the formation and development of a long wave. As Nielsen (1991) puts it, the 'socio-institutional' is clearly perceived as subordinate to the 'techno-economic', or, expressed differently, the macroeconomy is too narrowly reduced to its technical attributes.

The flexible specialization approach

This approach to 'industrial divides' is most closely associated with the work of American sociologists Charles Sabel, Michael Piore and Jonathan Zeitlin and, more recently, Paul Hirst (Sabel, 1982, and chapter 4 in this volume; Piore and Sabel, 1984; Sabel and Zeitlin, 1985; Hirst and Zietlin, 1989, 1991). Its use of abstract theory is less pronounced than in the preceding two approaches, in part because of a conscious attempt to avoid emphasizing the role of general structural tendencies in economic and social life, and to reject a deterministic account of historical evolution and transition. Indeed, such is the eagerness of Hirst and Zeitlin (1991) to insist on these differences that it has led them to oppose vehemently any attempt to link the approach to the others, and to insist zealously on the superiority of their own approach. The approach has a certain conceptual simplicity that is also due to its focus on the arena of production. As Nielsen (1991, p. 12) summarizes:

> Piore and Sabel (1984) base their argument on a simple conceptual distinction between two opposites of industrial production: mass production and flexible specialisation. 'Mass production' involves the use of special purpose (product specific) machines and of semi-skilled workers to produce standardised goods while 'flexible specialisation', or craft production, is based on skilled workers who produce a variety of customised goods.

At the heart of the approach lies the claim that the two industrial paradigms have coexisted since the nineteenth century, with neither exhibiting technological superiority or inevitable dominance over the other on grounds of economic efficiency. But, it is argued that at rare moments in history, when a stark choice between competing technologies and markets becomes available, one of the two paradigms may limit the other, to emerge as a prevailing international standard (although this does not necessarily mean the disappearance of the 'vanquished' paradigm). Thus, the adoption and diffusion of a paradigm is claimed to be a matter of historical circumstances and political choice rather than logical necessity. Central to this choice are claimed to be the policy decisions taken by different actors (from firms and unions to national and local government), which influence the diffusion of one or the other paradigm. At these rare historical turning points, or 'industrial divides', active choices taken in one direction or the other tend to consolidate into an epoch-making standard favouring either mass production or flexible specialization. Thus, one paradigm suffers because of the absence of supporting structures, while the other, it seems, gains in strength, because it comes to be seen as 'best practice' by industry, government and other institutions. Conceptually, it is not entirely clear how a moment of stark choice between paradigms is reached – whether it follows from the crisis of the dominant industrial paradigm, the rise of new options, a change in circumstances, or from forced policy and institutional choices with path-breaking consequences. When an explanation is offered, it tends to be based on a selective interpretation of events at such moments, rather than an analysis rooted in any theory of crisis and transition.

Piore and Sabel identify two 'industrial divides'. The first is at the turn of the century, when the emergence of mass production technology and techniques is said to have limited the growth of craft production methods in various regions of Europe. Thereafter, and particularly after the 1920s and 1930s, mass production dominated the leading countries and leading industries, and was reinforced as a standard by the introduction of Keynesian policies designed to sustain and stabilize demand. As in the regulation approach, the guarantee of the mass consumption norm is seen to be of crucial significance; a guarantee traced to a series of state measures seeking to maximize and match supply and demand, sustain mass consumerism, avoid underconsumption, stabilize prices, etc.

The present period, dating from the stagnation of the world economy in the early 1970s, is said to constitute the second industrial divide: an open choice, as in the past, between mass production and flexible specialization (see below). It is an opportunity which springs from the general crisis of the structures of mass production, symbolized by the crisis of US Fordism. This crisis is related to two main developments. The first concerns changes in the market, notably the stagnation of demand in the course of the long recession, growing uncertainty of demand owing to the breakdown of international regulatory mechanisms such as Bretton Woods and, above all, the threat to mass consumerism posed by the growth in demand for non-standardized, better quality, short shelf-life goods. These market trends are said to constitute a problem for mass production and an opportunity for flexible specialization. The second development, also an opportunity for flexible specialization, is the rise of non-specialist and highly flexible manufacturing technologies (numerically controlled as well as non-electronic) and flexible work practices. These are said to favour smaller batch production without loss of scale economies in industrial efficiency, thus reducing the historic disadvantage of small firms and smaller units of organization. The implication, therefore, is that on this occasion, such are market and technological circumstances that an epochal reversal in the industrial paradigm towards craft production might well be possible.

The approach has been widely debated, and its dualist logic has invited strong criticism (see Elam, chapter 3 in this reader; Asheim, 1992; Solo, 1985; Frankel, 1987; Williams et al., 1987; Sayer, 1989; Smith, 1989; Amin and Robins, 1990; Hyman, 1991; Pollert, 1991; Jessop 1992b; Leborgne and Lipietz, 1992; Curry, 1993; Harrison, 1994). A number of common arguments run through the critique. One is that the theory is constructed around dual oppositions (mass production versus flexible specialisation) which not only caricature each industrial paradigm (e.g. a rigid past versus a flexible future, unskilled Fordism versus skilled flexible specialization), but also reduce a great deal of diversity on either side of the divide down to narrowly defined paradigms. Another criticism concerns the tendency to slip too easily between voluntarism and historical logic in explaining the crossing of industrial divides – paradigms are ascribed their own developmental logic, but they are also made the object of choice, policy and politics: history by design and will. In addition, Piore and Sabel have been accused of being too naive in imagining the likelihood or possibility of a large-scale return to a craft industrial paradigm, on the grounds that the embedded structures of Fordism will persist and adapt to new circumstances rather than disappear (history is difficult to reverse). A fourth argument is that the approach makes the error of equating only industrial efficiency with competitiveness, thereby underestimating the power of the protagonists of Fordism (e.g. multinational firms) to continue to dominate markets via their grip over finance, market outlets, distribution networks, advertising and so on. Most controversial, however, has been its portrayal of a rosy, 'flexible' future across the second industrial divide, an issue taken up in the following section.

IMAGINING THE FUTURE: POST-FORDISM, NEO-FORDISM, 'AFTER'-FORDISM, FIFTH KONDRATIEV, FLEXIBLE SPECIALIZATION . . .?

All the approaches discussed above are rooted in different conceptual traditions, and all three generalize at different levels of analysis. Reading across the approaches, however, there emerges a considerable degree of consensus as regards the nature, dynamic and crisis of the passing era. In contrast, their speculations on the future are quite different from each other, varying in terms of not only the trends identified, but also the discernibility and 'fixity' of the new age, seen from the perspective of the present. This section outlines the competing visions, through a discussion of the major themes of change covered in the debate.

New macroeconomic designs

The regulationist and neo-Schumpeterian approaches are the two most rooted in economics, and most orientated towards analysis of the economy as a whole (i.e. production, distribution and exchange). The Schumpeterians consider information technology (microelectronics-based products, processes and communications networks) to lie at the core of the fifth Kondratiev. It is anticipated to be the key technology to drive future growth and to affect the behaviour of the entire economy by raising productivity and lowering input costs in all industries, creating new industries with high levels of demand, and securing a revolutionary onslaught on space and time constraints via electronic networking. Innovation will also involve transformation within prevailing managerial best practices (Dankbaar, 1992), and introduce a new set of inter-sectoral and inter-firm relationships. Thus, the fifth Kondratiev is speculated to be innovation- and knowledge-intensive; be based on information technology carrier branches such as computers, electronics capital goods, software, telecoms, robotics, electronic data banks and information services; involve a shifting emphasis in production from scale economies, rigid technologies and compartmentalization, towards scope economies, flexible manufacturing systems and integration of design, production and marketing; involve the development of new computer networks-based forms of intra- and inter-organizational collaboration and communication; see the rise of new patterns of work including tele-working, home-working and flexible hours; involve new patterns of consumption such as tele-shopping, enabled by advanced telecommunications systems; and give rise to new geographies of production and consumption based on distance-shrinking technologies.

The vision is of a new 'cybernetic' macroeconomy. The necessity of a fifth Kondratiev, along the lines outlined above, for the survival of capitalism is taken as given by the neo-Schumpeterians. However, the transition is not assumed to be inevitable, but one predicated on profound changes in attitudes and behaviour, and institutional priorities and policies. At a governmental level, it is argued that this requires careful, planned and strategic intervention in order to remove obstacles preventing the long-term development of the new techno-economic paradigm. Such a programme is required to provide: supply-side policies in training and education so as to encourage research, innovation and new skill formation; support for technological upgrading and industry–university research links; programmes to develop advanced telecommunications networks; strategic support for new industries and new services; and support for learning and adaptation of new management and organizational cultures. Indeed, cultural changes across the institutional spectrum are posited as an essential requirement for the consolidation of the new 'information economy'.

The regulation approach, while in agreement that long-term capitalist renewal requires radical change within both the regime of accumulation and the mode of regulation, is more reticent to predict the characteristics of what comes after Fordism (Tickell and Peck, 1992). This is because it sees the present as a period of experimentation with various strategies to resolve the bottlenecks of Fordism, a period in which particular solutions – more or less successful – will emerge. Thus against the certainty of both the neo-Schumpeterians and the flexible specialization approach (see below) concerning the 'ingredients' of a lasting solution, the regulationists argue that the shape of post-Fordism will emerge from the dialectical confrontation between rival forms. For this reason, this approach is less anxious to fix the name of the new era, hesitating between 'neo-Fordism' (to stress a strong element of continuity with Fordism), 'post-Fordism' (to denote a genuine resolution to the crisis of Fordism) and 'after-Fordism' (a translation of the original *après-fordisme*, to designate a period after Fordism rather than a new phase of capitalist development – see chapter 9 in this volume, by Peck and Tickell).

Some regulationists, however, are less reticent than the Parisian regulationists about the future. Hirsch and Esser, for example (chapter 3 in this volume; Hirsch, 1991), scan the array of dominant patterns of restructuring in Germany to outline a hauntingly pessimistic 'post-Fordist' scenario. Within the mode of accumulation, they outline five tendencies: new technology-based work, representing lay-offs, worker segmentation and social marginalization; a strengthened industrialization of the service sector, representing changes in the social structure towards white-collar strata, and the erosion of collective identities via the use of new technologies; enforced mobility in labour markets provoked by new geographies of employment, resulting in a breakdown of family and communal ties; growing social polarization between high productivity/high consumption strata and low-wage or no-wage strata; and an individualization and pluralization of lifestyles as the result of the preceding tendencies. This is a vision of the future quite at odds with the implicitly benign and socially inclusive growth model proposed by the neo-Schumpeterians, stressing, as it does, the socially divisive and alienating impact of a new technology-based era.

For Hirsch and Esser, the elements of a new mode of regulation, too, are discernible. This they characterize as a strengthening of monopolistic regulation and governance of the economy. They stress the role of advanced technologies in integrating firms and industries, of new small firm networks and of processes of international concentration and coordination in the hands of major firms and financial institutions. They signal the weakening of the trade unions as a 'regulatory' institution. They envisage a scaling down and reorientation of welfare services towards the 'economically active' groups in society. Finally, they anticipate a new corporatism involving state and industry alliances in the high technology sector and select groups of privileged workers. As with the regime of accumulation, they anticipate a post-Fordism which abandons the universal or collective principles that Fordism had come to embrace.

In contrast, Jessop's regulationist account of post-Fordism (chapter 8 in this volume; 1992a) draws together aspects of the neo-Schumpeterian futurology and that of Hirsch and Esser (although it lacks the bleakness of the German regulationists). He too argues that many new developments in the labour process, in the macroeconomy and in the mode of regulation can be said to be genuinely prefigurative of a post-Fordism (i.e. emerging out of Fordism *and* resolving its problems). However, and significantly, he is careful to stress that a well-developed and relatively stable post-Fordist system is yet in the making, because of the absence of a dominant or binding 'mode of societalization' comparable to the role played by 'Americanism' in the Fordist era. For Jessop, the absence of a strong ideology which secures a general acceptance of the 'rules of the game' makes it premature to announce post-Fordism as a relatively stable and self-reproducing growth regime.

In contrast to Jessop and the German writers influenced by the regulation approach, the Parisian regulationists tend to be more circumspect, couching discussion of the future in terms of 'ways out of the crisis of Fordism', and thinking of post-Fordism either as a coexistence of solutions based on sectoral or national specificity or as a compromise or conflict between competing scenarios. There is a certain openness which stems from a desire to retain a vision of the future as the product of contestation, of many possibilities and unforeseeable outcomes. This is an approach stressed especially by Boyer, Coriat, Lipietz, Leborgne and Petit.

Boyer, for example, in the context of labour markets and their regulation, identifies five possible post-Fordist scenarios: flexible specialization; international Keynesian attempts to underwrite employment; market-led labour flexibility; segmented labour markets; and negotiated attempts positively to develop skills and labour resources (Boyer, 1988b). At a broader level of analysis, he reviews different theories to propose that a new industrial paradigm might consist of a composite model, incorporating different organizational forms appropriate for individual contexts. He argues, for instance, that information technology as a techno-economic paradigm might be applied for flexible mass production in modern high-tech industries, while flexible specialization might revitalize declining or craft sectors, with new versions of Fordist mass production 'exported' to developing countries or applied to the traditional consumer services (Boyer, 1991). In a similar vein, Coriat and Petit (1991) anticipate a macro-scenario presupposing the growth of advanced services and the internationalization of markets and production processes, but they warn of a failure to change in this direction that could result from inward-looking, short-term adjustment policies by national governments.

The French regulationists are relatively open about the characteristics and likelihood of a post-Fordist macrodesign, and this is the result of on-going dialogue with other theories of transition and an appreciation of the diversity of contemporary 'on-the-ground' patterns of restructuring. Over a decade ago, however, Aglietta (1982), one of the pioneers of the regulation approach, was less equivocal about the characteristics of a durable solution to the crisis of Fordism. He imagined a *neo-Fordism*, involving the extension and deepening of the principles of 'intensive' accumulation which underpinned Fordism. Aglietta wrote of the application of Fordist methods in the service sector to raise productivity, the application of new technologies in production to increase the intensity of work and introduce new forms of labour control, and the globalization of firms with the aid of new information technology. With the passing of time, regulation theory has moved on from this position, and in so doing, it has come to imagine post-Fordist scenarios which are different from rather than an extension of Fordism.

New sociologies and geographies of industrial organization

Although the flexible specialization approach also discusses the possibility of a new macrodesign (via the pursuit of an international Keynesianism based on demand reflation), it is best known for its theorization of paradigmatic change in the nature of work and industrial organization. In presenting a stark choice between mass production and flexible specialization, it is also least equivocal about the future. Though Piore and Sabel are careful to stress that things may go either way depending on the strategic decisions taken by policy-makers and institutions, their analysis of contemporary technological and market developments tends to point the future in the direction of flexible specialization. There is a strong hint that the availability of flexible, numerically controlled machines and other multi-purpose technologies, together with the growth in markets for better quality, non-standardized products, will tip the balance in favour of flexible specialization as the staple industrial paradigm.

Flexible specialization is proposed as the industrial model best capable of producing quality goods for specialist and volatile markets, with the minimum of effort, time and cost. The principle which underlies the model is a reliance on skills, flexibility and networking between task-specialist units in order to produce changing volumes and combinations of goods without incurring productivity losses (resulting from not utilizing sections of the workforce or the productive apparatus at any given moment).

The ideal-type consists of a set of organizational arrangements which can sustain this principle. One is the division of tasks within the production cycle between specialist, autonomously run units or independent firms, so that each unit or firm may maximize the scale economies and expertise gained from specialization in one field, but, at the same time allow the final product to be varied in volume and shape without loss of overall efficiency. Another aspect is the reintegration of research and design, management, white-collar and blue-collar work – in order to maximize on inventiveness and speed of reaction to changing market signals. A third aspect is a reversal of the Fordist and Taylorist tendency towards deskilling and worker isolation, through greater reliance on skills, polyvalence, worker participation and collaboration in the pursuit of product quality and the flow of ideas, know-how and workers between task and product areas. A fourth aspect is the decentralization of decision-making authority, so as not only to reduce worker alienation, but also to raise responsibility and responsiveness in all areas of the work. A fifth aspect is the deployment of multi-purpose technologies (rather than task-specific ones) which can be used flexibly across task and volume commitments. Related to this is a broader shift in philosophy concerning the people–machine interface, away from skill substitution and human enslavement by technology, towards the craft idea of machines as tools of work. A final aspect is the sedimentation of a culture of cooperation, trust and negotiability between firms trading with each other, as well as within firms, as a key condition underwriting the interdependence and flexibility demanded by this model of industrial organization.

This is a much less technocentric industrial paradigm than that envisaged by the neo-Schumpeterians. Further, and this is part of its appeal, it proposes a less dismal picture of industrial relations than that offered by the neo-Fordist version of the regulation approach, which anticipates further new technology-led dehumanization and atomization of work (see Witheford, 1994, for a 'workerist' critique of celebratory theories of new technology and work). Flexible specialization promises to restore dignity and skills in the workplace, as well as to establish new democratic industrial relations based on cooperation, mutual respect, dialogue and 'studied trust' between employers and employees (Piore, 1990; Sabel 1992). It could thus prefigure a less contentious 'yeoman (artisan) democracy' that replaces the Fordist model of democracy which was based on mass representation (e.g. corporatist negotiation between unions, employer federations and the state) as a general standard for social interaction and political behaviour.

The principal question raised by this interpretation of the future concerns its likelihood and whether it is representative of the most powerful experimentations in work organization today. For Sabel (chapter 4 in this volume) and his colleagues the answer seems to be a positive one based on the observation that the new industrial patterns can be observed in a number of leading-edge industries. The examples quoted have become all too familiar: technopoles such as Silicon Valley in the high-technology industries; craft-based industrial districts such as those in the 'Third Italy' which have revitalized many traditional consumer industries; speciality niches within saturated, mass industries ranging from steel and chemicals to advertising and films (see Storper, chapter 6 in this volume, on the film industry); and 'lean', high performance German, Italian or Scandinavian large companies which draw extensively on innovation, high quality products and skills in order to dominate markets. Common to all these examples is said to be an organizational structure drawing on decentralized management, worker participation, polyvalence, skills and active labour–management cooperation.

Critics, on the other hand, argue that equally or more durable solutions, which have little to do with 'yeoman democracy' and a return to craft principles, can be observed in other industrial contexts. Leborgne and Lipietz (1988) identify three possibilities: a 'neo-Taylorist' solution in contexts of weak labour representation, involving hierarchical labour control, a rigid division of tasks and no worker involvement; a 'Californian' solution echoing the Silicon Valley model of no unions, flexible wages and worker identification with corporate cultures; and the 'Kalmarian' model which takes a leaf out of the Swedish experience of combining negotiated involvement, collective bargaining, rigid wages and labour flexibility. The point made by Leborgne and Lipietz and others (Lane, 1989; Tomaney, chapter 5 in this volume) is that especially in the arena of work organization and industrial relations, solutions are the product of situated socio-cultural traditions and balances of power; thus different local and national solutions may be expected. Conceding, however, that post-Fordist times presuppose a measure of organizational flexibility, Leborgne and Lipietz (1992) argue that an 'offensive' strategy of flexibility based on strong labour rights and worker involvement logically does not rule out a 'defensive' capitalist strategy based on low and flexible wages and individualized or reduced labour rights.

Other critics argue that no discussion of post-Fordist solutions is legitimate without reference to the highly successful combinations of flexibility and rigidity as well as quality and price competitiveness, within mass production, perfected by the Japanese. The argument here is that Japan offers a unique industrial paradigm that pulls together the scale economies and institutional advantages (e.g. industry–government links, inter-sectoral and inter-firm ties) of mass production and corporatist regulation, and the flexibility of scope and scale guaranteed through subcontracting, loose interdependencies within organizations, labour flexibility, team working, cultures of consensus and cooperation and so on. It is a model which defies the dualisms of the flexible specialization approach that force an artificial distinction between a rigid and confrontational past and a flexible and negotiated future (see Mahon, 1987; Dankbaar, 1992; Sayer and Walker, 1992; Tomaney, chapter 5 in this volume, for more on Japanization).

Observers of contemporary patterns of workplace restructuring also argue that experiments with simultaneous reliance on privileged and marginalized workers, separated by skills, gender, age and experience, is also characteristic of the West. Practices by firms involving the relocation of production in the labour markets of developing countries and less favoured regions, single-union or no-union deals, individualization of salaries, task flexibility and other erosions of worker solidarity are claimed to be symbolic of a new, and perhaps permanent, drive for flexibility and efficiency based on acute labour market fragmentation (Elger, 1991; Marginson, 1991; Pollert, 1991; Rainnie, 1993). For Alliez and Fehrer (1987), two French regulationists close to Aglietta's original line of reasoning, this new labour dualism should be interpreted as a process of further 'enslavement' of labour by capital, through 'marginalization' in the case of peripheral workers, and 'desubjectification' in the case of core workers now fully 'incorporated' by capital into its historic mission.

Another, equally polarized, debate which the flexible specialization approach has stimulated concerns the geography of post-Fordist industrial organization. Sabel (chapter 4 in this volume) makes the forceful claim that flexible specialization encourages the geographical clustering of productive activity, that is, the resurgence of locally integrated regional economies based around their specialization in particular products. Drawing on the examples of Italian industrial districts, Baden Württemberg and high-technology regions such as Silicon Valley, he suggests that the local agglomeration of the value-chain in an industry provides vital support for an industrial paradigm composed of loose confederations of specialist firms responding rapidly to changing market environments. Proximity is said to provide the social solidarity and trust, the face-to-face contact, the pool of skills and know-how, the easy access to input and output markets that such a paradigm needs. Similarly, product-based area specialization leads to the growth of specialist services and other inputs as well as institutional support for what amounts to a central industrial cluster for a locality, thus serving to provide individual firms with a range of external economies of agglomeration. If flexible specialization comes to replace Fordism, we can expect a reversal of traditional Fordist geographies of production, which were based on national and international hierarchies of command and task distribution that allocated only partial functions to individual locations. The new age, in contrast, promises a return to self-sustaining regional economies: a new inter-regional equilibrium.

The work of Californians Allen Scott and Michael Storper in the late 1980s draws a similar conclusion, but via a slightly different line of argument (Scott, 1986, 1988; Storper and Scott, 1989). Scott and Storper note a widespread tendency towards vertical disintegration (i.e. decentralization of production and management) within and between firms, not only in the context of specialized or new product markets, but also within once oligopolistic or mass markets such as the US film industry (see Storper's detailed account of vertical disintergration in Hollywood in chapter 6 of this volume). For Scott and Storper, the crisis of Fordism and the attendant uncertainty and instability in markets represent a decisive break with the industrial geography of large, vertically integrated, corporations relying upon internal scale economies to service secure markets. The crisis represents a general transition towards specialization and horizontal inter-firm networks as a basis for coping with risk and uncertainty (see Henry, 1992, for a critique of this assumption). It is suggested that, in time, external economies of scope and transaction cost reductions associated with externalization will irreversibly replace corporate reliance on internal economies, and set in train a transition towards flexibly specialized industrial systems. The economics of this transition are explained through a mixture of Marxist arguments concerning new developments in the technical and the social division of labour, arguments within the theory of the firm concerning decisions to 'make' or 'buy', and debates in economic geography relating to the salience of agglomeration economies in industrial organization (see chapter 6 by Storper). Reference to the latter allows the Californians to concur with Sabel that 'vertical disintegration encourages agglomeration and agglomeration encourages vertical disintegration' (Scott, 1988, p. 27). In their more recent work, Scott and Storper concede that the geography of vertical disintegration may involve internationalization of production, but they continue to stress the learning and innovation advantages of the regions of industrial agglomeration (Scott, 1992; Storper, 1992, 1993).

Against the 'localization' thesis, my chapter with Malmberg (chapter 7) in this reader suggests that contemporary patterns of industrial restructuring, particularly those involving multinational corporations, point in the direction of globalization of production and corporate reach (see also Amin and Dietrich, 1991). It reviews corporate and policy trends in Europe and the literature on contemporary international corporate strategies, to draw the conclusion that through increased merger activity as well as new forms of vertical disintegration and networking, multinational firms increasingly rely on the globalization of their activities to raise both efficiency and profitability. Thus, the development of global geographies, rather than local agglomeration, is considered to be a key driving force beyond Fordism.

The 'discovery' of global hierarchies and global networks need not, of course, contradict the idea of a return to regional economies if globalization is seen as a necklace of local industrial complexes (Storper, 1992). This view, however, is not consistent with other interpretations which see globalization as a threat to local autonomy and as a substitute for local linkage formation; a process, as in the past, of uneven distribution of growth opportunities between different types of region. For instance, Castells (1989) envisages a future of global economic flows and few local fixities; Sassen (1991) emphasizes the concentration of global power and influence in a small number of world cities; Dicken et al. (1994) fail to find convincing evidence to show that inward investment in a diversity of regional contexts has become sufficiently 'locally embedded' to constitute local growth poles; Amin and Thrift (1992, 1994) argue that localization tends to be confined only to a restricted number of cities and regions of the world which can offer information, innovation, knowledge and institution-rich environments; Cooke et al. (1992) deploy the concept 'global localization' to stress the uneven articulation between global forces and local opportunities; and Lipietz (1993, p. 16) reiterates the old truism that 'there can only be a certain "type of region" which wins . . . in international economic competition'. These observations, taken together, tend to interpret post-Fordist industrial geography as 'global times', bringing 'good times' to only certain localities rather than all regions.

Policy and politics beyond Fordism

Throughout the post-Fordist debate, there is agreement that no transition to a new industrial paradigm or a new macroeconomic growth regime will be successful or durable without appropriate changes in the regulatory environment. There is also widespread condemnation of contemporary market-led solutions, on the grounds that an infant macrodesign requires strategic, active and collective institutional support in order to develop and mature. Thus, neo-conservative liberalism, which manipulates markets in favour of the strongest economic and social actors, is rejected as a short-term, backward-looking and individualistic solution to a problem of structural transition that requires a lot more.

However, as regards the ingredients of an alternative regulatory solution, there remains considerable difference within the debate. For neo-Schumpeterians, public policy should seek to identify the emerging technologies of strategic importance and adopt programmes that favour their diffusion across the entire economy. It should seek to encourage new industries, the technological upgrading of firms, the diffusion of new standards and the installation of advanced communications networks, provide support for risk-taking Schumpeterian entrepreneurs who innovate but lack business acumen, and invest in education and training in new areas of knowledge, competence and skill.

Active supply-side intervention is also favoured by the flexible specialization approach, but beyond efforts simply to upgrade technological standards. Hirst and Zeitlin (1991) provide a useful summary of policy priorities for a new manufacturing paradigm. They argue that the challenge of flexible specialization must shift the focus away from classic Keynesian strategies of demand management (since mass consumption is no longer vital), state-directed industrial planning (since central institutions will prove to be inflexible) and state policies encouraging concentration of ownership and scale economies (since 'giantism' has proven to be inefficient and inflexible). They argue instead that strategies should seek to capture the institutional characteristics common to the regions in which flexible specialization has come to the fore. The emphasis thus falls on local solutions, and they isolate in particular one factor without which flexible specialization cannot be nurtured, namely 'the existence of political, normative and organisational means of creating relationships which foster co-operation and co-ordination' (Hirst and Zeitlin, 1991, p. 44). They stress that a local 'public sphere', drawing upon a culture of local identification and trust, is necessary both for strategies to develop small firm industrial districts and for strategies to stimulate the reorganization of multinational firms into constellations of semi-autonomous units embedded within the local economy:

> Trust needs to be institutionalised and co-operation presupposes forums
> in which it can be developed. This is the most important lesson for
> policymakers seeking to revitalise declining regions or to sustain
> previously successful industrial districts. . . . Politics in this sense is
> broader than the policies of public agencies; it involves the creation of
> a regional or sector 'public sphere' in which firms, labour interests,
> officials and politicians can interact and co-operate. *(Hirst and Zeitlin,
> 1991, pp. 44–5)*

Theirs is a solution requiring the construction of formal and informal
ties, networking between public and private agencies, the provision
of collective services and public policies to prevent encroachment by
investors threatening to break up the cohesiveness of industrial
districts: a firm-centred local communitarianism.

This utopia, of course, presupposes that a ubiquitous return to
a world of autonomous local economies and local commitments is
possible – an assumption which is difficult to sustain if it is accepted
that the modern world is composed of many fractured local economies,
disempowered regions and fragmented local cultures (Amin and Thrift,
1994). In such a context, the sufficiency of local, flexible specialization-
based institutional solutions is open to question. Lipietz (1987, 1992),
for instance, makes the case for a neo-Keynesian expansionary
programme at the international level, which would include a series
of financial, trade and political agreements designed to revitalize
demand in both developed and developing countries. Without such
intervention, the success of (local) supply-side interventions risks being
undermined by a lack of overall demand in the macroeconomy.

Regulationists, as regards the nature of supply-side intervention for
a new growth regime, identify the need for change in a broad range
of areas including the wage relation and labour markets, corporate
organizational norms, inter-firm relations, rules of competition, rules
in money and credit markets, and so on (see Jessop, chapter 8 in this
volume, for a summary). In other words, a case is made for a new mode
of regulation involving pervasive institutional change across the entire
economic system (production, distribution and exchange).

But within the approach, there remain strong differences of opinion
as regards the characteristics and geography of a post-Fordist mode of
regulation. The differences crystallize around discussions on the state,
and are well illustrated by the positions taken by Jessop, Peck and
Tickell, and Mayer in this reader. Jessop posits the transition from a
Keynesian welfare state to a 'Schumpeterian workfare state' which will
be governed by the aim 'to promote product, process, organizational,
and market innovation in open economies' (hence Schumpeterian) and

'to subordinate social policy to the needs of labour market flexibility and/or the constraints of international competition' (hence workfare). He identifies three variants of this principle in a post-Fordist future: neo-liberalism; neo-corporatist strategies drawing upon a selection of institutional interests, and mediated by the state; and neo-statism (state-guided economic reorganization).

A second aspect stressed by Jessop is the 'hollowing out' of the national state in an emerging context of a simultaneously internationalized and regionalized post-Fordist accumulation regime. The process is said to represent a reordering of state–economy relations and state functions in a dual direction. The first is an enhanced role for supranational institutions and political configurations in providing regulatory authority and strategic guidance for the world economy. The second is a transfer of authority downwards to the local state, which increasingly assumes the role of customizing local supply-side conditions to underpin Schumpeterian competitiveness. Peck and Tickell, on the other hand, argue that a coherent post-Fordist mode of regulation has yet to stabilize, which is why the crisis of Fordism continues, in a desperate search for a 'new institutional fix'. Seeing the present as a crisis of 'after-Fordism', they also dismiss the neo-liberal option which prevails today, as a crisis-prolonging political-economic programme serving only to promote 'systemic instability', as 'business cycles swing ever more violently, while localized growth is increasingly fragile and short-lived'. They therefore disagree with Jessop's portrayal of neo-liberalism as one potential post-Fordist regulatory option. In the same vein, they argue that the twin geographies of hollowing out belong to the 'after-Fordist crisis'. For them, the rise of local and supranational regulatory experiments is a symptom of absent systemic regulation and represents 'responsibility without power' in the case of the former and 'power without responsibility' in the case of the latter. They argue instead the case for a supralocal regulatory framework which would involve coordination at national and supranational level to harness and exceed the institutions thrown up by neo-liberalism.

Mayer, however, tends to share Jessop's evaluation of the increased salience of the local in a post-Fordist regulatory regime. Focusing on contemporary shifts in urban policy and politics, she draws the conclusion that many developments of the 1980s constitute a genuine reformulation of economic and social policies in the direction of a post-Fordist Schumpeterian entrepreneurialism. She notes the proliferation of local measures, institutions and coalitions, and their orientation towards 'the entrepreneurial mobilization of indigenous potential', as a genuine replacement for the overbearing, hierarchical Fordist state, serving to secure the conditions for a new, flexible growth model. Indeed, she goes so far as to suggest that such changes at the local level might be prefigurative of a new, post-Fordist, politics. Echoing the 'local communitarianism' of Sabel and his colleagues, she contends that a more inclusive, pluralist and democratic institutional politics could be in the making. Her argument is that the new urbanism is producing an innovative political culture which draws upon coordination between different policy areas (from technology policy to education and welfare policies), an expansion in the sphere of local political action (to involve unions, local authorities, investors, planners, research centres, training agencies, voluntary agencies, etc.) and the rise of 'new bargaining systems based on negotiation'. In short, a better form of democracy.

For regulationists, discussion of the shape of future institutional politics is relevant not only as an avenue for exploring beyond the authoritarian centralism of neo-liberal conservatism, but also in terms of its longer-term appropriateness for a new growth regime. The concept 'societal paradigm', theorized as a precondition for a stable growth regime, refers to common 'ways of doing things', including the nature of political discourse and representation. The nature of the relationship between post-Fordism and democracy is explored by Lipietz in this reader. He characterizes Fordism as a hierarchical democracy built around an 'organicist' (hierarchical, but collective) commitment to society-wide redistribution of the fruits of growth via a top-down politics. He identifies the 'liberal-productivism' of the 1980s, based on market solutions, individualism and entre-preneurialism, as a serious contender for the future, but rejects it as a model in which democracy will retreat in terms of both legitimating a philosophy of no societal obligations as well as placing restrictions on who may participate in politics. Lipietz argues that another, more democratic, alternative to both Fordism and liberal-productivism is possible, both as better politics and as new growth regime. He describes the 'alternative' as one which remains socially inclusive but non-hierarchical, and one which defends actively the principles of collective participation, negotiation, 'dynamic guarantee of employment', eco-logical sanity, the enhancement of free time, the defence of socially useful work and the transformation of the welfare state (based on income redistribution) into the 'welfare community' (in defence of the welfare of communities).

This is a vision of participatory democracy which draws upon aspects of institutional change identified by Mayer at the local level. But significantly, for Lipietz, it is a grand design, a model for the future, which will not follow inevitably from the new institutional configura-tions of today. Instead, he argues that it needs to be constructed and fought for. Lipietz calls it a democracy in the making, not a promised outcome, since it involves radically new, non-Fordist, forms of political engagement in pursuit of a radically new set of expectations of social and economic progress: 'a continent to be discovered'. Thus, with Lipietz, the transition to a new societal mode is made a question of politics and political choices. The importance of a need to construct actively an alternative vision of societal goals is too easily forgotten by some accounts seeking a new political project, which have conceded too much to the individualism, the consumerism, the fragmented politics and the subjectivism of contemporary neo-liberalism, seeing them as 'natural' outcomes of advanced society and therefore the stuff of an alternative socialist politics (e.g. Hall and Jacques, 1989).

One problem within Lipietz's analysis, however, relates to the tendency to see the politics of transition as relatively open and those of a new paradigm as relatively circumscribed. There is a hint that the period of transition between phases of capitalist development is the moment of confrontation between radical political alternatives, while once a 'societal mode' is established, the 'rules of the game' settle to delimit the political arena. Such an interpretation could be a sticking point for many critics on the Left, uncomfortable with the idea of stable political settlements, and choosing instead to view capitalist development as permanently crisis-ridden and a constant battle between irreconcilable interests. The latter perspective allows interpretation of the timing of political transition and the destabilization of a hegemonic project to remain an open question and a matter of permanent struggle. It thus allows one, 'from a political perspective, to theorise areas of antihegemony, of contradictory development, in order to create openings for projects of social transformation' (Graham, 1992, p. 409).

Post-Fordist city lives and lifestyles

A final theme developed in this reader relates to social and cultural change. Normally in the literature, the term 'post-Fordism' is associated with economic and institutional change, while the term 'post-modernism' is associated with change in the arena of consumption, aesthetics, culture and lifestyle. However, for observers concerned with the totality of change today, not only are the two arenas representative of a single, overarching transition, they are also inseparable. For Stuart Hall (1988, p. 28), one epithet captures both:

> If 'post-Fordism' exists then, it is as much a description of cultural as
> of economic change. Indeed, that distinction is now quite useless.
> Culture has ceased to be, if it ever was, a decorative addendum to the
> 'hard world' of production and things, the icing on the cake of the
> material world . . . Through design, technology and styling, 'aesthetics'
> has already penetrated the world of modern production. Through
> marketing, layout and style, the 'image' provides the mode of represen-
> tation of the body on which so much of modern consumption depends.

The 'aestheticization of commodities' and the 'commodification of
aesthetics' are two aspects of the emerging age which serve to blur
the traditional distinction between economic and cultural activity. The
first refers to the embellishment of products, artifacts, buildings, workplaces, infrastructure and so on, as a means of enlivening everyday
life at the same time as legitimating consumerism and social acceptance
of the imperatives of capitalism. The second refers to the increasing
transformation of culture and cultural activity, especially leisure and
recreation, into cultural industries, that is, commodities sold in the
market to individual consumers who, in turn, increasingly identify
cultural gratification with consumption, rather than as an independent
activity, geared towards, say, creative learning (Urry, 1990).

'Post-modernist' theory, in contrast, tends to focus on and 'celebrate
the penetration of aesthetics into everyday life and the ascendancy of
popular culture over the high arts' (Hall, 1988, p. 25). It notes that
the post-modern condition increasingly blurs image and reality, prefers
kitsch over high art, is interested in appearance and the superficial, and
celebrates cultural diversity, subjectivism and 'ideals of the moment'
over universal and collective metaphors of progress. The theory offers
a perspective on contemporary cultural transformation, without,
however, exploring in any depth the connections with the economic
and political changes identified in the post-Fordist literature.

One notable exception is the work of David Harvey (1989a, 1991,
and chapter 12 in this reader), who has sought to relate the rise of post-
modern culture and society to the imperatives of a post-Fordist
economy (which he calls 'flexible accumulation'). For Harvey, the
link and its contradictions are starkly represented in the city, that is,
in contemporary urban life. His chapter in this reader (chapter 12),
based on his observations on urban transformation in the United
States, considers three aspects of the post-Fordist/post-modern city –
aspects with worrying social implications. One aspect, which he calls
the 'production of symbolic capital', refers to the exploitation of
differentiated markets, through the enticement of middle and high
income groups into accumulating status-enhancing luxury goods. The

effect of this process is not only the spatial and social segregation within cities of the affluent from others unable to acquire 'symbolic' capital, but also the acquisition of greater power in urban politics by the former because of their privileged position in an urban economy increasingly based on consumption priorities (see also Zukin, 1992).

The second aspect, called the 'mobilization of spectacle', refers to the enormous proliferation in recent years, as a result of active support from the state (Harvey, 1989b), of shopping and leisure 'experiences', such as shopping complexes, marinas, Chinatowns and so on, as a means of boosting mass consumerism. This turning of cities into an arena of spectacle and play is seen to represent a further division between those who can and those who cannot take part in the spectacle, but also, more importantly, a redirection of urban policy and political priorities away from investment in production and from meeting social needs (see also chapter 10 by Mayer).

The third aspect of post-Fordist urban change stressed by Harvey (and echoing Esser and Hirch's analysis in chapter 3) is an epidemic rise in poverty and informal activity (from odd-jobbing and domestic work to drug-trafficking and prostitution) associated with post-Fordist deindustrialization and the emergence of the flexibly organized economy. It is a process which has created a vast underclass of low-income or no-income communities increasingly abandoned by welfare programmes, and isolated from areas of the city 'embellished' for the well-off. This aspect of urban social life, with its stark cultural outcomes related to crime, poverty, degradation, dehumanization and isolation, is conspicuously absent in post-modernist accounts of city life, focusing, as they do, on the new consumerism and on urban aesthetics. In Britain, an interpretation of city life celebrating cultural pluralism and cafe cultures is unashamedly proposed by theorists and planners keen to imagine the 'good' city (e.g. Mulgan, 1989; Montgomery, 1990).

Not all accounts of changing city cultures share this up-beat bias. The chapter by Featherstone (chapter 13) asks whether the emerging post-modern city cultures and lifestyles represent 'enclaved' experiences, for the better-off, in specific urban locations. Like Harvey, he argues that the principle of 'city as play-pen' conceals stark differences between the lifestyles of different social groups. However, he tends not to distance himself from the post-modernist interpretation of cities of tomorrow as centres of consumption, aesthetics and cultural activity. He appears to accept, perhaps because of his focus on cultural issues, that the city has become less a site of production and work and more a site of consumption and play – the most vivid symbol of the post-modern condition. He discusses, for instance, the greater aetheticization of the urban fabric and the daily lives of people, the development of new consumption and leisure activities (e.g. museums, theme parks, shopping centres) and the gentrification of selected city areas. His analysis thus tends to endorse the idea of the city as fun and spectacle, as its citizens become recast as consumers.

A very different story emerges from Christopherson's analysis of the contemporary American city (chapter 14). Echoing Harvey, Mike Davis (1990) on Los Angeles and other American urban political economists (e.g. Mollenkopf and Castells, 1991, on New York), she argues that the post-Fordist city has ceased to be a place of encounter, cultural mixture and a public sphere open to all citizens. Instead, she argues that the contemporary stress within urban policy and city politics on consumption and consumerism has destroyed the idea of social citizenship and the idea of public sphere which was present in the Fordist city, having replaced it with the credo that city spaces are privatized places of consumption (Davis, 1990, refers to 'Fortress LA' in relation to Los Angeles). She contends that this is a turn with nightmarish consequences for marginalized sections of society, now kept out of public spaces (libraries, streets, shopping centres, select neighbourhoods, parks, churches, etc.), as these areas are turned into 'safe' places open only to people valued as consumers or producers. Further exclusion, she points out, has come from the increasing orientation of local politics towards a defence of communities of self-interest and consumer rights, while the 'old' politics of universal access to housing, health care, public services and so on are abandoned. The post-Fordist city is thus conceived as an arena of exclusion and private spaces, as it 'comes to be dominated by security cages and a honeycomb of residential and business fortresses'. This vision of the city as a segregated and excluding setting contrasts starkly with the concept of the city as post-modern play-pen. The latter concept displays a certain complacence as regards the status quo, while the former demands urgent corrective action to restore social justice and social citizenship in our cities (Harvey, 1992).

Like the other themes of post-Fordist transition discussed in this book, here too the future is contested. The differences in perspective will need to be debated, questioned and tested against contemporary developments. Ultimately, perhaps only time and the forces of history will reveal the true phantoms and fantasies of post-Fordism. It is hoped, however, that this reader might help in laying down the conceptual foundations for making sense of the future as it unfolds.

NOTES

I am grateful to James Cornford, Andy Pike and John Tomaney for their helpful suggestions on an earlier draft.

REFERENCES

Aglietta, M. (1979) *A Theory of Capitalist Regulation*. London: New Left Books.
Aglietta, M. (1982) World capitalism in the eighties. *New Left Review*, 136, 3–41.
Alliez, E. and Fehrer, M. (1987) The luster of capital. *Zone*, 1/2, 315–59.
Amin, A. and Robins, K. (1990) The re-emergence of regional economies? The mythical geography of flexible accumulation. *Environment and Planning D: Society and Space*, 8(1), 7–34.
Amin, A. and Dietrich, M. (1991) From hierarchy to 'hiearachy': the dynamics of contemporary corporate restructuring in Europe. In A. Amin and M. Dietrich (eds), *Towards a New Europe? Structural Change in the European Economy*. Aldershot: Elgar.
Amin, A. and Thrift, N. (1992) Neo-Marshallian nodes in global networks. *International Journal of Urban and Regional Research*, 16, 4: 571–87.
Amin, A. and Thrift, N. (1994) Living in the global. In A. Amin and N. Thrift (eds), *Globalisation, Institutions and Regional Development in Europe*. Oxford: Oxford University Press.
André, C. and Delorme. R. (1982) *L'Etat et L'Economie*. Paris: Seuil.
Asheim, B. (1992) Flexible specialisation industrial districts and small firms: a critical appraisal. In H. Ernste and V. Meier (eds), *Regional Development and Contemporary Industrial Response: Extending Flexible Specialisation*. London: Belhaven.
Bonefeld, W. (1993) Crisis of theory: Bob Jessop's theory of capitalist reproduction. *Capital and Class*, 50, 22–47.
Bonefeld, W. and Holloway, J. (eds) (1991) *Post-Fordism and Social Form*. London: Macmillan.
Boyer, R. (1986) *La théorie de la régulation: une analyse critique*. Paris: La Découverte.
Boyer, R. (1988a) Technical change and the theory of regulation. In G. Dosi, C. Freeman, R. Nelson, G. Silverberg and L. Soete (eds), *Technical Change and Economical Theory*. London: Frances Pinter.
Boyer, R. (ed.) (1988b) *The Search for Labour Market Flexibility: the European Economies in Transition*. Oxford: Clarendon Press.
Boyer, R. (1991) The eighties: the search for alternatives to Fordism. In B. Jessop, H. Kastendiek, K. Nielsen and O. Pedersen (eds), *The Politics of Flexibility*. Aldershot: Edward Elgar.
Brenner, R. and Glick, M. (1991) The Regulation Approach: theory and history. *New Left Review*, 188, 45–120.
Castells, M. (1989) *The Informational City: Information Technolopy, Economic Restructuring and the Urban Regional Process*. Oxford: Blackwell.

Clarke, S. (1988) Overaccumulation, class struggle and the regulation approach. *Capital and Class*, 36, 59–92.

Clarke, S. (1990) New utopias for old: Fordist dreams and post-Fordist fantasies. *Capital and Class*, 42, 131–55.

Cooke, P., Moulaert, F., Swyngedouw, E., Weinstein, O. and Wells, P. (1992) *Towards Global Localisation: the Computing and Telecommunications Industries in Britain and France*. London: UCL Press.

Coriat, B. (1979) *L'atelier et le chronomètre* Paris: Christian Bourgois.

Coriat, B. and Petit, P. (1991) Deindustrialisation and tertiarization: towards a new economic regime? In A. Amin and M. Dietrich (eds), *Towards a New Europe?* Aldershot: Edward Elgar.

Curry, J. (1993) The flexibility fetish: a review essay on flexible specialisation. *Capital and Class*, 50, 99–126.

Dankbaar, B. (1992) *Economic Crisis and Institutional Change*. Maastricht: UPM.

Davis, M. (1990) *City of Quartz: Excavating the Future in Los Angeles*. London: Verso.

Dicken, P., Forsgren, M. and Malmberg, A. (1994) The local embeddedness of transnational corporations. In A. Amin and N. Thrift (eds), *Globalisation Institutions and Regional Development in Europe*. Oxford: Oxford University Press.

Dosi, G., Freeman, C., Nelson, R., Silverberg, G. and Soete, L. (eds) (1988) *Technical Change and Economic Theory*. London: Frances Pinter.

Dunford, M. (1990) Theories of regulation. *Environment and Planning, D: Society and Space*, 8, 297–321.

Elger, T. (1991) Flexibility and the intensification of labour in UK manufacturing in the 1980s. In A. Pollert (ed.), *Farewell to Flexibility?* Oxford: Blackwell.

Foster, J. B. (1988) The fetish of Fordism. *Monthly Review*, 39(10), 14–33.

Frankel, B. (1987) *The Post-Industrial Utopians*. Cambridge: Polity Press.

Freeman, C. and Perez, C. (1988) Structural crisis of adjustment, business cycles and investment behaviour. In G. Dosi, C. Freeman, R. Nelson, G. Silverberg and L. Soete (eds), *Technical Change and Economic Theory*. London: Frances Pinter.

Freeman, C., Clarke, J. and Soete, L. (1982) *Unemployment and Technical Innovation. A Study of Long Waves in Economic Development*. London: Frances Pinter.

Gertler, M. S. (1988) The limits to flexibility: comments on the post-Fordist vision of production. *Transactions, Institute of British Geographers*, 13, 419–32.

Gertler, M. S. (1992) Flexibility revisited: districts, nation-states and the forces of production. *Transactions, Institute of British Geographers*, 17, 259–78.

Graham, J. (1992) Post-Fordism as politics: the political consequences of narratives on the left. *Environment and Planning, D: Society and Space*, 10, 393–410.

Hall, S. (1988) Brave new world. *Marxism Today*, October, 24–9.

Hall, S. and Jacques, M. (eds) (1989) *New Times*. London: Lawrence and Wishart.

Harrison, B. (1994) *Lean and Mean: the Changing Landscape of Corporate Power in the Age of Flexibility*. New York: Basic Books.

Harvey, D. (1987) Flexible accumulation through urbanisation: reflections on 'post-modernism' in the American city. *Antipode*, 19(3), 260–86.

Harvey, D. (1989a) *The Condition of Postmodernity*. Oxford: Basil Blackwell.

Harvey, D. (1989b) From managerialism to entrepreneurialism: the transformation of urban governance in late capitalism. *Geografiska Annaler*, 71B(1), 3–17.

Harvey, D. (1991) Flexibility: threat or opportunity? *Socialist Review*, 21(1), 65–77.

Harvey, D. (1992) Social justice, postmodernism and the city. *International Journal of Urban and Regional Research*, 16(4), 588–601.

Harvey, D. and Scott, A. J. (1988) 'The practice of human geography: theory and empirical specificity in the transition from Fordism to flexible accumulation. In W. D. MacMillan (ed.), *Remodelling Geography*. Oxford: Blackwell.

Henry, N. (1992) The new industrial spaces: locational logic of a new production era? *International Journal of Urban and Regional Research*, 16(3), 375–96.

Hirsch, J. (1991) From the Fordist to the post-Fordist state. In B. Jessop, H. Kastendiek, K. Nielsen and O. Pedersen (eds), *The Politics of Flexibility*. Aldershot: Edward Elgar.

Hirst, P. and Zeitlin, J. (1989) Flexible specialisation and the competitive failure of UK manufacturing. *Political Quarterly*, 60(3), 164–78.

Hirst, P. and Zeitlin, J. (1991) Flexible specialisation versus post-Fordism: theory, evidence and policy implications. *Economy and Society*, 20(1), 1–156.

Holloway, J. (1988) The great bear, post-Fordism and class struggle: a comment on Bonefeld and Jessop. *Capital and Class*, 36, 93–104.

Hyman, R. (1991) *Plus ça change?* The theory of production and the production of theory. In A. Pollert (ed.), *Farewell to Flexibility?* Oxford: Blackwell.

Jessop, B. (1991) Thatcherism and flexibility: the white heat of a post-Fordist revolution. In B. Jessop, H. Kastendiek, K. Nielsen and O. Pedersen (eds), *The Politics of Flexibility*. Aldershot: Edward Elgar.

Jessop, B. (1992a) Fordism and post-Fordism: critique and reformulation. In M. Storper and A. J. Scott (eds), *Pathways to Industrialisation and Regional Development*. London: Routledge.

Jessop, B. (1992b) Post-Fordism and flexible specialisation: incommensurable, contradictory, complementary, or just plain different perspectives? In H. Ernste and V. Meier (eds), *Regional Development and Contemporary Industrial Response: Extending Flexible Specialisation*. London: Belhaven.

Kern, H. and Schumann, M. (1987) Limits of the division of labour: new production and employment concepts in West German industry. *Economic and Industrial Democracy*, 8, 151–70.

Lane, C. (1989) *Management and Labour in Europe*. Aldershot: Edward Elgar.

Lash, S. and Urry, J. (1987) *The End of Organized Capitalism*. Cambridge: Polity.

Lash, S. and Urry, J. (1993) *Economies of Signs and Space: After Organised Capitalism*. London: Sage.

Leborgne, D. and Lipietz, A. (1988) New technologies, new modes of regulation: some spatial implications. *Environment and Planning, D: Society and Space*, 6, 263–80.

Leborgne, D. and Lipietz, A. (1992) Conceptual fallacies and open questions on post-Fordism. In M. Storper and A. J. Scott (eds), *Pathways to Industrialisation and Regional Development* London: Routledge.

Lipietz, A. (1985) *The Enchanted World: Inflation, Credit and the World Crisis.* London: Verso.

Lipietz, A. (1987) *Mirages and Miracles: the Crises of Global Fordism.* London: Verso.

Lipietz, A. (1988) Accumulation, crises and the ways out: some methodological reflections on the concept of 'regulation'. *International Journal of Political Economy*, 18(2), 10–43.

Lipietz, A. (1992) *Towards a New Economic Order. Post-Fordism, Ecology and Democracy.* Oxford: Oxford University Press.

Lipietz, A. (1993) The local and the global: regional individuality or inter-regionalism? *Transactions Institute of British Geographers*, 18, 8–18.

Lovering, J. (1991) Theorising post-fordism: why contingency matters – a further response to Scott. *International Journal of Urban and Regional Research*, 15, 298–301.

Mahon, R. (1987) From Fordism to? New technology, labour markets and unions. *Economic and Industrial Democracy*, 8, 5–60.

Marginson, P. (1991) Change and continuity in the employment structure of large companies. In A. Pollert (ed.), *Farewell to Flexibility?* Oxford: Blackwell.

Meegan, R. (1988) A crisis of mass production? In J. Allen and D. Massey (eds), *The Economy in Question: Restructuring Britain.* London: Sage.

Meiskins Wood, E. (1989) Discussion on Manifesto for the New Times. *Marxism Today*, August.

Mistral, J. (1986) Régime internationale et trajectories nationales. In R. Boyer (ed.), *Capitalisme Fin de Siecle.* Paris: Presse Universitaire de France.

Mollenkopf, J. H. and Castells, M. (eds) (1991) *Dual City: Restructuring New York.* New York: Russell Sage Foundation.

Montgomery, J. (1990) Cities and the art of cultural planning. *Planning Practice and Research*, 5(3), 17–24.

Mulgan, G. (1989) The changing shape of the city. In S. Hall and M. Jacques (eds), *New Times.* London: Lawrence and Wishart.

Nielsen, K. (1991) Towards a flexible future – theories and politics. In B. Jessop, H. Kastendiek, K. Neilsen and O. Pedersen (eds), *The Politics of Flexibility.* Aldershot: Edward Elgar.

Nöel, A. (1987) Accumulation, regulation and social change: an essay on French political economy. *International Organisation*, 41, 303–33.

Perez, C. (1985) Microelectronics, long waves and world structural system: new perspectives for developing countries. *World Development*, 13, 441–63.

Perez, C. (1986) Structural change and assimilation of new technologies in the economic and social system. In C. Freeman (ed.), *Design, Innovation and Long Cycles in Economic Development.* London: Frances Pinter.

Piore, M. (1990) Work, labour and action: work experience in a system of flexible production. In F. Pike, G. Becattini and W. Sengenberger (eds), *Industrial Districts and Inter-firm Co-operation in Italy*. Geneva: ILO.

Piore, M. and Sabel, C. (1984) *The Second Industrial Divide: Possibilities for Prosperity*. New York: Basic Books.

Pollert, A. (1988) Dismantling flexibility. *Capital and Class*, 34, 42–75.

Pollert, A. (1991) The orthodoxy of flexibility. In A. Pollert (ed.), *Farewell to Flexibility?* Oxford: Blackwell.

Psychopedis, K. (1991) Crisis of theory in contemporary social sciences. In W. Bonefeld and J. Holloway (eds), *Post-Fordism and Social Form*. London: Macmillan.

Rainnie, A. (1993) The reorganisation of large firm subcontracting: myth and reality? *Capital and Class*, 49, 53–75.

Roobeek, A. (1987) The crisis of Fordism and the rise of a new technological paradigm. *Futures*, April, 129–54.

Rustin, M. (1989) The politics of post-Fordism: or, the trouble with 'New Times'. *New Left Review*, 175, 54–78.

Sabel, C. (1982) *Work and Politics: the Division of Labour in Industry*. Cambridge: Cambridge University Press.

Sabel, C. (1992) Studied trust: building new forms of co-operation in a volatile economy. In F. Pyke and W. Sengenberger (eds), *Industrial Districts and Local Economic Regeneration*. Geneva: ILO.

Sabel, C. and Zeitlin, J. (1985) Historical alternatives to mass production: politics, markets and technology in nineteenth century industrialisation. *Past and Present*, 108, 133–76.

Salvati, M. (1989) A long cycle in industrial relations, or: regulation theory and political economy. *Labour*, 3(1), 41–72.

Sassen, S. (1991) *The Global City*. Princeton, NJ: Princeton University Press.

Sayer, A. (1989) Post-Fordism in question. *International Journal of Urban and Regional Research*, 13, 666–95.

Sayer, A. and Walker, R. (1992) *The New Social Economy: Reworking the Division of Labour*. Oxford: Blackwell.

Scott, A. J. (1986) Industrial organisation and location: division of labour, the firm and spatial process. *Economic Geography*, 62, 215–31.

Scott, A. J. (1988) Flexible production systems and regional development: the rise of new industrial spaces in North America and Western Europe. *International Journal of Urban and Regional Research*, 12, 171–86.

Scott, A. J. (1992) The role of larger producers in industrial districts: a case study of high technology system houses in Southern California. *Regional Studies*, 26, 265–75.

Sivanandan, A. (1990) All that melts into air is solid: the hokum of New Times. *Race and Class*, 31(3), 1–30.

Smith, C. (1989) Flexible specialisation, automation and mass production. *Work, Employment and Society*, 3, 203–20.

Solo, R. (1985) Across the industrial divide. *Journal of Economic Issues*, 19, 829–36.

Sternberg, E. (1993) Transformations: the eight new ages of capitalism. Mimeo, Department of Planning and Design, State University of New York, Buffalo.

Storper, M. (1992) The limits to globalisation: technology districts and international trade. *Economic Geography*, 68, 60–93.

Storper, M. (1993) Regional words of production: learning and innovation in the technology districts in France, Italy and the USA. *Regional Studies*, 27, 433–55.

Storper, M. and Scott, A. J. (1989) The geographical foundations and social regulation of flexible production complexes. In J. Wolch and M. Dear (eds), *The Power of Geography: How Territory Shapes Social Life*. Winchester, MA: Unwin Hyman.

Thrift, N. (1989) New times and new spaces? The perils of transition models. *Environment and Planning, D: Society and Space*, 7, 127–9.

Tickell, A. and Peck, J. (1992) Accumulation, regulation and the geographies of post-Fordism: missing links in regulationist research. *Progress in Human Geography*, 16, 190–218.

Urry, J. (1990) *The Tourist Gaze*. London: Sage.

Webber, M. J. (1991) The contemporary transition. *Environment and Planning, D: Society and Space*, 9, 165–82.

Williams, K., Cutler, T., Williams, J. and Haslam, C. (1987) The end of mass production? *Economy and Society*, 16(3), 405–39.

Williams, K. and Haslam, C. (1991) Ford versus Fordism. Mimeo, Department of Economics, University of Wales, Aberystwyth.

Witheford, N. (1994) Autonomist Marxism and the Information Society. *Capital and Class*, 52, 85–125.

Zukin, S. (1992) Postmodern urban landscapes: mapping culture and power. In S. Lash and J. Friedman (eds), *Modernity and Identity*. Oxford: Blackwell.

Part I

New Macroeconomic Designs

2

Puzzling out the Post-Fordist Debate: Technology, Markets and Institutions

Mark Elam

INTRODUCTION

The post-Fordist debate is the contemporary expression of a classic debate. The debate is about capitalism's future; its dynamics and its survival. It is a debate which gains fresh impetus during periods of uncertainty and transition and the current post-Fordist appellation reflects a certain preoccupation with the changing fortunes of American capitalism and the decline of US hegemony in the global economy. New models for the future development of capitalism appear to be taking shape; new industrial paradigms signalling the end of the global diffusion of 'Fordism' and the 'American Way of Life'. However, the extent to which new technological possibilities add up to the basis for a new qualitatively different phase of capitalist development remains very much open to discussion.

Within the context of the post-Fordist debate we can bear witness to a thorough reappraisal and partial reformulation of some of the classic accounts of the historical development of capitalism. Argument centres on the continued relevance of the theories expounded by earlier observers of capitalist development and the possibilities for the revitalization and reaffirmation of their ideas in considerably revised

This chapter is a reprint of an article published in *Economic and Industrial Democracy* (1990), vol. 11, no. 1, pp. 9–37.

forms. In this chapter I shall take up three contrasting post-Fordist perspectives signifying renewed interest in three classic accounts of the nature of capitalist development.

Firstly, I shall discuss a *neo-Schumpeterian* perspective exemplified by the recent work of Christopher Freeman and Carlota Perez.[1] This perspective attempts to specify phases of capitalist development primarily in terms of their technological content. Thus, the history of capitalism is the history of technological revolutions and the post-Fordist era is synonymous with the dictatorship of information technology. Secondly, I identify a *neo-Smithian* perspective exemplified by Michael Piore and Charles Sabel, who in their book *The Second Industrial Divide*,[2] ultimately place the changing face of markets at the centre of the historical stage. The post-Fordist era is being ushered in by the contemporary instability, uncertainty and apparently irreversible fragmentation of core markets in the major capitalist economies. This far-reaching process of market fragmentation has fundamental consequences for the organization of production and the choice of technique. Thirdly, I will explore a *neo-Marxist* perspective exemplified by the recent work of both the so-called French Regulation School and Michael Burawoy.[3] This perspective moves beyond the sphere of 'techno-economic' determinations and points to the existence of a second constellation of dynamic forces in the historical development of capitalism; a largely autonomous sphere of 'politico-institutional' forces. Thus, we are confronted with *two* basic dynamics emerging out of the bedrock of capitalist social relations and the post-Fordist era is associated not only with technological transformations and a new 'regime of accumulation' but also institutional transformations and a new 'mode of regulation'.

A NEO-SCHUMPETERIAN PERSPECTIVE

The theoretical point of departure for this perspective is Schumpeter's reworking of Kondratiev's notion of 'long waves' in the development of capitalist economies. According to Schumpeter, these long-waves of roughly fifty years' duration reflect a process of 'creative destruction' and long-term changes in the technological base of the economy:

> The fundamental impulse that sets and keeps the capitalist engine in motion comes from the new consumers' goods, the new methods of production or transportation, the new markets, the new forms of industrial organisation that capitalist enterprise creates. *(Schumpeter, 1979: 83)*

Christopher Freeman and Carlota Perez have been responsible for the significant extension and refinement of Schumpeter's original formulations and have thereby greatly added to our understanding of the nature of technological change. For them, periodic gales of 'creative destruction' represent fundamental technological revolutions which bear with them 'quantum leaps' in industrial productivity. Each revolution is composed of a 'cluster of radical innovations' which introduces a new set of common sense principles into capitalist production and a clearly defined 'best practice' frontier. As a critical stage of advancement is reached it becomes very difficult for national economies and individual firms to opt out of the new technological regime; they become 'locked-in' to a universal developmental trajectory.

Techno-economic paradigms and technological determinism

The *systemic* nature of technological revolutions gives rise to the notion of 'techno-economic paradigms'; qualitative changes in capitalist production exceeding the simple sum of new engineering trajectories – completely new worlds of work with new standards of efficiency; new models for management; new locational patterns; new high growth sectors and a redefined optimal scale of production (Perez, 1985: 444). Each techno-economic paradigm hinges on a crucial input or 'key factor' in production which is able to play a 'steering role' because it fulfils the following conditions:

(a) clearly perceived low and rapidly falling relative cost;
(b) almost unlimited supply for all practical purposes;
(c) potential all-pervasiveness in the productive sphere;
(d) a capacity to reduce the cost and change the quality of capital equipment, labour inputs and other inputs to the system. (Perez, 1986: 32, Freeman and Perez, 1988b: 48)

Today, at the onset of the 'fifth Kondratiev' and the 'information technology paradigm' the key factor is considered to be micro-electronics which are increasingly 'steering' technical and organizational common sense. After 1930, this role was played by oil together with petro-chemicals. In the 1880s and 1890s, low-cost steel began to fashion the growth of the heavy engineering industries. The Victorian boom was correspondingly based on low-cost coal and steam-powered transportation, while the 'Industrial Revolution' (the first Kondratiev) revolved around cotton and pig iron (Freeman and Perez, 1988b). Clearly, the neo-Schumpeterian perspective is vulnerable to the charge of courting an excessive degree of *technological determinism*. There is a predominant tendency to reduce significant qualitative changes within capitalism to 'key factors' and very tangible technological content – the changing technological hardware of history. It would appear that Freeman and Perez are, themselves, aware of, and troubled by, this intrinsic *reductionism* and have consequently strived to complement (but not sacrifice) the overriding emphasis on the role of radical technical innovations with additional elements. Thus, Kondratiev's long waves are not simply defined as 'techno-economic' phenomena, they are: 'the manifestation, measurable in economic terms, of the harmonious or disharmonious behaviour of the *total socio-economic and institutional system* (on the national and international levels)' (Perez, 1986: 27, my emphasis).

The transition from one techno-economic paradigm to the next is considered to entail 'equally profound transformation of the institutional and social framework' (Freeman and Perez, 1988b: 57). However, despite this apparent sensitivity to the contextual environment, the history of capitalism remains one where 'new' techno-economic forces always do the initial acting and 'old' socio-institutional frameworks the eventual reacting:

> While in nature, it is the external environment that forces the adaption of the living species; in economic development, it would be the environment that is reshaped to suit the potential of the new genetic pool. Yet it must be emphasized that, in spite of appearances, we are not making an argument for *mere* technological determinism. The variety of suitable environments is quite large, and whatever specific form is arrived at, from the wide range of viable options, will in turn determine the preferred ways in which the latent technological potential develops through strong 'feedback' selective action and gradual mutual adjustment. *(Perez, 1985: 445, my emphasis)*

The 'socio-institutional' is clearly subordinate to the 'techno-economic' and its autonomy strictly bounded. Regarding the post-Fordist era, the nascent information technology paradigm has offered us a glimpse of the future and convinced us of the need for a 'full-scale reaccommodation of social behaviour and institutions' to facilitate a new harmonious period of sustained growth (Freeman and Perez, 1988b: 59). Although the notion of a socio-institutional context may broaden the neo-Schumpeterian perspective, it remains, at present, a diffuse and undervalued constellation (Kaplinsky, 1988a). This may in turn be seen as a reflection of a pre-existing reticence within the neo-Schumpeterian perspective to deal with social relations in general. Tangible but impersonal technologies have always been given precedence over the less palpable forces shaping economy and society. Even within the techno-economic sphere itself, the realm of *embodied* technology has continually dominated over that of *disembodied* technology which can now all too easily fall into a catch-all socio-institutional context (Kaplinsky, 1988a).

It would appear that Freeman's well-established 'taxonomy of innovations'[4] – based on a long history of empirical work at the Science Policy Research Unit, Sussex and out of which the notion of techno-economic paradigms has evolved – makes insufficient room for the less tangible *social innovations* which always coexist alongside the more hard and fast technical ones. Thus, significant innovations in the way in which the production process is 'materially organized' (Sayer, 1985: 15) have been seriously neglected in the neo-Schumpeterian perspective. In order to successfully take into account these social innovations, the neo-Schumpeterian perspective will have to shift attention away from generic technologies and the most accessible facts of production, towards specific patterns of social relations and the more opaque bases of different productive paradigms which can only be brought to light through studies of individual workplaces in particular socio-cultural contexts. The centrality of social innovations and the need to study specific patterns of social relations to gain a better understanding of broad processes of technological change has become increasingly apparent in the wake of recent studies attempting to account for the spectacular rise of Japan as an advanced capitalist economy.

The Toyota paradigm: 'automation with a human mind'

It is often thought that the Japanese superiority in automobile productivity arises from their more advanced utilisation of electronics-based automation technologies. Indeed, it is currently the case that with the possible exception of Fiat, a number of Japanese firms are the leaders in this type of automation. Yet this was not always the case and until 1983 or so, most of the Japanese firms were laggard in this respect. The point is that the major improvements in productivity arose *before* electronics technologies were widely used. *(Kaplinsky, 1988b)*

It is extremely difficult to explain the 'quantum leaps' in productivity made by Japanese industry in recent years in terms of a technological revolution in the neo-Schumpeterian sense. The most important features of Japanese production systems often appear to be simplicity and frugality rather than sophistication and daring (Schonberger, 1987). For this reason Japanese car production has been recently

conceived as having more in common with the running of a super-
market than the launching of a space rocket (Cole, 1985). At Toyota,
the largest Japanese car firm, the key process of automation has never
been 'steered' by microelectronics in any straightforward fashion
and has never been solely connected with the replacement of manual
labour by computer-controlled machines.[5] An important dimension of
automation and central element in the Toyota Production System has
been what Monden (1983) calls '*autonomation*' or 'automation with a
human mind'. In contrast to more sophisticated forms of automation
based on flexible manufacturing systems (FMS), computer-controlled
machine tools, robots and CAD/CAM systems, autonomation is
essentially a social innovation and relatively simple and inexpensive.
Its major advantages over a more ambitious 'high-tech' approach
to manufacturing lie in its often superior ability to assure quality,
flexibility and continuity in production. Crucially, autonomation
remains a much more *fluid* process than computer-controlled automation; in fact the latter can be accurately seen as *solidified* autonomation.

The basic aim of autonomation is an 'automatic control of defects'
making it impossible for defective parts to pass unnoticed along
the production line. Human judgement and discretion remain
central to autonomation, although these are usually augmented by
'mechatronic'[6] support systems which ensure the process is foolproof.
Foolproof autonomation means the realization of the goal of 'zero-
defects'. Two typical examples of autonomation at Toyota provided by
Monden (1983) appear as follows: (i) at a spot welding station a counter
records the number of welds automatically and sounds a buzzer if there
is a discrepancy between the number it has counted and the number
required; (ii) to ensure that a worker puts all the required parts into
a shipping-box, electronic eyes are installed in front of each parts
bin so that the worker's hand interrupts the light beam when he
removes each part. Unless all the beams are interrupted the box will
not be released and allowed to leave the worker's station. In both cases
operations are simplified and the work cycle becomes more uniform.
Therefore, in Toyota's autonomated factories smooth, faultless and
flexible production is not typically guided by advanced computer
systems, but human discretion aided by an assorted collection of
buzzers and beams like those mentioned above plus multicoloured
lights (andons) constantly indicating the state of the production line
and tag-like cards (Kanbans) passed upstream with instructions about
the quantities of parts and materials required at any particular time.
Kanbans are often singled out as the definitive ingredient in the Toyota
Production System and this is not surprising as they are literally
the symbol for a highly efficient 'low-tech' substitute for sophisticated

computer control. As one assistant manager at Toyota recorded by Robert Cole explained:

> Although we use computers for working out monthly production schedules and production volumes, our daily variations of production are all controlled by the movement of Kanban. If we were to use computers for the fine-tuning of the production schedule in lieu of Kanban, we would probably need a capacity 20 times what we now have. Moreover, even with such computer capabilities we would not be able to do all the jobs that Kanban does for us. No computer programme can predict the fluctuations in automobile production. *(Quoted in Cole, 1985: 103)*

On the basis of assertions such as this it is worth questioning the extent to which computer-controlled automation is the logical and inevitable extension of human-centred autonomation. Clearly the advantages of a fluid autonomation may persist and the risks and commitments involved in a move to more solid forms of computer-controlled automation may not prove worth taking or making. Provided a suitable workforce is available that is both willing and able to participate in autonomative practice and internalize its goals, the incentives to harden automation into its more sophisticated computer-controlled forms may well remain low. Therefore, we can conclude this brief discussion of Japanese industry by asserting that if the significant 'leaps' in productivity achieved by Japanese firms like Toyota are considered to reflect the initial crystallization of a new techno-economic paradigm for the post-Fordist era, then social innovations and complex changes in the material *organization* of production may demand just as much attention as technical innovations and the highly visible changes in the material *composition* of production.

Allocating social innovations a central role in the broad processes of technological change connected with the post-Fordist era means rejecting the neo-Schumpeterian preoccupation with microelectronics as a 'key factor' playing a 'steering role'. This preoccupation involves courting with an unacceptably hard and narrow technological determinism which an alternative focus on social innovations would largely neutralize. Such an alternative focus, which would give the 'techno-economic' a decisive social content, would also help to breathe new life and greater autonomy into the neo-Schumpeterian notion of a socio-institutional context. Clearly, if *both* 'new' technological forces and 'old' institutional contexts have an essentially social content then the character of qualitative change can be actively *negotiated* as well as passively accommodated.

A NEO-SMITHIAN PERSPECTIVE

While Freeman and Perez conceive the post-Fordist era in terms of the coming of the 'fifth Kondratiev', Piore and Sabel (1984) are satisfied with just the 'second industrial divide'. After an epoch of mass production and the rule of Fordist production systems, Piore and Sabel do not see a new 'long wave', but a new 'branching-point' – a 'brief interlude of openness' (Sabel and Zeitlin, 1985: 162) before the new technological trajectory is established. In similar fashion to the neo-Schumpeterian perspective, Piore and Sabel also take up the notion of 'technological paradigms'; but this time the tables are turned and the emphasis is very much on social innovation and only secondarily on embodied technology.

The passing era of mass production has been characterized by a paradigm of work organization based on an extreme division of labour; the limits of which have been reached and infamously stretched. Thus, the time is ripe for the introduction of new social innovations in production; Piore and Sabel see a constellation of these forming the basis for the new technological paradigm of 'flexible specialization' – a supposedly more efficient *and* humane world of work. However, flexible specialization is put forward as only one of many possible productive worlds that could accede Fordist mass production. Only a period of frantic technological competition can decide which paradigm will shape the future of capitalist production. Once the new technological trajectory is set and major infrastructural investments have been made, the other competitors will inevitably fall by the historical wayside. In the last instance, Piore and Sabel consider it to be political forces and exercises of economic power that decree which technological trajectory is to be followed; *not* the technological potential of the various paradigms in competition *per se* (Piore and Sabel, 1984: 40). Significantly, however, the most powerful political forces in their analyses of periods of transition tend to be reduced to *market forces* and the most decisive exercises of economic power to exercises of *market power*. Although the existence of a 'narrow track' of technological progress is rejected the spectre of market determinism looms large.

Industrial divides and dualist theory

In order to distinguish the conceptual origins of Piore and Sabel's work on a second industrial divide, it is necessary to return to Piore's earlier contributions to the theory of industrial dualism (Berger and Piore, 1980; see also Sabel, 1982: 34–7; Piore and Sabel, 1984: 26–8; Sabel and Zeitlin, 1985: 137–8). The notion of a pervasive dualism in industrial societies gained favour in the 1970s, especially in the United States. A series of dichotomies was identified spanning different economic systems and attempts were made to find a common explanatory focus. The dichotomies included:

(a) in the enterprise structure of modern industrial economies between a large, monopolistic sector and a small, competitive sector;
(b) in developing economies between a modern, organized sector and a traditional, informal sector;
(c) in the labour market, between a stable core of high-waged workers (typically white/male) and an unstable periphery of low-waged workers (typically black/female). (Piore, 1980: 55)

A clear political ambition behind dualist analysis has been to link the plight of the disadvantaged in the developed and developing worlds. Such a link has been seen by Piore as requiring a move away from the basic tenets of neo-classical economics and a return to classical political economy; or more precisely, to what he calls Adam Smith's theory of technology. While, in neo-classical theory, technology is treated as an exogenous or residual factor, Smith accounts for the development of productive forces with two central postulates: firstly, that productivity is an increasing function of the division of labour; and, secondly, that the division of labour is limited by the extent of the market (Piore, 1980: 59). In other words, economic progress is a matter of 'expanding markets and dividing labour'. The division of labour is seen as *the* definitive social innovation in the history of capitalism; an innovation which first gained significance during the 'proto-industrial phase' (Hudson, 1981; Berg, 1985) with the development of the Verlag or putting-out system, which tied individual households to merchant capital; and reached its apotheosis in Henry Ford's Highland Park factory (Hounshell, 1984). By the late eighteenth century, Smith had already recognized the central importance of the division of labour for raising productivity and he was able to isolate three principal reasons for such productivity gains:

(a) the dexterity of workers would improve as a smaller number of tasks allowed greater concentration;
(b) time would be saved as moving between tasks became unnecessary;
(c) by concentrating on single tasks workers would see opportunities for improvements that would otherwise go unnoticed. (Piore, 1980: 60)

Turning to Smith's second postulate, we find that this rests on the notion that the division of labour is *prefigured* by the number of items produced *and* sold. If the market for an item produced is small, the opportunities for an extended division of labour will be curtailed; if the market is large the opportunities will be greater. The optimal market size will be one that allows each worker to be fully employed executing a single task. It is on this second postulate, that the division of labour is limited by the extent of the market, that Piore has attempted to build a theory of industrial dualism. For this purpose he *enlarges the prefigurative influence of the market on the division of labour* by adding three other factors to that of 'extensiveness'. These are:

(a)   the standardization of output;
(b)   the stability of market demand;
(c)   the uncertainty of market demand. (Piore, 1980: 61)

The addition of 'degree of standardization' is largely a definitional refinement to the notion of 'extensiveness' of demand; a firm can supply a large number of different product models using the same standardized parts. Therefore, the reduction of complex products to standardized parts greatly facilitates the division of labour. Non-standardized and/or customized production defies an extended division of labour. The more fundamental factors for the theory of industrial dualism are *stability* of demand:

> each level of instability in a given total output is equivalent, in terms of the profitable division of labour to some smaller, stable level of output . . . to the extent that the division of labour involves increased capital investment and capital is so specialised that it cannot transfer to other uses during troughs in demand, the periodic unemployment of capital which instability entails will also deter the division of labour. *(Piore, 1980: 62)*

And the *uncertainty* of demand:

> Production schedules can be stabilized and economies of divisibility realised even in the face of instability in product demand through variations in inventories, but inventory investment will be discouraged when the fluctuations are unpredictable. People will not be willing to hold inventories when demand declines if the subsequent revival is problematic. Uncertainty will also discourage the investment of fixed capital which seems to accompany the division of labour. *(Piore, 1980: 62)*

With the separation of the market demand for any product into stable/predictable and unstable/unpredictable portions, Piore aims to provide us with the basis for an explanation of the co-existence of large- and small-scale producers in the same industry in developed economies. According to him, as productivity gains and corresponding reductions in costs depend on the division of labour which in turn is limited by the size of the market, a tendency for increasing economic concentration will become evident as individual firms merge to gain a greater share of the market. This process could continue until only one firm is left in the industry. But with significant degrees of market instability and uncertainty, the optimal size of the firm is reduced to something less than the size of the industry. Thus, the possibility for competition remains but only in this unstable and uncertain segment of the industry, where an extended division of labour can only be maintained if combined with such measures as lowered wages and an accelerated pace of work.[7]

Dualist theory is also considered helpful by Piore for the explanation of the structure of industries in developed economies which have failed to develop a large-scale monopoly sector. For example, in industries such as high-fashion garments, the division of labour has been curtailed apparently because demand has always been transitory and unpredictable. The degree of standardization of output is also put forward by Piore as a crucial factor for determining industrial structure and the persistence of certain instances of 'craft' production in such sectors as construction and glassware. In fact, it would seem as though the continued division of labour in predominantly large-scale industries like the car industry has often been dependent on the maintenance and even growth of specialized small-batch production in small-scale industries, like machine tools. Thus, the activities of modern craft producers have been a necessary complement to the activities of mass producers.

Flexible specialization: industrialization after industrialization?

But what if the dualist world that Piore depicts was turned upside down? What if the non-standardized, unstable and uncertain markets for goods like high-fashion garments and machine tools were the rule rather than the exception? Where would we be then? According to Piore and Sabel in *The Second Industrial Divide* we would be (and are?) in the post-Fordist world of 'flexible specialization'. By means of a simple inversion, dualist theory has been boldly wheeled into post-Fordist territory and been charged with greater historical explanatory power and broader geographical relevance (Lever-Tracy, 1984: 60; Pollert, 1988: 62). In the world of flexible specialization further division of labour is no longer an effective means for raising productivity – the greatest social innovation of modern times is defunct. At the heart of Piore and Sabel's analysis of global economic crisis in the 1970s and

1980s and the conditions favouring a transition from Fordist mass production to post-Fordist flexible specialization are the twin notions of the 'saturation' and 'break-up' of mass markets. These are seen as the results of long-term trends which offer a 'more fundamental explanation' of the economic history of the past two decades (Piore and Sabel, 1984: 184). Therefore, although Piore and Sabel may insist that a future of flexible specialization is by no means inevitable (1984: 38) and that a period of intense techno-economic competition will ultimately decide the technological paradigm for the post-Fordist era, the legacy of dualist theory in their analysis makes the result of such competition a foregone conclusion.

Just as proto-industrialization has been dubiously characterized as 'Industrialization before Industrialization' (Kriedte et al., 1981); flexible specialization can be adventurously seen as referring to 'Industrialization *after* Industrialization'! A qualitatively different type of industrialization able to flourish in a world where basic needs for food, clothing and shelter have been largely satisfied and more 'refined wants' can be expressed (Piore and Sabel, 1984: 189). But also a world where demand even for these basic items has become more 'diverse':

> One reason for the early success of mass production in the United States was the homogeneity – or rather the indefinition – of American taste. Conversely, one reason for the persistence of the specialised industrial districts in Europe was the diversity of continental taste. This diversity of taste was perpetuated by producers' and retailers' education of consumers to appreciate the fine distinctions among products. *(Piore and Sabel, 1984: 190)*

Today, apparently, if Piore and Sabel are to be believed, American consumers are developing tastes equal in diversity and discernment to those of the continental bourgeoisie in the last century. Karel Williams et al. (1987), however, do not accept their analysis of market trends. In answer to the claim that mass markets are reaching 'saturation point' they point to a large and stable replacement demand for established consumer durables and important product development by 'old' mass producers:

> It is salutary here to list some of the new durables which are now being sold in Britain in volume although they did not exist as mass market products ten years ago. In brown and white goods the list would include VCRs, new format cassette players like the 'walkman', CD players, microwave ovens, dishwashers and food processors. Most of these new products are complementary from the producers' point of view; they can be put together on new lines in existing factories and sold through existing distribution channels. *(Williams et al., 1987: 425)*

In relation to the critical notion of the break-up of mass markets, Piore and Sabel can be seen as failing to distinguish between extensive product differentiation by established large-scale producers and market fragmentation favouring new small-scale producers (Gough, 1986: 64). Most mass producers continue to survive today by providing families of interrelated products; Japanese industry has been leading the way by showing that previously unimagined degrees of product variety can be achieved within mass production enterprises (Williams et al., 1987: 422). Nissan's factory in north-east England is a case in point; where on the basis of social innovations similar to those at Toyota we discussed earlier, almost 200 variants of the Nissan Bluebird are produced for export to different countries (*The Economist*, 1988). In fact, it is to be seriously doubted whether mass production has ever consistently corresponded to the Fordist paradigm Piore and Sabel put forward. According to Houndshell (1984: chapter 7), the limits of archetypical Fordist mass production were reached already in the late 1920s when General Motors and 'Sloanism' successfully challenged Ford's market leadership based on the 'unchanging' Model T:

> The saturation of the Model T market and the rapid growth of GM's Chevrolet Division were part of a larger movement in the American economy characterized by increased consumer purchasing power to which Ford's earlier work no doubt contributed. Sloan and his managers came to see that growth would occur not by the production of basic needs or by a 'car for the masses' but by selling cars whose appearance, if not features, changed annually. . . . In this consciously orchestrated economy of change and consumption that stressed style and comfort *above utility*, mass production as Ford had developed it with the T was no longer suitable. (*Houndshell, 1984: 264; my emphasis*)

This early victory of 'Sloanism' over 'Fordism' in the formative years of the mass-production paradigm represents the early rule of marketing over pure production; it was pointless to revolutionize the ways of producing cars without also revolutionizing the ways of selling them. General Motors recognized the value of novelty and built a degree of variety and flexibility into mass production in order to realize that value. GM's Chevrolet production system, set up after 1927 under the guidance of a former Ford production expert, departed radically from the Ford idea of 'single-purpose manufacture' (Houndshell, 1984: 265). Standard or general-purpose machine tools to accommodate change were the rule; single-purpose 'dedicated' equipment was the exception. Alfred P. Sloan Jr was also well-versed in Piore and Sabel's language of flexible specialization: to fulfil General Motors' competitive strategy of 'keeping the consumer dissatisfied', he pointed to the need to recognize 'the "laws" of Paris dressmakers . . . in the automobile industry' (Houndshell, 1984: 267). It would appear that even during the era of mass production, producers and retailers have been greatly interested in the 'education of consumers to appreciate the fine distinctions among products'.

Although politico-institutional forces and exercises of economic power are introduced into Piore and Sabel's analyses of 'industrial divides' and the determination of new technological trajectories (or qualitatively different phases of capitalist production), their overwhelming attention to, and persistent preoccupation with, market trends means that politics and exercises of power are all too often reduced to the perceived actions of 'sovereign consumers' (Hyman, 1988: 58). Through the dubious medium of inverted dualist theory the ghost of Adam Smith and the prefigurative powers of the market have secured a central position in Piore and Sabel's metahistory of industrial transformation.

A NEO-MARXIST PERSPECTIVE

Unlike the two perspectives we have already examined, the neo-Marxist perspective we will refer to now does not concentrate on the renewal of capitalist forces of production, but rather the reproduction of capitalism *per se*, or the process of capitalist '*régulation*'.[8] The *régulation* perspective, developed in France during the 1970s, builds upon a critique of 'mechanical and catastrophic' interpretations of Marx (Boyer, 1988a: 70). In other words, it takes the question of capitalism's survival seriously. How is the broad assimilation of an aggressive new techno-economic paradigm possible? Why is it that the unavoidable chaos, instability and conflict in every structural crisis of capitalism (phase of 'creative destruction') does not prevail? How is social cohesion and economic stability achieved and maintained despite the unremitting pressures of disrupting cleavages? Interest is focused, therefore, on Gramsci rather than Lenin and the containment of capitalism's inherent 'animality' which results in the indefinite postponement of the 'impending catastrophe':

> The history of industrialism has always been a continuing struggle . . . against the element of 'animality' in man. It has been an uninterrupted, often painful and bloody process of subjugating natural (i.e. animal and primitive) instincts to new, more complex and rigid norms and habits of order, exactitude and precision which can make possible the increasingly complex forms of collective life which are the necessary consequence of industrial development. *(Gramsci, 1971: 298)*

Marrying Marxism and institutionalism

Implicit in the *régulation* perspective's desire to avoid mechanical explanations of capitalist development and techno-economic determinism is the aim of breaking down the compartmentalization of economics and politics and linking them in a dynamic integrated framework (Noël, 1987: 307). In order to achieve this aim, attention has progressively shifted away from value theory approaches in Marxist political economy towards a greater concern with the varying *social forms* of capital. This has, in turn, led to growing contacts with established institutionalist traditions in economics which have always worked on the assumption that the market mechanism in itself will never be able to maintain social and economic stability, and left to its own logic will threaten to destroy human society (Mjöset, 1985: 1).

The result of this marriage between Marxist political economy and institutionalist tradition is a conceptualization of qualitative change within capitalism which posits the existence of not one, but *two*, fundamental dynamics forcing change. Two dynamics growing out of the same discordant soil of capitalist social relations. One giving rise to specific *regimes of accumulation*, the other to particular *modes of regulation*. In contrast to the neo-Schumpeterian perspective which subjugates a diffuse and unspecified 'socio-institutional' framework to an irresistible and relatively articulate 'techno-economic paradigm', the *régulation* perspective offers genuine autonomy to institutional forms and fills both spheres (the 'institutional' and the 'technological') with an essentially social content. In contrast to the neo-Smithian perspective which superficially attempts to marry economics and politics but ultimately ends up subjugating politics and institutional arrangements to the invisible hand of the Market, the *régulation* perspective sees markets as institutions usually encompassed by other 'limiting institutions' (Mjöset, 1985: 20), which, being based on principles of reciprocity and cooperation, guarantee social cohesion through the coordination of private/individual activities.

Because the notion of a single universal dynamic in capitalist development is rejected and causal powers are allocated to specific cultural and political forms, the peculiarities of national capitalisms take on a new significance. Interest is stimulated in the unequal capacities of different capitalist nations to generate and assimilate new techno-economic systems[9] and a major concern becomes the qualitatively different impact of the same techno-economic forces in time and space. Although major structural crises are seen as inevitably taking on international dimensions, it becomes of importance to track down the historically specific conditions under which the determinants of crisis have collided – the *conjuncture* of general and particular determinants of crisis and transformation.[10]

Whereas the assorted members of the French regulation school have been interested in the problem of capitalist *reégulation* on the international level down to the national level, Michael Burawoy has been concerned with basically the *same issue* at the firm level up to the national level (Burawoy, 1979, 1985). His major concern is with historical and cultural variation in the 'micro-politics' of capitalism and he is severely critical of those labour process theorists who have failed to distinguish between the labour process as a particular social organization of tasks and a political apparatus conceived as its 'mode of regulation' (Burawoy, 1985: 125).[11] For Burawoy, it is not an easy operation to translate *labour-power* and the capacity to work into sufficient *labour* and the application of effort necessary to generate the required exchange value for the survival of the firm. Such an operation is considered to depend on the recognition of a degree of *mutuality* between wage-earners and employers as individuals:

> At the same time that they produce useful things, workers produce the basis of their own existence and that of capital. The exchange value added through cooperative labour is divided between the wage equivalent, which becomes the means of the reproduction of labour power, and surplus value, the source of profit which makes it possible for the capitalist to exist as such and thus to employ the labourer. (*Burawoy, 1985: 123*)

During the era of liberal capitalism in the last century, employers could typically rely on coercion and the 'economic whip' of the market, what Burawoy calls a *despotic* politics of production, to define the nature of mutuality; workers usually had no alternative means of livelihood other than the sale of their labour power. During the course of the twentieth century, however, coercion has not always proved as effective a means of securing sufficient labour and its use has often been curtailed. New political apparatuses of production have arisen, relying on more diplomatic means of guaranteeing sufficient labour. Diplomacy has been necessitated by changes in the balance of power between labour and capital and the partial separation of the reproduction of labour power from the process of production. Using Burawoy's terms, *hegemonic factory regimes* have largely replaced despotic ones under advanced capitalism; a fair deal of subtle persuasion is typically needed to draw workers into the production process as the state usually guarantees a minimal level of welfare irrespective of work performance.

During the uncertain and crisis-ridden transition to post-Fordism

some advanced capitalist nations have been more prone than others
to revert to despotic patterns of *régulation*. In Sweden, diplomacy and
gentle persuasion are still normal practice. Employers and trade unions
have together addressed the problem of an increasing unwillingness
among young Swedes to enter into industrial production (Madsén,
1988). School-leavers are wooed by the obsequious representatives
of both capital and labour and are flatteringly(?) classed as a 'bristvara'
('rare commodity'). In Britain, despotism would seem to have returned
with a vengeance. Against a background of concerted attempts to
exclude labour from the institutionalized apparatuses of production
(Crouch, 1986), revised Youth Training Schemes and a proposed
'Unified Training Scheme' threaten to constitute a new system of
'economic conscription' (Gray, 1988), where eligibility for social
security benefits depends on participation in special compulsory work
schemes.

Régulation: *the protection of capitalism against itself*

Let us now focus on the relationship between the *régulation* perspective
and institutionalist tradition and the perceived bases of institutional
dynamics. Mjöset (1985: 18–30) identifies the central position assumed
by Karl Polanyi within institutionalist tradition. Polanyi, in his book
The Great Transformation, provides a classic denunciation of liberalism
in theory and practice. According to him liberalism makes the fatal
error of first conceiving of the three basic factors of production –
labour, land and money – as simple commodities and then acting as
if this were so. These misconceived actions subsequently lead to a
serious threat against the human and material substance of society and
therefore *society will inevitably take measures to protect itself*:

> To allow the market mechanism to be the sole director of the fate of
> human beings and their natural environment, indeed, even of the
> amount and use of purchasing power, would result in the demolition of
> society. For the alleged commodity 'labour power' cannot be shoved
> about, used indiscriminately, or even left unused, without affecting also
> the human individual who happens to be the bearer of this peculiar
> commodity. . . . Robbed of the protective covering of cultural institu-
> tions, human beings would perish from the effects of social exposure;
> they would die as the victims of acute social dislocation through vice,
> perversion, crime and starvation. Nature would be reduced to its
> elements, neighbourhoods and landscapes defiled, rivers polluted,
> military safety jeopardized, the power to produce food and raw materials
> destroyed. Finally, the market administration of purchasing power

would periodically liquidate business enterprise, for shortages and surfeits of money would prove as disastrous to business as floods and droughts in primitive society. *(Polanyi, 1957: 73)*

As Mjöset (1985: 18) correctly points out, there is a strong flavour of functionalism in Polanyi's work betrayed by an unmistakable flair for biological analogy and physical threats to the 'substance' of society. We have already witnessed a similar flair for biological metaphor in the recent work of Carlota Perez within the neo-Schumpeterian perspective and it is interesting to compare her thoughts on the 'anatomy' of techno-economic forces with those of Polanyi.[12] The *régulation* perspective attempts to avoid institutionalism's weakness for functional explanations by balancing notions of structure and anatomy with an emphasis on the *openness* of historical process (Noël, 1987: 311; Boyer, 1988a: 69; Lipietz, 1987: chapter 2). In other words, it rejects the notion of an equilibrium position for the social 'organism', or as Jessop (1988: 151) puts it, regimes of accumulation and modes of regulation are seen as 'always relative, always partial and always provisional'.

Although the *régulation* perspective may reject Polanyi for his functionalism, it is in agreement with him when he asserts that neither human beings, nature nor money are produced for sale and that their 'commodity character is entirely fictitious' (Polanyi, 1957: 72). It would also agree that the *relative* stability of 'techno-economic' systems depends on the introduction of 'protective' measures and that without such measures these systems will soon threaten to destroy the bases of their own existence. In similar fashion to Polanyi, the *régulation* perspective sees 'labour' and 'money' as especially important arenas for institutional formation and mediation. Lipietz and Aglietta are two members of the French Regulation School who have devoted special attention to the institutional codification of *monetary and credit relationships*. In his *A Theory of Capitalist Regulation*, Aglietta (1979) also pays special attention to the transformation of wage-earners' conditions of life or what Boyer calls the *'wage-labour nexus'*, this being a crucial institutional constellation, central to every mode of regulation, defining the relationship between wage-earners and employers. Other important fields of institutional formation identified within the *régulation* perspective are: *inter-firm relations* (the centralization or decentralization of production; competitive versus cooperative relations); and *forms of state intervention* (a large versus a minimal state, scale and nature of defence spending; the orientation of the educational system, etc.). Clearly, *régulation* is not reducible to state regulation as this is only one dimension of many. The *régulation* perspective consciously strives against an 'over-politicization' of the state and 'under-politicization' of the other arenas where social cohesion is secured.[13]

By concentrating on the need for 'protective measures' we are able to gain some key insights into the 'paradoxes' of liberalism and the so-called 'competitive regulation' of techno-economic systems. The recent neo-liberal mood in Britain and the USA can be understood as ultimately having very little to do with long-term '*de*regulation', as the established rules of the game governing (and protecting) capitalist production are not being widely abolished but simply rewritten. During the classic period of liberal capitalism and competitive regulation in the last century, when a regime of 'extensive' accumulation was established (based on the rapid growth of the capital goods sector), a decisive but largely unacknowledged protective framework consisted of essentially pre-capitalist institutional constellations.

Strange as it may seem when considering the work of contemporary neo-Schumpeterians, Schumpeter, himself, was an important analyst of this old 'protecting strata' (or '*régulation à l'ancienne*'). He (mistakenly) saw its sad decline as clearing the path for the triumph of a despicable socialism (Schumpeter, 1979: chapter 12). According to him the emerging bourgeoisie had assumed an ambivalent position relative to the institutional arrangements of the feudal world, they were both fettered and sheltered by these arrangements. The aristocracy possessed a 'mystic glamour': the ability and habit to command and be obeyed. Their prestige was so great and *valuable* that, as a class, they were able to 'outlive' the socio-economic conditions in which they had been rooted and adapt by means of a transformation of their class function to quite different conditions (Schumpeter, 1979: 137). Generally, the bourgeoisie were considered by Schumpeter to lack both political credibility and the ability to defend their own interests: they have been ill-equipped to deal with the problems, both domestic and international, which confront a nation-state. Therefore, they have tended to thrive best within a protective framework *not* made of bourgeois stuff. The significant symbiosis of the techno-economic forces of nascent capitalism with an established politico-institutional framework was necessary for the sustainment of the initial growth of the productive forces and by campaigning for the removal of this original framework, liberalism sought to break down not only the barriers that impeded capitalism's further expansion but also the 'flying buttresses that prevented its collapse' (Schumpeter, 1979: 136).

Unlike the neo-Schumpeterians we have referred to in this chapter, Schumpeter himself did not neglect the centrality of institutional dynamics for qualitative change within capitalism. He saw the concentration of capital and absentee ownership as eroding perceptions of the 'material substance' of private property and breaking down 'moral allegiance' to capitalism. The Carnegies and the Vanderbilts, not the intellectuals and the agitators, were making entrepreneurs obsolete and expropriating the bourgeoisie as a class (Schumpeter, 1979: 134). Schumpeter saw capitalism's chances for survival as limited and its days numbered.

However, not every entrepreneur in the last century was as politically impotent as Schumpeter would have us believe. A prime example of a successful entrepreneur who also became deeply involved in the reform and *extension* of the 'protecting framework' is given by Joseph Chamberlain, who as liberal mayor of Birmingham became associated with what has been called 'the municipal ideal' or somewhat inappropriately 'municipal socialism' (Fraser, 1987; Smith, 1982). Chamberlain came to symbolize an innovative movement within Victorian local government which relied on local legislation rather than national dictate, to gradually build up an impressive range of local social and economic services. Education was one important area for local government intervention; voluntary educational systems were seen as inadequate to meet new 'educational needs'. Chamberlain, however, gained most renown for the municipalization of Birmingham's gas and water supplies. Although, in the 1870s, such municipal control was not unique in England, Birmingham was the first city to include these measures in a coherent strategy based on 'modern' administrative techniques to combat contemporary urban problems (Fraser, 1987: 37). The relatively successful implementation of this strategy led one distinguished American visitor to christen Birmingham 'the best governed city in the world' (Smith, 1982: 229). Therefore, despite the inappropriateness of the notion of 'municipal socialism', we can nevertheless conceive of Birmingham under Chamberlain as taking the first tentative steps on an alternative 'local road' to welfare capitalism.

The end of a Golden Age of capitalism

Post Second World War welfare capitalism is in the eyes of the *régulation* perspective the 'Golden Age' of capitalism, a period without historical precedent when steady economic expansion was 'propelled by a simultaneous evolution of productivity and real wages' (Boyer, 1988a: 82). According to regulationists, there is nothing 'late' about welfare capitalism as some alternative neo-Marxist perspectives have insisted. It was only with the post-war marriage of 'intensive' accumulation and 'monopolistic' regulation that capitalism became a universal experience and a fully integrated system. The move to a regime of intensive accumulation meant that the continued growth of capitalist economies had become dependent not only on dynamic production goods sectors (the precondition for extensive accumulation), but also on dynamic *consumption goods* sectors. The move to monopolistic regulation meant that workers were fully rather than partially integrated into capitalist systems as both producers *and* consumers. The *combination* of intensive accumulation and monopolistic regulation conceived as a historical mode of development is what the *régulation* perspective sees as constituting 'Fordism'. It does so in tribute to Gramsci, who, in his prison notebooks at the beginning of the 1930s, introduced the notions of 'Americanism and Fordism' as shorthand for what he perceived as a new historical 'epoch' or 'passive revolution' which appeared to have the potential capacity to sweep away the last remnants of the 'Old Regime' in Europe (Gramsci, 1971: 279–318). Therefore, the *régulation* perspective, with its respect for Gramsci, accepts an extremely *broad* definition of Fordism, encompassing not only an industrial or technological paradigm but also a particular institutionalized 'way of life'.

Different definitions of Fordism (broad or narrow, technologically or institutionally oriented) obviously provide the bases for different periodizations of capitalism. While Piore and Sabel, with their primary focus on Fordism as mass production, would probably class the inter-war period as the period when a qualitatively different capitalism (or industrialism) emerged, the regulationists, with their primary focus on Fordism as a new way of life for wage-earners, would probably date the completion of the 'passive revolution' as late as the beginning of the 1950s! As far as the regulationists are concerned, neither the productive genius of Henry Ford nor the salesmanship of Alfred Sloan was capable of securing a 'passive revolution' within capitalism; only the effective linking of wages to increasing productivity after the Second World War was able to achieve this end.

Therefore, the 'Golden Age' of capitalism was based on the crystallization of a new wage-labour nexus which recognized wages not only as a cost but also an outlet for expanding capitalist production. This has been perceived by some as constituting a significant victory for labour and an important step towards its 'de-commodification' (Esping-Andersen, 1985). However, it is probably more accurate to say that the Fordist wage-labour nexus meant workers won the recognition of their employers for embodying not only labour-power but also purchasing-power. De Vroey summarizes the general pattern well:

> In most countries, the golden age was a period of social consensus, interrupted by only short phases of social upheaval. Capitalist societies

had not of course foregone their invariable features: exploitation and domination were still present. However, the two main classes, employers and wage-earners, had come to a mutually advantageous compromise. Workers benefited from a stronger institutional and political collective position. Regular increases in wages gave them across to a consumption pattern undreamt of by their parents. Unemployment was low, while workers were provided with insurance systems and a network of collective goods and services . . . For the capitalist class, the advantages were obvious: the attainment of social peace and class collaboration; minimizing halts in production and gaining outlets for the increased production. (*De Vroey, 1984: 56*)

Post-Fordism, therefore, is within the *régulation* perspective primarily considered to refer to the breakdown of these 'growth compromises' and the dissolution of the 'protective frameworks' established in the post-war period. Some compromises may have weathered the crisis of Fordism better than others but all have been seriously affected.[14] What have been the limits of Fordism leading to its crisis? Boyer (1988b: 199–203) provides perhaps the most precise answer. He identifies four tendencies which have led to structural crisis. Firstly, increased division of labour within the firm has become largely counter-productive. During the late 1960s and throughout the 1970s, productivity gains decreased as worker resistance to the excesses of 'scientific management' grew. A consequent slowdown in investment depressed productivity growth even further. Secondly, the continued expansion of mass production and the pursuit of even greater economies of scale has led to an increasing globalization of production and sales. Competition between countries has intensified and domestic markets have been penetrated, making economic management at the national level increasingly difficult. Thirdly, Fordism has led to growing social expenditure. The logic of mass production is not applicable to areas of collective consumption like education, health and housing. This has meant that their relative cost has progressively increased, leading to imbalance and destabilizing inflationary pressures. Fourthly, the consumption patterns of the 'affluent worker' have gradually changed; a greater variety of use-values is demanded which cannot be satisfied by conventional means of standardized production. Clearly, this fourth tendency contributing to crisis is reminiscent of Piore and Sabel's emphasis on the 'saturation' and 'break-up' of mass markets. But, in general, the regulationists' account of contemporary structural crisis is broader and more *politicized* than that given by either the neo-Smithian or the neo-Schumpeterian perspective. Although the regulationists accept that we have reached a watershed in the history of capitalism, no definite vision of the future such as the 'information technology Kondratiev' or 'flexible specialization' is advanced. The shape of post-Fordism today is considered to be as ambiguous and open as the shape of Fordism was for Gramsci in the 1930s. This is why the new mode of capitalist development remains, as yet, nameless within the *régulation* perspective.

CONCLUSION

> The move toward the ethnographic in American political economy, I would argue, is related to a widely perceived decline of the post-World War II international order in which America has held a hegemonic position and to an undermining of the American form of welfare state itself. A sense of profound transition in the foundations of domestic and international reality, as seen from the American perspective, has in turn been reflected intellectually in a widespread retreat from theoretically centralized and organized fields of knowledge. *(Marcus, 1986: 167)*

This quote from George Marcus, the American ethnographer, situates the post-Fordist debate fair and square in its global context. The breakdown of Fordism has been registered in the social sciences by a 'crisis of representation' (Marcus and Fischer, 1986) and a pervasive loss of confidence in the established frameworks for describing/ explaining reality. The contemporary social scientist is confronted with a chaotic and disordered world; the strict and regular rhythms and routines of the Golden Age of capitalism have been significantly eroded and patterns of life which were increasingly conceived as 'natural' have turned out to have been merely ephemeral. The three perspectives examined in this chapter can be seen as concerted attempts to recast the classic theories of Schumpeter, Smith and Marx on capitalist development into social scientific languages which allow us to unravel global chaos and get to grips with the post-Fordist era. How promising are these attempts? Do they offer convincing bases for making sense of post-Fordism?

In both the neo-Schumpeterian and neo-Smithian perspectives we have examined, individual firms, specific groups of workers and the various national economies under study are predominantly portrayed as isolated units with 'outside' forces (technology and markets) impinging upon them. It is impossible to resist the new technological and competitive 'realities' of post-Fordism – the 'hard and irresistible facts' ushering in a new way of life. These 'facts' are typically *pre-given* and derived from self-contained theoretical constructs, such as a taxonomy of innovations or a transhistorical division of the economy into rigid and flexible sectors. Instead of informing, these constructs ultimately dictate over the history of capitalist development. It is only within the *régulation* perspective that there appears to be a genuine attempt to integrate 'outside' forces into the construction/constitution of the individual units themselves. Even larger forces and global crises are seen as having essentially local origins. The *régulation* perspective probably comes closest to an understanding of individual units as: '*always* in flux, in a perpetual historically sensitive state of resistance and accommodation to broader processes of influence that are as much inside as outside the local context' (Marcus and Fischer, 1986: 78).

The *régulation* perspective encourages greater faith in micro-level analysis to conceptually inform problems that the other two perspectives still persistently phrase in terms of macro-concepts alone. Instead of charting the progressive diffusion and dictatorship of the information technology paradigm or flexible specialization, the *régulation* perspective poses the question of how emergent trends in the global economy (e.g. social innovations) are produced and then complexly 'inscribed' in the productive practices and political consciousness of distant locations. It is only with such an enhanced interest in the peculiarities of historical/cultural contexts and greater attention to 'ethnographic detail' that we can begin to translate the abstract notions of system, trajectory and paradigm into more concrete human terms.

Because the regulationists, in agreement with institutionalists like Karl Polanyi, see the commodity status of labour and capital as entirely fictitious and are willing to imbue techno-economic forces with a decisive social content, a generic interest arises in the *mutual* determination of economic and political processes. The future of capitalism is considered to be relatively open and new techno-economic imperatives less stringent than the neo-Schumpeterians and neo-Smithians would have us believe. In fact, *strategic resistance against new technology and the Market may well be essential if a new period of stable capitalist growth is to be secured.* Therefore, it is not surprising that the *régulation* perspective is hesitant in giving the new era of capitalist development a name; this era is still considered to be very much in the making. While the neo-Schumpeterian and neo-Smithian perspectives tend to see the information technology paradigm and flexible specialization as pervasive *ready-made* disciplines for the post-Fordist era, the *régulation* perspective sees the new rulebook of capitalist life as only partially written with room for many more co-authors.

NOTES

1 The references relied on are Perez (1985, 1986), Freeman and Perez (1988a, 1988b) and Freeman (1988).

2 Apart from Piore and Sabel (1984), other important references for understanding this perspective are considered to be Sabel and Zeitlin (1985), Piore (1980 and Sabel (1982).

3 The references relied on here are Boyer (1988a, 1988b), Noël (1987), Mjöset (1985), Jessop (1988), Lipietz (1987), Aglietta (1979), De Vroey (1984) and Burawoy (1979, 1985). It is considered acceptable to group together Burawoy with the French Regulation School as both are striving towards the same interdisciplinary end (albeit at different levels of analysis); the breaking down of the 'compartmentalization of the politics and economics' and their union in a dynamic integrated framework.

4 This taxonomy encompasses incremental innovations, radical innovations, new technology systems and new techno-economic paradigms. Social innovations perceived as learning by doing/using are seen largely as incremental innovations and therefore of least significance.

5 Nissan appear to have developed a production system very similar to Toyota's. In their factory in the north-east of England there are as yet only twenty-four robots, twenty-one of them assembling car bodies (*The Economist*, 1988).

6 Mechatronics is more or less a unique Japanese phenomenon. It is a process of technology 'fusion' involving the marriage of mechanical and electronics technology (see Kodama, 1986).

7 In the developing economies, the coexistence of modern and traditional industries is explained in terms of the same underlying relationships. Traditional industries are seen as restricted to small domestic markets, while modern industries are usually tied into world markets. The division of labour in the two sectors of the economy therefore reflects the 'extensiveness' of their respective markets (see Piore, 1980: 69).

8 The French word '*régulation*' does not carry such a narrow meaning as the English word 'regulation'. It refers more to the preservation of a set of norms and a 'way of life', than a process of conscious adjustment (see Boyer, 1988a: 68).

9 In this context it is interesting to note a relatively recent concern within the neo-Schumpeterian perspective with 'national systems of innovation' (see Freeman, 1988; Andersen and Lundvall, 1988).

10 In recent work, Boyer illustrates this conjunctural approach by showing how the contemporary search for labour market flexibility, as a general response to crisis, is tending to reveal and emphasize historically inherited features in each country's system of wage/labour relations which largely disappeared from view during the 'Golden Age' of sustained growth in the 1950s and 1960s (Boyer, 1988b: 213). The rise of this elaborate patchwork of contextually dependent solutions to the 'flexibility problem' aggravates the need for further conceptual elaboration to counter the persistence of composite conceptions of labour-market flexibility which

lump together essentially unrelated phenomena observed in different contexts.

11 According to Burawoy, Braverman totally ignores the political moments of production, while Edwards, Littler and Friedman tend to collapse them into the labour process.

12 Compare our quote from Polanyi with that from Perez on page 46. The contrast would seem to be between the need to accommodate or civilize 'techno-economic' forces in society – accept progress or fight against barbarity.

13 In this context, it is worth noting that a definitive feature of the renowned 'Swedish Model' of wage/labour relations in its golden years after 1936 was the successful *exclusion* of the state from the major negotiations between the central organizations of labour and capital (Johansson, 1989). The two 'finely balanced power-groupings' in the labour market were able to pursue a flexible, agreement based, problem-solving strategy for over twenty years without either side feeling the need to draw upon state power and the threat of legislation to achieve its particular aims.

14 Although the Fordist wage-labour nexus in Sweden seems to have survived relatively intact into the post-Fordist era, it remains strongly dependent on external developments and offers no ready-made solutions to the problem of stabilizing a new mode of development (Andersson and Mjöset, 1987).

REFERENCES

Aglietta, M. (1979) *A Theory of Capitalist Regulation*. London: New Left Books.

Andersen, E. S. and B.-Å. Lundvall (1988) 'Small National Systems of Innovation Facing Technological Revolutions: an Analytical Framework', in C. Freeman and B.-Å. Lundvall (eds) *Small Countries Facing the Technological Revolution*. London: Pinter.

Andersson, J.-O. and L. Mjöset (1987) 'The Transformation of the Nordic Models', *Cooperation and Conflict*, 22(4): 227–43.

Berg, M. (1985) *The Age of Manufactures*. London: Fontana.

Berger, S. and M. Piore (eds) (1980) *Dualism and Discontinuity in Industrial Societies*. Cambridge: Cambridge University Press.

Boyer, R. (1988a) 'Technical Change and the Theory of "Régulation"', in G. Dosi et al. (eds) *Technical Change and Economic Theory*. London: Pinter.

Boyer, R. (1988b) *The Search for Labour Market Flexibility*. Oxford: Clarendon.

Burawoy, M. (1979) *Manufacturing Consent*. Chicago: Chicago University Press.

Burawoy, M. (1985) *The Politics of Production*. London: Verso.

Cole, R. (1985) 'Target Information for Competitive Performance'. *Harvard Business Review*, 63(3): 100–9.

Crouch, C. (1986) 'Conservative Industrial Relations Policy: Towards Labour Exclusion?', in O. Jacobi et al. (eds) *Economic Crisis, Trade Union and the State*. London: Croom Helm.

De Vroey, M. (1984) 'A Regulation Approach Interpretation of Contemporary Crisis', *Capital and Class*, 23: 45–66.

Dosi, G., C. Freeman, R. Nelson, G. Silverberg and L. Soete (eds) (1988) *Technical Change and Economic Theory*. London: Pinter.

Economist, The (1988) 'When "Made in Europe" Isn't', 8 October.

Esping-Andersen, G. (1985) *Politics Against Markets*. Princeton: Princeton University Press.

Fraser, D. (1987) 'Joseph Chamberlain and the Municipal Ideal', *History Today*, 37 (April): 33–9.

Freeman, C. (1988) 'Japan: a New National System of Innovation?', in G. Dosi et al. (eds) *Technical Change and Economic Theory*. London: Pinter.

Freeman, C. and C. Perez (1988a) 'Long Waves and Changes in Employment Patterns', paper prepared for the ALC Conference, Saltsjöbaden, Stockholm, 6–9 June.

Freeman, C. and C. Perez (1988b) 'Structural Crises of Adjustment, Business Cycles and Investment Behaviour', in G. Dosi et al. (eds) *Technical Change and Economic Theory*. London: Pinter.

Gough, J. (1986) 'Industrial Policy and Socialist Strategy', *Capital and Class*, 29: 58–81.

Gramsci, A. (1971) *Selections from the Prison Notebooks*. London: Lawrence and Wishart.

Gray, A. (1988) 'Resisting Economic Conscription', *Capital and Class*, 34: 119–46.

Houndshell, D. (1984) *From the American System to Mass Production 1800–1932*. Baltimore: Johns Hopkins University Press.

Hudson, P. (1981) 'Proto-industrialization: the Case of the West Riding', *History Workshop*, 12: 34–61.

Hyman, R. (1988) 'Flexible Specialization: Miracle or Myth?', in R. Hyman and W. Streeck (eds) *New Technology and Industrial Relations*. Oxford: Basil Blackwell.

Jessop, B. (1988) 'Regulation Theory, Post-Fordism and the State', *Capital and Class*, 34: 147–68.

Johansson, A. (1989) *Tillväxt och klassamarbete (Growth and class co-operation)*. Stockholm: Tiden.

Kaplinsky, R. (1988a) *Automation*, 2nd edn.

Kaplinsky, R. (1988b) 'Restructuring the Capitalist Labour Process: Some Lessons from the Automobile Industry', *Cambridge Journal of Economics*, 12.

Kodama, F. (1986) 'Japanese Innovation in Mechatronics Technology', *Science and Public Policy* 13(1): 44–51.

Kriedte, P., H. Medick and J. Schlumbohm (1981) *Industrialisation before Industrialisation*. Cambridge: Cambridge University Press.

Lever-Tracy, C. (1984) 'The Paradigm Crisis of Dualism: Decay or Regeneration?', *Politics and Society*, 13(1): 59–89.

Lipietz, A. (1987) *Mirages and Miracles*. London: Verso.

Madsén, T. (ed.) (1988) *Vem skall göra jobben? (Who will do the work?)* Lund: Studentlitteratur.

Marcus, G. E. (1986) 'Contemporary Problems of Ethnography in the Modern World System', in J. Clifford and G. E. Marcus (eds) *Writing Culture*. Berkeley: University of California Press.

Marcus, G. E. and M. M. J. Fischer (1986) *Anthropology as Cultural Critique*. Chicago: University of Chicago Press.

Mjöset, L. (1985) 'Regulation and the Institutionalist Tradition', in L. Mjöset and J. Bohlin (eds) *Introduksjon til reguleringskolen*. Aalborg: Nordisk Sommeruniversitet.

Monden, Y. (1983) *Toyota Production System*. Industrial Engineering and Management Press.

Noël, A. (1987) 'Accumulation, Regulation and Social Change: an Essay on French Political Economy', *International Organization*, 41(2): 303-33.

Perez, C. (1985) 'Microelectronics, Long Waves and World Structural System: New Perspectives for Developing Countries'. *World Development*, 13: 441-63.

Perez, C. (1986) 'Structural Change and Assimilation of New Technologies in the Economic and Social System', in C. Freeman (ed.) *Design, Innovation and Long Cycles in Economic Development*. London: Pinter.

Piore, M. (1980) 'The Technological Foundations of Dualism and Discontinuity', in S. Berger and M. Piore (eds) *Dualism and Discontinuity in Industrial Societies*. Cambridge: Cambridge University Press.

Piore, M. and C. Sabel (1984) *The Second Industrial Divide*. New York: Basic Books.

Polanyi, K. (1957) *The Great Transformation*. Boston: Beacon Hill.

Pollert, A. (1988) 'Dismantling Flexibility', *Capital and Class*. 34: 42-75.

Sabel, C. (1982) *Work and Politics*. Cambridge: Cambridge University Press.

Sabel, C. and J. Zeitlin (1985) 'Historical Alternatives to Mass Production: Politics, Markets and Technology in Nineteenth Century Industrialisation', *Past and Present*, 108: 133-76.

Sayer, A. (1985) 'New Developments in Manufacturing and Their Spatial Implications', *Sussex Working Papers in Urban and Regional Studies*, 49. University of Sussex: Brighton.

Schonberger, R. (1987) 'Frugal Manufacturing', *Harvard Business Review*, 65(5): 95-100.

Schumpeter, J. (1979) *Capitalism, Socialism and Democracy*. London: Allen and Unwin.

Smith, D. (1982) *Conflict and Compromise*. London: Routledge and Kegan Paul.

Williams, K., T. Cutler, J. Williams and C. Haslam (1987) 'The End of Mass Production?', *Economy and Society*, 16(3): 405-39.

3

The Crisis of Fordism and the Dimensions of a 'Post-Fordist' Regional and Urban Structure

Josef Esser and Joachim Hirsch

INTRODUCTION

The radical processes of social change as a result of the most recent world economic crisis do not merely alter the face of towns and the scenario of urban conflicts. They have also forced reorientations of theory to be made, which has meant drawing nearer to urban sociology (again) and general social theory, as well as more strongly interlinking their basic approaches to the formation of theories and research. More then ever, urban and regional research has been forced to make certain of its reference framework of social theory and to take as a central theme the relationship between historical changes in the capitalist development of society and the change in spatial structures.

Imposing new types of technology and production concepts, with the radical change in the international division of labour which this entails, causes 'tertiarization' processes to be accelerated and accentuates the gulf between expanding 'global cities' and stagnating old industrial towns. Associated with this, especially in the expanding towns, is a considerable economic and social heterogenization, which is distinguished by new types of inner urban processes of marginalization and division. A new type of social movement and political behaviour

This chapter is an update of an article published in the *International Journal of Urban and Regional Research* (1989), vol. 13, no. 3, pp. 417–36.

(e.g. green parties) has its essential social basis in the urban 'tertiarized' middle classes, who are themselves subject to strong restructuring processes and have, in part, formed 'alternative' milieux with particular forms of socialization and politics. Under pressure from international competition, strategies introduced for the restructuring of capital are particularly targeted at urban development, which leads to an ideological revaluation of local government politics, whilst it is subject to increasingly strong external determination. Strategies of local government politics, under the recurring formula 'urbanity', stand beside urban economizing processes, which are aimed at developing new forms of labour, social classes and consumer models. Urban 'cultural and educational policy' is becoming an important instrument of economic restructuring policy in the race between locations; planned 'urbanity' is becoming an economic strategy (Bachmann, 1985).

The break in the development and structure of the metropolitan towns which became apparent in the 1960s and 1970s also forced urban research to concentrate once more on global and long-term social developments: secular processes of crisis, radical changes, which were supported by technology, in the organization of production and labour, and the formation of new classes, became the subjects of empirical research and theoretical considerations in critical urban sociology. This happened initially in the USA, where processes of urban restructuring were pushed through sooner, more forcibly and more incisively than in Europe (Fainstein and Fainstein, 1982; Mollenkopf, 1983; Gregory and Urry, 1984; Szelenyi, 1984; Timberlake, 1985; Walton, 1985; Blake, 1985; Castells, 1985; Harvey 1984; Smith and Feagin, 1987). The efforts which took place in the same historical context to formulate a comprehensive materialistic theory of capitalist development were able to find support here from rich material prepared by urban research and a whole series of new ways of formulating the question, whilst critical urban sociology had to consider itself more and more clearly as an integral part of a theory and analysis of society as a whole (e.g. Læpple, 1985; 1986; Hæussermann and Siebel, 1986a; Ipsen, 1987; Marcuse, 1988; Lipietz, 1991; Mayer, 1991; Keil, 1993).

We will first of all sketch a theoretical basic approach for analysing capitalist development and the historical changes in it which were forced by secular processes of crisis. A few preliminary thoughts lead on from this on the connection between the development of society and spatial structure in the transition from Fordism to post-Fordism. Against this background, we will then investigate the predominant capitalist reorganization concepts in the FRG, with its foreseeable consequences for regional and urban structure. Finally, we outline a few theses for the future development of regional and urban conflicts.

THE CAPITALIST DEVELOPMENT OF SOCIETY: A THEORETICAL SKETCH

With the formulation of a 'nonlinear' theory of capitalist development, we pick up social analytical approaches which were developed within the framework of the 'school of regulation', as it is called (Aglietta, 1976; Lipietz, 1985, 1987; Boyer, 1986; see also Jessop, 1985, 1990; Hirsch and Roth, 1986; Hirsch, 1990; Jessop, 1990). In doing this, we oppose an interpretation of Marxist theory which sees history as the unfolding, according to laws, of a 'logic' set in the economic nuclear structure of the capitalist mode of production, and reduces the complex structure of society to a simple base–superstructure model. Instead of this, we work on the assumption that the history of capitalism on the world scale is characterized by a sequence of specific social formations, which differ from each other greatly, based on an unvarying basic structure (private production, waged labour, the appropriation of surplus production through the exchange of goods) in their forms of production and exploitation, conditions of socialization and class, as well as in the character of the state and the political rule. The transitions between these capitalist developments take the form of acute 'secular' crises, which are determined by long-term fluctuations in profit rates. The development of the profit rate, the outbreak and form of secular crises do not, however, follow a simple 'objective' logic, but are determined by specific economic, social and political relationships. The process of the formation and crisis of developments is conveyed through the international market and through the competition of capitals, closely associated with national social conditions, including differences in national structure and a lack of synchronization within global development.

Each capitalist development of society is characterized by a specific *mode of accumulation* (accumulation regime) and a *method of regulation* associated with it. By 'mode of accumulation', we mean a form of surplus value production and realization, supported by particular types of production and management technology. It includes the type and method of organizing production and labour and the national economic reproduction of labour power and capital. This includes investment and capital devaluation strategies, branch structures (in particular the ratio between the producer goods sector and consumer goods sector), wage conditions, consumer models and class structures, the relations between the capitalist and non-capitalist sectors of work in society and the mode of integration into the international market. Regulation describes the way in which the elements of this complex relationship between production and reproduction are related to each other socially, i.e. based on the behaviour of the social participants. It is 'the way in which the system as a whole functions, the conjunction of economic mechanisms associated with a given set of social relationships, of institutional forms and structures' (Boyer, 1986: 100). It includes a multifaceted configuration of economic and sociopolitical institutions and norms, which gives a certain equilibrium and stability to the reproduction of the system as a whole or 'the totality of institutional forms, networks, explicit or implicit norms, which ensure the compatibility of types of behaviour within the framework of an *accumulation regime*' (Lipietz, 1985: 121). We use *hegemonic structure* to describe the concrete historical connection between the *mode of accumulation* and the *method of regulation*, which endows the economic form of capital reproduction (ensuring valorization) and political-ideological (legitimation, force and consent) reproduction of the system as a whole, under the domination of the ruling class(es), with relative durability (Boyer and Mistral, 1983). In this way, each capitalist development is characterized by a specific hegemonic structure, i.e. a particular form of valorization and class conditions and their institutional and normative reproduction. This does not rule out the possibility that fairly long-lasting 'non-hegemonic' phases may occur, following the crisis of a development, and the struggles for a new mode of accumulation and regulation may persist during these phases.

With the concept of the mode of accumulation, method of regulation and hegemonic structure as categories of social analysis, we depart from the abstract opposing of 'economics', 'politics' and 'ideology', from 'base' and 'superstructure'. This enables us to see, within the context of a comprehensive theory of social development, the town as a historically specific connection between production and reproduction, socialization, politics and ideology, whose form is determined by a complete method of regulation, interwoven into the international mode of accumulation, and its spatial expression.

A secular crisis of capitalist development, i.e. of a hegemonic relationship between accumulation and regulation, must be distinguished from economic crises within a method of accumulation and regulation (Lipietz, 1985). It occurs because, within a relatively tightly structured, institutionalized, hegemonic structure, which is only flexible to a limited degree, the stability of profit rates is certainly guaranteed for quite long periods of time, but never permanently. In general, crises in development can be traced back to the fact that the dynamics of the valorization process and the socioeconomic consequences of a mode of accumulation are on a collision course with the limits of the method of regulation, which is strengthened both institutionally and normatively. The effects of the accumulation of capital, which are socially and technologically revolutionary, must demolish these, at least in the long run. The structural disturbance in reproduction caused by this expresses itself in a 'secular' fall in profit rates.

Crises in a hegemonic development characterized by a specific mode of accumulation and regulation are accordingly to be understood as complex processes, which are connected with each other economically, politically and ideologically. They may show a specific lack of synchronization in their occurrence, relationship and course, i.e. 'economic', 'political' and 'ideological' crises can occur relatively independently of each other and displaced in time. Only when they join together or deteriorate does this lead to a secular crisis in development. The secular crisis, which is characterized by an incompatibility between the mode of accumulation and the method of regulation, forces a new mode of accumulation, a new method of regulation and thus a new hegemonic structure to be imposed.

CRISIS IN FORDISM AND THE CHANGING OF CONDITIONS OF REGULATION

Fordist capitalism, i.e. the hegemonic structure which had imposed itself as internationally dominant after the Second World War under the leadership of the USA, regardless of national differences and a lack of simultaneity, has been in a crisis since the seventies (Lipietz, 1985, 1987; Hirsch and Roth, 1986; Hirsch, 1990). The immediate phase is characterized by serious argument about fundamentally reforming society, i.e. the imposition of a 'post-Fordist' mode of accumulation and regulation. The Fordist phase of capitalism was marked by the imposition of Taylorist labour processes in important sectors, associated with a considerable extension of wage labour (by repressing subsistence-economic forms of production in the agricultural and domestic sector); whilst at the same time making labour conditions relatively similar ('employee society'). The industrial mass production of consumer goods became the basis for an extensive capitalization of the sphere of reproduction, i.e. the reproduction of the work forces became the integral part of the reproduction of capital on the basis of a generalized consumer model. Great advances in productivity and the linking of mass incomes to productivity increases facilitated strong growth in the national product and the general standard of living. The forced capitalization of the sphere of production and reproduction led to the accelerated disintegration of the traditional sociocultural milieux.

This mode of accumulation joined together with a 'monopolistic' method of regulation, which was very different from the rather liberal-competitive form of regulation which had been widespread until then (Boyer and Mistral, 1983: 49 ff; Lipietz, 1985: 121 ff). It consisted of strong processes of concentration and the formation of new mass industries (in particular the car and electronics industries), the development of bureaucratized and centralized trade unions with a tendency for all workers to be included in the right to representation and thus to have the opportunity to conclude comprehensive pay agreements, and the expansion of the bureaucratized welfare state. The latter not only greatly changed the conditions of the reproduction of the work force, but also made a distinct contribution to the stabilization of the model of mass consumption. On this basis, a centralized corporatism was able to develop, based on social-contractual cooperation between commercial associations, trade unions, parties and state administrations, and a Keynesian state interventionism supported by it. The assurance of full employment and growth, the expansion of the welfare state and global control of the economic process of reproduction, supported by the extended apparatus of financial and fiscal state intervention, corporate negotiation structures and national economic prognoses, were determinate characteristics of the Fordist hegemonic structure. It guaranteed the stability of profit rates, the raising of the general standard of living and a relative balance in the economic processes of reproduction for a fairly long phase. The essential characteristic of this 'Keynesian' regulation relationship was the inclusion, obtained by the social democratic (or similar) parties, of the workers, organized into trade unions, in the processes of state administrative decisions, and a stable legitimation of the sociopolitical relationships, supported by growth, consumption and a class conflict institutionalized in a reformist way.

The crisis of Fordism in the 1970s led to the worldwide collapse of the mode of accumulation and regulation which were its characteristics. This crisis continues: a new, stable, international, hegemonic 'post-Fordist' development has so far been unable to impose itself. In a national and an international context, the situation is characterized rather by a complex mixture of alternative strategies for overcoming the crisis, which are at the same time the subject of deep political–social conflicts. National and regional development concepts have stepped in to replaced the 'global Fordism' of the 1950s and 1960s; these diverging and, at the same time, hotly disputed concepts may eventually be realized and implemented. Thus, there can hardly be any talk of a restabilized 'post-Fordist' capitalism or indeed even an international 'post-Fordist' capitalism. At best, there are tendencies towards it and starting points for it. But these can at least be specified on a national level and their chances of implementation and consequences can be evaluated. This is done here with reference to Germany (specifically, western Germany).

The following are characteristics of the new *mode of accumulation*:

1 The transition to *post-Taylorist forms of organization of production and labour*, on the basis of new information and communications technologies. This does not in any way lead to the 'end of mass production', but to a new technological constitution of it which is, however, associated with a massive laying-off of the work force, far-reaching processes of social marginalization and a strong fragmentation of the relationships between work and wages.

2 A strengthened *industrialization of the service sector*, based on the new information and communications technologies ('hyperindustrialization'), which leads to a great many changes in service industry jobs, and radically changes the social structure of the workers (e.g. the relationship between workers and white-collar workers). At the same time, changes in information and communications have strong, individualizing effects on the form of socialization. Associated with this are shifts in regional structure, especially in the relationship between thriving 'new' and stagnating 'old' industrial locations, and the formation of new urban service-industry centres with inhabitants who are socially highly polarized ('global cities').

3 A *new thrust* of capitalization which is based on the industrialization of services and a further industrialization of agriculture, which leads to an increase in forced mobility and a rapid breakdown of family relationships.

4 A *decoupling of increases in productivity and the income of the masses*, and thus the transition to accumulation at a low level of growth, which is linked to an increase in differences in income and an increased differentiation of the consumer model.

5 An *'individualization'* and *'pluralization of lifestyles'*, based on a fragmentation of the relationships between wages and work, socialization according to information technology, consumer differentiation, increased competition for jobs whilst, at the same time, there is a relaxation in the disciplining effects of standardized waged work and sociopyschological processes of redundancy.

Associated with this is the formation of a *method of regulation*, which gives a new emphasis to elements of monopolistic regulation, and combines them with a stronger control of the market, still controlled by the government. Its characteristics are:

1 *New relationships integrating branch structure and industry on the basis of advanced production technology*, associated with strong international processes of

concentration and a reorganization of the relationship between industrial and finance capital. Small businesses which are close to the market and innovative become more significant. Both in the high-technology sector and in the marginalized areas of the economy, there is an increasingly blurred border line between self-employment and waged work.

2   *A quantitative reduction and institutional fragmentation* of the system of social security, resulting in a further division into different categories of waged workers.

3   The *weakening of the trade unions* through mass unemployment, processes of tertiarization, the heterogenization of working relationships and processes of social division within waged workers.

4   The formation of *new corporate forms*, which are characterized by a close interweaving between the state and industry in the technology sector, a *selective* inclusion of privileged sectors of the workers in corporate arrangements, ('selective-decentralized corporatism').

DEVELOPMENT OF SOCIETY AND SPATIAL STRUCTURE

The various historical developments of capitalism are also marked by a specific structuring of space in each case. The imposition of a historically dominant form of capitalist production–work relationship, the level of consumption and types of socialization, produce a characteristic spatial structure on an international, regional and local level. This affects the spatial localization of work – the relationship between 'town' and 'region' – as well as the spatial/social form of the towns themselves. Thus, specific forms of political regulation of space are required in the context of changing processes of differentiation in centralization, peripheralization and function. Regional and local spaces, partly lying across national state boundaries, are incorporated into the worldwide relationships between accumulation and regulation in different ways.

Fordist capitalism in the developed cities was marked by the imposition of an 'intensive' mode of accumulation on the basis of Taylorist mass production, an extensive capitalization of the sector of reproduction, a standard model of mass consumption, the accelerated breakdown of traditional life milieux, the generalization of the labour condition and a contradictory social homogenization and individualization associated with this. The accumulation, supported by the internal capitalization of the cities, produced a centre–periphery relationship on a world scale, which was spatially structured, relegating the peripheral countries of the 'Third World' into the neocolonial status of suppliers of simple manufactured goods and raw materials. Accumulation and international trade was concentrated in the developed capitalist cities. A worldwide polarization of 'town' and 'region' matched the industrial capitalization of the cities, based on the exploitation of natural resources and forms of subsistence reproduction. The regional structure of the cities was marked by the dominance of Fordist industrial locations (e.g. steel industry, car industry, chemical industry, electrical equipment industry), a drastic fall in the agricultural population with the partial industrialization of agriculture and an internal peripheralization, which allowed regions threatened by depopulation to become, at best, branch plant economies.

The image of the Fordist town was characterized by strong agglomeration processes, the standardization and industrialization of construction, the nuclearization of the family and far-reaching processes of social disintegration, resulting in the erosion of the traditional sociocultural milieux (e.g. workers' settlements). Supported by the large-scale imposition of the car, extreme spatial-functional differentiations developed, characterized by suburbanism, the formation of satellite towns, the depopulation of the inner cities, the dying out of smaller production and business operations, whilst at the same time stores and discount supermarkets blossomed in parts of the inner city. Life in the nuclear family, standardized labour, television and cars became the basis of a new model of life and consumption and structured urban space. The 'uncongeniality' of the standardized towns, whose spaces were differentiated according to function, became a central issue for critical urban sociology. State and local government administrations supported this process with their traffic development and subsidy policies. Serious social conflicts were caused by the process of turning residential areas near the city into slums as a preliminary step towards commercial use for predominantly 'tertiary' functions, the extension of inner-city branches of industry, the loss of infrastructure and the expulsion of the population from deep-rooted residential areas and the drastic reduction in 'quality of life'.

The 'crisis of Fordism' was therefore also a crisis of the Fordist town. Here the economic, political and ideological dimensions of the crisis crystallized into an explosive mixture. In its course, driven on by extensive restructuring processes in production technology and new social movements and conflicts, the contours of a 'post-Fordist' development of society are to be seen, and their imposition greatly modifies the arrangement of spaces and the spatial matrix of social conflicts.

On the world scale, a new international division of labour is developing. This is characterized by an internationalization of production which is driven by the multinational concerns. Production processes, management and control operations can become extremely fragmented on the basis of new production, information, communications and transport technologies, allow varying aspects of location to be exploited flexibly (cheap or qualified workforce, 'highest' capacity environment – 'worldwide sourcing'). Capital becomes more flexible, major spatial heterogenization processes mark this: enforced industrialization in former peripheral regions ('threshold countries' or 'new industrializing countries') go along with the deindustrialization of metropolitan regions. High-tech producers leave the capitalist centres, whilst, at the same time, the Taylorist mass production of simple goods can be relocated in these places. New production technologies, supported by the 'microelectronic revolution', lead to a heterogenization and 'flexibilization' of working conditions and the spreading of a multitude of forms of peripheral work in urban centres. A result of this is intensified division in society, characterized by continuing mass unemployment, increased differentiation in qualifications and income, and the formation of a new, hierarchical model of consumption. Whilst social heterogenization and the imposition of new communication technologies drive Fordist individualization on, new 'alternative' forms of production and socialization have appeared at the same time. 'Lifestyles' multiply – yuppies, boutique-bourgeoïsie, 'new poverty' and 'alternative living'. Associated with the internationalization of production and the communication revolution, expansive urban administration centres are developing as the nodal points of connection between internationalized production, circulation and finance ('global cities'). The advantages of these locations are based less on their geographical situation, but increasingly result from the availability of a qualified workforce, the combination of specific industrial services and research capacities, advantages of contacts and agglomeration, as well, of course, as favourable political conditions for capital. The 'post-Fordist' metropolitan city is less than ever the product of natural conditions of location but rather of economic strategies.

At the same time, some traditional industrial locations and regions are threatened by stagnation and decline. The international and regional heterogenization of work and living conditions, however, is also reproduced in the expanding 'tertiary' towns of the services industry: inner-city sectors of high technology, high consumption and high culture mingle with ghettoes of ethnic minorities, the socially marginalized etc. 'Revaluation' and 'cultural enlivening' of the inner cities, 'gentrifying' and economic 'revitalizing' of quarters near the city count as important tools of locational policy, which aims above all at the tertiarized 'industries of the future', with their need for a highly qualified workforce. However, this does not eradicate the demand for poorly qualified, marginalized and peripheral production and service sector personnel. Extensive functional differentiation gives way to small-scale heterogenization. Within the urban area, the forms of labour, socialization and cultural orientation multiply. Further socio-economic division, produced by the imposition of the new mode of accumulation on a global level, are reproduced in the 'post-Fordist' town in a politically and socially explosive fashion.

Thus, new conditions arise for urban development policy. It encounters the increased pressure of restructuring and adaptation processes determined by the market, and the advancing inter-nationalization of production and circulation, and is forced to actively encourage this. During this process, spatial-social disparities arise as well as social conflicts which bring about changed political forms of regulation.

STRATEGIES FOR OVERCOMING THE CRISIS IN THE FEDERAL REPUBLIC OF GERMANY: SOCIO-SPATIAL CONSEQUENCES OF THE MODERNIZATION OF THE 'EXPORT MODEL' FOR GERMANY

Although the secular crisis of the Fordist model of socialization is penetrating all capitalist countries, and although they all face the increased pressure of the technical–economic restructuring determined by the world market, the ideal way for all countries to enter into post-Fordist capitalism has so far failed to be identified. No new hegemonic centre – a role which the USA had assumed for the Fordist phase – is recognizable as a starting point, rather a state of hegemonic instability (Arrighi, 1986) can be detected. Thus, the politico-economic strategies of all the capitalist cities involve adapting to new conditions, on the basis of their former specializations. To this extent, the analysis of the socio-spatial effects of this restructuring process in the Federal Republic of Germany (FRG) must take the historically specific condi-tions of the 'export model of Germany' as a starting point. Post-Fordist capitalism is far removed from a 'Japanization', 'Germanization' or 're-Americanization' on a global scale.

If we now try to outline the FRG's variant of the post-Fordist strategy of accumulation, the distinction between 'deindustrialization' (the loss of economic activities and functions to other regions of the world), 'reindustrialization' (regaining an industrial base of one's own) and 'neoindustrialization' (building up new high-technology industries) proves problematic. German business has tried to defend its existing profile of specialization (see Esser et al., 1983). This involves first of all the internationalized industrial core sector, which is strongly competitive, especially technologically advanced engineering, plant and vehicle construction, chemical processing, mineral oil and plastic processing, electrotechnology and optoelectronics. These are to be modernized, specialized and made more flexible. Secondly, there is an even closer interweaving in this industrial core of all branches of industry with each other and the functional integration of small and average-sized industries, as well as of the private and public services sector (banks, insurance, marketing, engineering, export insurance).

This means that small and average-sized businesses are involved even more closely in the production and product innovations of large businesses operating worldwide, but above all that the functional and structural linking of the industrial and tertiary sectors is being deepened considerably. Without being able to describe this strategy here in great detail, its form can be summarized as follows: the entire industrial core sector, from steel to cars, machine tools, chemical products to communications and the computer industry, is to profit from the revolution in microelectronics and information technology, the sectoral coherence of all branches and sectors (including the so-called traditional industries: steel, shipyards, textiles, etc.) is to be retained and deepened, rather than given up in favour of fewer types of product as in the Japanese model or more distinct concentration on the services sector in accordance with the US model (Esser, 1986). Thus far, a distinction can be made between deindustrialization, reindustrialization and neoindustrialization for the German strategy of accumulation analytically. In reality we find all three variants present in all branches and sectors at the same time.

The next question concerns what socio-spatial consequences arise from this state of affairs. Social-scientific investigations into German regional and urban development have suggested that a heterogenization of regions and towns has resulted from this technical–economic restructuring process. The heterogenization of the regions involves a south–north division, the heterogenization of cities involves their division into two or three parts (Häussermann and Siebel, 1986b). However, our thesis is that this description of the post-Fordist spatial structure of the FRG is inaccurate, because it fails to take into account the specificity of the accumulation strategy.

The tendency towards a south–north division, i.e. towards splitting the FRG into an area of prospering *Länder* in the south (Bavaria, Baden-Württemberg, Hessen) and a stagnating impoverished, area in the north (Schleswig-Holstein, Hamburg, Bremen, Niedersachsen, Nordrhein-Westfalen) (Brune and Koeppel, 1980; Commerzbank, 1983; Voss and Friedrich, 1986) was assumed, above all by Häussermann and Siebel, to be already complete: 'The distribution of modern industry in favour of few centres [of industry] in southern Germany is established to a great extent.' The concentration of electronics, microelectronics, aircraft construction and aerospace industries in the area of southern Germany has, in the meantime, set off the sort of gravitation dynamics which we know from the agglomeration tendencies of industry. The extension of research capacities and the services companies which go with them, as well as the development of a specific labour market in the Württemberg or upper Bavarian area has in the meantime progressed so far – supported by a massive policy of investment and orders from the FRG, especially with defence orders – that it is impossible to foresee where or how further major centres should form in this technological sphere in the FRG (Häussermann and Siebel, 1986b: 106).

Even though there are considerable differences between the *Länder*, especially in the unemployment levels, this state of affairs is still unable to support the thesis of the south–north division. Häussermann and Siebel claimed, without evidence, that the future key industries of the FRG will essentially be determined by the dynamics of the defence sector, and, accordingly, include only electronics, aircraft construction and the aerospace industry. They overlooked the fact that German capitalism continues to have good chances of surviving within world capitalism through investment goods and durable consumer goods in the civil sector. This means that chemical engineering and plant construction, and vehicle construction, besides the electronics and optoelectronics industry, will further form the core parts of the export industries.

With reference to spatial structure, this means that since these core branches, including the supply and services spheres subordinated to them, are situated in all regions of the FRG, all regions of the FRG will profit from their growth, albeit in different ways. Our own studies into industrial policy in different *Länder* confirm the findings of other empirical research into the structure and development of branches and sectors of German industry, that industries which have strong or weak growth are, despite regional variances in the rate of growth, almost identical in all the *Länder*. Even the structure and development of industrial sectors in individual *Länder* have very many common features. Manufacturing has remained the largest industry in the majority of *Länder*, even in the 1980s, although it has lost some importance – like agriculture – compared with the so-called 'service sector'. However, since this service sector can only develop in functional subordination to the goods-manufacturing trade (Hack and Hack, 1985), the shifts between the two areas confirm the thesis presented here. Against this background it is also understandable that an overall comparison of the *Länder* shows enormous similarities in the level, structure and development of the most important economic indications: production, employment, income and unemployment. Each *Land* has both strengths and weaknesses (Koerber-Weik and Wied-Nebbelling, 1987). Finally, the thesis of the 'south–north division' fails to recognize that because of different branch structures the differences in their overall level of development are not so dramatic because of the fact that so-called streamlining processes in the traditional industries of the north – shipyards, steel, coal – have already progressed a long way; a 'stabilization of the north' can succeed in the long term (Wettmann, 1986). So it does not make sense to characterize the changes in spatial structure in the FRG as a south–north division. It is more accurate to talk of a division in the north and the south, for within individual *Länder* there are greater disparities than between the *Länder*. In other words, winner and loser regions are to be found distributed throughout the entire FRG.

Against the background that winners and losers in the technical-economical restructuring process are distributed across the FRG, a development towards a two or three part division in cities noted by Häussermann and Siebel could arise. This would involve:

1   The internationally competitive urban area, which predominantly takes on functions which are aimed at internationally orientated business people, visitors to conferences and meetings etc. (airports, museums, the conference and hotel sphere, expensive cultural facilities, luxurious accommodation, administrative complexes of firms aimed at the international market) and is in competition with other cities.
2   The 'normal' residential urban area for the middle class, with the function of a principal regional centre.
3   The marginalized urban area, in which fringe groups, the permanently unemployed, the poor, foreigners and drug addicts (if possible isolated and monitored by the security police), eke out their miserable existence.

To be sure, the 'mixing' of these three areas, in each case according to the economic structure of the surrounding area and the winner–loser relationship associated with it, will be different – and certainly the internationally competitive area will be missing from many towns, which is why the distinction between towns divided into three or two parts seems meaningful. However, increasing social segmentation and segregation, and increased political control and monitoring, characterizes all towns. The unification process sharpened these developments. So we have to add new and different processes of segmentation: the splitting between East and West Germany.

POLITICAL-IDEOLOGICAL PATTERN OF REGULATION:
FROM THE VERTICAL INTEGRATION OF POLICY
TO THE 'BREAK-UP OF THE REGIONS'

The FRG can be split into central, federal and municipal political-ideological levels of regulation. Here we leave aside the problems of the central level (see Hirsch and Roth, 1986; Esser, 1986). But according to our thesis the federal level is currently increasingly becoming strategically important in the search for, and experimentation with, political–ideological forms of regulation adequate for post-Fordism. This is supported by the fact that German *Länder* recently succeeded in establishing their codetermination in European Union politics. In contrast, there can hardly be any talk yet of an independent and autonomous urban policy.

In the Fordist phase of West German capitalism, an attempt was made to link urban and regional policy functionally to the central-corporational regulation model. This reached its peak as a result of the first great economic recession of 1966–7, when a strengthened world market offensive by the Germany economy to overcome worsened conditions of capital valorization proved ever more inevitable (Hirsch, 1986). The entry of the SPD (German Social Democratic Party) to power brought about the necessary restructuring of the forms and institutions of state intervention in the economic reproduction process. Efforts were made to bring about a strict centralization and rationalization of cooperative federalism (Lehmbruch, 1976), as well as an extension of the Keynesian state control apparatus (law of stability) and the stronger binding of the unions into the development of informed opinion and decision-making (liberal corporatism). The aim was to create new structural and industrial–political decision-making bodies, which could be cut off from the 'disturbing' influences of regional and local authorities. Resistance to structural–political measures by the central state which occurred within local or regional political institutions was to be neutralized, just like the protests of social groups who attacked the destruction of towns and countryside. Moreover, the belief was that central state planning organizations could unify regional development and living conditions in the whole of the FRG.

In detail, the financial independence of *Länder* and municipalities was cut back, central state legislation and administrative authorities were extended, municipalities and administrative districts were merged into general planning and administrative areas and municipal and *Land* parliaments lost power to new central institutions like the Finance Planning Council, the Economic Council and regional planning societies. The most important parts of this 'vertical integration of policy' were communal projects to improve agricultural structure and protection of the coastline, to improve the regional economic structure, extend higher education and improve training and research policy. Planning committees were created by federal and *Land* governments to formulate and impose these policies. The funding of plans was taken over by the federal government and the *Länder*, half each. This 'technocratic planning model, which tried to join the power and financial potential of the central state with the basis of information and competence of implementation of the decentralised state entities' (Garlichs, 1980: 72), failed when, as a result of the world economic crisis of the mid-1970s, the central state scope for regional funding assistance decreased, the potential for conflict between the *Länder* for regional aid increased and the level of consensus dropped (Scharpf et al., 1976). In the ever-tougher competition between the *Länder* and the municipalities to attract industry, the *Länder* set up their own promotion programmes, each according to their own financial situation and administrative skills, their own tax cuts and subsidies, their own technology parks, etc. The vertical integration of policy thus failed due to the autonomy of the *Länder*, which entered the field of structural and industrial politics with high hopes of their own image and in a 'race between the regions' (Esser, 1989).

In fact, every federal *Land* in the FRG would like to 'spearhead innovation and progress' – the rhetoric sounds the same, regardless of the party-political composition which the respective *Land* government has. And they all believe that they have good opportunities to do this because of their particular industrial structures. No difference can be distinguished between individual *Länder* strategies with regard to their technical–economic content. Everywhere it is a question of pushing forward the high-technology sphere by sponsoring engineering companies, founding technology parks, etc.; financing small and medium dynamic companies; safeguarding financial help for the modernizing and restructuring of production plants for the traditional industrial core and dealing with 'streamlining' processes socially and politically; linking the industrial sector more efficiently with the so-called services sector. The adaptation to world market conditions and the assurance of international competitiveness remains the unquestioned imperative of the industrial policy of each *Land*. It also goes without saying that private capital – above all large businesses operating worldwide (supported by banks, insurance, business organizations) – with small and medium-sized businesses in tow, determine the content and direction of this restructuring process. The task for *Land* governments will be to set legal administrative and fiscal limits, and if necessary to strengthen the capability and readiness of businesses to risk more flexibility and deregulation ('the dismantling of encrusted structures'). Moreover, it is their task to produce the social and political consensus for this policy, and thus fasten social integration and politico-ideological legitimation.

It can be said, with some exaggeration, that all *Land* governments now behave like the management of a business, attempting to direct their entire policy at the needs and requirements of the *Land* as an industrial location in post-Fordist world capitalism. However, two differences can be noted between *Länder* with different party political compositions: one with regard to the limit of the level of state activity, the other with regard to the concrete mode of political-legitimizing integration. The basic types of Christian Democratic Inc. and Social Democratic Inc. are illustrated by the two states of Baden-Württemberg and Nordrhein-Westfalen.

In the conservative plan of Baden-Württemberg, more faith is placed in the market than in the state, from the point of view of efficiency. This was not fundamentally changed by the establishment of a 'big coalition' government, combining Christian Democrats and Social Democrats in 1992. Whilst the state must, above all, look after the construction of a scientific-technical infrastructure, and dismantle state-bureaucratic 'encrustments' which could hinder the company's freedom to develop on the market, it is to refrain from exerting any influence on decisions about the products or the concrete formulation of production processes. Therefore, any political dialogue about the social usefulness of or damage caused by products/production processes is to be rejected. Technocorporate alliances between the state, economy and science are to serve the purpose, above all, of aligning businesses with market developments more quickly, efficiently and smoothly than those of competitors. The leadership of such alliances is left to the large concerns operating worldwide. Their market knowledge, including their comprehensive information systems, offers the best guarantee of identifying new market developments swiftly and reacting to them. The unions also have to subordinate themselves to this private capitalist leadership. Their role can at best be that of being kept informed about imminent developments and seeing that the employees accept the inevitable. Should they refuse to accept this limited role, and demand codetermination in the use of new technologies or even that technology be structured in a social-contractual way, then acceptance must be pursued over their heads, i.e. directly from factory committees on site.

This policy is politically and ideologically safeguarded by a discourse of technological optimism. According to this, by quickly and efficiently

changing the products and production processes required by the
market, not only is a top position in the world market guaranteed,
but at the same time, it enables all social needs and interests to be
harmonized, ecological damage to be removed and the 'correct'
balance to be reached between regional and local disparities.
Admittedly, the individual human being must change before this
combination of technical, economic and social progress, the outbreak
of the harmonious technopolis, can be fully realized. The farewell to
the society of the masses has been announced, the rise of the new
individual is on the agenda (Drescher et al., 1986; Esser and Fach,
1986). The requirement is for the flexible, mobile, brave, risk-taking
worker businessman, active at all times. He stands in his place, active
and ready to work with his own people in the factory, family,
neighbourhood, community, region, and forms small communities
which show solidarity and a willingness to make sacrifices to overcome
difficulties, but helps only himself first of all, before he calls on the
larger association. Finally there is the individualized, market-based
and active society (corporation), linked by decentralized corporate
structures. For potential deviants and those who cannot be integrated,
the strong state, with extended political and administrative information
and decision-making capacities, stands prepared to come using a new
social order policy and an efficient 'ministry for welfare and social
policy', so that 'alternative futures' cannot spread, ensuring that there
are limiting conditions 'within which the reasonable nature of the
"competent" individual can develop and prove himself, freely and
securely' (*Zukunftsperspektiven*, 1983: 45; Bulling Commission, 1985:
18 ff; Esser, 1987).

Efficiency, rather than humanitarian perspectives, also determines
the Social Democratic alternative project, as illustrated by Nordrhein-
Westfalen. Here also, it is a question of the operating capability of the
private company on the capitalist world market. Admittedly, the
policies are reminiscent of the industrial–political selective corporatism
of the Social Democratic 'model Germany' of the 1970s (Hauff and
Scharpf, 1975; Esser and Fach, 1981) and more faith is placed here
in state and union 'common-sense capitalism'. But it is also the prime
task of private enterprise to press on with structural change in
Nordrhein-Westfalen: 'In all spheres of the economy, the factories
must make increased efforts to raise their capacity for competition
and performance, and to develop new sales markets which encourage
growth. The *Land* government sets particular store by the flexibility,
innovative force and potential for developing markets of the middle-
class economy' (Der Minister für Wirtschaft, 1985: IV). However, 'the

market alone does not help as an instrument of choice, for the market cannot recognize values' (Rau, 1985; similarly Spoeri, 1987).

Only a cooperation partnership between the state, companies and unions can wring a value-orientated – and thus sensible – political economic world market strategy out of the market. This means that in practice, a strategy oriented towards the world market must be worked out, under the leadership of the companies, which makes positive use of the new technologies but integrates environmental and social contractual attitudes. Two aims can thus be realized at the same time: a specific advantage in competition on the world market, on the one hand, ecological and 'economic renewal of the industrial *Land* of Nordrhein-Westfalen', on the other hand.

Apart from the fact that private capital in Nordrhein-Westfalen has so far acted no differently from that in Baden-Württemburg and neither government nor unions have political plans to bring them to 'reason' and encroach upon their autonomy, the state and unions also do not know which world market products are ecologically and socially acceptable. Therefore, efforts are being made first to build up research capacities. This involves a programme of 'socially acceptable structuring of technology', which is to establish the problems resulting from new types of technology and to 'change the reality'; an institution for 'labour and technology'; and a cultural–scientific institution, which is to investigate the multifaceted influence of culture and technology. Also:

> urban development policy, communications policy, economic and environmental policy are to be even more effectively linked with each other, so that we can keep our towns and communities as homes worthy of our love and worth living in. The *Land* government has presented a framework for ecologically orientated urban renewal with the concept of 'urban ecology'. In view of stagnating and sinking net incomes, and permanently high unemployment, there are too few reasonably-priced flats. . . . The total plan of the *Land* government for building flats lays emphasis on making available value-for-money old buildings, and protecting stocks of council housing; it will include environmental criteria. *(Rau, 1985: 25)*

If operations in Baden-Württemburg are ideologically those of the 'conciliation corporation,' in Nordrhein-Westfalen the 'solidarity corporation' involves the alliance of all reasonable and responsible people in the economy, the unions, and communities. The key points of this social pact to be forged were: a shortening of working hours, a labour market qualifications policy, ecological and economic renewal.

The conservative conciliation option involves an 'activity corporation' which links individualized, flexible and small communities from the bottom, admittedly supervised by the 'realized policy of order' by the state. However, in Nordrhein-Westfalen the traditional, Social Democratic approach is followed: the social pact is to be produced from the top. Even the desired individual initiative requires state encouragement: 'We will create the basis for a foundation for the "protection of nature, the homeland and culture". Like the National Trust in Great Britain, we want to challenge the individual initiatives of our citizens for nature, culture and their homeland. For the state cannot, should not, do everything alone' (Rau, 1985). With the deepening of the economic crisis since 1992, the solidarity aspects of the social pact withered away even in the Social Democratic strategy. Shortening of working hours and comprehensive social security arrangements for the 'victims of modernization' are now off the agenda.

In relation to the heterogenization tendencies associated with the technical–economic restructuring processes in regions and towns, neither 'right-wing' nor 'left-wing' industrial–political techno-corporatism proposes to counteract these, but merely to seek to ensure their legitimation in a different ways. The question is whether urban policy can.

URBAN POLICY AND URBAN CONFLICT

In all localities, due to the requirement for economic growth, increased efforts to establish industries and infrastructural modernization measures are on the agenda. However, there can hardly be talk of an independent local government economic policy. Rather, towns in competition to establish industries adapt themselves passively to conditions set by the world market. Moreover, they increase the trend towards their internal heterogenization through these actions (Blanke, 1991; Bullmann, 1991; Esser, 1992). However, new social movements and political conflicts must also be expected.

With the crisis of Fordism the nature of urban conflict has also changed. The traditional workers' movement was deradicalized in the bureaucratically overstructured mass consumption culture and institutionalized in the corporate regulation battle, so new social movements developed in the 1960s with new organizational forms and objectives. Their most important social basis was the 'tertiarized' new middle class above all in the social and services professions, which had grown in the wake of the advancing economy. Under conditions of relatively full employment, the expansion of standardized and institutionally safeguarded labour and expanded mass consumption, the area of 'reproduction' now became the primary field of conflict. Sexual inequality and repression, the environment, living conditions, the prevailing model of consumption and the 'quality of life' developed into important themes. Under the pressure of extensive processes of social disintegration and individualization and in the face of the growing 'lack of congeniality' of standardized and function-differentiated towns, the search increased for new, self-initiated social relationships, forms of communication and publicity. In decaying quarters in particular, threatened with redevelopment, alternative 'movement milieux' arose with their own economic and political structures, whose 'class basis' is rather diffuse and whose appearance and development show strong characteristics of a political self-constitution which is relatively separated from social status (Hirsch and Roth, 1986: 168 ff).

At the same time, new forms of socio-political linkages between town and *Land* arose, between 'alternative' urban and rural 'villages'. The urban protest against environmental destruction, paradigmatically in the Anti Nuclear Weapons Movement, joined with the resistance of those who were affected by the impact of industry on rural regions and gained an explosive quality. The perceived link between the building of the Frankfurt airport runway and the nuclear reprocessing plant in Wackersdorf, to name but one example, had the consequence of linking conflicts personally and politically which were at a great spatial distance from each other. 'Alternative' perspectives spread into the rural regions as well, supported by close communications with the urban milieu. At the same time, the flight from the towns in the 1970s led to new social mixing. This produced a comprehensive urban critique and a critique of civilization (but also 'antimodernistic' orientations with regressive tendencies).

In the meantime, the crisis of Fordist development also leaves its traces in these 'new' movements. Although the Fordist 'dream of everlasting prosperity' has been shattered and permanent mass unemployment as well as a worsening of incomes are apparent, a revival of a workers' movement on the traditional pattern seems unlikely in view of increasing heterogeneity and division. Of course, the 'ageing' of these 'new' movements should also be noted. They have been 'gentrified' and integrated economically, culturally and politically to a certain extent. This is accompanied by the breaking-out of new conflicts, characterized by ethnic conflicts, made more acute by the pressure of unemployment, and the appearance of new, radicalized groups, largely consisting of marginalized young people. Their forms of action are violent, their understanding of politics and society radically anti-institutional; they hardly develop 'reformist' concepts of society and politics which are scarcely comprehensive, and they meet less in the form of tightly structured 'alternative' milieux than in public places, rather accordingly to the tribalistic pattern of streetfighters. The very strong squatter movements and militant conflicts in Hamburg (Hafenstraße) and Berlin (Kreuzberg) are examples of this. The newest development in this field is the rise of militant right-wing groups throughout the country since the beginning of the 1990s, mainly caused by the effects of unification politics. This is an outcome of both intensified economic, social and cultural marginalization processes and the nationalist and populist ideology adopted by the leading parties to legitimate their political and economic strategy. In addition, the right-wing mobilization, and more generally the intensification of cultural and ethnic conflicts, is linked with the wave of migration which has followed the decline of peripheral capitalist regions and the Eastern European countries, after the break-down of the Soviet Union. Explosive urban conflicts like those in Los Angeles are not likely yet in the politically highly regulated and controlled German cities, but the general tendencies are the same. The transition to the 'post-Fordist' town is thus marked by a great heterogenization and division in the milieu of the social movements, the active groups and the areas of conflict.

One of the most important tasks of local government policy today seems to be to ensure and manage the division of the town ideologically into three or two parts (Haeussermann and Siebel, 1986a). This includes the restructuring and repressive isolation of oppositional social spaces (the repression of deviancy, strategies of gentrification, measures to create no-go areas, regulation of the drug trade), selective measures for employment and economic aid (welfare, cold-weather support, support for the poor, etc.) in order to keep at least the worst needs of the 'new poor' below a certain level (Blanke et al., 1986). This is linked with efforts to assimilate elements of the 'alternative culture' and a corresponding depoliticization of opposition movements. This 'culturalization of protest' is becoming an important part of the cultural 'revitalizing' of towns. The integration of an 'established' and 'alternative' culture, supported by an experimental and relatively unorthodox modernization of traditional culture, is becoming the focus of a new urban 'us feeling' which smooths over the conflicts handed down from, and associated with, the protest movements of the 1960s and 1970s and seems to leave only violent alternatives for the new marginalized population. The cultural policy of Frankfurt, which has been extremely successful and has now achieved international fame, provides a fine example of this (Bachmann, 1983). In addition there is the parliamentarization of protest on a municipal and state level, promoted above all by the appearance of the green party. The Greens, who still have their most important base in the alternative milieux, see themselves exposed to the pressure of observing the 'parliamentary rules of the game', distancing themselves from violence, which is 'extra-'institutional, i.e. from practically any behaviour which is at all against the rules. This leads to enormous internal conflict and also advances the political separation of the protest movements.

The ever more perfectly equipped arsenal of repressive monitoring and pacification strategies is directed above all at radical anti-institutional groups and their forms of protest, which are barely cohesive politically and ideologically, and tend towards violence. The arming of the police, which is becoming more and more evident in the towns, is accompanied by the expansion of the state monitoring and preventive capacities in the face of conflict which is becoming increasingly unpredictable. The modern service centres, culturally highly stylized and full of boutiques, are becoming fortresses full of weapons at the same time. Chic shopping precincts and pedestrian zones are planned from the very beginning to accommodate water cannons and commando troops. The small-scale social divisions in the towns increasingly make it necessary to prevent the ghettoes and marginalized subcultures from spreading to the islands of 'high technology', 'high consumption' and 'high culture' which are their immediate neighbours.

It does, however, remain to be seen which spatial, social and political structure the 'post-Fordist' town will finally adopt. It is likely that it will be far more varied than the standardized type of town marked by Fordism, because of the social and regional heterogenization process. It is not only 'objective' tendencies and capital strategies, determined by the world market, which will be important but also the outcomes of political–social conflicts in the towns themselves. The boundaries of the repressive subordination of deviating minorities are known, but it remains to be seen how far the political-ideological integration strategies towards opposition movements and groups will take hold. The fact that the social–spatial structure of towns is always the result of political–social power relations, conflicts and compromises under given economic–structural conditions, which vary historically and in the context of particular struggles, is more true today than ever before.

REFERENCES

Aglietta, M. (1976) *Régulation et crises du capitalisme. L'éxperiece des Etats Unis.* Paris: Calman Lévy.

Ahfeldt, H., Siebel, W. and Sieverts, T. (1983) Frankfurt im Jahr 2000 – eine Horrorvision? *Frankfurter Rundschau*, No. 304, 21 December.

Arrighi, G. (1986) Eine Krise der Hegemonie. In S. Amin et al. (eds), *Dynamik der globalen Krise*. Opladen: Westdeutscher Verlag, 36–75.

Bachmann, D. (1985) Kampagne in Frankfurt. Wie man die Kultur einer Stadt umkrempelt *Tages-Anzeiger Magazin (Zürich)*, No. 8, 23 February, 6–13.

Blanke, B., Evers, A. and Wollmann, H. (eds) (1986) *Die zweite Stadt*. Leviathan, Sonderheft 7.

Blanke, B. (ed.) (1991) *Staat + Stadt*. Politische Vierteljahresschrift, Sonderheft 22.

Boyer, R. (1986) *La théorie de le régulation: une analyse critique*. Paris: Edition la Découverte.

Boyer, R. and Mistral, J. (1983) *Accumulation, Inflation, Crises*. Paris: PUF.

Brune, R. and Köppel, M. (1980) Das Nord-Süd-Gefälle verstärkt sich. *Mitteilungen des Rheinisch-Westfälischen Instituts für Wirtschaftsforschung*, April, 225–47.

Bulling Kommission (1985) *Bericht der Kommission 'Neue Führungsstruktur Baden Württemberg'*, 3 Volumes. Stuttgart: Reclam.

Bullmann, U. (1991) *Kommunale Strategien gegen Massenarbeitslosigkeit*. Opladen: Leske and Budrich.

Castells, M. (ed.) (1985) *High Technology, Space, and Society*. Beverly Hills, London and New Dehli: Sage.

Commerzbank (1983) Bundesländer: Süden holt auf. *Bericht der Abteilung Volkswirtschaft*, No. 155, 17 October.

Commerzbank (1986) Bundesländer: dynamischer Süden. *Bericht der Abteilung Volkswirtschaft*, No. 177, 28 February.

Drescher, A., Esser, J. and Fach, W. (1986) *Die politische Ökonomie der Liebe*. Frankfurt: Suhrkamp.

Esser, J. (1986) State, business and trade unions in West Germany after the 'political Wende'. *West European Politics*, 9, 198–214.

Esser, J. (1987) Dem 'Aufbruch der Teilstaaten' politisch Beine machen – zur Reorganisation des Staatsapparats im Spätkapitalismus. Mimeo, Frankfurt.

Esser, J. (1992) Globalisierung der Ökonomie – Regionalisierung der Politik? In J. Mayer (ed.), *Die Produktion von Stadt-Land-Schaft*. Loccum: Evangelische Akademie, 217–28.

Esser, J. and Fach, W. (1981) Korporatistische Krisenregulierung im 'Modell Deutschland'. In U. von Alemann (ed.), *Neokorporatismus*. Frankfurt: Campus, 158–79.

Esser, J. (1989) Does industrial policy matter? Land governments in research and technology policy in Federal Germany. In C. Crouch and D. Marquard (eds), *The New Centralism*. Oxford: Basil Blackwell, 94–124.

Esser, J., Fach, W. and Dyson, K. (1983) 'Social market' and modernization policy: West Germany. In K. Dyson and S. Wilks (eds), *Industrial Crisis*. Oxford: Martin Robertson, 102–27.

Esser, J. and Fach, W. (1986) Das Prinzip 'Gemeinheit' – über die volkstuemelnde Rechte in der Bundesrepublik. In H. Dubiel (ed.), *Populismus und Aufklärung*. Frankfurt: Suhrkamp, 190–210.

Fainstein, N. I. and Fainstein, S. S. (eds) (1982) *Urban Policy under Capitalism*. Berverly Hills: Sage.

Garlichs, D. (1979) Grenzen zentralstaatlicher Planung in der Bundesrepublik. In D. Wollmann (ed.), *Politik im Dickicht der Bürokratie*. Leviathan Sonderheft 3, 71–102.

Gregory, D. and Urry, J. (eds) (1984) *Social relations and spatial structure*. London: Macmillan.

Hack, L. and Hack, I. (1985) *Die Wirklichkeit, die Wissenschaft*. Frankfurt: Campus.

Harvey, D. (1985) *The Urbanization of capital*. Baltimore: Johns Hopkins University Press.

Häußermann, H. (1984) Der Wandel der Wohnverhältnisse von Arbeitern – eine Problemskizze. In R. Ebbinghausen and F. Tiemann (eds), *Das Ende der Arbeiterbewegung in Deutschland*. Opladen: Westdeutscher Verlag, 646–60.

Häußermann, H. and Siebel, W. (1985) Die Chancen des Schrumpfens. Plädoyer für eine andere Großstadtpolitik. *Die Zeit*, No. 33, 22 March.

Häußermann, H. and Siebel, W. (1986a) Die Polarisierung der Großstadtentwicklung im Nord-Süd-Gefälle. In J. Friedrichs, H. Häußermann and W. Siebel (eds), *Süd-Nord-Gefälle in der Bundesrepublik?* Opladen: Westdeutscher Verlag, 70–96.

Häußermann, H. and Siebel, W. (1986b) Zukünfte der Städte. In B. Blanke et al. (eds), *Die Zweite Stadt*. Leviathan Sonderheft 7, 102–18.

Hauff, V. and Scharpf, F. W. (1975) *Modernisierung der Volkswirtschaft – Technologiepolitik als Strukturpolitik*. Köln und Frankfurt: Europäische Verlagsanstalt.

Hirsch, J. (1986) Spaltung? Alte Bewegungen und neuer Protest. *Links* No. 190, 15–16.

Hirsch, J. (1990a) *Kapitalismus ohne Alternative?* Hamburg: VSA.

Hirsch, J. (1990b) Regulation theory and historical-materialistic societal theory. *Economies et Societës, Série Theorie de le Régulation*, No. 5, December, 97–113.

Hirsch, J. and Roth, R. (1986) *Das neue Gesicht des Kapitalismus*. Hamburg: VSA.

Ipsen, D. (1987) Phasen der Modernisierung. Regulationsregime und räumliche Entwicklung. Mimeo, Kassel.

Jessop, B. (1990) Regulation theories in retrospect and prospect. *Economy and Society*, 19(2), 153–216.

Keil, R. (1993) *Weltstadt – Stadt der Welt. Internationalisierung und lokale Politik in Los Angeles*. Münster: Westfälisches Dampfboot.

Körber-Weik, M. and Wied-Nebbeling, S. (1987) Gefälle in Nord und Süd *Wirtschaftswoche*, No. 13, 114–18.

Läpple, D. (1986) 'Süd-Nord-Gefälle'. Metapher für die räumlichen Folgen einer Transformationsphase auf dem Weg zu einem post-tayloristischen Entwicklungsmodell? In J. Friedrich, H. Häußermann and W. Siebel (eds), *Süd-Nord-Gefälle in der Bundesrepublik*. Opladen: Westdeutscher Verlag, 97–116.

Lehmbruch, G. (1976) *Parteienwettbewerb im Bundesstaat*. Stuttgart: Kohlhammer.

Lipietz, A. (1985) Akkumulation, Krisen und Auswege aus der Krise. Einige methodologische Anmerkungen zum Begriff der 'Regulation'. *PROKLA*, No. 58, 109–37.

Lipietz, A. (1987) *Mirages and Miracles. The Crisis of Global Fordism*. London: Verso.

Lipietz, A. (1991) Zur Zukunft der städtischen Ökologie. In M. Wentz (ed.), *Stadt-Räume*. Frankfurt.

Lipietz, A. and Leborgne, D. (1987) New technologies, new modes of regulation: some spatial implications. Mimeo, Paris, CEPREMAP.

Marcuse, P. (1989) 'Dual city': a muddy metaphor for a quartered city. *International Journal or Urban and Regional Research*, 13(4), 697–708.

Mayer, M. (1991) Politics in the post-Fordist city. *Socialist Review*, 21(1), 105–24.

Minister für Wirtschaft, Nordrhein-Westfalen (1985) *Politik für den Mittelstand*. Düsseldorf: Olbrysch.

Mollenkopf, J. (1983) *The Contested City*. Princeton, NJ: Princeton University Press.

Rau, J. (1985) *Wir erneuern Nordrhein-Westfalen – ökologisch und ökonomisch*. Düsseldorf: Olbrysch.

Scharpf, F. W., Reissert, B. and Schnabel, F. (1976) *Politikverflechtung: Theorie und Empirie des kooperativen Föderalismus in der Bundesrepublik*. Kronberg: Athäneum.

Smith, M. P. (ed.) (1987) *Cities in transformation. Class, Capital, and the State*. Beverly Hills, London and New Dehli: Sage.

Smith, M. P. and Feagin, J. R. (eds) (1987) *The Capitalist City*. Oxford: Blackwell.

Sorokin, M. (ed.) (1987) *The Postmodern City*. New York: Pantheon.

Spöri, D. (1987) Rede des Spitzenkandidaten Dieter Spöri auf dem Landesparteitag der SPD Baden-Württemberg am 16.5.1987, Mimeo.

Szelenyi, I. (ed.) (1984) *Cities in Recession. Critical Responses to the Urban Policies of the New Right*. London: Sage.

Timberlake, M. (ed.) (1985) *Urbanization in the World Economy*. New York: Academic Press.

Voss, R. von and Friedrich, K. (eds) (1986) *Das Süd-Nord-Gefälle*. Bonn: Verlag Bonn Aktuell.

Walton, J. (ed.) (1986) *Capital and Labour in the Urbanized World*. London: Sage.

Wettman, R. W. (1986) Das Süd-Nord-Gefälle – Realität und Perspektiven. In R. von Voss and K. Friedrich (eds), *Das Süd-Nord-Gefälle*. Bonn: Verlag Bonn Aktuell, 23–43.

Zukunftsperspektiven (1983) *Bericht der Kommission 'Zukunftsperspektiven gesell-schaftlicher Entwicklungen'*, Stuttgart: Erstellt im Auftrag der Landesregierung von Baden-Wïttemberg.

Part II

New Sociologies and Geographies of Industrial Organization

4

Flexible Specialisation and the Re-emergence of Regional Economies

Charles F. Sabel

INTRODUCTION

Until at least the mid-nineteenth century, the region was a natural unit of economic activity and analysis. Lyons produced silks, Sheffield and Solingen cutlery, Birmingham and St Etienne guns and hardware. These regions were both flexible and specialised. They constantly varied their products to satisfy changing tastes and extend their markets by defining new wants. They developed general-purpose technologies and a highly skilled work-force to cut production costs without inhibiting flexibility. To discourage price competition, they created institutions to police working conditions, set minimum wages and detect the use of inferior materials. To encourage competition in new products and processes, they created co-operative banks willing to give failing firms credit for reorganisation and vocational schools to ensure the supply of skilled labour. Even the strongest firms in these systems of flexible specialisation depended on extensive co-operation with their competitors either directly through complex, rapidly changing subcontracting relations or indirectly through joint participation in the institutions regulating the municipal economy.[1]

The success of each agglomeration depended almost exclusively on

This chapter is a reprint of chapter 1 in P. Hirst and J. Zeitlin (eds) (1989) *Reversing Industrial Decline? Industrial Structure and Policy in Britain and Her Competitors*. Oxford: Berg.

its ability to respond to the rapidly changing international markets which absorbed much of its output. The national economy was a category in the thought of the mercantilists and their heirs, the political economists. But in fact, the nation's economy was the sum of its parts. National economic development was only marginally controlled by central political authorities. Even as late as the 1920s, Alfred Marshall, a founder of neo-classical economics, was fascinated by the regional character of much industrial production. He spoke of Sheffield and South-East Lancashire for example, as 'industrial districts' to emphasise that the matrix of production there was an area, not a firm.[2]

By the 1960s, the region had become at most a derivative category of analysis and a secondary locus of economic activity. Despite continuing differences in national industrial structure, there was widespread agreement that the most effective productive unit was the giant corporation, which at the limit integrated in one physical structure the activities of independent firms in the industrial districts. A system of mass production incorporated as subcontractors the pieces of the older regional economies which it had not already swept aside. Products were standardised, production routinised and decomposed into simple operations performed by product-specific or dedicated machines tended and supplemented by semi-skilled workers. Nationally, states increasingly used their fiscal and monetary powers to stabilise the long-term growth of demand. The aim was to induce firms to expand by ensuring markets for their increased output. National social welfare and unemployment-insurance programmes protected individuals against personal disasters and further stabilised demand by guaranteeing minimum levels of purchasing power for persons with no income. The drive for Keynesian macro-economic control and social welfare insurance was, like the drive for mass production, as much programme as reality. National differences in the speed and mode of implementation persisted here too. But even allowing for the wide gap separating aim and actuality, between the microcosm of independent firms and individuals and the macrocosm of the self-sufficient national economy, there was a near vacuum in theory and a jumble of confused activities in practice.[3] Regional and local governments increasingly became subordinate agencies in the national social welfare administrations.

But in the early 1970s, as international competition increased and world markets fragmented, firms became more and more wary of long-term investments in product-specific machinery. The product's market often disappeared before the machinery's costs were recovered. The more volatile markets became, the more firms experimented with flexible forms of organisation which permitted rapid shifts in output.

As they did, they encouraged the reconsolidation of the region as an integrated unit of production.[4]

Five developments, each expediting the others and influenced by them, contribute to this result. The first is the emergence of conspicuously successful, twentieth-century variants of industrial districts in Italy, West Germany, Japan, Denmark, Austria, France, and the United States. The second is the reorganisation of large, multinational firms. Product lines are being concentrated in single operating units which have increased authority to organise their own sales, subcontracting, and even research.

The next development, the double convergence of large- and small-firm structures, is a clear extension of the preceding two. As large firms reorganise, they try to recreate among their specialised units the collaboration characteristic of relations among firms in the flexible-specialisation economies. As these latter expand, they create centralised laboratories, marketing agencies and technology consultancies inspired by large-firm models. And as this reciprocal borrowing proceeds, flexible large firms and their smaller counterparts enter direct alliances. One form such alliances take is a long-term subcontracting relation between the newly consolidated operating unit of multinational and a nearby network of flexible subcontractors. Another is the formation within one or several areas of flexible specialisation of an industrial group composed of a large firm (where large is defined by local standards) with expertise in marketing and finance and smaller firms with expertise in production. Either way, the fabric of the local economy is reinforced at the same time as local firms are more directly tied in international markets.

A fourth sign of the re-emergence of the region as an economic unit is the slow transformation of local governments from welfare dispensaries to job-creation agencies. This transformation is a response to the pressure for new services imposed by the growing networks of large and small firms and the pressure for increased social insurance outlays imposed by failing businesses. In extreme cases, these reorganised authorities resemble the nuclei of local welfare states loosely tied to the national political centre.

The fifth development can be viewed as circumstantial evidence of the pervasiveness of the preceding four. It is that plant- or regional-level officials of American, West German and Italian trade unions are co-operating – often under duress – in the industrial reorganisation just described. As they do they are coming to defend labour's interests through agreements in which the work-force accepts constant reorganisation of the work-place in return for the right to participate in and review the results of local strategic decisions affecting its fate. Willy nilly, labour is reshaped by its association with the newly autonomous local management.

It is unclear what will come of these changes. Not all firms in the advanced industrial countries will tie their future to specialisation and regional co-operation. There are, we shall see, forces driving many in a contrary direction. Nor will the complex, closely connected structures of local and national government automatically adjust to the needs of firms that do regroup regionally. National political responses to the crisis have often obstructed such adjustment; and where local institutions have accommodated company reorganisation, their reaction has been more a reflex of prior institutional developments than a strategic choice. Similarly, national unions have often blocked plant-level adjustment even where local circumstance favoured it.

Finally, even if numerous regional economies do emerge, it is unlikely that they will survive without the help of still undefined national institutions. Flexibly specialised production systems seem better able to survive the current economic turbulence than the mass-production systems they are displacing. Yet that hardly means that each of the new territorial systems can resist all shifts in demand or production technology. To adjust, crisis regions will have to depend on assistance, from flourishing ones; and this could well require the creation of a new national system of resource allocation. No one has a clear idea of how such a system would work, still less of how to integrate it with the institutions of parliamentary democracy. To make matters worse, the *de facto* devolution of responsibility for national economic policy to firms and local unions and governments weakens just those institutions – national employers' associations and trade unions, and the state agencies with whom they treat – which might well play a central role in reconstructing the machinery of co-ordination.

But these considerations do not alter the fact that the relation between the economy and its territory is changing. In the late 1960s and early 1970s, almost all the advanced industrial societies responded to the first disruptions of the post-war boom by trying to reinforce the existing system of macro-economic control and mass production. Governments, umbrella associations of employers, and trade union confederations created or augmented the authority of tripartite, neo-corporatist institutions to co-ordinate national wage and price levels.[5] Firms pursued the logic of mass production and tried to cut costs by increasing economies of scale: products intended for domestic sale were standardised for sale in world markets, as in the introduction of 'world cars' by Ford and General Motors. Production was reorganised to allow decentralisation of labour-intensive processes to low-wage areas.[6]

Neither strategy was successful. In some cases the comprehensive efforts at macro-economic control were stillborn because of opposition within the labour movement (the USA) or from key state institutions (the Bundesbank in West Germany). In others, ongoing programmes were wrecked by labour's dissatisfaction with the results (the British 'winter of discontent' in 1978-9), or by capital's (the Italian employers' opposition in the late 1970s to wage indexation formulae agreed on only a few years earlier). In the remaining cases, aggressive policies for reducing unemployment through reflation, subsidisation of state industry, and vocational training were abandoned when they threatened to bankrupt the national treasury. This was the story in Austria, France and Sweden. Treatment of the unemployed and youth entering the labour market was better in these three countries than in the United States or the United Kingdom, for there the failure of Keynesianism was often accompanied by a brutal attack on the social welfare rights of the poor.[7] But the idea that improvements in institutional design – more comprehensive trade unions with correspondingly greater interest in the general level of employment, for example – would make it possible to pursue the old macro-economic strategy was almost everywhere discredited.

The firms' world-car strategy of market stabilisation was no more successful than state co-ordinated, macro-economic efforts. Fluctuations in oil prices and differences in national tastes make it extremely difficult to develop models with universal appeal. Long-distance decentralisation hindered the timely detection of defective parts, and raised the costs of remedying the defects. Maintenance of large buffer stocks to hedge against the disruption of long supply lines became prohibitively expensive as interest rates rose with inflation. Workers in low-wage areas demanded pay increases much sooner than expected.[8] By the late 1980s, executives at Ford and General Motors often attributed the idea for the world car in conversation to their competitors.

The almost complete defeat of neo-corporatist efforts to relaunch growth is, of course, proof that promising strategies are not self-executing. But it would be foolhardy to dismiss the change as a mere change of fashion. A novel strategy commands attention as a sign that those with the most to lose think the conditions of their survival have changed.

This chapter considers the possible consequences of this strategic reorientation for relations among the state, the economy, and the organisations connecting the two. It leaves aside discussion of the decay of the nineteenth-century regional economies and the rise and decline of the mass-production system. Rather, the core of the essay concerns the reaction of firms and local authorities to the continuing, current economic turbulence. The focus is on industrial firms, but the argument applies to important segments of the service sector and banking and insurance as well.[9] The chapter begins with a look at developments from the vantage point of small and medium-sized firms. It treats cases where such firms have formed or revitalised internationally competitive, technologically sophisticated regional economies. It then moves on to consider the way multinationals have adjusted as new products are introduced more rapidly and development costs soar. Together these sections argue that an emergent corporate form which blurs familiar distinctions between large and small firms is spreading – in different variants and speeds in every country – through the advanced capitalist world. The next section focuses on co-ordinate changes in the job-creation strategies of local authorities, whose past failures lead them to dream of new regional economies, just as the luckiest among them discover that such things are already flourishing in their own countries.

The final sections address the future of these inchoate economic forms. The question for the fifth section is this: assuming that regional economies enjoy competitive advantages under conditions of continuing economic uncertainty, can political intervention encourage their formation where tradition has not? The conclusion discusses the role the state, trade unions, and employers' associations could play if the advanced economies did become confederations of flexible regional economies, and the problems that arise in constructing such a confederal state from the institutional fragments of the mass-production system.

A RENAISSANCE OF REGIONAL ECONOMIES

Perhaps the most dramatic response to the continuing instability of international markets has been the formation or revitalisation of regional economies that strongly resemble the nineteenth-century centres of flexible specialisation. These districts escape ruinous price competition with low-wage mass producers by using flexible machines and skilled workers to make semi-custom goods that command an affordable premium in the market. Their technological dynamism distinguishes them from the small firms that emerged during the Great Depression of the 1930s. Whereas the firms of that volatile epoch used traditional tools and skills to maintain existing goods, the new industrial districts constantly renew their products and production methods.

The first conspicuous case was the Third Italy, identified – in contrast to the impoverished South and the old industrial triangle of Genoa, Turin, and Milan – by Bagnasco.[10] It is a string of industrial districts stretching from the Venetian provinces in the North through Bologna and Florence to Ancona in the South, and producing everything from knitted goods (Carpi), to special machines (Parma, Bologna), ceramic tiles (Sassuolo), textiles (Como, Prato), agricultural implements (Reggio Emilia), hydraulic devices (Modena), shoes, white goods, plastic tableware, and electronic musical instruments (Ancona). But the example of the Third Italy is conquering the first two as the organisational practices of the industrial districts spread to Turin (factory automation)[11] and the Canavese (software and computer equipment) in Piedmont,[12] the Milanese provinces (furniture, machine tools) in Lombardy[13] and Bari in the South.[14]

And besides the many Italies there is a 'Second Denmark': Jutland, the traditionally poor agricultural West of the country, is now a patchwork of textile, garment, furniture, machine-tool, and shipbuilding districts that are outgrowing the established centres of industry surrounding Copenhagen in the East.[15] The Swedish metalworking producers in Småland are another Scandinavian case in point.[16] In West Germany, industrial districts in the *Land* of Baden-Württemberg are flourishing in textiles, garments, textile machinery, machine tools, and automobile components.[17] The metalworking firms there are doing substantially better than similar firms in northern *Länder* that dominated the national economy during the heyday of mass production.

The United States is known for two high-technology industrial districts: the centre of semiconductor production in Silicon Valley, south-east of San Francisco, and the concentration of mini-computer producers along Route 128 circling Boston.[18] But in Los Angeles, too, there are growing, often technologically advanced, agglomerations of firms specialising in processes required in the closely related motion-picture, television, video-game, and music-recording industries – as well as in injection moulding, garments, and (in neighbouring Orange County) aerospace products.[19] Geographers are beginning to see these assemblies of industrial districts as a new model of urban reindustrialisation, and to speak of Los Angeles as the 'capital of the late twentieth century'.[20] Officials in the Port Authority of New York City, which has traditionally operated as a kind of economic development agency for that city, are having similar thoughts regarding the garment, printing, publishing and financial industries. In Japan the remote mountain village of Sakaki – to take one of many possible examples – has 0.02 per cent of the national population, but 0.2 per cent of the entire national stock of numerically controlled (NC) machine-tools.

Almost every household has at least one machine, and the village sets its prices collectively.[21] In France, studies of industry in the Lyons area have brought to light a town (Oyonnax) of injection moulders that is indistinguishable from equivalent areas of the Third Italy,[22] as well as substantial metalworking sectors that use NC machine-tools on the lines of the flexible specialisation model.[23] Researchers studying the eastern Valles near Barcelona explicitly liken the cotton textile, wooden furniture, and metalworking complex situated there to the Italian industrial districts.[24]

A proverb has it that 'for example is not a proof'. A list of modern industrial districts much longer than the preceding one would still not warrant general conclusions about the expansionary potential of the small-firm systems. Systematic efforts to assess the weight of such productive systems in the advanced economies are in their infancy.[25] But evidentiary problems aside, there is something arresting about the proliferation in such different industries and locations of an industrial system, novel for this century, and able to hold its own against the world's most powerful enterprises.

One indirect indication of the transformative potential of the new industrial districts is that during the last decade their development has repeatedly redefined managers' and researchers' understanding of competitive efficiency. Almost no one expected rapidly growing clusters of new firms to emerge where they did. Many of the first researchers to notice these developments found the new factories almost literally before their front doors. Brusco was living in Modena when he began writing about the Third Italy; Saglio, who studied the plastic firms of Oyonnax, heads a research team in Lyons; the geographers who proclaim Los Angeles the 'capital of the late twentieth century' are talking about their home city; Hull Kristensen, who writes about the transformation of Danish industry, is a native of Jutland; among the first insightful reports about Baden-Württemberg was a book of political self-advertisement by the governor of the *Land*, Lothar Spaeth.[26]

Other researchers happened on industrial districts while evaluating statistical anomalies only loosely connected with questions of industrial structure. Bagnasco found the Third Italy while sorting through industrial census data. Borken, a township in the north-west of the Federal Republic of Germany which converted textile mills to the production of speciality fabrics, attracted attention because of its low unemployment rates.[27] Baden-Württemberg appeared as a unified entity in a study of the spatial preconditions for the diffusion of new metalworking technologies in West Germany.[28]

Precisely because the discoveries were so unexpected, it was almost inevitable that the first reports of the industrial districts reduced them to something familiar, be it malignant or benign. To many Western Europeans, and particularly the Italians, the development of a huge informal or underground economy seemed a return to turn-of-century sweatshop conditions; to many Americans, the growth of the high-technology areas looked like a return to pristine *laissez-faire*. There was substantial truth in both views. Many of the new firms in the Third Italy were founded in the early 1970s expressly to avoid the unions' growing control of the large factories. Many of the new firms evaded taxes, refused to pay social welfare benefits, imposed long hours, used toxic materials hazardously, and paid substandard wages.[29] Conversely, many of the new, high-technology firms in the USA were created by real-life entrepreneurs possessed by new ideas and in revolt against the existing corporate structures – including the corporations' compromises with trade unions and the state.[30]

During the last decade, however, views on both sides have been substantially modified. The lesser part of this change resulted from a better understanding of how these industrial systems worked. In Italy, for instance, much of what first seemed child labour proved to be the carefully monitored initiation of children in their parents' work-day world. In Japan, the gap between high-wage large firms and low-wage small firms in some sectors of the metalworking industry is substantially reduced once *lifetime* earnings of cohorts in the two different sized firms are compared: in some Japanese industrial districts, as many as one-third of the workers in small firms go into business for themselves; but their high earnings are recorded as profits or salaries, while the less successful members of their age group report wages below those of comparable workers in large firms.[31] In the United States it became clear that, in addition to all their Schumpeterian attributes, the new entrepreneurs depended on ties with one another, universities and local government for their success.

The greater part in the change in perception of the industrial districts reflected successive changes in the organisation of the new regional economies. From the early 1970s to the early 1980s the small and medium-sized firms learned to make efficiently flexible use of the new microprocessor-based technologies and elaborated extensive but generally informal co-operative practices. From the early 1980s to the present they have begun to formalise relations among themselves by entering explicit but loose business alliances while also collectively expanding the range of services provided to the district as a whole.

In many parts of the Third Italy, for example, by the late 1970s wages and investment per capita approached or exceeded those in the traditionally advanced areas of the country.[32] Prato and Carpi became two of the largest concentrations of modern looms in the world, as well as centres for the development of many specialised pieces of textile machinery.[33] In Japan, Sakaki was only one of many industrial districts which turned to the massive use of NC equipment.[34] Baden-Württemberg was one of the first areas of West Germany to make massive use of computer-controlled equipment.[35]

Equally important, during this period the new regional economies began to elaborate or revitalise systems for regulating co-operation between firms and workers that recalled the earlier controls on competition in the nineteenth-century industrial districts. Bagnasco's[36] and Contarino's[37] accounts of the elaborate combination of conflict and consensus at the root of wage determination in the Third Italy are clearly echoed in Hildebrandt's[38] reports from Baden-Württemberg and Saglio's from Lyons. The general practice became that minimum pay scales and acceptable working conditions are set through collective bargaining. Subsequent, frequently informal, negotiations regarding wages or other matters exclude demands that imperil the flexible use of labour or capital equipment. This did not mean that labour relations in the industrial districts became harmonious, let alone joyously communal. Bagnasco and Trigilia note that the strike rate in the Third Italy is among the highest in the country.[39] But it did mean that conflicts were conducted and concluded with respect for the preconditions for continuous redisposition of resources. Strikes in the Third Italy thus tend to be shorter than in other areas of Italy, and to eventuate in agreements in principle rather than detailed rules. Similarly, metalworkers in Baden-Württemberg supported what became, at the national level, a bitter strike in 1984; but the conflict had by all accounts no repercussions on labour relations in the small shops, where workers quickly recouped production losses by putting in overtime once labour peace was restored.[40]

Nineteenth-century notions of partially formalised but still flexible relations among firms with overlapping interests have also been reinvented or reaffirmed in the new industrial districts. In Italy, firms formed consortia to secure cheap credit, buy raw materials, bid on public projects, commercialise their products and conduct research;[41] in Lyons firms began to exchange information in a way that would have been 'unthinkable' thirty years ago.[42]

Trade associations in Baden-Württemberg, continuing practices well established by the 1920s, did the same things more formally. They policed co-operation within each industry by seeing to it that firms kept to their specialities. These specialisation cartels or finishing associations have made the firms more dependent on their neighbours' complementary products, and hence more willing to exchange information with them and to support the vocational schools, research institutes and marketing agencies that serve the industry as a whole. This co-operation is facilitated by the entrepreneurs' frequent meetings as members of the supervisory boards of local co-operative banks, a common occurrence in Italy as well.[43]

The changes characteristic of the second period – from roughly 1980 to the present – amount to a more conscious elaboration of the traditions and spontaneous experiments which proved themselves in the turbulence of the preceding decade. As managers and workers came to a more systematic understanding of their success, they became more decisive in judging what the industrial districts required or excluded. The cumulative effect of those decisions is to create structures which resemble and sometimes mesh with those we will see emerging in large firms.

In the region of Emilia-Romagna, for instance, provinces such as Modena substantially expanded the technical consulting services provided to the small and medium-sized firms.[44] In Baden-Württemberg, the already excellent public technical consulting services and vocational and technical education system have been substantially improved. Vocational high schools (*Berufsschulen*) once gave elementary instruction to apprentices. Now they are teaching the skills formerly taught to technicians and engineering students in community colleges or polytechnics (*Fachhochschulen*). Meanwhile, the latter are beginning to do the kind of research and teaching once reserved for technical universities.[45] On the other hand, when the Christian Democratic *Land* government tried to gain control over the co-operative banks and create agencies with omnibus powers for industrial policy similar to those supposedly concentrated in the Japanese Ministry of International Trade and Industry, industrialists, local bankers and bureaucrats blocked the reorganisation as a threat to the region's system of decentralised decision-making.[46]

Such changes have been accompanied by less conspicuous ones in relations among firms. To gain access to technical expertise and sometimes the capital necessary to apply it, small- and medium-sized firms in the industrial districts appear to be seeking long-term, collaborative relations with larger partners inside or outside the industrial district. Sometimes these relations take the form of long-term subcontracting arrangements; sometimes the larger firm purchases equity in the smaller. Benetton, a huge clothing company, is a frequently cited example here. The firm orchestrates relations among a vast network of subcontractors in the Italian industrial districts – whence it itself came – and a second network of franchisees who retail the finished goods in Western Europe and the United States.[47] It is even harder to assess the growth of these networks within the industrial districts than to weigh the role of the latter in national economies. But scanty as it is, the evidence suggests that they are numerous and rapidly multiplying. In Prato, for instance, there are about 800 'industrial' firms with an average of 25 employees and 7,000 'artisan' firms with on average 2.5 employees. Trigilia reports that these roughly 8,000 firms are formed in some 400 groups.[48] My own discussions with entrepreneurs in many parts of Italy, Baden-Württemberg and western Massachusetts suggest that the specialist firms are seeking and often finding allies who will teach them new production technologies, not abandon them during downturns, and yet not try to reduce their autonomy.[49] Sometimes these alliances are contractual, but more often they are informal matters of fact. The logic of these relations is a topic for the next section.

Of course not all the established regional economies have institutionalised co-operation among specialists as extensively as Baden-Württemberg or Modena. The textile producers in Prato have been unable to agree on how to introduce a telecommunication system which would in theory lead to more efficient capacity utilisation: the *impannatori* – brokers who collect orders from final customers and then assemble networks of small firms to fill them – fear that such a system would ultimately make their vast knowledge of the area's productive capacity superfluous.[50] In Los Angeles, the trade unions formed inside the vertically integrated movie studios are having difficulty incorporating the workers employed in the highly specialised shops dispersed throughout the city.[51] In the absence of strong trade associations like those in Baden-Württemberg or even traditions of long-term collaboration, large firms in Silicon Valley and Route 128 pursue contradictory subcontracting policies. At times they promise to co-operate with their small suppliers, at times they try to crush them through direct competition.[52]

And there are, furthermore, emergent regional economies which seem unlikely to proceed even as far down the path to flexible specialisation as Los Angeles, Silicon Valley, or Route 128. For example, Benton found shoe firms in Madrid more interested in the advantages of tax evasion, low wages and bankruptcy laws than in investment in more productive equipment. (Small firms in the electronics sector of the same city, however, showed signs of consolidating into a technologically dynamic industrial district.)[53]

Yet, despite these qualifications, the view that the decentralisation of production and technological innovation resulted from a capitalist strategy to subdue an unruly work-force or a renaissance of untrammelled entrepreneurship is wide of the mark. Christopherson,

Morales, Scott and Storper thought their studies of Los Angeles would vindicate the first hypothesis. Instead of finding capital in flight, they found the disintegration of vertically integrated manufacturing systems, and their reconstruction as regional economies. Hildebrandt and his colleagues expected managers in the machine-tool industry in Baden-Württemberg to use the introduction of flexible manufacturing systems to control a highly skilled work-force. They found instead that managers and workers had consciously agreed to a complex informal 'social pact'; and their use of the technology was subordinated to the maintenance of that agreement. And, as we shall see, even conservative Republican governors in the USA now admit 'entrepreneurship' cannot flourish without complementary state support.

But what is to replace these discredited views? What, exactly, are the general principles governing the relations among firms, and between firms, workers and government in the new industrial districts? It has proved much easier to exemplify and typologise the flexibly specialised regional economies than rigorously to explain them. Many observers, myself included, have relied on what anthropologists delicately call the ethnographer's privilege – the right to ask the reader to believe in what the author has seen – in asserting the distinctiveness of this form of production; and the most diverse efforts at rigorous explanation, despite indubitable advances, seem for the moment stalemated.

Thus attempts to arrive at even a rough characterisation of the logic of the industrial districts by following the writings and practices of late eighteenth- and early nineteenth-century artisan-radicals like Paine, Proudhon, or the French societies of *compagnons* produce only a fuzzy picture of an artisan republic in which the exercise of property rights is subordinated to principles of social equity, particularly prohibitions against using accumulated property to deprive others of their independence.[54] Monographic descriptions of nineteenth-century industrial districts add institutional detail to this picture without framing it analytically.

Nor do ethnographies of the new industrial districts based on interviews or survey questionnaires produce uniform, analytically precise self-explications. Efforts to solicit such self-characterisation are, except in areas (such as parts of the Third Italy) with strong mutualist or co-operative traditions, almost always disastrous. Businesses, especially small businesses, prize their autonomy. Asking proprietors who *do* co-operate whether they in fact do is like asking members of a loving family whether they commit incest. They are so offended by the question that it is almost impossible to discern amidst the expostulations their offhand references to collaboration – which they take as self-evidently compatible with complete autonomy. Friedman, for example, reports that the small-shop owners in Sakaki vehemently denied that they co-operated in any way – the customary right of each shop-owner to run parts-cutting programmes on the idle machines of the others for free and the *de facto* existence of a municipal price list for products (justified by reference to the quasi-collective utilisation of the machine park) notwithstanding.[55] Herrigel and I found machine-tool firms in Baden-Württemberg insisting on their autonomy – despite the fact that they frequently sit on the same boards of directors of local co-operative banks, grant one another loans, and thus become in effect stockholders in a joint enterprise.

Not surprisingly, then, analytic efforts by historians, sociologists, political scientists or industrial economists that begin with ethno-graphic interrogation and direct observation have produced inconclu-sive results. Certainly, markets in the new industrial districts are 'socially constructed'[56] in that they form 'productive communities'[57] which limit competition to encourage innovation by means of 'social pacts'.[58] But should these regional economies be considered a negotiated alliance of fundamentally distinct groups, or integral communities with a fluid but discernable division of labour? If the latter, does the community operate according to a single logic – the logic of permanent innovation – expressed in a vocabulary of solidarity provided indifferently by religious, political, or local tradition? In that case it might approximate Rousseau's ideal republic, in which the young (following the pedagogy of *Emile*) are socialised to see the constraints on individual behaviour required for the innovative good of all as a condition of personal freedom. Or does the community depend on the fusion of more fundamental, distinct principles – for example, the principles of self-regarding market exchanges and familial solidarity? Each conceptualisation suggests different potential fault lines in the industrial districts – class against class, individuals or factions against the whole, families against one another or against merchants – and different principles for remediating conflict. All are plausible, none wholly persuasive.[59]

Sociologists studying organisational behaviour and economists studying industrial structures as instruments for minimising the costs of transaction among production units or as solutions to the related problems faced by principals in controlling their agents have also detected something significantly novel in the kinds of arrangements associated with the new industrial districts. But their analyses seem no more trenchant than the preceding ones. For example, Williamson once held that, depending on circumstances, transaction costs could be minimised by markets or hierarchies.[60] The argument was that frequent, product-specific exchanges – sales of, say, components for a certain make of automobile as against bushels of wheat or boxes of standard screws – led to the integration of the suppliers into the hierarchies of their large customers. This eliminated the dependence of the latter on the former (a problem that always arises when the number of potential parties to a bargain is small) and reduced the customers' costs of monitoring performance (which are high so long as the supplier has exclusive knowledge of production costs and hence the ability to act on an allegedly fundamental propensity for selfish opportunism). Now, influenced by Ouchi, he allows that *networks* of firms or managers, perhaps bound together by a 'clan culture', may sometimes be the more competitive form of organisation. Why do current conditions favour the latter to the detriment of the former?[61]

Drawing on work in population biology, organisational theorists provide models supporting the equally broad conclusion that 'generalist' organisations have advantages over 'specialist' ones under various combinations of environmental instability and institutional flexibility: for example, when the period required to specialise resources is long relative to the frequency of environmental change.[62] But we already know that industrial districts adopt generalist organisations because they know that by the time they have dedicated resources to meet one situation, they will face another. The question is, how do the generalist organisations work?

Information economists such as Grossman and Hart[63] explain the creation of networks of firms linked through exchange of equity as a collective strategy of risk reduction. They argue that boundaries among firms will depend on the costs or gains associated with events that cannot be anticipated in contractual provisions. The greater the uncovered risk in its dealings with its partners, the greater will be the company's interest in purchasing the residual contract rights – the rights to decide matters not governed by the formal agreement. Acquisition of these rights is tantamount to purchase of a property right in the partner. On this view, as uncertainty increases, novel forms of property – such as those observed in the industrial district – will distribute residual rights so as to spread risk among the relevant parties without reducing their flexibility. But the precise forms of property will depend on the sources and nature of the uncertainty. The mass-production corporation was often formed through the fusion of smaller firms in an effort to accommodate fluctuations in the level of demand for standard items. What precisely in the current environment leads to an exchange of property rights short of fusion? On this question the theory is silent. Thus, like ethnographic accounts, the economic models are more descriptive and suggestive than predictive. They, too, seem as much an expression of the new developments as an explanation of them.

A more promising line of attack regards the learning advantages of network systems as industrial organisation. Johanson and Mattson[64] argue that firms which have stable but not exclusive relations adjust most rapidly to each other's needs and hence to market demand. Familiarity facilitates co-operation; autonomy allows each to benefit from the novel experiences of the other. Long-term development costs are reduced because an important by-product of current production is knowledge about potential new products and processes. The argument suggests that the spreading of risks and the minimisation of transaction costs are not the causes of network formation but rather the consequences of the networks' superior learning capacity. But Johanson and Mattson also do not provide a precise enough account of the relation between the structure of the network and its environment. How is learning organised? Why do firms increasingly think they need to learn this way? To answer these questions it is necessary to look at the lessons large firms have drawn from their experience since 1973, and to see why they are imitating and allying with the industrial districts.

THE REORGANISATION OF THE MULTINATIONALS

In the last fifteen years, many of the largest multinationals have shifted strategy. Often without explicitly repudiating the mass-production model, they have begun to organise production on the lines of flexible specialisation.[65] They have been moved to do this by their previous failures, by the exemplary successes of the new industrial districts, and by their fear of Japanese competitors – who are themselves perfecting systems of flexible production. West German, Italian and Japanese firms have moved most quickly in this direction because they never fully switched to mass production, and, where they did, they institutionalised it in a way which did not impede subsequent reorganisation. American corporations have moved most slowly because they had profited longest from mass production of a kind which proves particularly recalcitrant to piecemeal reform. The world-car strategy was an emblem of their traditional attachments, and its costly failure a further impediment to reorganisation. It is all the more significant, then, that the American firms – and the French companies such as Renault which most faithfully imitated them – are now pursuing flexible strategies as well.

To grasp the reorientation of strategy it will be helpful to add some detail to the notion of the separation of conception and execution which defines the mass-production corporation. In the textbook case, an elite corps of strategic planners at company headquarters allocated investments among current businesses, research into new products, and stabilising revenues – through the acquisition of firms whose profits rose and fell during phases of the business cycle when the new parent company's did the opposite. A central research laboratory made 'break-through discoveries' leading to 'blockbuster industries'. One hierarchy of engineers applied the breakthroughs in the design of new products – Nylon and transistors were favourite examples.[66] A second, subordinate hierarchy of engineers translated the designs into instructions; the company's own relatively unskilled work-force or outside contractors then executed the directives.

This division of labour had to be elaborately policed. Supervisors made sure that workers followed the rules; a quality-control division monitored the supervisors' success. Purchasing agents played subcontractors off against each other to assure they met elaborate specifications at the agreed price. An industrial relations department managed disputes between managers and workers arising over the interpretation of the rules. Unions defended workers in these disputes, using selected cases to advance their members' common interests and incidentally making the rules still more complex.

Because tasks changed slowly and their definition was tied to the manufacture of particular products, most learning by workers and managers was done on the job, regardless of their formal education. Workers advanced up a hierarchy of semi-skilled jobs, each requiring familiarity with the preceding one. Managers progressed up the ranks of their operating units as they became more adept at applying standard operating procedures in varying circumstances.

This division of conception and execution made sense only if the huge costs of building such organisations could be amortised over huge production runs. But the more markets fragmented in the 1970s, the more difficult this became. Here, too, the failure of the world-car strategy is emblematic. Firms learned to expect the unexpected from the market. Once they assumed that they could not foresee which products would succeed, they introduced more new items to increase the chances of finding a winner. To speed up the development of new products and assure that winners selected by the market could be manufactured in time to meet the demand, the firms then had to learn to cut the costs of reorganising production. In a word – their word – they had to become more flexible. To do that, they had to reintegrate conception and execution, thereby blurring the distinction between planning and production at all but the highest levels of the corporation, and reducing costs and time required for both.

In the textbook case this has meant reconcentration of strategic power in the hands of senior managers. All but truly strategic decision-making authority is decentralised to operating units. Specialised bureaucracies within the operating units are reintegrated into normal chains of command. The workers and subcontractors are treated not as programmable automata but as (junior) partners in production with some capacity to reshape the product or the production process.

Headquarters therefore shrink dramatically. Strategic planners go as senior managers regain control of planning. Many of the officers who oversaw the finances or purchases of the operating units are eliminated as final authority for most of these matters is pushed down to the units themselves. Central research facilities either cease to grow or are dismantled as operating units build their own local laboratories and wholly new technologies are introduced into the corporation through joint ventures or participation in new firms.

The operating units, meanwhile, come to resemble autonomous small or medium-sized firms. The parent corporation often transforms itself into a holding company, and treats its subsidiaries as quasi-independent companies whose profits and losses are obscured by intra-firm transfers of goods or funds. Ideally, each operating unit is the corporation's unique representative in a distinct market. To meet the changing needs of that market, production is reorganised to permit continuous reorganisation of production.

Products must be designed rapidly, and so that they can be efficiently produced. Design engineering and production engineering are therefore combined in a process – integrated or simultaneous engineering, of course – which accelerates product development and requires fewer engineers because the designers help the production experts, and vice versa. Similarly, supervisors and workers no longer respectively enforce and obey rules. Rather, like the merged groups of engineers, they co-operate in solving common problems. The supervisors who policed the old system are either eliminated or made part of work teams which define their members' jobs as they perfect their work. Flexible capital goods often replace product-specific machines. Or the costs and time required to produce dedicated equipment are so reduced that it can be scrapped without compunction when the market shifts: the higher the scrapping rate, the more a succession of product-specific machines resembles a single piece of flexible equipment.

These changes entail broader training of workers and collaborative industrial relations. Workers are encouraged to learn many tasks so that they can move quickly from job to job as reorganisation requires. They are given some fundamental instruction in the theoretical background of their work – metallurgy, chemistry, electronics – to facilitate this more applied training. In unionised firms the unions negotiate general standards which reflect the demands of local circumstance and periodically verify that continuous reorganisation of work respects those standards. To do this they must be so fully informed of business decisions and so empowered to veto or amend them that they assume some limited but undeniable responsibility for management. In non-union firms the company establishes an employee participation system to elaborate the standards.

The decentralisation of the corporation and the blurring of hierarchical distinctions also require a reorientation of management training. Because the operating units are so autonomous, it is important that their managers' responses to change be motivated by such similar concerns that local strategies are mutually reinforcing. To cultivate this spontaneous co-ordination, corporate headquarters insists that managers not only encourage co-operation within their own operating unit, but also learn enough about the others to anticipate corporate needs in their separate decisions. The rotation of managers through different units thus becomes an administrative instrument for guaranteeing corporate unity.

The transformation of the operating units extends, finally, to their relations with subcontractors. As product cycles shorten, development costs of new products and production processes go up. The operating units have to share those costs with outsiders, without, however, assuming ultimate responsibility for the latter's survival. The large corporations concentrate their expertise in co-ordinating the design and assembly of the final product, and in advancing a few key technologies. They develop complementary parts, products and processes in collaboration with selected subcontractors. In the paradigmatic case, the product is redesigned so that it is constructed of a set of modules, each available in a number of variants, which can be recombined into many versions of the basic item. Principal subcontractors then become responsible for whatever modules the large corporation does not reserve itself.

This strategy requires the creation of inter-industry production networks. When a subcontractor works for, say, five large firms in as many industries, a customer need not fear that information passed to its supplier will circulate to its competitors. At the same time, the customers profit from the subcontractor's experience in other industries. The diversified subcontractor is hedged against slumps in any one line of business.

Subcontractors in the new flexible system are thus expected to become both more and less closely integrated with their large-firm customer. They become more integrated in the sense that major subcontractors are expected to enter long-term contracts with their customers, share the burden of designing parts and components and guarantee delivery of defect-free products as they are needed – the just-in-time system which reduces the customer's inventory costs and facilitates rapid detection of defects. They become less integrated in that the corporations oblige subcontractors to seek outside customers and, in effect, demonstrate the capacity to survive without their most important client. Customers and subcontractors therefore share information much more freely than before, but the former impose ceilings on the percentage of the latter's output they will buy. Major subcontractors in turn apply these rules to *their* subcontractors, and so on down the chain of production.

The cumulative result of these changes is the twofold convergence of large- and small-firm structures I spoke of earlier. The quasi-independent operating units have the agility, dedication to circumscribed markets, and informal operating procedures usually associated with small firms, whatever their exact size as measured by turnover or number of employees. Moreover, the operating units are inserted into and dependent upon a network of still smaller firms whose procedures are increasingly similar to their own.

This account of the strategic reorientation of the large corporation supports and extends the tentative conclusion that network production is best viewed as a learning system. Not volatility *per se* but the fragmentation of markets overwhelmed the adaptive capacities of the hierarchical corporation. In particular, the drive to spread development costs among subcontractors strongly suggests that even the largest firms no longer know exactly what to produce or how. To track changes in the market, the corporations or the managers in each operating unit must learn from their subordinates (respectively the subcontractors or workers); and they must teach the subordinates how to teach them what they need to know.[67] The optimal learning system also diversifies the participants' risk: one example is the inter-industry subcontracting network which cross-pollinates technologies while hedging both suppliers and their customers against the risk of excessive mutual dependence; analogous cases are the use of broadly skilled workers and flexible or easily scrapped special machines.

This same learning system also minimises transaction costs by fostering high-trust relations typical of clans, socially constructed markets, and productive communities. The premise that all economic exchanges must also be occasions for reciprocal learning implies that the parties anticipate problems, and that the problems will be solved jointly. This is the definition of a high-trust relation, and in the current economic environment it minimises transaction costs by freeing the parties from the impossible task of precisely specifying their respective rights and responsibilities through elaborate contracts (as in markets) or bureaucratic rules (as in hierarchy).

But here the argument is moving too fast. In drawing theoretical conclusions from a textbook picture I have proceeded as though the possibility of diversified learning systems assured their realisation. The trope is familiar from the ontological proof of the existence of God. The proof asserts that God exists because we can conceive of an omnipotent being, and such a being will inevitably exercise the power to exist which omnipotence implies. But on this earth theories are not self-realising, and it is therefore necessary to assess the correspondence between the textbook picture of corporate reorganisation and a composite picture of actual practice. In the absence of comprehensive evidence it is helpful to establish two polar reference points – cases where corporate reorganisation matches the foregoing description, and cases where the goal is a clear alternative – and then scrutinise intermediate developments for clues about the viability and potential diffusion of the extremes.

First, as in the case of the industrial districts, it is significant that many companies look like a stylised picture no one could have drawn a decade ago. Take the example of Montedison at Ferrara studied by Bordogna.[68] Here the firm – itself recently reconstituted as a holding company – divided a single chemical complex into five companies. Four (of which one was ceded to the public-sector chemical corporation, Enichem) manufacture well-defined product lines. The fifth provides services to the others. These services range from the technical – maintenance of equipment, planning of new facilities, testing of feed stocks and final products – to the administrative – collective bargaining with unions, management of layoffs (workers dismissed from the production plants pass through the service firm before being expelled onto the external labour market). Production work is organised by teams; skill levels are rising; wherever possible capital goods are designed to facilitate changes in the product and product mix. In one case – Himont – a new polyproplene technology developed at Ferrara is both more flexible and cheaper to build and operate than its competitors. Senior managers are trained (according to a model developed by the American firm Johnson and Johnson, and carefully adapted to local conditions) reflexively to coordinate the goals of the operating units and the corporation. The whole system looks, in fact, like one of the small-firm districts described earlier, with the difference that the service company rather than the municipality and employers' associations provides the production units with whatever they cannot provide themselves.

Among the large American firms, Xerox comes closest to the ideal picture.[69] There is a regional reconcentration of production at Rochester, NY; product lines are grouped by geographic area (the Japanese subsidiary specialises in small copiers, the Rochester complex in large ones); production work is organised in teams that include engineers; subcontractors are being taught to innovate, and so on. The Ford Motor Company is moving in this direction as well. Magna, the Canadian automobile parts supplier described by Herzenberg, is an extreme case in point. Each of its seventy-two plants (with an average of 100 employees) has full responsibility for its business plan, capital budgeting, profitability and recruiting. Each plant makes one product, family of products, or works with one customer. The aim is to meet shifting demands through continuous specialisation. The corporation maintains research facilities and raises capital for the operating units.[70] In the American computer industry, large circuit board manufacturers and assemblers such as Flextronics are building regional production facilities to serve clusters of customers in the same way.[71]

In West Germany, Robert Bosch, the largest West German manufacturer of automobile parts, has consciously pursued many elements of the textbook strategy since the early 1970s. Indeed, the preceding account of a diversified subcontractor network is an elaboration of company policy as described in conversation with the firm's director of purchasing; I will refer to such systems as the Bosch model.[72]

But second, many corporations have adopted elements of the decentralised model without breaking fully with the organisational principles of the mass-production firm. Here, as with many of the newer industrial districts, it is hard to decide whether the firms are progressing towards flexible specialisation, have been obstructed in their efforts to move in that direction, or are successfully pursuing a long-term strategy which amounts to a modification – and not a repudiation – of past practice.

Many American firms, for example, appear to be pursuing what might be called a Japanese (as opposed to world-car) variant of this strategy of flexible mass production. The aim is to increase the variants of production without abandoning the distinction between conception and execution. The corporation still assumes that it can anticipate demand. Rather than expecting the unexpected and learning to organise permanent reorganisation, it simply tries to accommodate larger market fluctuations than before. Product development is still centralised, but development time is reduced through the use of computer-aided design. Some supervisory levels are eliminated at corporate headquarters. But operating units – even if consolidated according to product line – are still regarded as divisions of the parent company, not independent firms. Programmable automation is used to reap the benefits of dedicated equipment in the manufacture of a few closely related variants of a part or product instead of one. Workers are taught to operate the full range of new equipment so that they can shift jobs easily; but because the range of products is already well defined and the machines programmed accordingly, there is little incentive to teach them the fundamentals of the new technology. The emphasis instead is on giving workers the knowledge and autonomy necessary to operate just-in-time delivery systems, which includes teaching them to detect defects and help identify and eliminate their source.

Subcontractors are treated analogously. They are no longer pitted against one another in brutal price wars; they can expect advice from their customers on how to use new technologies, maintain quality control and organise just-in-time delivery. But they are still regarded as executors with little capacity to take the initiative in the design of products or production processes. At most they are seen as possessing a single innovation which the corporate customer will appropriate through collaboration.

Managerial training, finally, is also a hybrid of old and new. Low and middle-level managers progress up narrow hierarchies within their operating units as in the mass production system. Only a small number of potential high-flyers are selected by corporate headquarters for a programme of rotation through various divisions which prepares them for one of the reduced number of supervisory positions at the top of the company later in their careers.

The American power-tool manufacturer Black and Decker comes closest to embodying this model. But firms such as General Motors, Kodak and the appliance division of General Electric might be cited as instances as well. However traumatic the introduction of this understanding of Japanese manufacturing methods may be for such American firms, it is surely more a matter of perfecting the mass-production system than of abandoning it.[73]

But this second model appears unable to accommodate the currently necessary pace of product development. Firms which once applied it successfully – first and foremost the large Japanese manufacturers of automobiles and integrated circuits – are increasingly adopting the organisational forms of the more decentralised large corporation. These piecemeal changes are hardly proof of an inevitable rejection of mass production, but they are the best guide to the drift of current developments.

A conspicuous sign of change in the Japanese model of mass

production is the redefinition of subcontracting relations. As the pace of new-product introduction increased, the large corporations began radically to extend and thereby change the terms of their collaboration with their subcontractors in two ways. First, Nishiguchi has shown that they are delegating complete assembly of small-lot products to leading suppliers, a practice called *itaku seisan* or contract assembly. Thus while Toyota produces high-volume cars in its own plants, the Kanto Auto Works, once an autobody supplier to the firm, now alternately produces a sports car, luxury saloon, and middle-class passenger car on the same extremely flexible assembly line in its Higashifuji factory.[74] Ikeda reports similar examples from the automobile industry and in consumer electronics as well.[75] Contract assembly also leads to contract development, with the supplier elaborating the customer's initial idea and producing the eventual product. Second, the large corporations ask subcontractors to manufacture prototypes of end-products under extremely tight deadlines.

In both cases these subcontractors must be substantially more independent than before; and when the existing suppliers do not seem able to assume the greater responsibility – perhaps because their loyalty to their chief customer makes it hard for them to conceive of themselves as operating in more open markets – new ones are created which can. Aoki reports many large corporations laying off their own managers and encouraging them to form legally autonomous firms with the capacity for innovative production. He calls this process, which recalls the corporate drive for cost reduction and increased flexibility which contributed importantly to the rise of the Third Italy, 'quasi-disintegration'.[76] One prototype manufacturer of small appliances, for another example, has established an 'educational factory' where skilled workers from the firm learn to use a variety of machines while taking their first steps as independent producers. Their lessons consist of turning out parts on machinery purchased with a loan from their employer. Fully thirty of the prototype manufacturer's subcontractors were firms established by former employees who had attended this school.[77]

A natural result of the increased design capacity, flexible production facilities, and more versatile supplier network is that the subcontractors begin to diversify into new industries. The prototype manufacturer supplies many segments of the electrical equipment industry, and it is not unusual for second- or third-tier suppliers in the automobile industry to work for computer manufacturers. Aoki's new subcontractors frequently worked for clients outside their parent's group. In short, the Japanese subcontracting system as understood in Western managerial circles is beginning to look like the Bosch model, and this shift is indicative of a general redirection of the Japanese manufacturing sector towards more specialised and flexible production.

Evidence regarding several large metalworking firms in the North of the Federal Republic of Germany gives a further indication of the strength of the forces driving firms to adopt more flexible production set-ups. Firms such as Demag (construction equipment) and Krupp (steel, special machines) have always been speciality producers, collaborating closely with their customers in the design of capital goods. But unlike the Baden-Württemberg firms, with their ever more extensive subcontracting networks, these large combines have traditionally pursued a policy of corporate autarky. The vast majority of necessary parts were produced in the firms' semi-independent workshops. Workshops with slack capacity acted as subcontractors, preferentially for other units in the company. Flexibility was thus compatible with insulation from the local economy. Recently, however, the firms have for the familiar reasons begun to decentralise whenever they could make use of qualified suppliers without jeopardising relations with their skilled workers. Krupp, for example, does not integrate newly acquired companies into the existing network of workshops, allowing them instead to choose suppliers freely among local firms. Demag has begun to delegate more and more responsibility to its subcontractors; Gildermeister, a leading machine-tool maker, has decentralised operations in Bielefeld along South-West German lines. Thus the Bosch model and the drive for maximum flexibility and integration into the regional economy with which it is associated appear attractive to firms that were already highly flexible by American standards. Moreover, distressed companies which do not adopt the model themselves may be forced to by others. There are signs that the southerners are toying with the idea of purchasing pieces of wrecked firms in Bremen and Hamburg and integrating them into their own production network.[78]

If the experience of these Japanese and West German companies indicates a trend, then the shift towards the textbook picture will be self-reinforcing. The more the Toyotas of the world pin their strategies to flexibility and diversity through decentralisation, the more they undercut the economies of scale in production and design of the neo-Fordists – the 'Japanese' corporations of much current debate – by fragmenting the latter's markets. The more the neo-Fordists try to meet the new competition, the more they are driven to use their equipment and work-force in new, flexible ways – or the more likely they are to fall victim to competitors who do. Even in the limiting case, of course, many neo-Fordist firms would continue to supply standard, multi-purpose capital goods or components for more flexible firms.

But subject to this reservation, the activities of the giant corporations would more closely resemble and actually blend into the activity of the industrial districts. An engine plant which participates in the design of the engine and depends on highly specialised local suppliers to produce it is both part of a multinational car firm *and* an independent industrial district. To pursue the implications of such developments for relations between industry and local government we have to shift perspective again and look at the changing self-perception of local economies.

THEORY IN SEARCH OF PRACTICE: THE CHANGING PERCEPTION OF THE REGION AS A CATEGORY OF ANALYSIS

Independent of the emergence of the new industrial districts and the shift in large firms' strategy, there has been a striking reorientation in the thinking of regional planners, local development officials, and the geographers, urbanists and regional economists who are their exponents and advisers. In the heyday of mass production poorer regions were conceived as blank spaces on the national map of industry, to be filled by the same development strategies as such voids were filled in the Third World. In more prosperous areas the region or municipality was seen as an administrative unit suited to dispensing welfare services.[79] Today, as increasing competition undermines the sense of security of even the most well-to-do areas and national welfare systems strain to meet their obligations, these two perspectives are giving way to a single view of the region as an economic entity full of underused or unused resources that range from traditional artisanal skills to petty commerce. Prosperity depends, according to the new doctrine of endogenous growth, on developing these resources rather than importing the equipment and skills of a mass-production economy from the rich exterior.

Much of this reorientation is just talk – sincere, often desperate talk, but detached from concrete projects. But in exceptional cases, the talk has inspired or been inspired by promising deeds. In any case, the new doctrines are so much of a piece with developments in the industrial districts and the corporations that, should these latter continue in the indicated directions, they will likely prompt elaboration of the idea of endogenous growth, which would in turn affect the new industrial organisations.

The new doctrine, like the old, is partly a reflection of current thinking about the Third World. The failure of many industrialisation projects, combined with the intractable problems of trade relations with the advanced countries, have encouraged 'neo-populist' calls for 'South–South' alliances based on semi-automatic strategies of growth 'from below'. Centres of declining industry at the mercy of uncontrollable markets can sympathise as easily with the spirit of such ideas as can perennially poor First World regions who have lost the ear of fiscally strapped central authorities.[80]

But the new doctrines have deeper domestic sources. The failure of mass-production development strategies, combined with the welfare state's repudiation of its guarantee of prosperity – often expressed as decentralisation of authority for creating jobs and caring for the unemployed – have forced local communities to discard one promising growth model after another. The first to go was the notion of creating 'growth poles' and a regional 'export surplus' by attracting outside firms through subsidies.[81] Many of the new firms were low-wage, technically unsophisticated subsidiaries of larger corporations. They pulled up stakes at the first downturn, leaving few skilled workers or experienced managers behind. Fewer firms are currently willing to relocate (a result of slower growth and, presumably, the failures of the original corporate strategy of decentralisation to low-wage areas). Subsidies, as it turns out, seldom influenced location decisions: the unsophisticated firms were ignorant of them. The sophisticated ones found that every locality matched the others' offers.

These views are held clear across the political spectrum and in virtually all the advanced countries. In 1982 the British Labour Party's 'Alternative Regional Strategy' found 'with hindsight' that while the strategy of premiums 'succeeded in diverting new industry' to depressed areas until the mid-1970s, it 'failed to build up an economy capable of generating long-term growth'.[82] In 1984, the Council of State Planning Agencies, the research bureau of the US National Governors' Association, published a book on state development strategy which opened with an admonitory review of Mississippi's Balance Agriculture with Industry Program, established in 1936 to reduce the state's dependence on cotton. According to its authors:

> The most comprehensive financial incentive program of its time, BAWI proved to be a mixed blessing. It accelerated the pace of business diversification, but it also trapped Mississippi into a tradition of low-wage industries and denied tax coffers the resources for basic investments in education, infrastructures, and public health at levels enjoyed elsewhere. And, despite its leadership in establishing the prototype for state development economic strategy, Mississippi remains one of the poorest states in the nation.[83]

And this Prologue was introduced by an approving Foreword by the conservative Republican governor of New Hampshire, John H. Sununu.[84]

The second doctrine to go was what might be called municipal Keynesianism. During the late 1970s and early 1980s cities (or, in some West German cases, city-states) like Marseilles, London, Dortmund, Bremen, Hamburg, and Detroit tried to reduce or at least stabilise the local unemployment rate by funding public works – hospital construction, road improvement, and the like – or subsidising local employers on the verge of failure. The results were disappointing. Public works expenditures leaked from the region, so that most of the jobs they created were in other jurisdictions; the subsidies were insufficient for successful reconversion, or created too few jobs to justify the expense; the training programmes led to dead-end jobs or no jobs at all.[85]

The third false hope was the idea of a forward flight into the sunrise world of high-technology industrial parks. In the late 1970s and early 1980s almost the only industries with a future in the advanced industrial countries seemed to be related to micro-electronics, genetic engineering and such exotic materials as high-performance ceramics. Desperate to do something about rising unemployment rates, politicians tried to imitate the success of Silicon Valley and Route 128. But it soon became commonplace that the new firms created fewer jobs than anticipated; that industries like semiconductors and computers were as cyclical as other capital goods industries; that much of the money in high technology was to be made not by investing in breakthroughs, but by applying them to traditional products (as in the use of microprocessors to regulate motor-car engines). Moreover, even the successful regions did not have an institutionalisable understanding of their own success. To help revitalise depressed areas of the state, Massachusetts established university 'centres of excellence' modelled on Ohio's efforts to imitate the success of MIT and Route 128. Western Europeans – who were matching American industrial technology just as they discovered a new and thus more disconcerting technology gap – still worried about keeping pace with the Americans and Japanese; but for most politicians, the blush was off the rose of high-tech industrial parks by the mid-1980s.

These pressures for reconsideration of development strategy were augmented, finally, by the new financial strains on local governments: the national state's willingness to cover shortfalls in local budgets declined as tax revenues from business activity decreased. In these cases the national state pursued a carrot-and-stick strategy. The stick was a reduction of subsidies to distressed firms and social welfare and vocational training benefits for displaced workers. The carrot was partial devolution of authority over vocational training, economic development, and social welfare programmes to local or regional authorities. The *Loi Defferre* of 1982–3 consolidated centrally controlled, piecemeal subsidies to local authorities into block grants which were to be principally under the latter's control.[86] The American Job Training Partnership Act (JTPA) of 1983 decreased the financial contribution of the federal government to vocational training, but increased the state's powers to dispose of the funds. It mandated that decisions about the allocation of grants be made in consultation with local Private Industry Councils (PICs) – boards created by the Act, and composed of representatives of local industry and government (but not, as the name already suggests, labour).[87] West Germany has pursued an analogous, though less unabashedly pro-industry, reduction of vocational training funds accompanied by increased subsidies to economically distressed regions.[88] Denmark and Sweden have been especially aggressive in what they explicitly call the 'regionalisation' of labour-market policy.[89] In other countries, however, there has only been the stick: in its efforts to reduce tax rates, the Thatcher government severely limited the power of local authorities to tax – in the case of Greater London, by abolishing the municipal council entirely.

Together, these changes created a new orthodoxy of endogenous local development that parallels the emergent orthodoxy in corporate strategy. Like the firms, the localities know that they must survive in a turbulent economic environment; like the firms, they must accommodate volatility through flexibility, though for localities this naturally means facilitating the recombination of resources among companies, so that the latter may better redeploy them internally. And as with the firms, many localities will renovate themselves only with the greatest difficulty.[90]

Certainly there are grounds for pessimism. Despite reduced resources, publicly discredited subsidies often continue new names. As usual, decentralisation by decree has had unspectacular results. The *Loi Defferre* has hardly allowed the regions to seize control from Paris;[91] in the Massachusetts state government no one, so far as I have been able to determine, has a comprehensive picture of what the PICs do, and the most informed persons say that many do nothing. Sustained efforts to diversity local (heavy) industrial 'monocultures' have frequently foundered, as in the now scandalous case of the state-owned Austrian steelmakers, because trade unionists, managers and local politicians from all parties have branded together to block change rather than trade old troubles for new.[92]

There are, however, also signs that the new ideas are combining in unanticipated ways with the firms' spontaneous efforts at restructuring to produce results akin to the reformers' intentions. Sometimes the successes are due largely to the capacity of local industrialists, bankers and development officials to co-ordinate many government programmes originally addressed to distinct economic problems. This is the case in Borken, where the head of the local development agency helped convince the local notables to restructure the old textile mills.[93] Elsewhere in West Germany, the district hospital, which depends on a strong local economy to keep firms' medical insurance payments within acceptable limits and hence its own finances in balance, could well become a nerve centre of economic planning. Because the hospitals' governing boards are composed of leading local industrialists and politicians whose own fate reflects the institutions', these committees provide a natural forum for discussion of the problems of co-ordination.[94]

Similar networks are forming in such traditional metalworking and garment districts of Massachusetts as Springfield (where labour participation is minimal) and Fall River (where it is substantial). In Springfield, the metalworking firms are creating a new apprenticeship system. The starting point is a demanding curriculum in machining technology planned in collaboration with the local community college. In combination with shop experience, this programme is designed to attract youngsters by validating metalworking as a 'computer' profession of the future, and provide them with high-level skills. In Massachusetts these developments are being encouraged by state programmes – the Cooperative Regional Industrial Laboratories – which provide for a discussion of local problems through the organisation of conferences and councils.[95] Governors in the American Mid-West encouraged a new generation of community activists to develop programmes for preserving the states' industrial base. Often the first step in such programmes – and an indication of how ill-prepared the states were for the task – was simply to take a detailed census of manufacturing establishments in key sectors. But many such programmes soon began to organise consulting services to individual firms, co-ordinate dispersed training facilities, and promote sustained, fundamental discussion of strategies for modernising the second- and third-tier supplier network: the firms most likely to be displaced by foreign manufacturers when the first-tier suppliers scramble to meet *their* customers' demands for a just-in-time delivery system.[96]

In France the major banks are becoming more willing to finance locally owned firms. Loans to the national champions proved riskier than anticipated, and the regional authorities, whatever their limitations, do have the power to secure the bank debt of firms in their jurisdiction. Of course, the guarantees could prop up hopelessly weakened firms; but given the banks' interest in profits and the state's general disappointment with policies of subsidisation, the result could be the promotion of regional economies.[97] Even in the UK, despite the central government's restrictions on local authorities, there are faint signs that a combination of strategic reorientation by the firms and local government is encouraging the formation of flexible, competitive industrial systems.

In extreme cases, local or regional authorities have comprehensive plans for economic revitalisation which overlap substantially with the more conscious practices of the new industrial districts. On the one hand, they encourage the formation of consortia of firms with complementary specialities. On the other, they provide an infrastructure of permanent innovation at the service of the new firm groups. At a minimum, the infrastructure plans call for vocational schools and research institutes. But they also provide for superbly maintained roads and other transportation facilities to ensure operation of just-in-time production systems; 'one-stop' negotiation of health and safety, unemployment insurance; and other social welfare regulations which take account of the ways firms are beginning to reduce insurance costs to the public through preventive medicine or job guarantees.

Here again the results are as provocative as they are inconclusive. There are signs of regional reconsolidation, but significant obstacles to it as well. Even in countries such as West Germany and Denmark with strong federalist traditions, prior efforts at administrative rationalisation of local governments, as instruments of the welfare state efforts to impose national fiscal discipline, obstruct efforts to increase regional autonomy. And these are the most favourable cases. But in these countries, and others as well, the new localists are pressing for an extension of their legal powers and no one is to say which forces will prevail.[98] But it is possible, I think, to indicate some ways political intervention can and has already encouraged the formation of successful regional entities. That is the task of the next section.

THE POLITICS OF MEMORY:
CREATING REGIONAL ECONOMIES

To discuss the prospects of endogenous development and the multiplication of industrial districts it is necessary to return to the earlier questions about the constitution of the social solidarity on which both regional economies and the flexibly specialized corporations depend. The argument was that flexible economies rely on high-trust relations which they reinforce through their operation but cannot generate themselves: in a low-trust world no one wants to take the first step towards the high-trust alternative for fear of being caught out when others do not follow, so no one moves. If this initial, catalytic trust arises only under highly unusual conditions, flexibly specialised economies will be overshadowed by less exiguous neo-Fordist arrangements. Conversely, if there are many sources of trust, or rather if it is possible, as a common expression has it, to 'build' trust from diverse experiences, then there is more reason to think that efficiency considerations as currently defined will encourage their diffusion. The arguments for a restrictive view of the generation of trust have been developed most elaborately with regard to small-firm industrial districts; I shall therefore concentrate on these, although parallel claims and counter-claims can be made regarding trust relations in large corporations.

The explanation of the origins of trust in the regional economies focuses on the relation between pre-industrial land-tenure patterns and traditions of artisanal by-employments with their connections to world markets. In the Third Italy,[99] Jutland,[100] and Baden-Württemberg,[101] the argument in synthesis goes, agrarian conditions were similar to those which gave rise to flexible specialisation in the regional economies of nineteenth-century France. Land holdings were so small that proprietors had to supplement agricultural income with income from artisanal work (weaving, knitting, furniture making) or industrial employment (in, say, the urban construction industry during the agricultural off season). The property regime and connection to international trading networks which fostered these relations were different from case to case. *Mezzadria*, or sharecropping, combined with handicraft production exported via trade routes first opened by the Renaissance city states, was typical of parts of the Third Italy. In Jutland, eighteenth- and nineteenth-century state regulations kept peasants tied to land, allowed them to capture the return on their investments, but not to enlarge their holdings. This situation combined with proximity to the old Hanseatic sea routes to produce similar incentives and opportunities. The common results were the formation of entrepreneurial families which survived by shifting resources quickly from activity to activity, and the creation of local institutions such as banks and small merchant houses which helped the families move rapidly into national and international industrial markets when the opportunity arose. By contrast, areas in Denmark (Falster), Germany (East Elbia), and Italy (Sicily) where large estates were cultivated by farm labourers or peasants with scant possibilities for familial accumulation through astute management, have not produced modern industrial districts.

But such comparisons are misleadingly narrow. The finding that some areas are quick to adopt certain organisational forms does not warrant the conclusion that the history of the advantaged regions defines the only possible path to those forms. Nor does it warrant the conclusion that slower-moving regions lack the institutional or cultural reserves which could enable them to convert after some time to the promising alternative. In fact, even a slightly broader canvas of current cases is enough to show that there is no plausible list of the necessary and sufficient conditions – rare or otherwise – for the emergence of flexible economies. Moreover, many of the cases which suggest at first glance that such economies are the results of unreflective responses to the accidents of economic history are in fact full of just the kinds of political struggle over corporate, union, and state policy familiar from current debates. Some regions and firms have had an easier time than others adjusting to a volatile environment. But even the most favoured ones faced, and knew they faced, critical strategic choices. If they now appear to have arrived at their present organisation by following immemorial traditions, this is not least because they resolved those conflicts by redefining their past as traditionally harmonious or necessarily culminating in harmony. This is a kind of political intervention which is almost undetectable because it deliberately covers its tracks, but it is politics nevertheless.

The earlier discussion of new industrial districts immediately suggests the shortcomings of any current list of structural determinants of flexibility. Alongside Baden-Württemberg, Tuscany, the Marches, and Jutland are the cases of industrial automation in Turin, the electronic entertainment industry in Los Angeles, application-specific integrated circuits or engineering work-stations in Silicon Valley, and mini-computers in Route 128. None of these can be assimilated to the model of small-holder, family agriculture as the matrix of co-operative entrepreneurship which certainly helps explain the development of the former. Rather, trust is established through common educational and professional experiences, reinforced at times by ethnic allegiances or – cause or consequence of economic success? – local pride. These common experiences are often expressed in the language of family, as when certain persons or firms are said to be in the lineage of or descended from established laboratories, companies or researchers. But this metaphoric use of family is meant to mark off certain particularly intimate and formative professional experiences from others, not to identify and mystify them as 'truly' familial. Indeed it is conceivable that the understandings of 'family' will eventually converge in what I am here calling urban and rural industrial districts: biological family connections could come after several generations to play a greater role in structuring economic relations in the former (this has already happened in the Los Angeles entertainment industry), while metaphoric family ties spread in the latter to resolve their recurrent succession crises.[102] But even if there is no convergence, professional solidarity is apparently an alternative to familial solidarity as a source of that mixture of individual responsibility and mutual dependence on which flexible economic relations depend. This conclusion is reinforced by Capecchi's observation that in Emilia-Romagna there is a distinct *urban* artisan tradition articulated and transmitted through publicly supported technical schools. Indeed, he found that the small-firm owners he surveyed were more likely to be children of workers or artisans and to have attended these schools than to have rural origins.[103]

The same point about solidarity as a social construct can be made the other way around by noting the cases of apparently traditional productive community which resulted in fact from repeated political compromises. In the nineteenth-century cases, conflicts arose out of efforts to construct an institutional regime which fostered flexible work relations and transmission of knowledge to succeeding generations through the old solidary craft organisations, while removing guild restrictions which blocked introduction of new technologies and products. The small manufacturers, who were as a rule the old guild masters or their heirs, pressed for substantial freedom; their employees, the guild journeymen or their descendants insisted on observation of traditional practices as their protection against the masters' caprice. The successful compromises in many of the German, Danish and French crafts typically depended on an exchange of rights: the journeymen granted the masters greater freedom of action in return for contractual guarantees to minimum wages and participation in dispute-resolution systems patterned on old-regime guild tribunals (for instance, the bipartite *conseils de prud'hommes*, established first in Lyons in 1806 as a court and 'quasi-legislature' for the regulation of the local silk-working industry).[104] Sometimes the state smoothed the way for these compromises by offering (as in Denmark)[105] aid to vocational schools under joint control of the parties or (as in the nineteenth-century Kingdom of Württemberg)[106] creating technical consultancies and information-gathering services which improved the competitive position of the small-firm sector and thus reduced pressure on the masters to insist on concessions.

The compromises were the result of conflicts. In Denmark it took a series of bitter strikes and lockouts from 1885 to 1899 as well as decades of struggle within the state ministries and between them and parliament to establish the rules of the new game.[107] Boch traces analogous conflicts at the municipal level in the Solingen cutlery industry.[108] And if conflict was an unavoidable prelude to compromise it was no guarantee of success. The Sheffield cutlery industry and the Birmingham hardware trades were competitively crippled by the kinds of dispute which led to renewal elsewhere.[109] The issue in all these disputes was precisely the meaning of traditions of co-operation; and however much the parties might in retrospect insist on the fidelity of their agreements to established principle, their conclusions could hardly be traditional in the conventional sense of a shared, indubitable, and self-explicating understanding of their rights and responsibilities.

Similar constitutive conflicts are common in the modern industrial districts, but, if anything, harder to trace. First, there is the obvious problem that making peace often entails reinterpreting the events which led to conflict as an unfortunate misunderstanding best worth forgetting. Thus, despite his intimate knowledge of Prato and its post-war history, Triglia only recently discovered that between the time the integrated woolen mills began decentralising production in the 1940s and the consolidation of the decentralised system in the early 1960s, *no* collective bargaining agreements were signed between a union and employers' association currently regarded as traditionally co-operative.[110]

Second, the dominance of mass production has meant that unions and firms in the industrial districts have become extremely cautious about advertising their conflicts or co-operation to outsiders. The more the mass-production model spread as a standard of behaviour, the more deviant the craft practices of the industrial districts appeared to trade unions and employers' associations bent on negotiating standard agreements fixing working hours, wages and work conditions for entire economic sectors. For example, through the early 1970s the industrial unions accepted in principle that progress in the division of labour meant elimination of skill from manufacturing. Their strategy (frequently compromised by concessions to the craft workers who often remained their most loyal cadre) was to reduce pay differentials among different skill grades and raise the average wages of the increasingly central group of semi-skilled workers, whose augmented purchasing power helped ensure expansion. One consequence was that highly paid semi-skilled workers were particularly likely to be laid off during downturns, with uncertain prospects for re-entering the firm or industry. In contrast, unionised workers in the industrial districts often pursued a strategy of *de facto* job sharing. The contractual wage was set low with respect to the employers' general capacity to pay, reducing the probability of layoffs during downturns and assuring the continuous participation in the industry and thus access to current information essential to flexible work practices. A complementary strategy was to invent administrative fictions allowing use of national unemployment insurance funds to support workers during slack seasons or periods. During upturns, the workers used the bargaining power conferred by their skills to raise wages without endangering employment.[111]

To avoid interference from the national organisations, local trade unions and employers' associations in the industrial districts made a policy of keeping to themselves. They typically have loosely formalised arrangements for settling differences over pay, working conditions and hours for the local labour market, and the establishment and maintenance of these arrangements is often accompanied by conflicts at that level rather than firm by firm. But such municipal unionism and the constant adjustment of rights and responsibilities on which it rests usually come to light as the accidental by-product of research directed to other questions. In the Baden-Württemberg machine-tool industry, Hildebrandt and his colleagues discovered that managers only realised how easily perturbed their relations with the work-force were when their daily inspection tours that were informally used for elaborating the implicit social pact between the parties were replaced by information-gathering technologies – and conflict increased as a result.[112] In Denmark, Hull Kriestensen found in the course of a study of individual reorganisation that the *tillidsmæn* or shop stewards in the metalworking industry were struggling to invent new payment, training and classification systems to increase the flexibility of production and increase the general skill level. Even though these efforts frequently entailed innovative use of public labour market institutions, the stewards were reticent to talk with national trade union officials about these matters for fear of inviting unwanted intervention.[113] Kochan, Katz and I have observed the same combative inventiveness and detachment from the national union in frequent discussion with local officials of the United Automobile Workers from General Motors plants.

But this situation is changing rapidly. As the success of flexible economies attracts scholarly attention and as national unions and employers' associations increasingly look to local experiments as a guide to rethinking their strategies, the informal or concealed practices of the regional economies are coming to light. Contarino's[114] study of local strategies of the Italian textile workers' union and Locke's[115] more recent work on the Italian textile, chemical and automobile workers are two examples of the studies to come.

But it may be objected that these arguments show at most that traditions of solidarity are in need of political repair under changing circumstances, not that it is possible to create such traditions once they have been totally destroyed. What, then, about the hard cases where the long-standing fragmentation of tasks in a mass-production regime has undercut the opportunities for acquiring the skills and exercising the initiative necessary in a system of flexible specialisation?

The evidence here is scant but dramatic. At Freemont, California, Toyota and General Motors have recently rebuilt an abandoned General Motors assembly plant, reorganised work according to Toyota's principles, and rehired selected employees from the old facility – which had a history of bitter labour disputes – to operate the new one. The New United Motors Company is currently almost 50 per cent more efficient than the old General Motors plant on the same site, almost 50 per cent more efficient than comparable GM assembly plants which were modernised while Freemont was closed, and more than 90 per cent as efficient as an equivalent Toyota plant in Japan meeting the same standards of quality.[116] The difference in productivity, moreover, seems attributable to the Japanese plant's shorter supply lines for some components. This success is no proof that the workers could disperse to form a network of co-operating independent firms; but it does show that it is possible to reverse in an astonishingly short time a history of strife typical of mass production in its most exasperated form and move toward the kind of co-operation which makes the acquisition of skill and the exercise of initiative likely rather than exceptional. Studies of new, flexible firms growing up amidst the ruins of old Austrian centres of mass production such as Wiener-Neustadt[117] and Mürzuschlag[118] as well as the traditional centre of heavy industry in Sesto San Giovanni[119] near Milan point towards the same conclusion.

These empirical counter-examples, however, obscure the more fundamental point that the question about hard cases rests on an untenable assumption. It is misleading to ask about the prospects of regeneration of production systems when all forms of co-operation are destroyed because there can be no production – at least no industrial production – without some minimal degree of co-operation. Shop-floor managers and sociologists of work have long recognised that even the most exact plan of production must constantly be readjusted to meet changing circumstances; and that semi-skilled workers must draw on a large stock of 'tacit' – officially unrecognized – knowledge about particular machines, their workmates, or, say, the effect of humidity and heat on certain materials in order to maintain the flow of production. Workers demonstrate the indispensability of this knowledge every time they shut down a plant simply by working precisely according to rule.[120]

The *source* of this co-operation is a matter for debate. A *Marxisant* explanation is that work is collective in character and constitutive of individual identity; hence participation in production creates solidarity which cannot be fully destroyed even when the organisation of production belies its existence. Liberal explanations emphasise that parties which frequently contract with one another learn that the benefits of co-operation outweigh those of opportunism. Once it is generally understood that it pays to assume that the other party will not breach the agreement, contracts take on the cast of trust relations.[121] Efficiency-wage theories, for example, assume that by paying workers a premium above the rate necessary to elicit blind obedience to rules it is possible to induce them to use their initiative productively. Indeed, the exchange of a wage premium for an implicit promise to co-operate in raising efficiency is regarded in some of these theories as a 'quasi-gift' relation to underscore the break with purely contractual dealings.[122] On both views, however, co-operation in production is always necessary and possible, and the practical question is how to re-elaborate it according to the needs of the moment, not how to create it from nothing.

The numerous discredited theories of industrialisation are, moreover, so many admonitions against efforts to draw up a short list of necessary and sufficient conditions for competitive adjustment. To industrialise first meant to imitate Great Britain and the United States. When Germany, Russia, and Italy industrialised later in the nineteenth century, they defined new routes to mechanisation and cast doubts on explanations that overlooked the possibility of their success.[123] The growth of South Korea, Taiwan, Singapore and Brazil reveals still other paths and raises further explanatory questions.[124] No matter that an alleged precondition of industrialisation was a break with pre-industrial traditions of economically paralysing community; the issue here, on the contrary, is the (re)constitution of solidarity. The lesson is that structural explanations which simply make established cases into universal models overlook substantial reserves of organisational plasticity.

To argue that there are always diverse traditions which can serve as the source of high-trust social solidarity and that each of these is itself a political artefact is not to say that some situations are not more propitious than others for the emergence of flexible economies. Structural explanations such as the small-holder model of solidarity would have no bite were there no developmental regularities. But the arguments of this section do shift the burden of proof in debate over the expansive potential of flexible economies. To ask why flexible economies should not diffuse under competitive pressure is as reasonable as to ask why they should. The most disadvantaged regions or countries might adjust so slowly that they are ruined by swifter competitors. The winners, however, would be flexible economies, though they would not be identical: like the giant corporations of various nations in the heyday of mass production, each would bear the marks of its history and accordingly react (as did the mass producers) differently to future shocks. But all would be characterised by the greater integration of conception from execution which sets the new system off from the old.

Suppose that a short supply of solidarity does not impede the diffusion of industrial districts. Could these districts by themselves come to form a national economy? Or might their long-term survival require some armature of higher-level, national institutions? These questions return attention to possible connections between changes in the organisation of production and the reconstruction of the welfare state.

THE LOCALISED WELFARE STATE?
TWO FUTURES FOR FLEXIBLE ECONOMIES

Macro-economic regulation is at bottom a problem of reinsurance. Its aim is to reduce or spread the market risks which firms alone or in combination cannot escape or bear themselves. Mass-production corporations in the 1920s tried to stabilise their markets one by one through segmentation strategies or industry by industry through cartels. The lesson of the Great Depression was that control of aggregate purchasing power was a precondition for the success of any of these particular measures. The very nature of flexible specialisation suggests that it too will require complementary macro-economic institutions, different in kind but not in ultimate purpose from the Keynesian reinsurance system. And because of the conditions which favour its diffusion, furthermore, it is likely that even abstracting from the additional problems of creating an appropriate international trade regime, national economies will have no easier a time, and perhaps a harder one, discovering why and how to construct such institutions.

Flexible specialisation has been defined in two ways. It was introduced as the inverse of mass production: the manufacture of specialised goods by means of general-purpose resources rather than vice versa. Later it was defined as a system in which firms know that they do not know precisely what they will have to produce, and further that they must count on the collaboration of workers and subcontractors in meeting the market's eventual demand. This second definition clarifies some questions concerning the advantages of network production. It also better captures the actors' own fundamental strategic considerations, thus permitting a fuller understanding of their tactics in particular instances.

To draw out the macro-regulatory implications of flexible specialisation, however, it is necessary to examine more carefully the relation between flexibility and specialisation. The key point is that the former depends on the latter. In order to shift rapidly from product to product within one area of the economy, it is necessary to focus on that area to the neglect of others. The chief virtue of Bosch-model subcontracting systems is to free even the largest companies to concentrate on developing that portion of their expertise which they value most. Flexibly specialised firms are flexible by comparison to mass producers, and hence more competitive in volatile environments. But there are limits. They are hardly materialising machines capable of making any and all goods.

Specialisation of course entails market risk. Even the most flexible producer of woollens is in trouble when fashion shifts to other fabrics; and the sections of the Prato textile industry which currently face this situation know that their problems are not simply resolved because of their vast experience in running a network production system. If many governments subsidise domestic steel producers and block entry of imports, then, as West German steelmakers have discovered, even the most far-sighted strategy of specialisation will not guarantee security in the steel business.

These sorts of risk are mitigated for two reasons. First, specialisation can itself lead to diversification, which reduces reliance on any single type of market. For example, Trumpf, a West German manufacturer of sheet-metal bending and cutting equipment, recently developed an industrial laser for its own purposes, discovered additional applications, and now plans to stabilise its earnings by entering new markets whose behaviour is not strictly tied to the demand for working sheet metal.[125] Second, there are always analogies or overlaps between the manufacturing processes, materials, products or distribution channels serving one market and those serving others. Thus firms are constantly pulled by opportunity or pushed by crisis to shift their area of specialisation by playing on the affinities between what they know and what they need to know. But even under favourable circumstances reconversion takes time, which firms under duress do not have.

Hence the need for a system of macro-regulatory stabilisation. In theory, the system as a whole should be flexible enough so that price changes – particularly the fall in interest rates accompanying a drop in economic activity – should lead to the redeployment of resources and the revival of investment which classical economics regarded as the re-equilibrating response to slowdowns. But no single district could rely on this mechanism to assure its long-term prosperity. Industrial districts which have already in effect insured themselves against substantial shifts in demand by increasing their internal flexibility should therefore want to reinsure themselves by pooling resources with other equally flexible regions. Such a confederation would be able to aid a distressed member by helping to provide the capital, technical assistance, vocational training, and unemployment payments required for reconversion to new markets. Whereas the Keynesian reinsurance system spread the residual risks of changes in the level of demand, this one spreads the uncovered risks of changes in its composition.

There is nothing novel about the idea of pooling resources to facilitate structural adjustment. Keynes and others in his camp hoped the International Monetary Fund created after the Second World War would collect funds from countries with a balance-of-payments surplus and lend it long-term to nations running a deficit. The debtors could then rebuild their industry and improve their trade balance by improving their export performance. This would have been a substitute for the austerity measures for reducing imports and increasing the share of public funds available to service foreign debt which the IMF in fact came to favour.[126] Within single countries, policies to aid poor regions, protect distressed industries from foreign competition, promote technological modernisation or ease labour market dislocations have long operated to facilitate structural adjust-ment.[127] But with a few marginal exceptions such as the confedera-tions of Israeli *kibbutzim* (producer co-operatives which increasingly operate on flexible lines and pool resources in the indicated way),[128] these policies have been regarded at best as complements or correctives to the dominant Keynesian strategies. At worst they have been considered – sometimes correctly – as political payoffs to economic interests which have the ear of influential parties or ministries.

But the breakdown of Keynesianism and the concomitant spread of flexible production makes it less likely that such programmes can operate in the shadows; and the state, industry, and labour will come to clarify their motives for pursuing them. In Scandinavia, for example, regional labour-market policy was viewed from the capitals for most of the post-war period as, among other things, a way of reducing the danger of wage inflation associated with demand stimula-tion by eliminating shortages of critical skills. At the same time, of course, these programmes contributed to the consolidation of regional economies; but these were not identified in public debate as such, and the effectiveness of the programmes was judged by their effect on national unemployment levels, not local reconversion. Today regional labour-market policy, understood broadly to include vocational and continuing education, is increasingly seen by the national political elite itself as part of regional programmes of job creation. Programmes to transfer technology from universities to industry or to encourage exports are being reinterpreted there and elsewhere in analogous ways. And these reinterpretations have their echoes in the internal discussions of national trade unions and employers' associations. Thus debate about the national implications of the emergent regional economies is slowly taking shape even as the regions begin to debate a future in which they can count less and less on the nation.[129]

Two contrary lines of development are imaginable. In the first, debate leads to the decision to reject systematic reform of the macro-regulatory institutions, or sputters out even before there is a considered judgement to do nothing. In that case, if the flexible economies spread, time will test how resilient to shocks each in isolation truly is. In the second, a new reinsurance system emerges with correspondingly new distribution of responsibility among national and local governments and the various levels of employers' associations and trade unions. Tracing these two lines of development points to the preconditions for two radically different kinds of industrial society based on flexible local economies.

The first possibility is a grim extrapolation of the most divisive tendencies in the diffusion of flexible specialisation. In this line of development, industrial districts combining small-firm networks and corporate operating units expand substantially as more and more regions discover the political secrets of reconversion. But this expansion stops short – depending on circumstances, far short – of encompassing the economically active population. Above all, there are no institutional incentives to extend the system past the limits reached by local initiatives. The new firm complexes depend as much on international as domestic markets; and in any case their flexibility protects them against shifts in the market. In contrast to the Keynesian epoch, they therefore have no interest in a steady, general increase of purchasing power, still less the expansion of employment which would make it possible. On the contrary, because they have to give something like an employment guarantee to the skilled workers on whom they depend, they are extremely chary about expanding the work-force even in boom times. As the power of national trade unions and industry associations declines with the atrophy of centralised macro-economic management, power in these organisations slides to the local level. Both begin to look out for the members in their industrial district or, at most, their branch narrowly defined (not metalworking, but medical instrument making, for example). They too have no interest in pressing for the extensions of vocational training, technical consulting services, or credit facilities which could help create additional industrial districts and expand the circle of prosperity.

The welfare state would look like a more ramshackle version of its current self. The industrial districts would half surreptitiously reshape its services locally to meet their needs; wherever possible they would try to reduce their contributions to public revenues with the plausible argument that through their job guarantees and training programmes they already bear many of the risks and responsibilities once born by the state. At the same time, the national state would support the excluded – primarily unskilled workers, many of them women – through some combination of unemployment insurance and poor relief. In northern European countries with strong democratic traditions some alliance of progressives urging the attractive possibilities of leisure in a post-material society and conservatives anxious to keep the poor off the streets might press for a legal right to a minimum income, thus removing poverty from the national political agenda and legitimating the silent co-existence of those inside and outside the new economies. In classically liberal societies such as the USA, much of the new underclass would scrape by serving the privileged. The rest would be grudgingly provided for, and constantly tested to determine their propensity to respond to various incentives to join the active labour force.

If this system is not shaken by the social divisions it tolerates, it is likely to fall victim to the very decentralisation of authority which makes possible competitive success through flexibility. The dilemma and the danger are the macro-social analogues to Perrow's account of the paradox of operating a potentially explosive continuous process plant.[130] To operate the unit efficiently, it is necessary to give operating teams authority to compensate for disturbances immediately so that problems are not amplified as they move from station to station. But if control is thus decentralised, it is unlikely that any central authority will have the knowledge, experience, or competence to stabilise situations which exceed the control of a sequence of stations. The price of higher efficiency under normal conditions is an increased chance of catastrophe. Similarly, the industrial districts could in this picture be lulled into a false sense of security by their superior resilience in the same way as the national institutions – state, trade unions, employers' associations – which could respond to shocks beyond local control atrophy.

The second line of development supposes that circumstances favour the institutionalisation of motives to extend flexible specialisation through the economy. In the rare cases such as Austria or Denmark where the trade unions have the *de facto* power to block major economic reform, the labour movement could almost achieve this unilaterally: if the unions insist – as they currently do – on expansion of vocational and technical training, with particular attention to requalification of the semi-skilled, as their price for acquiescence in industrial restructuring, the consequence will be an abundant supply of craft labour. The easy availability of skilled labour could then induce firms to use equipment in the most flexible way possible, thereby reinforcing the network production systems and creating demand for additional skills. This is the variant of Say's Law, frequently observed in West Germany, in which the supply of craft labour creates its own demand.

A more likely development concerns collaboration between national unions and national employers' associations faced with the common problem of unruly increases in local autonomy. Both have reason to identify and provide the industrial districts with services they can not provide themselves. In their search they come to see the benefits of co-operating with each other. Thus each can plausibly argue that the interests of its members and the other's are best served if the industrial districts do not cut too many ties to the national economy. To stay with the crucial example of education: the more broadly skilled a firm's workers, the less likely it is to lay them off and the more likely they are to find acceptable alternative employment if they are laid off. But any highly specialised group of firms and workers, however dedicated to training in principle, is likely to draw the circle of vocationally relevant skills too narrowly precisely because of its detailed knowledge of how much needs to be known to maintain current production. Managers and workers alike in such a setting will naturally discount the value of training in collateral or emergent skills with no clear connection to the indisputable core of necessary knowledge. In a period where technologies are constantly being recombined as each is advanced, however, these apparently marginal skills can suddenly decide the fate of reconversion projects. National institutions with sources of information in many sectors of the economy are of course in a better position to anticipate such possibilities than local ones. Hence the industrial districts have prudential motives for integrating into national training programmes monitored or advised by trade unions and employers' associations. The motives are all the stronger when, as typically happens, state subsidies are available to educational institutions which meet criteria set in consultation with the umbrella associations. And even when employers and trade unionists establish rival training programmes, the effects are similar: in this case, too, their respective members are forced to acknowledge bonds extending beyond regional boundaries, and these ties can become the first strands in a net of broader solidarity.

If the pooling of knowledge succeeds, it can easily become the political metaphor and matrix for the pooling of other resources as well. The more knowledge available to each industrial district, the less the probability of any being tripped up by costly ignorance; the greater the number of prosperous industrial districts, the more likely that each can draw on the resources of the others in its moments of distress. If firms, workers, trade associations and trade unions come to define their interests this way, then they will press for those policies – modelled perhaps on co-operation in education – which encourage the diffusion of regional economies. The result would be to draw currently marginal groups into the flexible economy while strengthening the armature of supra-local institutions which would eventually have to construct the macro-regulatory system of flexible specialisation. The division of labour between central and local authorities in such a system would differ from case to case, as would the organisation of flexibility in firms of different nations. But the emergent confederal states would all recognise in their constituent regions the same increased integration of conception and execution in economic strategy which is the distinguishing feature in flexibly specialised firms.

There is nothing utopian about this prospect. Many of the constitutive institutions of an eventual reinsurance system already exist, and national associations and agencies have not decayed beyond repair. Surely the situation is not very different from the decades that preceded the consolidation of the Keynesian model of macro-regulation, a model which was – typically – scarcely conceivable until it became almost self-evidently necessary.

Here my will to speculation is exhausted. If, as I have argued, flexible economies continue to spread through the fusion of large and small firms into industrial districts, the advanced capitalist societies are heading for a crisis. Either the circle of prosperity will remain closed to many, and the struggles between rich and poor, by themselves or in combination with the instability of uncoordinated economic decentralisation, will shake the foundations of divided societies. Or else the circle of prosperity will enlarge as both consequence and cause of new forms of institutionalised confederation. Then the capitalist democracies will face the problem of reconciling the new mechanisms of redistribution with their traditions of parliamentarism and equal treatment under law. Better the problems of prosperity.

NOTES AND REFERENCES

1   See, on these regional economies, Charles Sabel and Jonathan Zeitlin, 'Historical Alternatives to Mass Production: Politics, Markets and Technology in Nineteenth-Century Industrialisation', *Past and Present*, 108 (August 1985).

2   Alfred Marshall, *Industry and Trade* (London, 1919), pp. 283–8. For a detailed account of Marshall's ideas, see Giacomo Becattini, ed., *Mercato e forze locale: Il distretto industriale* (Bologna: Il Mulino, 1987).

3   For an account of the rise of mass production and Keynesianism which emphasises the link between the use of product-specific technologies, corporate organization and Keynesianism, but also the diversity of national experience, see Michael J. Piore and Charles F. Sabel, *The Second Industrial Divide* (New York: Basic Books, 1984).

4   See ibid., pp. 165–93, for an analysis of the changes in the international conditions of competition.

5   The *locus classicus* of the neo-corporatism discussion is Philippe C. Schmitter, 'Still the Century of Corporatism?' *Review of Politics* 36.1 (1974), pp. 85–131. See also Gerhard Lehmbruch, 'Liberal Corporatism and Party Government', *Comparative Political Studies*, 10.1 (April 1977), pp. 91–126.

6   For a clear formulation of the world-car strategy, see Marina von Neumann Whitman, 'Automobiles: Turning Around on a Dime?' *Challenge*, 24 (May–June 1981), pp. 37–39.

7   For a survey of the fate of neo-corporatist arrangements as of the early 1980s, see John Goldthorpe, ed., *Order and Conflict in Contemporary Capitalism* (Oxford: Clarendon Press, 1984); and Robert J. Flanagan, David Soskice and Lloyd Ulman, *Unionism, Economic Stabilization, and Incomes Policy: European Experience* (Washington, DC: The Brookings Institutions, 1983).

8   For shifting views of the world-car strategy within the American automobile industry, see John Wormald, 'The World Car: Lessons of an Evolutionary Manufacturing Process', *Outlook*, 8 (1985), pp. 12–18. *Outlook* is the journal of the consulting firm Booz-Allen & Hamilton, New York.

9   See, for example, on banking and computer software, Sarah Kuhn, 'From Back Office to the Front Lines: The Computer Software Development Labor Process in a Changing Business Environment', unpublished PhD dissertation, Department of Urban Studies and Planning, MIT, Cambridge, MA, May 1987.

10   Arnaldo Bagnasco, *Tre Italie: La problematica territoriale dello sviluppo italiano* (Bologna: Il Mulino, 1977).

11   Angelo M. Michelsons, 'Turin between Fordism and Flexible Specialization', unpublished PhD dissertation, University of Cambridge, 1986; M. L. Bianco and A. Luciano, *La sindrome di Archimede* (Bologna: Il Mulino, 1982).

12 Giuseppe Berta and Angelo M. Michelsons, 'Olivetti' in Marino Regini and Charles F. Sabel, eds, *Strategie di flessibilità: Imprese, sindecati, governi locali* (forthcoming).

13 Gioacchino Garofoli, 'I sistemi produttivi in Lombardia: Meccanismi di funzionamento e politiche di intervento', in U. Leone, ed. *La rivalorizzazione territoriale in Italia* (Milano: Franco Angeli, 1986), pp. 83–110.

14 Serious scrutiny of the diffusion of these industrial systems to the South of Italy is just beginning. See Marcello Messori, 'Sistemi di imprese e svilluppo meridionale', unpublished paper, Program in Science, Technology and Society, MIT, Cambridge, MA, 1987.

15 Peer Hull Kristensen, 'Udkanternes industrielle miljo', unpublished manuscript, Copenhagen, 1987; P. Hartoft-Nielsen, *Den regionale erhverstruktur og Beskæftigelsudvikling* (Copenhagen: Landvistkommisionens Sekretariat, 1980).

16 See Bengt Ake Gustafsson, 'Kultur for entreprenorskap' in Bengt Johannison and Olav R. Spilling, ed, *Lokalnaeringsutvikling* (Oslo: Universitetsforlaget, 1982), pp. 79–96.

17 On the textile-machinery industry as a typical example of industrial organization in Baden-Württemberg see Charles F. Sabel, et al., 'How to Keep Mature Industries Innovative', *Technology Review* 90.3 (April 1987), pp. 26–35.

18 See AnnaLee Saxenian, 'Silicon Valley and Route 128: Regional Prototypes or Historical Exceptions?' in Manuel Castells, ed., *High Technology, Space and Society* (Beverly Hills, CA: Sage, 1985), pp. 81–105.

19 See, for example, the excellent study, Michael Storper and Susan Christopherson, 'Flexible Specialization and Regional Agglomerations: The Case of the US Motion Picture Industry', *Annals of the Association of American Geographers* (March 1987), pp. 104–17.

20 E. W. Soya and A. J. Scott, 'Los Angeles: Capital of the Late Twentieth Century', *Society and Space* (September 1986).

21 David Friedman, *The Misunderstood Miracle: Politics and Economic Decentralization in Japan* (Ithaca, NY: Cornell University Press, forthcoming).

22 Marie-Françoise Raveyre and Jean Saglio, 'Les systemes industriels localisés: éléments pour une analyse sociologique des ensembles de PME industriels', *Sociologie du travail*, 2 (1984), pp. 157–77.

23 Jean Saglio with the collaboration of Pierre Garrouste, Marie-Françoise Raveyre, and Geraldine Richoilley, 'Relations professionelles, strategies économiques et innovations technologiques dans les ensembles de PME,' Groupe Lyonnais de Sociologie Industrielle, Lyons, n.d.

24 Ma Theresa Costa Campi and Joan Trullen Thomas, 'Decentramiento productivo y difusión industrial', unpublished manuscript, Universidad de Barcelona and Universidad Autonoma de Barcelona, 1987.

25 For the most comprehensive and careful recent effort, see Werner Sengenberger and Gary Loveman, 'Smaller Units of Employment: A Synthesis Report on Industrial Reorganization in Industrialized Countries', Discussion Paper, International Institute for Labour Studies, Geneva, 1987.

26   Lothar Spaeth, *Wende in die Zukunft* (Hamburg: Rowohlt, 1986).

27   Chris Hull, 'Making Small Firms Grow: German Final Report', International Institute of Management, West Berlin, May, 1985.

28   Hans-Jürgen Ewers and Josef Klein, 'The Interregional Diffusion of New Processes in the German Mechanical Engineering Industry', Discussion Paper IIM/IP 83-2, International Institute of Management, West Berlin, January, 1983.

29   On the background of Italian developments see Charles F. Sabel, *Work and Politics* (New York: Cambridge University Press, 1982), pp. 145-67 and 220-1, which indicate further references.

30   A typical celebration of the new entrepreneuralism, which nevertheless casts interesting light on its unexpected communitarian aspects in Everett M. Rogers and Judith K. Larsen, *Silicon Valley Fever: Growth of High-Technology Culture* (New York: Basic Books, 1984).

31   Friedman, *The Misunderstood Miracle*.

32   Arnaldo Bagnasco and Rosella Pini, *Sviluppo economico e trasformazione sociopoltiche dei sistemi territoriali a economica diffusa*, Quaderni Fondazione Giangiacomo Feltrineilli 14 (Milan: Feltrinelli, 1981) especially Table 4.1b, p. 105 (for wage data), and Table 3.9, p. 54 (for investment data).

33   This view, held widely in Prato and Carpi, was confirmed by textile-machinery producers whom Gary Herrigel and I interviewed in Baden-Württemberg in July 1986.

34   Friedman, *The Misunderstood Miracle*.

35   Ewers and Klein, 'The Interregional Diffusion'.

36   Arnaldo Bagnasco, 'La costruzione sociale del mercato: strategie di impresa e esperimenti di scala in Italia' *Stato e mercato*, 13 (April 1985), pp. 9-45.

37   Michael Contarino, 'The Politics of Industrial Change: Textile Unions and Industrial Restructuring in Five Italian Localities', unpublished PhD dissertation, Department of Government, Harvard University, May 1984.

38   Rudiger Selt and Eckart Hildebrandt, 'Production, Politik, und Kontrolle - Arbeitpolitische Varianten am Beispiel der Einführung von Productionsplanung and Steuerungssystemen im Machinenbau' in Frieder Naschhold, ed., *Arbeit und Politik* (Frankfurt am Main: Campus, 1986), pp. 91-125.

39   Arnaldo Bagnasco and Carlo Triglia, eds, *Società e politica nelle aree di piccola impremsa. Il caso del Valdesa* (Milan: Franco Angeli, 1985), pp. 462-4.

40   'Die Armel hochkrempelt. Baden-Württemberg ein Jahr nach dem Streik', *Frankfurter Allgemeine Zeitung*, 22 August 1985, p. 11.

41   See Carlo Triglia, 'Il caso di Prato' and Paolo Perulli 'Il distretto industriale di Modena' in Regini and Sabel, *Strategie di flessibilità*.

42   Saglio, 'Relations professionelles', p. 17.

43   Sabel et al., 'Keeping Mature Industries Innovative', pp. 30-4.

44   See Perulli, 'Il distretto industriate di Modena'.

45 Sabel et al., 'How to Keep Mature Industries Innovative', p. 32.
46 Interviews conducted by the author and Gary Herrigel with indus-
    trialists, bankers, and officials of the *Land* from several ministries, July
    1986.
47 Fiorenza Belussi, 'Benetton: Information Technology in Production
    and Distribution: A Case Study of the Innovative Potential of Tradi-
    tional Sectors', Occasional Paper Series, no. 25, Science Policy Research
    Unit, University of Sussex, 1987.
48 Triglia, 'Il caso di Prato', pp. 6–7.
49 For an excellent study of the vitality of small manufacturing firms in
    traditional sectors in Massachusetts, see Peter B. Doeringer, David G.
    Terrkla, and Gary Topakian, 'Crossing the Post-Maturity Frontier:
    Specialization, Product Cycles, and Other Invisible Factors in Local
    Economic Development', Institute for Employment Policy, Boston
    University, Boston, October 1986.
50 Triglia, 'Il caso di Prato'.
51 Michael Storper and Susan Christopherson, 'Flexible Specialization and
    New Forms of Labor Market Segmentation: The United States Motion
    Picture Industry', unpublished paper, Graduate School of Architecture
    and Urban Planning and Department of Geography, University of
    California, Los Angeles, January 1987.
52 On, for example, the fragmentation of the capital-goods producers in the
    American semi-conductor industry, and their uncertain relations with
    their customers, see Jay Stowsky, 'The Weakest link: 'Semiconductor
    Production Equipment, Linkages, and the Limits to International
    Trade', Working Paper, Berkeley Round Table on the International
    Economy, Berkeley, August 1987.
53 Lauren A. Benton, 'The Role of the Informal Sector in Economic
    Development: Industrial Restructuring in Spain' unpublished PhD
    dissertation, Department of Anthropology, Johns Hopkins University,
    Baltimore, MD, 1986.
54 See the excellent study, William H. Sewell, Jr, *Work and Revolution in
    France* (New York: Cambridge University Press, 1980).
55 Friedman, *The Misunderstood Miracle.*
56 Bagnasco, 'La costruzione sociale del mercato'.
57 Piore and Sabel, *The Second Industrial Divide.*
58 Seltz and Hildebrandt, 'Production, Politik und Kontrolle'.
59 These questions have been provoked by discussions with Luc Boltanski
    and Laurent Thevenot. See their *Les Economies de la grandeur* (Paris:
    Presses Universitaires de France, 1988).
60 Oliver B. Williamson, *Markets and Hierarchies, Analysis and Antitrust
    Implications: A Study in the Economics of Internal Organization* (New York:
    Free Press, 1975).
61 See Oliver E. Williamson and William G. Ouchi, 'The Markets
    and Hierarchies Program of Research: Origins, Implications, Prospects'
    in Andrew Van de Ven and William Joyce, eds, Perspectives on

Organizational Design and Behaviour (New York: Wiley, 1981); William G. Ouchi, 'Markets, Bureaucracies, and Clans', *Administrative Science Quarterly*, vol. 25 (March 1980), pp. 120–42; and Oliver E. Williamson, *The Economic Institutions of Capitalism: Firms, Markets, Relational Contracting* (New York: The Free Press, 1985).

62   Michael Hannan and John Freeman, 'The Population Ecology of Organizations', *American journal of Sociology*, 82 (1977), pp. 929–64.

63   Sanford Grossman, Oliver Hart, 'The Losses and Benefits of Ownership; A Theory of Vertical and Lateral Integration', *Journal of Political Economy*, 94.4 (1986), pp. 691–719.

64   Jan Johanson and Lars-Gunnar Mattson, 'Interorganizational Relations in Industrial Systems: A Network Approach Compared with the Transaction-Cost Approach', *International Studies of Management and Organization*, 17 (Spring 1987), pp. 34–48.

65   Except as otherwise noted, the following contrast between old- and new-model corporations is based on interviews with managers in American, West German, and Italian multinationals between 1985 and 1987. The firms are regarded as innovative leaders of the motor car, automotive parts, chemical, machine-tool, telecommunications, computer, and food-processing industries. Many features of the new-model corporation have been described in management journals. See, for example, the following articles in the *Harvard Business Review*: Arnold O. Putnam, 'A Redesign of Engineering', 3 (May–June 1985), pp. 139–44; J. L. Bower and E. A. Rhenman, 'Benevolent Cartels', 4 (July–August 1985), pp. 124–32; D. N. Burnt and W. R. Soulcup, 'Purchasing's Role in New Product Development', 5 (September–October 1985), pp. 90–97; and, more synthetically, Hirotaka Takeuchi and Ikujiro Nonaka, 'The New Product Development Game', 1 (January–February 1986), pp. 137–46.

66   On the changing organization of corporate research and development, see John Frian and Mel Horwitch, 'The Emergence of Technology Strategy', *Technology in Society*, 7 (1985), pp. 143–78; and on the rise and fall of stregic planning, see Mel Horwitch, *Post-Modern Management: Its Emergence and Meaning for Strategy* (New York: Free Press, forthcoming).

67   This view of subcontracting has obvious affinities with Granovetter's view of 'weak' – frequent but not exclusive – social ties as a means of spreading information in labour markets. Familiarity facilitates co-operation; autonomy allows each partner to learn from the other's experiences. The expansion of network systems, and hence innovative capacity, is self-reinforcing in the same way as job mobility, 'The more different social and work settings one moves through, the larger the reservoir of contacts he has who may mediate further mobility'. Mark S. Granovetter, *Getting a Job: A Study of Contacts and Careers* (Cambridge, MA: Harvard University Press, 1974), p. 85.

68   Lorenzo Bordogna, 'Il caso del petrochimico Montedison di Ferrara' in Regini and Sabel, eds, *Strategie di flessibilità*.

69 Joel Cutcher-Gershenfeld, 'The Collective Governance of Industrial Relations', unpublished PhD Dissertation, Alfred P. Sloan School of Management, MIT, Cambridge, MA, November, 1987.

70 Stephen Herzenberg, John Chalykoff, and Joel Cutcher-Gershenfeld, 'But Does the Union Get the Management it Deserves?', unpublished paper, Department of Economics, MIT, Cambridge, MA, February, 1987, pp. 13–19.

71 Ann Lee Saxenian, personal communication, February 1988.

72 Interview with Horst Sandvoss, Purchasing Director, Robert Bosch GmbH, Gerlingen-Schillerhöhe, 10 July 1986. For that matter, the system might be the Olivetti model, since that firm publicly follows identical principles. See the interview with Eliserino Poi, Head of the Office of General Strategy and Development, Olivetti, in *Industria Oggi*, 4 (March 1987), pp. 60–1. For a discussion of incipient tendencies in this direction in large French firms, see M. F. Raveyre, 'Une première approche du dispositif d'aide aux PME de Saint-Gobain Développement'. Groupe Lyonnais de Sociologie Industrielle, September, 1986, p. 43. For an overview of emerging subcontracting practices in the USA as an indicator of the changing relations between large and small firms, see *Electronics Purchasing*, special issue on *How Industry Buys Electronics*, 1987, and various numbers and special issues of its sister publication, *Purchasing Magazine*.

73 For an account of 'flexible mass manufacturing', see Michael J. Piore, 'Corporate Reform in American Manufacturing and the Challenge to Economic Theory', paper presented to the Conference on the Economics of Organization and Management, Yale School of Management, New Haven, CT, 24–25 October 1986.

74 Toshiro Nishiguchi, 'Competing Systems of Automotive Supply: An Examination of the Japanese "Clustered Control" Model and the "Alps" Model', paper prepared for the First Policy Forum, MIT International Motor Vehicle Program, Niagra-on-the-Lake, Canada, 5 May 1987, pp. 10–12.

75 Masayoshi Ikeda, 'An International Comparison of Subcontracting Systems in The Automotive Components Manufacturing Industry', paper prepared for the First Policy Forum, MIT International Motor Vehicle Program, Niagara-on-the-Lake, Canada, 5 May 1987; idem, 'The Japanese Auto Component Manufacturer's System for the Division of Production', Briefing Paper for the MIT Internal Motor Vehicles Program, 1987; idem, 'Small and Medium-sized Firms: Evolution of the Japanese subcontracting System', *Tradescope*, vol. 7, no. 7 (July 1987), pp. 2–6; idem, 'Production Network of Big Firms and Smaller Subcontractors in Japan', paper submitted to *Euro-Asian Business Review*, INSEAD, Paris, March, 1987.

76 Masahiko Aoki, 'Innovative Adaptation Through the Quasi-Tree Structure', cited – incorrectly – in Alexis Jacquemin, *The New Industrial Organization* (Cambridge, MA: MIT Press, 1987), pp. 150–1.

77 Nishiguchi, 'Competing Systems of Automobile Supply', p. 31.
78 Gary B. Herrigel, 'The Political Economy of Industry', paper prepared for 'The Case of the West German Machine-Tool Industry' in Peter Katzenstein, ed., *Industrial and Political Change in West Germany* (Ithaca, NY: Cornell University Press, forthcoming).
79 The rationalisation of the region as an administrative unit and the creation of regional economic development programmes from the 1950s until the 1970s intertwined in various complex ways in different countries depending on their constitutional history and the ways reform could alter the balance of local and national power. See, for example, on the UK, F. D. Lindley, 'The Framework of Regional Planning, 1964-1980' in Brian W. Hodgewood and Michael Keating, eds, *Regional Government in England* (Oxford: Clarendon Press, 1982), pp. 169-90; On France, J. C. Thoenig, 'Local Government Institutions and the Contemporary Evolution of French Society' in Jacques Lagraye and Vincent Wright, eds, *Local Government – Britain and France: Problems and Prospects* (London: George Allen & Unwin, 1979), pp. 74-104.
80 An excellent, historically sophisticated elaboration of the new development doctrines is Dieter Senghaas, *The European Experience* trans. by K. H. Kimmig (Leamington Spa and Dover, NH: Berg, 1985).
81 For a good review of this literature, see John B. Parr, 'Growth Poles, Regional Development, and Central Place Theory', *Papers of the Regional Science Association*, 31, 1973, pp. 173-212. A survey of findings on this topic and an excellent account of changing perceptions of regional development is Friederike Maier, 'Beschäftigungspolitik vor Ort: Die Politik der Kleinen Schritte, unpublished PhD dissertation, Department of Political Science. Freie Universtität Berlin, November 1987.
82 'Alternative Regional Strategy: A Framework for Discussion', Parliamentary Spokesman's Working Group, September 1982, p. 10.
83 Roger Vaughan, Robert Pollard, and Barbara Dyer, *The Wealth of States: Policies for a Dynamic Economy* (Washington, DC: SPA, 1984), pp. xi.
84 Ibid., pp. v-vii.
85 For a discussion of these problems in relation to job-creation programmes in, for example, Hamburg in the early 1980s, see Kurt Wand, 'Beschäftingungspolitische Initiativen in der nord-deutschen Küstenregion', unpublished manuscript, GEWOS, Hamburg, January 1984.
86 For an account of the French reforms, see Yves Meny, 'Local Authorities and Economic Policy' in Howard Machin and Vincent Wright, eds, *Economic Policy and Policy-Making Under the Mitterand Presidency, 1981-1984* (London: Frances Pinter, 1985), pp. 187-99; for a discussion of the Socialists' goals at the time, Dominique Schmitt, ed., *La Region à l'heure de la decentralisation. Notes et études documentaires* (Paris: La Documentation Française, 1985).
87 For the history and structuring principles of the JTPA, see Robert Gutman, 'Job Training Partnership Act: New Help for the Unemployed', *Monthly Labor Review*, 106 (March 1983), pp. 3-7.

88 For a survey of West German labour-market policy in the 1970s and early 1980s, see Gunther Schmid, 'Arbeitsmarktpolitik in Schweden und in der Bundesrepublik' in Fritz W. Scharpf et al., eds, *Aktive Arbeitsmarktpolitik. Erfahrungen und neu Wege* (Frankfurt am Main: Campus, 1982), pp. 29–62.

89 Per H. Jensen, 'Arbeidsloshedspolitiken i sverige' and Henning Jorgensen, 'Muligheder og grænsninger for regionaliseret arbeismarkedsog geskaeftigelsespolitik' both in Henning Jorgensen and Jens. Chr. Tonboe, eds, *Fagbevægelse, stat, og kommuner* (Aalborg: Aalborg Universitetsforlag, 1985), pp. 77–102 and 138–83, respectively.

90 For a lapidary statement of the new orthodoxy and a good sample of the research, out of which it grows and to which it contributes, see David Keeble and Egbert Wever, eds, *New Firms and Regional Development in Europe* (London: Croom Helm, 1986). A critical view is Ernst A. Brugger, ' "Endogene Entwicklung": Ein Konzept zwischen Utopie und Realität', *Information zur Raumentwicklung*, 1–2 (1984), pp. 1–19.

91 Michael Keating 'Comment' on Meny, 'Local Authorities and Economic Policy', in Machin and Wright, *Economic Policy and Policy Making*, pp. 200–4.

92 Franz Summer, *Das VOEST Debakel* (Vienna: Orac, 1987).

93 Hull, 'Making Small Firms Grow'.

94 See Albrecht Goeschel, 'Krankenkassen Kommunalkörperschaften und Regionalwirtschaft, *Die Ortskrankenkasse*, no. 1 (1985), pp. 12–19.

95 Dicussions with government officials, trade unionists, and industrialists participating in the Machine Action Project (Springfield) and the Needle Trades Action Project (Fall River), 1987. Both projects are part of the CRIL programme. One of the few studies of emerging inter-firm relations in the state metalworking industry is Sacha Page, 'Massachusetts' Policy Toward Changing Business Relationships in the Metalworking Industry', unpublished manuscript, Kennedy School of Government, February 1988.

96 Discussions from 1984 to the present with Jack Russell, founder of the Auto-In-Michigan (AIM) project, and other initiatives currently addressing these problems.

97 Didier Salvadori, 'Le financement des systèmes productifs régionaux', *Revue d'économie industrielle*, vol. 35, no. 1 (1986), pp. 127–41.

98 For an example of new localists' attention to the complexities of tax reform in relation to their programmes, see A. Drack, 'Kommunale Steuerreform und dezentrale Autonomie' in U. Bullman and P. Gitschman, eds, *Kommune als Gegenmacht* (Hamburg: VSA, 1985), pp. 130–45.

99 For an excellent discussion of Italian debates on this subject, see Marzio Barbagli, Vittorio Capecchi and Antonio Cobalti, *La mobilità sociale in Emilia-Romagna* (Bologna: Il Mulino, 1988), especially Chapter 3.

100 For a synthesis of the literature on Danish agrarian structure in relation to the formation of the artisan classes, see Peer Hull Kristensen and

Charles F. Sabel, 'The Agrarian Background of the Small-Holders' Republic', unpublished paper, Program in Science, Technology, and Society, MIT, Cambridge, MA, September 1987.

101 Klaus Megerle, *Württemberg im Industrialisierungsprozess Deutschlands* (Stuttgart: Klett-Cotta, 1982), pp. 71–150, 197–242.

102 This view of the possible convergence of real and fictive kinship ties as the foundation of industrial structure arose in conversation with Michael Storper.

103 Barbagli et al., *La mobilità sociale in Emilia-Romagna*, Chapter 3.

104 Alain Cottereau, 'Justice et injustice ordinaire sur les lieux de travail d'après les audiences prud'homales (1806–1866)', *Le Mouvement social*, 141 (October–December 1987), pp. 25–59. The phrase 'quasi-legislature' is from p. 51.

105 Kristensen and Sebel, 'The Agrarian Background'.

106 J. J. Lee, 'Labor in German Industrialization' in M. M. Postan, D. C. Coleman, and Peter Mathias, eds, *The Cambridge Economic History of Europe vol. vii, pt I* (New York: Cambridge University Press, 1978), pp. 442–90, especially pp. 453–71. See, for a comparison with France, Jürgen Schriewer; 'Intermediäre Instanzen, Selbstverwaltung und berufliche Vergleich', *Zeitschrift für Pädegogik*, 32.1 (1986), pp. 69–113; For Baden-Württemberg, see Hermann Schindler, *Die Routlinger Wirtschaft von der Mitte des neunzehnten Jahrhunderts bis zum Beginn des Ersten Weltkrieges* (Tübingen: J. C. B. Mohr, 1969), especially pp. 13–30.

107 Kristensen and Sabel, 'The Agrarian Background'.

108 Rudolph Boch, *Handwerker-Sozialisten gegen Fabrikgesellschaft. Lokale Fachvereine, Massengewerkschaft und industrielle Rationalisierung in Solingen 1870 bis 1914* (Göttingen: Vandenhoeck & Ruprecht, 1985).

109 On the decline of Sheffield see Sidney Pollard, *A History of Labour in Sheffield* (Liverpool: Liverpool University Press, 1959), pp. 65–77, 134–58; and G. I. H. Lloyd, *The Cutlery Trades* (London: Longmans, Green and Co, 1913), pp. 199–200, 348–9.

110 See Carlo Triglia, *Grandi partiti e piccole imprese. Communisti e democristiani nelle regioni a economia diffusa* (Bologna: Il Mulino, 1986), especially pp. 133–205; and on the decade of conflict between the textile unions and the small firms, idem. 'Il caso di Prato' especially p. 18. The Ilongot headhunters of northern Luzon in the Philippines provide a dramatic case of such negotiated forgetfulness. When their blood feuds threaten the survival of their tribes, the aggrieved parties reinterpret their kin relations so that insults exchanged by their ancestors do not require murders of the descendants. See Renato Rosaldo, *Ilongot Headhunting, 1883–1974: A Study in Society and History* (Stanford CA: Stanford University Press, 1980).

111 See, for example, the discussion of American practices in Piore and Sabel, *The Second Industrial Divide*, pp. 111–20.

112 Seltz and Hildebrandt, 'Production, Politik, und Kontrolle', especially pp. 102–3.

113 Peer Hull Kristensen, *Teknologiske projekter og organisatoriske processer* (Roskilde: Forlaget Samenfundsokonomi og Planlægning, 1986), pp. 414–16.

114 Contarino, 'The Politics of Industrial Change'.

115 Richard M. Locke, 'Redrawing the Boundaries of Italian Union Politics', paper presented to the American Political Science Association, Chicago, August, 1987.

116 John Krafcik, 'Learning from NUMI', Internal Working Paper, MIT International Motor Vehicle Program, Cambridge, MA, September, 1986. 1986.

117 See 'Die andere Obersteiermark', *Trend*, 1 (1987), pp. 96–101; Hans Glatz and Hans Moser, 'Innovationsorientierte Regionalpolitik Förderungsmoglichkeiten von kleinen und mittleren Unternehmen in der Obersteiermark', Institut für Höhere Studien, Vienna, February, 1987.

118 Gernot Grabher, 'Betriebliche Reorganisation in einer traditionellen Industrieregion Theoretische Grundlagen und empirische Ergebnisse für die Region Wr. Neustadt/Neukirchen', unpublished PhD dissertation, Department of Urban Studies, University of Vienna, 1987.

119 Ida Regalia, 'Processi di riaggiustamento nell'area di Sesto S. Giovanni' in Regini and Sabel, *Strategie di flessibilità*.

120 The classic reference is Stanley Bernard Mathewson, *Restriction of Output Among Unorganized Workers* (Carbondale: University of Southern Illinois Press, 1969; first published in 1931 by Viking Press, New York).

121 For a recent game theoretic exposition of this view see Robert M. Axlerod, *The Evolution of Cooperation* (New York: Basic Books, 1984). The clearest general formulation of this position is Arthur L. Stinchcombe, 'Norms of Exchange' in *Stratification and Organization* (Cambridge: Cambridge University Press, 1986), pp. 231–67. His key argument is that 'there are a lot of paths to complex normative developments in which an evolutionary sequence of Pareto-rational movements exists. In short, the pre-contractual element of contract can perfectly well be a previous contract.'

122 George A. Akerlof, 'Labor Contracts as Partial Gift Exchanges', *Quarterly Journal of Economics*, 97 (November 1982), pp. 543–69.

123 For a theory which generalised from these cases, see Alexander Gerschenkron, *Economic Backwardness in Historical Perspective* (Cambridge MA: Harvard University Press, 1966). A review of the criticism of the argument is Clive Trebilcock, *The Industrialization of the Continental Powers, 1780–1914* (London: Longman, 1981), especially pp. 403–25.

124 See, for example, Alice M. Amsden, 'The State and Taiwan's Development' in Peter Evans et al., eds, *Bringing the State Back In* (Cambridge: Cambridge University Press, 1985), pp. 78–106.

125 Interviews with managers of Trumpf GmbH and Co., Stuttgart, July 1986.

126 On Keynes's plan and its opponents, see Fred L. Block, *The Origins of*

International Economic Disorder (Berkeley: University Of California Press, 1977), pp. 1–108.

127   For a survey see Douglas Yuill, Kevin Allen, and Chris Hull, eds, *Regional Policy in the European Community* (New York: St Martin's Press, 1980).

128   On the intricate interregional links among *kibbutzim* belonging to the same political groupings, see Bernd Biervert and Beate Finis, 'Zur Bestandssicherung des Kibbutz als relativ autonomes, offenes sozialsystem in einer kapitalistischen Umwelt', *Archiv für öffentliche und freigemeinnützige Unternehmen*, 14 (1985), pp. 1–19. For an overview of these extremely complex debates, see Jorgensen and Tonboe, *Fagbevægelse, stat, og kommuner*. On the rise of flexible technologies on the kibbutzim, see Menachem Rosner, 'New Technologies in the Kibbutzim', *Jerusalem Quarterly*, 39 (1986), pp. 82–9.

129   Jorgensen and Tonboe, *Fagbevægelse, stat, og kommuner*.

130   Charles Perrow, *Normal Accidents: Living with High-Risk Technologies* (New York: Basic Books, 1984).

5

A New Paradigm of Work Organization and Technology?

John Tomaney

INTRODUCTION

This chapter critically examines the claim, advanced from various quarters, that fundamental changes have occurred in the organization of work and production over recent years in the industrialized countries. The aim is to assess whether *new* principles underlie the reorganization of work in the present period and whether the changes described amount to a fundamental reorganization of the labour process as well as guaranteeing a new and better deal for labour.

Three main positions are evaluated, each of which anticipates the rise of more benign forms of production organization and labour practices in the post-mass production ('post-Fordist') economy. They are: the theory of flexible specialization; claims concerning the 'Japanization' of industry; and the debate surrounding the alleged emergence of 'new production concepts' in Germany. I suggest that the evidence for a new organizing principle of work and production is flawed: while certain changes can be identified these are less dramatic than implied by this 'new orthodoxy'. Rather than representing a radical break, they tend, in many cases, to represent an intensification of existing tendencies. However, the general context for developments in the advanced capitalist world has been a shift in the balance of power in the workplace and in the labour market in favour of employers rather than workers. This has a crucial influence on the pattern of change and one that 'new optimists' generally neglect.

My argument is that the changes identified by the 'new optimists' express many possibilities, including the continuity of elements of Fordism. Trajectories of workplace change, it is argued, cannot be understood simply as a product of new technological and organizational developments, but are conditioned by deeply embedded traditions of industrial practice, which are themselves the product of specific histories and geographies.

TAYLORISM AND ITS CRITICS

During the 1970s debates over workplace change were concerned largely with the perceived growing dominance of Taylorist methods of industrial organization and control, which were based on the separation of conception and execution and extreme task fragmentation. What was remarkable about this debate was the extent to which it influenced discussion in almost all the advanced industrial countries. Perhaps the key text in this debate was Braverman's (1974) *Labor and Monopoly Capital*. For Braverman, Taylorism extended managerial control and allowed the speed-up of work with its search for the 'one best way' of work simplification through the rigid separation of manual and mental functions. Under monopoly capitalism, Taylorist scientific management secured a dominant position in management ideology and was seen as the characteristic form of production organization. Braverman saw Taylorism as representing the unfolding of capitalist rationality in the work process.

However, Braverman's position was much criticized. He was accused of romanticizing a past craft idyll and failing to recognize that management balanced the extension of control with the need to win consent and cooperation from the workforce (e.g. Burawoy, 1979, 1985). Critics argued that Taylorism was not the only means of workplace organization (Friedman, 1977). Marxists criticized Braverman for implying that capital, through its domination of the labour process, had secured complete control over society, pointing out that the rise of social democracy had been important in securing working class political assent in the advanced capitalist societies (Elger, 1979).

Today, however, a 'new orthodoxy . . . seems set to dominate the sociology of industry and organizations' (Hyman, 1988, p. 48); one which suggests a very different analysis and vision of the labour process. In contrast to the approach which sees 'deskilling' as a universal and immutable expression of the logic of capitalist development, the new orthodoxy sees the principles of 'scientific management' established earlier in the twentieth century as a contingent response to historically specific circumstances. This 'new orthodoxy', celebrating such concepts as craft and flexibility, suggests that a new organizing principle is emerging. It proposes that 'old' forms of work and production based on 'Taylorist' and 'Fordist' forms of control are increasingly counterposed to 'new' flexible work patterns characterized by loosened (or even abandoned) central managerial control of the labour process. In some accounts these new forms of work and production are ascribed liberating powers for labour and in others they are linked to wider processes of societal transformation. In most cases changes in skills and work patterns are linked to changes in production technologies, contributing to 'the popular impression . . . that the introduction of microelectronics will improve the quality of work in manufacturing industry (Dankbaar, 1988a, p. 25). It is the elements of the argument proposed by the new orthodoxy which are outlined and criticized in this chapter.

FLEXIBLE SPECIALIZATION AND THE RE-EMERGENCE OF CRAFT WORK

The theory of flexible specialization originally developed by Piore and Sabel (e.g. Sabel, 1982; Piore and Sabel, 1984), has gained a pervasive influence over Anglo-American debates concerning the nature of contemporary industrial change, to the degree that some writers see it as the centrepiece of the new orthodoxy described above (Hyman, 1988, 1991). According to Piore and Sabel the advanced industrial societies are witnessing the emergence of a new form of industrial organization which is altering all facets of economic activity, including the nature of markets, relations between firms and relations between industry and the state. Central are changes alleged to be occurring in the organization of work itself, and in the relations between capital and labour; changes in the direction of more skilled, more humane, more flexible and more efficient working practices based around the potentialities of both revitalized craft practices and advanced manufacturing technologies.

For Piore and Sabel the present is a period of breakdown of the hitherto dominant system of Fordist mass production – a system based on the production of long runs of standardized commodities for stable 'mass' markets, and involving the progressive erosion of craft skills and the growing demand for unskilled or semi-skilled operatives. The breakdown is attributed to the saturation and subsequent disintegration of the markets for mass produced goods. With the rise of increasingly differentiated and segmented markets combined with more discriminating consumer tastes, the rigidity of mass production methods in their dedication to the production of standardized commodities has been exposed.

Sabel identified the re-emergence of craft forms of production in the networks of small 'artisan' firms of central Italy. The experience of these clusters of Italian small firms was later taken as evidence of the birth of a new organizing principle in industrial production – 'flexible specialization' – wherein craft production is replacing mass production as the industrial paradigm (Piore and Sabel, 1984, p. 206). While craft production was 'marginalized' during the ascendancy of mass production (the first industrial divide), Piore and Sabel (1984, p. 205) now identify 'the re-emergence of the craft paradigm amidst the crisis' and argue that capitalist societies stand abridge a 'second industrial divide', where the possibility exists for a new phase of industrial development based on these principles.

Parallel changes, which Piore (1990) describes as 'analogous' to those occuring in the small firms sector, are identified in large-scale industries. As Sabel (1989) puts it, the industrial structures of large firms and industrial districts are 'converging'. For instance, in the car industry mass production methods are said to be giving way to flexible specialization, where firms are increasingly engaged in the manufacture of 'specialized vehicles tailored to meet the needs of particular consumer groups', with a tendency for specialized goods to be produced by means of general purpose machines – 'broadly skilled workers using capital equipment that can make various models' (Katz and Sabel, 1985, pp. 297–8). This new labour requirement compels firms to offer job security as an inducement to workers to acquire the company-specific skills associated with new technology, leading to 'a preoccupation with the reorganization of industrial relations and the redistribution of rights within the factory' (Katz and Sabel, 1985, p. 299). Thus: 'Instead of treating labor predominantly as a cost, the company began to consider reform of labor relations as part of flexible production linking new technologies, polyvalent workers, and more specialized products' (Katz and Sabel, 1985, p. 303). The separation of conception and execution, which Braverman saw as inherent under capitalist production, is rescinded under the new forms of production. Similarly, job hierarchies considered characteristic of 'mass production' are said to be disintegrating with the 'decentralisation of power and authority' (Piore, 1990, p. 60). The 'return' to craft is deemed to be inherently beneficial for labour even if labour is not organized:

> Thus the production worker's intellectual participation in the work processes is enhanced and his or her role revitalized. Moreover, craft

production depends on solidarity and communitarianism. Given these conditions of working life in craft production, there is a case for preferring it to mass production, regardless of the place accorded to unions within craft production. *(Piore and Sabel, 1984, p. 278)*

A return to craft?

The theory of flexible specialization is an ambitious one. It seeks to explain changes in markets, state activity and the geography of production as well as changes in the organization of work and industrial relations. The discussion below, however, is restricted to claims concerned with the workplace.

One area of doubt about the trend to flexible specialization concerns claims about the diminishing importance of scale economies. On the basis of a theoretical and empirical review Coriat (1991) questions the idea that flexible specialization will 'replace' mass production. In particular, he criticizes the notion that economies of scope (the ability to shift cost-efficiently from the production of one good to another) are triumphing over those that draw on economies of scale:

> Where output is increasing everything depends on the relative importance of scale of specific products and the economies of scope. Once the former are larger and greater than the second it will be more efficient to produce in two specific plants with longer runs the two joint products formerly made with a flexible technology. In practice – and it is the empirical argument with which one can oppose Piore and Sabel – firms in sectors with increasing demand really do adopt strategies that involve a search for scale economies and the cost reductions that scale economies allow. *(Coriat, 1991, p. 150)*

It seems likely that the proponents of flexible specialization overstate the flexibility of the new technologies. The costs recommissioning for model changeover remain high and, as Williams et al. (1987, p. 430) note: 'Robots cannot be re-programmed for new models by pressing a few buttons. That is a myth.' Such costs can be borne only by the largest companies and require a large scale of production. According to Williams et al., the more likely trend established by the introduction of flexible manufacturing systems (FMS) is for batch production to become more capital intensive. However, whatever variety is planned for, it remains crucial to obtain volumes that guarantee high rates of capacity utilization, given the high fixed costs of FMS.

It seems clear that where advanced production technology is being introduced often it involves large-scale investment in new computer controlled production technologies, the general character of which is different from that suggested by the flexible specialization thesis. Wood (1989), for instance, drawing from evidence from the Massachusetts Institute of Technology study (Altshuler et al., 1984) into the future of the automobile industry, found that managers tended to stress the use of technology in the improvement of quality and the enhancement of central coordination and control of the production process. In the car industry, new technology appears to be used mainly for reducing bottlenecks, production volumes and programming flexibility within existing capital installations. In general, it seems that computerization of mass production processes facilitates an improved control and integration of the labour process rather than rapid product switches. Similarly, Murray (1983, p. 88) in an earlier study of the Bologna engineering industry, suggested that systems such as computer-aided manufacturing were being used in a way 'that ensures the maximum saturation and coordination of labour time'.[1]

Within the flexible specialization thesis, in addition to the limited priority given to the enduring importance of scale economies, the computer is endowed with a questionable emancipatory potential. This view of the possibilities of the computer is used to support a view of craft work which echoes that of Braverman:

> The computer is thus a machine that meets Marx's definition of an artisan's tool: it is an instrument that responds to and extends the productive capacity of the user. It is therefore tempting to sum the observations of engineers and ethnographers to the conclusion that technology has ended the dominion of specialised machines over un- and semiskilled workers, and redirected progress down the path of craft production. The advent of the computer restores human control over the production process; machinery is again subordinated to the operator. *(Piore and Sabel, 1984, p. 261)*

Such an analysis fetishises technology and leads to some important gaps in Piore and Sabel's analysis of contemporary change in workplace organization.

Many writers point to the limited nature of much of what passes for 'enskilled' work. This is particularly true of attempts to upgrade semi-skilled work processes in the 'mass production' industries. Case study evidence exists to suggest that the new skilled occupations entail flexibility across a range of what were previously demarcated skills or tasks, what Hyman refers to as 'an expanded portfolio of competences' (quoted in Thompson, 1989, p. 226; see also Elger, 1991, for a review). This may be as true of 'intellectual skills' as of manual ones. Here, in many cases, it seems that the scope and depth of such jobs are often:

'so routinised that they could be picked up easily by other workers' (ibid.). Whether this amounts to 'humanization' or the 're-emergence of craft work' is contentious.

It seems, therefore, that what flexible specialization theory identifies as the emergence of humane, 'enskilled' work might actually signal a more limited, if none the less important, development in mass production industries. A relative shift may be occurring in management's attempt to engage the creative capacities of the workforce. This is related to the introduction of new technology insofar as increased capital intensity leads to a heightened concern with utilization rates. Attempts to engage the workforce in the struggle to improve utilization rates have become significant. But what are the terms on which such innovations are being pursued? According to Thompson, efforts to engage the creative capacities of workers represent 'a highly constrained form of empowerment that is far removed from either of the traditional agendas of industrial democracy or job enrichment. These constraints arise from the subordination of participation within management decision-making processes, efficiency criteria and power relations that have largely remained untouched' (Thompson, 1988, p. 226).

Second, while it is possible that in certain cases technical change may create demand for new kinds of competences which might 'enskill' particular groups of workers, the flexible specialization thesis overlooks the possibility that skilled work too may be subordinated to managerial control. While Braverman postulated the progressive erosion of craft skills ('deskilling') and growing managerial control of the labour process, criticism of his position has tended to point to the continued survival of 'craft' labour processes and the more general capacity of workers to resist managerial initiative (see Elger, 1979; Thompson, 1989, for a review). While Piore and Sabel suggest that the mass production paradigm was characterized by pervasive managerial control (which is a caricature), the absence of managerial control over 'craft work' tends to be assumed rather than demonstrated. In practice, various kinds of labour process will coexist at any one time, characterized by varying levels of managerial control, often reflecting the local balance of forces between management and labour and the particular character of product and processes (Shaiken et al., 1986). Moreover, forms of specialized expertise and craft competence may also be embedded within a complex structure of collective labour effectively subordinated to managerial control.

A third major problem area for the flexible specialization thesis is the neglect of the possibilities of work intensification in contemporary changes. As already seen, attempts to broaden semi-skilled work processes, for instance, may often represent simply a grouping together of several related tasks. Given the limited nature of these changes, important evidence exists to suggest that managements' concern with enskilling is mainly an attempt to intensify work processes. While some grouping together of tasks may reflect changed technical requirements, much of this change is concerned simply with eliminating downtime and waiting time from production processes. This can be achieved by requiring production workers to perform minor maintenance or inspection tasks. Intensification may also underlie attempts to alter craft demarcations. As Shaiken et al. (1986, p. 179) note: 'the classification issue is primarily a battle over the intensity of work'. Apparent tendencies towards more skilled work may be facilitating intensification on a large scale and may, therefore, be a Trojan horse for workers.[2]

In summary, it is possible to identify three major problem areas emerging from flexible specialization theory in its application to changes in the production process. These are: first, the utility of the mass production/flexible specialization dichotomy itself; second, the inability to account for diverse outcomes to the process of restructuring and to deal with the political implications of this; finally, the fact that even where instances of flexible specialization can be identified it does not necessarily have the benefits for labour which they assume.

JAPANIZATION

Japanese manufacturing techniques have exerted a mesmeric hold over the imagination of many British and North American commentators. The competitive success of Japanese manufacturing industry, often at the expense of Western producers, has prompted this heightened interest. Japan has been described as the quintessential 'post-Fordist' society (e.g. Kenney and Florida, 1988, p. 122). Moreover, the industrial principles which are said to underpin Japanese competitive success are said to be transferable to other countries (e.g. Schonberger, 1982). Kenney and Florida go even further, arguing that Japanese production methods are the new organizing principle for industrial production:

> The successful implementation of Japanese work organization indicates that postfordist production is generalizable across quite different national contexts. . . . Far from being unique to the Japanese context, social organization of postfordist production appears to be setting in motion a dramatic transformation of work organisation, industrial structure, and labor relations across much of the landscape of advanced industrial capitalism. *(Kenney and Florida, 1988, p. 144–5)*

Relatedly, some writers have suggested that, compared to 'Fordist' labour processes, the Japanese approach 'offers a much more humane working environment' (Kaplinsky, 1988, p. 468).[3] In what follows, then, the ever-growing debate on Japanese production techniques is addressed in relation to the question of whether it symbolizes the alleged radical departure in industrial organization and whether it presages a trend towards the humanization of work.[4]

Turning Japanese? Innovative aspects of Japanese production methods

The argument that Japanese production methods signal the end of mass production is particularly difficult to sustain. It seems clear that far from being a manifestation of a resurgent 'craft paradigm' as claimed by Piore and Sabel (1984), Japanese competitive success has turned on the performance of large enterprises practising the production of 'high volume *repetitively* produced goods' (Schonberger, 1982, emphasis in original; see also Naruse, 1991, p. 38). Furthermore, the idea that contemporary restructuring is determined essentially by technical innovation is not supported by the Japanese case. While it is true that Japanese enterprises make use of advanced technology (Japan is the world's largest user of robots) there seems broad agreement that the significance of these methods lies not in the nature of the technology but in the way it is used (e.g. Sayer, 1986; Morroni, 1990). As Jürgens observes:

> The Japanese production system is based on three principles: flexibility in utilization of facilities; minimization of quality problems as they arise; minimization of production-flow buffers, whether material, manpower or time-buffers. The realization of these principles is not apparently dependent on a specific technology; in fact, most experts conclude that the Japanese 'competitive edge' is not based on a specific technology. One of the most important factors is, in fact, the intense manpower utilization resulting from the interaction of the above mentioned production principles. (*Jürgens, 1989, p. 208; cf. Dohse et al., 1985; Kaplinsky, 1988: 462; Naruse, 1991*)

The cost-efficient core of Japanese production management and ongoing productivity improvement is generally viewed as arising from the adoption of just-in-time production and total quality control, which are held to challenge some of the assumptions of 'Western orthodoxy' in mass production industries. The latter is said to have traded off volume and quality in ways which led to wasted output and wasted production time (e.g. Sayer, 1986). In contrast, Japanese production methods ('just-in-time production', or JIT) are said to be based on a special concern with the elimination of wasted output and wasted time in production. This is pursued through attempts to build quality control functions into production (rather than testing for faults at the end of a production run) and through attempts to eliminate sources of disruption which lead to lost or unproductive time (Schonberger, 1982). The activities of the workforce itself are central in these processes. Managerialist literature stresses the extent to which such a system requires a 'skilled' and cooperative workforce (Monden, 1981; Schonberger, 1982). This last feature of the system is the foundation for claims about the 'progressive' features of Japanese production practices.[5]

The 'just-in-time' system is conceptualized as a 'semi-horizontal operational coordination' method (Aoki, 1990), which requires shop level flexibility in adjusting the amount, kinds and timing of in-process materials. The minimal use of inventories necessitates effective control of low level disruptions, such as machinery malfunctions, worker absenteeism, quality defects and so on, in order to minimize their effects on the smooth operation of production. This is aided by a form of work organization in which job demarcations are minimal and job rotation is maximized.

The emphasis on employee involvement and high motivation levels in managerial literature has led to the argument that Japanese methods are a 'respect-for-human system where the workers are allowed to display in full their capabilities through active participation in running and improving their own workshops' (Sugimori et al., 1977, p. 553). Moreover, this is seen to gel with key features of the Japanese industrial relations system: 'Customs such as lifetime employment system, labour unions by companies, little discrimination between shop workers and white-collar staff and chances available to workers for promotion to management positions, have been of great service in promoting the feeling of unity between the company and workers' (Sugimori et al., 1977, p. 553). Koike (1987, p. 287) argues that shop-floor employees of large firms have 'white collarized skills' and that these form a 'crucial foundation' of Japanese industrial success. These workers, moreover, 'think of themselves as belonging to the middle class' (Koike, 1987, p. 329). Wide ranging on-the-job training, supplemented by short, theory-oriented off-the-job instruction, lasting for several years is the foundation of this work organization. Shop-floor workers in large firms, therefore, share with white collar workers the promise of a 'career' with their company (Koike, 1984, 1987).

The existence and role of lifetime employment and seniority (or merit) wage systems (*nenko*) combined with company unions are seen as reflecting and reinforcing this system of skill formation and worker participation. Lifetime employment motivates both employers and employees to share the costs of investment in this team-oriented approach to workforce development. Seniority-related pay and long-term employment guarantees have been developed as devices through which both management and labour can reap returns from their respective investments over time. In order to protect his skill development – the workers to whom these comments apply are invariably men – the worker is seen as having a special interest in the economic situation of the firm: 'Even without any loyalty to the firm, he has to pay attention to the firm's productivity to prevent it from being bested by rivals' (Koike, 1987, p. 307). Enterprise unions, with their well-known cooperative attitude to management, merely reflect these concerns of the workforce.

However, there is a less celebratory view of Japanese production methods which emphasizes that the continuous flow and constant rationalization inherent in these techniques are based on the extreme intensification of work. For Dohse et al. (1985) the existence of company unionism is indicative of the untrammelled power obtained by Japanese management in the workplace, which results in continual rationalization of production – often through quality circles and the like – using workers' own knowledge. They term this process 'Toyotism' but suggest that it 'is simply the practice of the organizational principles of Fordism under the conditions in which management prerogatives are largely unlimited' (Dohse et al., 1985, p. 141) as the result of defeats inflicted on the independent union movement, which had posed a radical challenge to Japanese capital and state power following the end of the Second World War (Cusumano, 1985).

Kenney and Florida (1988) give perhaps the boldest critique of what they term the 'super-exploitation thesis', to present the Japanese case as an example (or the example) of post-Fordism and as more humane than Taylorism. They view lifetime employment guarantees and *nenko* as part of the 'unwritten terms' of a 'class accord', and the 'white collarization' of shop-floor work, participation in quality circles and rationalization of production as the outcome of successful struggles by company unions. They conclude that, in large firms, the strategies of company unions have rendered capital dependent on labour to an unprecedented degree. The success of this strategy is reflected in the relative absence of industrial conflict over the issue of technical change in Japanese enterprises.

Other writers, however, have stressed the limited workplace role played by company unions in the phase of rapid industrial expansion:

> Generally speaking, while labour unions in Japan express the primary concern over the wages, they pay little attention to the amount of labour supplied in return for the wages . . . [the] union function is very feeble or rarely seen in such areas as the regulation of production schedules, manning levels, standard output quotas, speeds of production and so forth. At least, unions scarcely pick up these issues as the agenda for the formal collective bargaining. *(Shirai, quoted in Kumazawa and Yamada, 1989, p. 117)*

To the extent that negotiations occur they do so informally. Deutschman (1987, p. 483) notes the 'congruence of union and management hierarchies' and argues that negotiations are dominated by the concerns of management, with the company union's role limited to 'preparing acceptance for the new technology and an atmosphere of smooth cooperation for its implementation' (Deutschmann 1987, p. 470). For Deutschmann, Japanese unions have failed to act as a 'countervailing power' to the interests of management at every level.[6] Indeed, it was precisely the absence of limits on management's ability to rationalize production and intensify work processes that was the foundation of rapid productivity increases in Japanese industry after 1960. Moreover, it was on this foundation of rising productivity that long-term employment guarantees were introduced. But far from being part of the 'unwritten terms' of the class accord, 'lifetime' employment has always been a gift of management and more often than not a response to endemic labour shortages.[7]

Furthermore, lifetime employment has been preserved for core workers in large firms only through the dualistic nature of the Japanese production system and labour market. Lifetime employment traditionally has been the preserve of employees in the largest firms and 'white collar skills' rarely extended into the periphery of subcontractor firms, which account for a significant proportion of labour hours and added value (see Koike, 1987; also Deutschmann, 1987; Sayer, 1986).

The company orientation of unions also limits the value of the 'skills' which are seen as central to *nenko* practices. This means that far from being indicative of worker security and company dependence, they are precisely the opposite. The company-specific nature of the skills means there are no nationwide social arrangements against which workers' skills can be evaluated across the dividing lines of firms organized, as they are, in a powerful hierarchy (Kumuzawa and Yamada, 1989). Thus, far from guaranteeing the economic security of workers, the Japanese industrial relations system actually limits it. As Deutschmann (1987) observes, the lack of vocational labour markets denies 'exit' options for those employees not able or willing to comply with rationalization measures. This has two implications. First, it means that firms can safely invest in 'human capital' with a guarantee of good returns. Second, it means that workers must comply with rationalization measures to guarantee the prosperity of 'their' firm. The company unions themselves are rendered more committed to the competitive struggle of the firm: in fact in a real material sense the interests of workers, unions and companies are at one.[8]

Kenney and Florida explicitly reject the notion that a tendency to intensification is built into the Japanese work practices. In a key passage they argue:

> The objective of the JIT system is to increase productivity not through super-exploitation of labor but rather through increased technological efficiency, heightened utilization of equipment, minimal scrappage or rework, decreased inventory and higher quality. It thus increases the 'value' extracted in production, decreases materials consumed per unit and minimizes circulation time, making the actual production process much more efficient. *(Kenney and Florida, 1988, p. 136)*

This is a neat argument but one which fails to address the main point of the critics that the search for precisely these time economies in the production process is premised upon and contributes to a more intensive use of labour. The pursuit of stockless production is based upon the elimination of all wasteful motions in the performance of work. The continued reduction of batch sizes allows tighter control of the production process and work allocation, greater utilization of residual labour and the further standardization of job tasks, coupled with an expectation that workers will assume a greater range of these tasks.[9] This is the basis of Schonberger's (1982, p. 193) rejection of the idea that JIT is more 'humanistic' than 'Taylorism': 'but the Japanese out-Taylor us all – including putting Taylor to good use in QC circles or small group improvement activities.' The continued removal of in-process buffers intensifies work even further.[10]

Furthermore, the specialized tasks which are devolved to the shop-floor are often of a limited character:

> Some of them may be probably highly routinized so that other workers can perform them without any real training. Furthermore, it is not unusual that frequent mobility in a workshop arises because of the management policy of operating with minimal manning levels. What can safely be said is only that 'skill' scarcely emerges as a source of workers' autonomous power to regulate how and how much workers should work. *(Kumuzawa and Yamada, 1989, p. 124)*

The case for Japanese work methods as a form of 'super-exploitation' remains strong. Moreover, the version of Japanese work methods outlined here would appear to resolve the discrepancy between those accounts which emphasize features such as 'learning by doing' and so on (e.g. Koike, passim; Sayer, 1986), and those accounts which stress intensification: intensification can be seen as the outcome of efforts to engage the participation of the workforce in the rationalization effort.

Despite various attempts to mobilize 'Japanization' as supporting evidence for flexible specialization or post-Fordism, it seems that these methods do not suggest the 'end of mass production'. Rather they suggest an innovation within mass production industry and its development into a more continuous process (Schonberger, 1982, pp. 104–5; also Shaiken et al., 1986, p. 176). JIT and its supports can be seen as a variant of the integrated mass production process to which I drew attention at the end of the previous section. In the Japanese case, though, the central emphasis is on shop design and intensive utilization of labour and the mobilization of workers' creative capacities, rather than a particular technology. The absence of a countervailing power to management is also central to the operation of this system. As Kumuzawa and Yamada (1989, p. 102) argue, 'The set of popularly perceived productivity advantages of so-called Japanese-style management largely rest on management's unchallenged power to reorganize the existing production process more efficiently.' Thus, there are strong grounds for viewing JIT – and the forms of work organization with which it is associated – as a form of work intensification.

NEW PRODUCTION CONCEPTS?

The notion that key areas of manufacturing industry are seeing the emergence of 'new production concepts', which raise the possibility of reskilling and, more importantly, the possibility of a new bargain between capital and labour, is associated with the work of Horst Kern and Michael Schumann. The possibility, however, that the new forms of technology and work organization offer positive signs for organized labour has been more widely heralded (see, for instance, Sorge and Streeck, 1988; Streeck, 1989). Debates about the value of this conception of contemporary workplace restructuring in manufacturing have dominated European sociology, in much the way that the debate about flexible specialization has dominated Anglo-American discussions (see Campbell, 1989, for a review). While superficially similar to the concept of flexible specialization, the 'new production concepts' idea is significantly different, insofar as it is firmly grounded in the recent experience of the (former) West German economy (hereafter referred to as 'Germany') and the development there of a the 'high-wage/high-productivity coalition'.

The end of the division of labour?

The end of the division of labour: that is what development in an important part of industrial production could lead to under the influence of the new production concepts. *(Kern and Schumann, 1987, p. 163)*

New experiments in work organization of the 1980s represent a radical break with Taylorism[11] and mean that skilled work, 'which during a process stretching over many years has been forced into secondary sectors' is seen as returning 'to the primary production area' (Schumann, 1987, p. 46).

The re-emergence of skilled work and an associated valorization of labour is ascribed to several reasons: because the fully automated factory is seen as a false hope; because technical change and the nature of markets requires more flexibility from workers; because the 'old' methods of securing control over the workforce have lost their credibility; and because of a general demand for more satisfying forms of work (e.g. Schumann, 1987, p. 57).

Kern and Schumann's thesis is based on research into changes occurring in three 'core' areas of German manufacturing: motor vehicles, machine tools and chemicals (Kern and Schumann, 1984a, 1987, 1989; Schumann, 1990). While the concrete forms of work organization differ in each case, they feel able to offer some claims about developments which are common to all and which constitute the 'new production concepts'. A new 'consciousness of the qualitative significance of human work performance' (Kern and Schumann, 1987, p. 160) arises principally with the trend towards flexible forms of automation. Where automation is occurring a 'holistic principle of labour skill appropriation' is emerging because the introduction of new technology 'frequently allows – or even demands – the tailoring of jobs for higher qualifications as well as broader responsibilities or at least a less detailed division of labour' (Kern and Schumann, 1984b, p. 59).

Despite differences which are the product of sectoral specificities a generally increased demand for a new type of skilled worker arises from the process of contemporary restructuring in the view of Kern and Schumann. There is a common factor underlying this new skilled work: 'What is required is a man who is manually gifted and theoretically talented, able to diagnose and to act effectively', one who 'must be in a position to compensate for weaknesses in the technical system by practical action' (Schumann, 1987, p. 47-8). Schumann has used the generic term 'systems controller' to capture the nature of the new skilled work emerging in manufacturing:

> The worker supports technical autonomy and intervenes if machinery does not function at an optimal level or if breakdowns occur. His actions are subsidiary. In the case of deviation from the optimum or failures the worker may take direct control of the process, always with the aim then, to give control back to the machinery. . . . If the technical system should work perfectly, the main responsibility of a systems' controller is to check and to service the machinery. He himself does a perfect job if he succeeds to anticipate deviations and breakdowns in the technical system and proceeds to initiate prevention. *(Schumann, 1990, p. 19)*

In short, the requalification of the workforce is necessary to guarantee the smooth operation of increasingly complex and costly items of plant.

Increasingly, as sections of management come to see the value of the new production concepts, labour's strategy should be to make alliance with the 'modernizers' in their battle with the 'traditionalists' who are stuck in outmoded, Taylorist lines of thought.

Limits to new production concepts

Controversy surrounds the evidence for 'new production concepts'. Kern and Schumann have been accused of 'a lack of empirical data in supporting their far-reaching conclusions' (Wiedermayer, 1989, p. 63). As Wiedermayer notes: 'the manner of their presentation conveys the impression of a virtually inexorable development process (not only in some core sectors but in the economy as a whole).' Similarly, Altmann and Düll (1990) suggest that the 'new production concepts', as described by Kern and Schumann, amount to only limited, isolated experiments, not an emerging trend.

A further point made by sceptics concerns Kern and Schumann's focus on the 'core' sectors, as this tends to ignore the fact that in other sectors alternative rationalization strategies may be dominant. Moreover, even within their restricted choice of sectors, Kern and Schumann have been accused of emphasizing, in the case of the car industry, trends in highly automated areas (where tendencies towards a more skilled workforce are more evident) while having less to say about areas like final assembly, where the obstacles to automation are great and the evidence for radical changes in work organization less strong (Berggren, 1989).[12]

The discussion that follows concentrates on the debate which surrounds the key features of restructuring in the 'core' sectors where the evidence for new production concepts is said to be strongest. The first question concerns the nature of the new skilled work which is emerging. Critics of 'new production concepts' make three related points. First they point to the difficulty of generalizing about the impact of technical change – even in its most advanced forms (cf. the discussion of flexible specialization). They also suggest that where production workers are gaining new skills these tend to be of a more limited kind than suggested by Kern and Schumann. Finally, the critics, echoing the criticisms of flexible specialization reported earlier, point out that even 'enskilled' work processes can be subject to high levels of managerial control and that this has implications for other important issues, such as work burdens. An examination of critical research in two important areas – robotization in key areas of the production process and the emergence of team-working, the two often being closely related phenomena – highlights these issues.

Windolf's (1985) study of the introduction of robots in three different car plants owned by separate firms concluded that general prognostications were difficult because of the impossibility of assessing the consequences of new technology independently of the particular circumstances under which it is implemented. New technology, it is argued, may be implemented within a 'traditional' division of labour as well as within relatively autonomous work groups. Malsch et al. (1984) studied the introduction of robots into the German car industry, largely in relation to spot welding. They argue that for those who retained their jobs after automation the range of skills involved the addition of 'small tasks', such as the preparation of work materials and the care and maintenance of electrodes in welding guns, or quality control tasks, the effect of which was to eliminate certain 'indirect' tasks. But 'there is no basic change in the unskilled character of the work' (Malsch et al., 1984, p. 40). To an extent there is a shift, associated with robotization to a more 'autonomous, comprehensive automation worker' as opposed to 'a drilled, segmented one' (Maisch et al., 1984, p. 43). However, this is a limited innovation rather than a radical break because little control over the work process has been ceded. The new 'comprehensive' worker, they argue, is subject to 'comprehensive control', made possible by the widespread use of information technology based on computer-integrated control of production and personnel information systems.

This point is reiterated by Dankbaar's (1988a) study of team-working in the (West) German car industry. The use of modular production for certain forms of off-line assembly work, for instance, allows longer work cycles for the completion of sub-assemblies than does a moving assembly line, and this can be taken as evidence of work humanization. But the use of AGVs (automatic guided vehicles) is double-edged because the technology embodies surveillance devices. The potentiality is clear and is ignored by the optimists: 'skilled' work may also be integrated into the machine system. This is not to impute a crude 'control imperative' to management. It is, instead, a recognition that capital intensification is requiring new efforts to increase machine utilization. Increased use of monitoring technologies reflects this broader imperative rather than a simple desire to control the workforce. The heightened concern with machine utilization, however, is often related by the critical research to the process of intensification – a process facilitated by the assignment of extra tasks to production workers. This is exemplified in the pronouncements of management in relation to team-working – usually taken as the ultimate expression of humanization. Thus, according to V. Haas of GM, Austria, in relation to that company's most advanced experiments:

> Generally stated, each of the individual departments named has its own personnel that can be divided with respect to labour deployment into active time and idle or waiting time. This is mainly caused by more or less rigid departmental boundaries in the sense of a division of labour and areas of responsibility. The team concept has this as a starting point. The concept leads to production teams, that means that all those directly participating are 'in one boat', and all can do all of the tasks within the area of responsibility of the team – quality, production, volume and capacity utilization. The joining together of previously separated individual areas of responsibility in a team opens up possibilities for reducing the sum of time lost. Or, expressed differently, *to achieve the highest possible ratio of time worked within the working time of the individual employee.* The ideal leads automatically to the formation of a team based on different areas of responsibility. *(Quoted in Jürgens et al., 1988, p. 269; emphasis added)*

This intensification of the work process arising from the new forms of work organization is a feature which is stressed in the critical accounts. The work of Kern and Schumann, however, is characterized by varying degrees of ambivalence or silence on the subject (see also Lane, 1988).

A further aspect of the conflict over intensification relates to the conflicts surrounding weekend working and flexible shift patterns. Arising partly as a result of the success of the metalworkers' union, IG Metall, in winning a reduction of the working week in the metalworking industry to 35 hours in 1984, management's expressed desire for weekend working reflects a wish to raise levels of utilization of expensive capital equipment: 'The traditional form of time arrangement could not easily be applied to the new constellation of production and time economy within industry' (Schüdlich, 1989, p. 32).[13]

The work of Kern and Schumann is provocative and its main benefit has been in terms of the debate it has inspired, but the idea of new production concepts has been subject to telling criticism. The argument that sweeping changes are transforming the 'core' sectors of the German economy needs to be treated with caution. However, the argument that rather less dramatic, more piecemeal and contradictory changes are occurring in those industries is sustainable. Kern and Schumann's focus on new forms of work organization overstates their novelty. This overstatement can be explained by their attempt to draw a contrast between new production concepts and the previous pattern of skill polarization. This perspective on the past, however, leaves the impression of a German industry that had been thoroughly imbued with Taylorism. In reality, though, German industry was relatively less influenced by Taylorism than that in other European countries (Lane, 1988). In fact, craft types of labour endured to a greater extent than elsewhere – a product, to a large degree, of the industrial strengths of the German economy in high value-added sectors. Thus, the trajectory of technical change should be located within the specificities of the German economy.

BEYOND THE LIMITS OF THE NEW OPTIMISM

The aim of the foregoing sections has been to outline and criticize the contributions which have gone to make up the new orthodoxy.[14] This new orthodoxy is founded on a basic optimism that the direction of technical change is forcing employers into establishing more cooperative relations with labour. This has had the effect of reversing the preceding emphasis on the degradation of labour which hitherto dominated industrial sociology, but on the basis of the evidence presented in the previous sections the proposition that the new direction of workplace change is inherently beneficial for labour needs to be treated with caution. Such doubts necessitate an alternative explanation of the nature of contemporary workplace change. On the basis of a synthesis of earlier criticisms of the new orthodoxy, and drawing on the alternative propositions outlined, the last section of this chapter seeks to outline the basic elements of an alternative interpretation of change.

Despite the criticisms made against their optimistic assertions, post-Fordist writers have not dulled in their enthusiasm for their version of contemporary workplace change. But, as we have seen, this view is firmly challenged by the evidence of the preceding sections, from which a number of general propositions emerge. First, where computer technology is being introduced, there is little evidence that its introduction signals the re-emergence of craft work. Far from facilitating the resurgence of artisanal production, the computerization of processes is occurring in ways which consolidate large-scale production.[15] Generally, computerization of industrial processes reflects the growing capital intensity of large-scale industry. In this context computerization of production processes also appears to be as much concerned with improving the control and integration of the productive flow as with facilitating rapid product changes. Moreover, while improved production flows in mass production are a general aim of management, there are several ways to achieve this end. Japanese managements achieve a smoother production flow through innovations such as JIT which appear unconnected to any specific technology.

Second, the 'post-Fordist' thesis may be right to draw our attention to changes in the content of work, but it frequently overstates the extent of change and misconstrues its nature. The pattern of change, moreover, is more incremental and evolutionary than is implied by concepts such as 'post-Fordism'. Kern and Schumann, in their rejection of the idea of 'revitalized craft work', come close to capturing the new content of work in capital-intensive production when they stress the extent to which increasingly the worker 'supports the technical autonomy of the system', noting that the worker is less materials oriented and more concerned with technical and organizational procedures.[16] The new 'skills' associated in different ways with the German and Japanese models, however, are of a limited nature. Although the range of specific dexterities and competencies may be extended under these systems, in principle they reflect little more than the erosion and recasting of demarcations between direct and indirect jobs.

The post-Fordist approaches also neglect the issue of how these new 'skilled' jobs are integrated into the wider, centrally orchestrated, division of labour. They tend to overlook, therefore, the extent to which 'reskilling' may facilitate an intensification of the labour process. This tendency, which seems so central to current developments in all their forms, is largely ignored in the post-Fordist accounts.

At a more conceptual level, the argument that the capitalist labour process has been characterized by sharp discontinuities in industrial practice – expressed in the transition to Fordism and from Fordism to post-Fordism – is difficult to sustain. Ever since the Industrial Revolution the capitalist labour process has undergone continuous transformation, the nature of which is not captured by simple dichotomies such as Fordism and post-Fordism. Fordism, as defined by the new orthodoxy, consisted of the twin processes of the fragmentation of tasks (Taylorism) and the growth of mechanization around dedicated machinery. However, the extent to which these developments represented a radical departure from existing tendencies in the transformation of the capitalist labour process is dubious. Marx, for instance, drawing on the work of Charles Babbage and Andrew Ure, analysed the emergence of large-scale industry (machinofacture) in the nineteenth century, precisely in these terms. Tendencies within 'manufacture' for the break-up of complex, skilled tasks into simplified, deskilled ones, through a deepening of the detailed division of labour, culminated in machinofacture, which was concomitant with the 'real subordination of labour'.[17] This rendered the labour process more continuous through a 'closer filling up of the pores of the working day' or a 'condensation of labour' (Marx, 1974a, p. 534; cf. Thompson, 1967).

Taylorism and Fordism were forms of work organization which led to the further integration of production. In particular, Ford's adoption of the assembly line represented a breakthrough in the historic problem, identified by Marx among others, of the rationalization and mechanization of the transfer of material and assemblies (Hounshell, 1984; Walker, 1989). Taylorist and Fordist principles tended to be applied most extensively in conditions of mass markets, mass production and high velocity of throughput. Taylor advocated bureaucratization of the shopfloor (through time and motion study) as a means to solve the problems of coordination and reintegration raised by the increasingly complex division of labour. Ford's innovation was to propose technical solutions which established a rationalization pattern for mass production industries. The essential underlying principle of both Taylorism and Fordism, though, was the institution of a flow line, designed to ensure high rates of utilization of fixed capital.

Fordism and Taylorism, however, were not universally applicable. There were technical limits to mechanization in some industries (Walker, 1989). Indeed, some factories may have been partly rationalized along Taylorist lines, while other parts of the factory (or process) remained untouched (Littler, 1982). Limited market size also precluded extensive mechanization and the pursuit of rationalization in some cases (Littler, 1983; Walker, 1989). The decomposition of tasks had its limits, as Adam Smith noted. Chris Smith (1989) notes that the false dichotomy of craft and mass production (or Fordist and post-Fordist production) conveniently ignores established industrial classifications of unit, batch, mass and process production and the fact that general purpose machines, far from replacing dedicated ones, have a history that is separate from Fordism. Many industries were never Fordist (Sayer, 1985; Clarke, 1988):

> The decades spanning the turn of the century, then, marked a period of major capitalist initiatives concerned to secure adequate valorisation and accumulation in the context of intensifying international oligopolist competition and increased worker organisation. A substantial deepening of the real subordination of the labour process to capital, accomplished through a combination of mechanisation and Taylorist specialisation and simplification of labour, was and remains central to, but not exhaustive of, the strategy of capital. *(Elger, 1979, p. 81)*

Taylorism and mechanization did not 'create a simply homogeneous mass of deskilled labour' but rather 'a complex, internally differentiated apparatus of collective labour which contained an uneven variety of narrow skills and specific dexterities' (Elger, 1979, p. 82). The post-Fordist thesis, however, presents the mass production 'paradigm' as one of homogenized deskilled labour in order to highlight the contrast with 'new' skilled work.

What Taylorism and Fordism do express, however, is a particular solution to an essential capitalist problem, resulting from the growing capital intensity of production and the need to ensure continuous production. As Alfred Sohn Rethel (1978, p. 144) noted, 'Growing capital intensity and a rising organic composition of capital leads, at a certain point, to a changing costing structure of production, amounting to an increasing dominance of the so-called indirect or fixed element of cost.' Moreover:

> The dominance of overhead cost is associated with a specific economy of time relating to the labour process of production. The more highly the production capacity of a given plant is utilised, that is to say, the more products are turned out in a given time and, as a consequence, the quicker the capital can be turned over, then the lower is the unit cost of the output and the greater the competitive struggle for profit under conditions of monopoly capitalism. *(Sohn Rethel, 1978, p. 148)*[18]

Fordism and Taylorism, according to Sohn Rethel, represented a particular 'economy of time' based on the mechanization of transfer: 'The flow method of manufacture is the mode of production most perfectly adapted to the demands of the economy of time in monopoly capital. The entirety of a workshop or factory is integrated into one continuous process in the service of the rule of speed' (Sohn Rethel, 1978, p. 161).[19] What the new orthodoxy takes as evidence of the 'end of Fordism' is a set of more limited, but none the less significant, developments of this broad tendency. The role of innovations in microelectronic technology in this process is important.

The nature of contemporary change

Fordist assembly lines were the ultimate expression of the capitalist necessity of achieving a continuous production flow in large-scale industry. However, contemporary developments illustrate that this is a historic capitalist pursuit, which is subject to periodic development reflected in the continued transformation of the labour process. Under Fordism, mechanical lines, for instance, created a new set of problems with flow coordination, work pace equalization and fixed task sequencing. Taylorist methods attempted to integrate production through work study, recording of information and the creation of bureaucratic strata of management, but have often merely exacerbated the problem of production imbalances and idle periods. The availability of information technology, however, has given rise to new attempts at integrating the production through the 'mechanization' of information that is achieved with on-line monitoring for continuous data collection: 'Mechanization of information flows may be more important for overall productivity than the mechanization of individual tasks' (Walker, 1989, p. 67).

These innovations address certain technical limits of Fordist production methods which gave rise to increased porosity of the working day. The integration of discrete and diverse elements of production into a more unified and smoother productive flow has implications for the nature of work. The 'mechanical principle of fragmented labour discipline by hierarchical direction' is replaced by an 'informational principle' of work organized in semi-autonomous groups, disciplined by the direct constraint of production itself' (Aglietta, 1979, p. 167). The application of microelectronics to production, according to Coriat (1984, p. 40), makes possible 'new forms of time management and flow control on the shopfloor', which 'result in considerable time-savings in production as well as increased efficiency in the utilisation of machines and tools'. Thus: 'The new principle of work organisation is that of a totally integrated system in which production operations properly so called, as well as measurement and handling of information, react upon one another as elements in a single process, in successive and separate steps of an empirical process of heterogeneous phases' (Aglietta, 1979, p. 124).[20]

The application of information technology to production, however, has been uneven, reflecting different technical and economic limits (Walker, 1989). Automation was established as a trend in series and process industries, for instance, long before 'the crisis of Fordism', while it had a much more limited application in batch industries. The significance of information technology is that it raises the possibility of automating non-mass production. As Williams et al. (1987) suggest, the likely outcome of this process is to establish in batch production principles akin to those of mass production and to make it more capital intensive. In process industries and mass production, while there is little evidence for an 'automation revolution' (Littler, 1983), information technologies do allow a further integration of the production process – a further extension of flow principles. A certain technological convergence appears to be occurring between batch, mass and flow production industries. Coriat, for instance, has argued that 'the automated Fordist workshop' is beginning to 'take on certain features of process type work' (Coriat, 1981, p. 100, my translation; cf. Malsch et al., 1984).[21] Information technology unites traditional management concerns with the integration of production and extended control over the productive flow:

> By virtue of their large capacity for reproducing and extending information processing operations, computer technologies can be used to take over planning functions associated with organisation and control. *They offer a new level of integration of the production process*, for example, through the integration of partial work functions into a continuous process, through matching temporally the insertion of the different production factors, and through transforming the demands of the market into optimal production commands (processing data on market situation, orders and delivery times). The result is a significant step forward in the penetration of both time economy and of the real subsumption of labour under capital. Subsumption now tends to reach out to include complex, mental functions, thereby giving new impetus to automation and the prospect of direct control of the production process through external data and planning. *(Campbell, 1989, p. 264, emphasis added)*

This process is seen as especially important in batch production, where flexibly deployed skills have traditionally been important. Computer technology is seen as overcoming these features to give greater control over production and as subjecting these processes further to the imperatives of valorisation.

Given the existence of these continuities it is more accurate to see contemporary technical change and new forms of work organization more as developments of existing trends: 'the modification of Taylorism' (Altmann and Düll, 1990, p. 112; see also Düll, 1989), 'flexible Taylorism' (Berggren, 1989, p. 193), 'automated Fordism' (Coriat, 1981; Malsch et al., 1984) or 'neo-Fordism' (Palloix, 1976; Aglietta,

1979). The dominant tendencies are towards the creation of new types of semi-skilled production work (rather than craft work) and towards the integration of work tasks into predetermined processes.[22] These dominant processes are incremental and uneven, rather than radical and universal, but remain important nevertheless.[23]

While the impact of technical change on skill formation is likely to be diverse and complex, generally, growing capital intensity and automation is leading to a growing importance, for management, of creating active vigilance, responsibility and initiative among workers on its behalf, as a result of increasing integration, interdependency and capital intensity (see Elger, 1979).[24] However, the forms of limited expertise and empirical skill arising from this imperative are subordinated to the demands of valorisation (e.g. Brandt, 1986; Hoss, 1986; Papadimitriou, 1986; Düll, 1989; Altmann and Düll, 1990).

Japanese work methods have at their centre the elicitation of workers' knowledge of production. As Naruse (1991, p. 42) puts it, 'We can say that if the Toyota production system has some significance with regard to the modern labor process, it is as a reconfirmation that any improvement in production methods depends ultimately on the experience and creativity of the combined laborers.'[25] To the extent that new production systems attempt to harness the subjective aspects of workers' abilities, this is seen as overcoming certain limitations in hierarchical forms of work organization in ways which reflect a continuing logic of rationalization:[26] 'that is to utilize the resources inherent in labour power and new technologies in an isolated and fragmented manner while at the same time integrating and optimizing them by organizing the production framework and structuring the collective worker' (Düll, 1984; translated in Hoss, 1986, p. 254).[27] For the critics it is the subordination of the new forms of work organization to the imperatives of the process of valorization which gives them their characteristic tendency toward intensification.[28]

However, far from leading inexorably to a new social bargain in the workplace, the development of semi-autonomous teamwork is an attempt to 'subordinate labour power also on the level of motivational abilities to capitalist exploitation' (Hoss, 1986, p. 254). This process is perhaps best exemplified by the Japanese case, where the mobilization of workers' creativity in the struggle for corporate success is more extensive and systematic than that achieved in countries like Germany (Jürgens, 1989). Whether such developments lead to improvements in workers' conditions is seen as highly contingent. However, under the conditions prevailing in Germany in the 1980s, the critics observe that additional responsibilities without relaxation of time standards is leading to a general process of intensification. This process is not accompanied by improved occupational status or systematic retraining because 'the skill problem is solved by selection' (Hoss, 1986, p. 256). Moreover, the new production concepts are restricted to strategically significant sections of the production process and autonomy is limited by increased power delegated to lower parts of the managerial hierarchy (see Dankbaar, 1988, p. 36). According to Hoss (1986, p. 257), the new production concepts in both limited and advanced forms are seen as 'a further decisive aspect of the "real subsumption" of labour under capital'.

It is important, though, to recognize the limits of this subsumption. As Elger puts it,

> [It] is necessary to recognise that the continually revolutionised character of modern mechanised production persistently renders 'incomplete' the subordination of labour to capital (in the sense of total direction and control by capital). On the one hand it creates new skills competencies and other opportunities for bargaining leverage arising from the complex coordination and interdependence of the collective labourer; on the other hand in phases of rapid accumulation unaccompanied by massive displacement of living labour by dead labour, it depletes the reserve army and provides the basis for powerful worker organisation. *(Elger, 1979, pp. 65–6; see also Marx, 1974c, pp. 1019–28)* [29]

Thus, although it is characterized by certain essential capitalist concerns, the transformation of the labour process remains open and subject to contest.

Of the theories which seek to make sense of contemporary transformations in the labour process, that which most accurately captures these concerns is the Regulation approach. Early work by advocates of regulation theory emphasized the role of workplace conflict in the 'crisis of Fordism' and efforts to resolve it. As noted earlier, Aglietta's (1979) use of the term 'neo-Fordism' (see also Palloix, 1976) appeared to denote a belief that contemporary reorganization of the workplace reflected attempts to overcome certain rigidities within Fordist labour processes, rather than a radical break with them. Aglietta's (1979) analysis gave an important role to class struggle in determining the crisis of the Fordist labour process, highlighted the trend towards saturation of the working day using new information technology and stressed the potential for intensification in contemporary patterns of restructuring. These developments formed part of the break-down of the post-war intensive regime of accumulation based on mass production and productivity deals leading to rising working class incomes and mass consumption. [30]

Lately, however, some 'regulationist' writers have begun to identify a 'flexible regime of accumulation', while others have highlighted what they perceive as possibilities for workers to gain from these tendencies as a consequence of attempts by management to accommodate workers' 'paradoxical involvement' in production (Leborgne and Lipietz, 1988, p. 265). For the regulation approach the neo-Fordist labour process provides one of the necessary elements of a new regime of accumulation, the coherence of which is characterized by a distinctive mode of regulation.[31]

It seems likely, however, that the regulation approach overestimates the contribution of Fordism to post-war economic growth. In the regulation approach the growth of mass production is linked to the expansion of mass markets and mass consumption. However, as Clarke (1988) notes, this view of post-war growth underestimates the degree to which post-war growth was fuelled by middle class consumption and demand from the military. Moreover, as noted earlier, only part of manufacturing was ever truly Fordist. The Marshall Plan contributed to the 'Americanization' of European industry by generalizing Fordist production methods and industrial relations, but these were only partially implemented in any one country. Finally, the notion that post-war growth was underpinned by productivity bargaining ignores the fact that such practices flowered only briefly after a long period of austerity and military Keynesianism. Thus, as Clarke (1988, p. 69) argues, 'Modes of regulation are better understood as institutional forms of class struggle, which certainly define the character of accumulation, but which do not define qualitatively different 'regimes of accumulation.'

This chapter has shown that contemporary restructuring is both complex and highly varied but remains rooted in specific histories and geographies. Such diversity belies attempts to offer them as examples of an unfolding logic of 'post-Fordist' restructuring. A determining characteristic of the nature of workplace change is the balance of forces existing between management and labour – be it at the level of the firm, industry, region or nation. This observation implies that, despite certain common concerns born of an age in which capital-intensive forms of production are of heightened importance, unevenness is embedded in the process of change at every level. A sensitivity to the historicity and spatiality of restructuring is essential.

The distinguishing feature of the post-war economic growth was not so much that it was 'Fordist' (based on mass production for mass markets), but that it was underpinned by 'the institutionalization of a particular balance of class forces, in which rising wages and rising levels of social expenditure were the price paid for the industrial and political integration of the working class' (Clarke, 1988, p. 85; see also Clarke, 1989). It is the character of this accommodation, which varies significantly from place to place, that is the decisive factor in accounting for variations in the national patterns of change in the past and that will be so in the future.

NOTES

Earlier versions of this chapter benefited from the comments of Ash Amin, Tony Elger and Andy Pike.

1   Even within Sabel's celebrated industrial districts, however, the notion that 'computer' technology is sustaining the emergence of 'a craft paradigm' is difficult to sustain as a general principle. Lazerson (1990), who otherwise has sympathy for the features of industrial districts, questions their designation as areas of 'high technology cottage industry'. He found only very limited application of new technology in his study of the Modena (Emilia) knitwear industry.

2   Piore and Sabel argue that the regions and countries with surviving craft skills are the most likely front-runners in the race to develop economic development strategies based on flexible specialization. However, their discussion of the rise of skilled work ignores the uneven distribution of skills throughout the workforce. To this extent, they choose not to recognize the 'undesirable and costly downside' of the strategy they advocate, namely, the extent to which it will foster new divisions within the workforce (Jenson, 1989, p. 141). The 'unity of the abstract and the concrete' within the artisan firm may simply express a growth in polarization of skills in the external labour market. As Jenson notes, different types of labour are used in different ways: women workers, for instance, are obstructed from obtaining access to the jobs that characterize those parts of the artisan sector which Piore and Sabel admire.

3   The view that Japanese work organization is more humane than that said to prevail in Western countries has been advanced from within the flexible specialization camp and offered as evidence of the 're-emergence of the craft paradigm' (e.g. Piore and Sabel, 1984, pp. 205–8).

4   A version of the Japanization thesis is found in discussions of 'lean production' as a solution to the competitive failure of the US and European car industry (Womack et al., 1990). As Williams et al. (1992, pp. 312, 352) note in their critique of this idea: 'Lean production is the most widely used of the competing organizing concepts for post-modern times: concepts such as flexible specialisation, new competition or post-Fordism circulate mainly in and around academic journals but lean production has been taken up by journalists, industry executives and policy makers who are otherwise not followers of intellectual fashion' and 'represents the apotheosis of the business school's fascination with Japan'. The lean production debate is not addressed directly here, although where relevant points of contrast and parallels are drawn.

5   Monden (1981), Schonberger (1982) and Sayer (1986) provide more detailed discussion of the principles of 'just-in time' and the extent to which it addresses problems in the operation of 'mass production' processes. See also Aoki (1984, 1987).

6   Kawanishi (1986, p. 152) goes so far as to describe enterprise unions as an 'auxiliary instrument' of personnel administration in large firms.

7 As Tokunaga (1983, p. 316) observes, 'the lifetime employment system was not prescribed in collective agreements, but existed only by custom: thus, if a management considered a situation serious, it could dismiss even regular employees (*honko*)' (for a similar interpretation see Kumuzawa and Yamuda, 1989, p. 123).

8 This situation explains why examples of worker militancy in post-war Japan have usually been associated with the issue of lay-offs. The major strikes at Nissan and Toyota in the early 1950s – the defeat of which was a prelude to the development of the contemporary industrial relations system – concerned lay-offs (Cusumano, 1985). The famous strike of the traditionally militant Mitsuii-Miike coalminers in 1959–60 also concerned this issue, and is usually regarded as the last attempt to halt the rationalization offensive which underlay the economic growth of the 1960s (Tokunaga, 1983; Muto, 1984, 1986).

9 'Since making line workers multifunctional is linked with the diminution of the number of the number of workers, the more multifunctional they become, the higher is the labor intensity of each worker' (Naruse, 1991, p. 43).

10 'The Japanese no longer accept the buffer principle. Instead of adding buffer stocks at the points of irregularity, Japanese managers expose the workforce to the consequences. The response is that workers and foremen rally to root out the causes of irregularity. To ignore it is to face the consequences of work stoppages. The Japanese principle of exposing the workers to the consequences of production irregularities is not applied passively. In the Toyota kanban system, for example, each time that workers succeed in correcting the causes of recent irregularity (machine jamming, cantankerous holding devices, etc.) the managers remove still more buffer stock. The workers are never allowed to settle into a comfortable pattern; or rather, the pattern becomes one of continually perfecting the production process' (Schonberger, 1982, p. 32; cf. the comments of Abernathy et al., 1983, p. 176). On this point see also Williams et al's critique of 'lean production'. They emphasize: 'In high flow factories, of the kind which Toyota and Honda operate, labour also generally acts as the elastic resource which maintains flow in the absence of buffer stocks and spare capacity'. They conclude that 'an ever more intense exploitation of working time' lies at the centre of the Japanese production system (Williams et al., 1992, p. 342).

11 Kern and Schumann's identification of 'new production concepts' around 1984 was a remarkable change from their previous position, which had identified the progressive 'polarization of skills' at the plant level.

12 Kern and Schumann (1987) note the absence of 'new production concepts' in 'old' industrial sectors such as shipbuilding, steelmaking and coalmining. The sectors, they argue, are distinguished by a simple struggle for survival and descending position in the economic hierarchy. Elsewhere I have challenged this statement in relation to restructuring in coalmining (see Tomaney, 1991).

13   'The interest of management in implementing more flexible working times is explicitly explained as a question of the "economic necessity" to avoid "idle times" of employees and extra payments for overtime work. Flexible working times would contribute to overcoming the "counter-productive effects of rigid working time arrangements", make it easier to cover peaks in work volume and increase the utilisation of plant. With working hours no longer linked to operating times, cost saving regulation of the use of labour would be possible' (Schüdlich, 1989, p. 35).

14   It is worth noting the lines of conceptual convergence that are bringing these apparently separate approaches together. For example, see the collaboration between two of the principal exponents of 'new production concepts' and 'flexible specialization' respectively (Kern and Sabel, 1991). Also see Morgan et al.'s (1992) attempt to apply the concept of 'lean production' to German industry.

15   As far as flexible specialization is concerned, Coriat (1991, p. 151) sees it as limited to 'certain competitive conditions relating to the lifecycles of products and the characteristics of demand'. Specifically, it allows dynamic small firms to develop 'constantly recreating (small) mono-polistic rents, but it lacks the generality that Piore and Sabel claim for it' (Coriat, 1991, p. 150).

16   This 'new' work content, however, was identified as a growing tendency in large-scale industry in the mid-nineteenth century: 'Labour no longer appears so much to be included within the production process; rather, the human being comes to relate more as watchman and regulator to the pro-duction process itself' (Marx, 1973, p. 705).

17   That is, the thoroughgoing domination of the labour process by the exclusively, capitalist imperative of valorization. Marx discusses this tendency in his 'Resultate' (see Marx, 1974a, 1019–28).

18   This reflects an essential capitalist concern identified by Marx: 'The value of fixed capital is reproduced only in so far as it is used up in the produc-tion process. Through disuse it loses its use value without its value being passed onto the product. Hence, the greater the scale on which fixed capital develops, in the sense in which we regard it here, the more does the continuity of the production process or the constant flow of reproduc-tion become an externally compelling condition for the mode of produc-tion founded on capital' (Marx, 1973, p. 703).

19   For an attempt to situate the work of Sohn Rethel, see Elger and Schwarz (1980).

20   Here I am drawing on certain insights of regulation theory in relation to contemporary transformations in the labour process. In some respects, however, regulation theory could be characterized as an element of the 'new orthodoxy' criticized earlier. In particular, most variants posit a radical break between historical eras based on Fordism and post-Fordism. I have already questioned the conceptual value of this dichotomy. However, the work of some regulation theorists, notably that of Coriat (1979, 1981, 1991), who is careful to talk about transformations within 'mass production industries', does contain important insights (see below).

21 In general terms the 'computerization' of industrial processes gives rise to a relative homogenization of conditions between mass and batch production and reflects the heightened importance attached to capital utilization. This in turn leads to the emergence of a new type of semi-skilled work: 'This seems similar to the type of complex semi-skilled tasks (like monitoring and controlling production equipment) which has long existed in the steel industry and the chemical industry. . . . This type of industrial work is above all characterised by a discrepancy between specific requirements and work stress: as long as the production process proceeds trouble-free, work is neither physically nor mentally challenging whereas contingencies strain concentration and perception as well as intellectual and reactive capacity to the utmost' (Papadimitriou, 1986, p. 43; cf. Altmann and Düll, 1990).

22 The penetration of time economy, however, is uneven, occurring 'neither simultaneously nor with the same dynamic and intensity'. Instead, 'the targets, course and degree of reorganisation processes seen from the angle of the economy of time, are in the end determined by the economic, technical and material conditions of production, which are varying from industry to industry' (Benz-Overhage et al., 1982, p. 89; translated in Papadimitriou, 1986, p. 38).

23 Japanese production systems are also characterized by the pursuit of a smoother and more integrated production flow, although information technology is less central than is reorganization of work itself (Sayer, 1986; Jürgens, 1989). Japanese methods signal 'a redirection from the classic Fordist obsessions with specialized conversion machinery or automated transfer toward the integration function in general' (Walker, 1989, p. 68). The pursuit of 'continuous flow' is the central aim but it is achieved through incremental improvements to work practices and technical systems (Schonberger, 1982).

24 As Marx noted, 'The capitalist's fanatical insistence on economy in means of production is therefore quite understandable. That nothing is lost or wasted and the means of production are consumed only in the manner required by production itself, depends partly on the skill and intelligence of the labourers and partly on discipline enforced by the capitalist for the combined labour' (Marx, 1974b, p. 83).

25 The character of the contemporary Japanese work process reflects less the unfolding logic of post-Fordism and more the conditions under which Taylorist and Fordist work methods were introduced into Japan and, in particular, the structural weakness of workplace trade unionism in Japan (Moore, 1983; Shirai, 1983; Dohse et al., 1985; Jürgens, 1989; Naruse, 1991).

26 Current attempts to reorganize work are seen as an attempt to come to terms with the 'paradoxical involvement' of semi-skilled workers (Leborgne and Lipietz, 1988, p. 265). Even under Taylorism shop-floor workers continued to intervene in order to optimize the production process, even against the instructions of the organization and method office: 'They do so to assert their autonomy as human beings' (ibid.). Current

experiments are a recognition of this and an attempt to exploit this aspect of workers' knowledge for the purposes of valorization. For Lipietz (1978) the crisis of Fordism is also a 'crisis of informal involvement of workers in production'.

27 Work is becoming more 'abstract' in the sense that it is becoming less concerned with particular skills of material conversion and more with machine optimisation. Conversion itself is a function of the entire process. Marx (1973, p. 709) noted this tendency within large-scale industry: 'the product ceases to be the product of the isolated direct labour and the combination of social activity appears, rather, as the producer'.

28 'Thus, a reduction of the transfer times and the losses associated with the assembly line model; the conversion of all or part of this time into effectively productive time; the new possibility for the worker to accumulate small time-gains in relation to "theoretical" production times. All this is based on the intensification of labour, by the increase in the number of productive actions in the course of the working day' (Coriat, 1980, p. 40). For Coriat this represents a 'new economy of time and control'.

29 While identifying an important trend toward computerisation, one should not underestimate the difficulties of using such technologies in practice (e.g. Walker, 1989; see also Tomaney, 1991).

30 The stress on the importance of class struggle was a feature of other work in the regulation approach. Coriat, for instance, traces the origin of the crisis in France to the period 1966–74. The central feature of this period 'is the relative instability of capitalist industry based on repetitive Taylorized labor, an instability brought about by frequent and forceful struggle by workers in the workplace' (Coriat, 1984, p. 40). The period was characterized, moreover, by a shift from wage-related demands to demands for the reorganization of work processes and improved conditions. Coriat (1984, p. 41) argues: 'Taken together, these demands constituted something close to a program for revision of workplace relations, a program for which the working class actively fought and struggled.' 'Neo-Fordism' and management's pursuit of flexibility were seen as an attack on workers. According to Boyer (1987, p. 115), 'in these times of crisis, flexibility strategies have entailed under various euphemisms, the downward adjustment of most hitherto established conditions of employment of workers.'

31 'The *regime of accumulation* describes the stabilization over a long period of the allocation of the net product between consumption and accumulation; it implies some correspondence between the transformation of both the conditions of production and the conditions of the reproduction of the conditions of the wage earners. . . . There must exist a materialization of the regime of accumulation taking the form of norms, habits, laws, regulating networks and so on that ensure the unity of the process . . . this body of interiorized rules and social processes is called the *mode of regulation*' (Lipietz, 1986, p. 19).

REFERENCES

Abernathy, W. J., Clark, K. and Kantrow, A. (1983) *Industrial Renaissance: Producing a Competitive Future for America*. New York: Basic Books.

Aglietta, M. (1979) *A Theory of Capitalist Regulation: the US Experience*. London: New Left Books.

Altmann, N. and Düll, K. (1990) Rationalization and participation: implementation of new technologies and the problems of the works councils in the FRG. *Economic and Industrial Democracy*, 11(1), 111–27.

Altshuler, A., Anderson, M., Jones, D., Roos, D. and Womack, J. (1984) *The Future of the Automobile*. London: George Allen and Unwin.

Aoki, A. (1984) Aspects of the Japanese firm. In A. Aoki (ed.), *The Economic Analysis of the Japanese Firm*. Amsterdam: Elsevier Science Publishers.

Aoki, A. (1987) The Japanese firm in transition. In K. Yamamura and Y. Yasuda (eds), *The Political Economy of Japan. Volume 1: the Domestic Transformation*. Stanford, CA: Stanford University Press.

Aoki, A. (1990) A new paradigm of work organization and coordination? Lessons from the Japanese experience. In S. Marglin and J. Schor (eds), *The Golden Age of Capitalism*. Oxford: Clarendon Press.

Benz-Overhage, K., Brandt, G. and Papadimitriou, Z. (1982) Computertechnologien in industriellen Arbeitsprozess. In G. Schmidt et al. (eds), *Materialen zur Industriesoziologie (Sonderheft 24/1982 der Zeitschrift fur Soziologie und Sozialpsycologie, Opladen)*, 84–104.

Berrgren, C. (1989) 'New production concepts' in final assembly–the Swedish experience. In S. Wood (ed.), *The Transformation of Work?* London: Unwin Hyman.

Brandt, G. (1986) Technological change, labour market change, and trade union policy. In O. Jacobi et al. (eds), *Technological Change, Rationalisation and Industrial Relations*. London: Croom Helm.

Braverman, H. (1974) *Labor and Monopoly Capitalism*. New York: Monthly Review Press.

Burawoy, M. (1979) *Manufacturing Consent*. Chicago: University of Chicago Press.

Burawoy, M. (1985) *The Politics of Production*. London: Verso.

Campbell, I. (1989) New production concepts? The West German debates on restructuring. *Labour and Industry*, 2(2), 247–80.

Clarke, S. (1988) Overaccumulation, class struggle and the regulation approach. *Capital and Class*, 36, 59–93.

Clarke, S. (1989) *Keynesianism, Monetarism and the Crisis of the State*. Aldershot: Edward Elgar.

Coriat, B. (1979) *L'Atelière le Chronométre*. Paris: Bourgeois.

Coriat, B. (1980) The restructuring of the assembly line: a new economy of time and control. *Capital and Class*, 11, 34–43.

Coriat, B. (1981) L'atelier Fordien automatisé. *Non!*, November/December, 90–101.

Coriat, B. (1984) Labour and capital in the crisis: France 1966–82. In

M. Kesselman (ed.), *The French Workers Movement: Economic Crisis and Political Change*. Boston: Allen and Unwin.

Coriat, B. (1987) Information technologies, productivity and new job content – skill as competitive issue. Paper presented to the BRIE meeting on comparative productions, Berkeley, 11–13, September.

Coriat, B. (1991) Technical flexibility and mass production. In G. Benko and M. Dunford (eds), *Industrial Change and Regional Development*. London: Belhaven

Cusumano, M. (1985) *The Japanese Automobile Industry*. Cambridge, MA: Harvard University Press.

Dankbaar, B. (1988a) New production concepts, management strategies and the quality of work. *Work, Employment and Society*, 2(1), 25–50.

Dankbaar, B. (1988b) Teamwork in the West German car industry and the quality of work. In W. Buitellar (ed.) *Technology and Work*. Aldershot: Gower.

Deutschmann, C. (1987) Economic restructuring and company unionism – the Japanese model. *Economic and Industrial Democracy*, 8, 463–88.

Dohse, K., Jürgens, U. and Malsch, T. (1985) From 'Fordism' to 'Toyotism'? The social organisation of the labour process in the Japanese automobile industry. *Politics and Society*, 14(2), 115–46.

Düll, K. (1984) Les nouvelles formes d'organisation du travail – la voie royale? Report to the International Workshop on New Forms of Work Organisation, Vienna Centre/Institute of Labour Research Budapest, Lake Balaton (Hungary), 13–17 May.

Düll, K. (1989) New forms of work organisation: case studies from the Federal Republic of Germany, France and Italy. In P. Grootings et al. (eds), *New Forms of Work Organization in Europe*. New Brunswick, NJ: Transaction Books.

Elger, T. (1979) Valorisation and 'deskilling': a critique of Braverman. *Capital and Class*, 7, 58–99.

Elger, T. (1991) Task flexibility and the intensification of labour in UK manufacturing in the 1980s. In A. Pollert (ed.) *Farewell to Flexibility?* Oxford: Blackwell.

Elger, T. and Schwarz, B. (1980) Monopoly capitalism and the impact of Taylorism: notes on Lenin, Gramsci, Braverman and Sohn Rethel. In T. Nichol (ed.), *Capital and Labour: a Marxist Primer*. London: Fontana.

Friedman, A. (1977) *Industry and Labour: Class Struggle at Work and Monopoly Capitalism*. London: Macmillan.

Hoss, D. (1986) Technology and work in the two Germanies. In P. Grootings (ed.), *Technology and Work: East and West*. London: Croom Helm.

Hounshell, D. (1984) *From the American System to Mass Production*. Baltimore: Johns Hopkins University Press.

Hyman, R. (1988) Flexible specialisation: miracle or myth? In R. Hyman and W. Streeck (eds), *New Technology and Industrial Relations*. Oxford: Blackwell.

Hyman, R. (1991) *Plus ça change?* The theory of production and the production of theory. In A. Pollert (ed.), *Farewell to Flexibility?* Oxford: Blackwell.

Jenson, J. (1989) The talents of women, the skills of men: flexible specialization and women. In S. Wood (ed.), *The Transformation of Work?* London: Unwin Hyman.

Jürgens, U. (1989) The transfer of Japanese management concepts in the international automobile industry. In S. Wood (ed.), *The Transformation of Work?* London: Unwin Hyman.

Jürgens, U., Dohse, K. and Malsch, T. (1988) New production and employment concepts in West German car plants. In S. Tolliday and J. Zeitlin (eds), *The Automobile Industry and Its Workers*. Cambridge: Polity Press.

Kaplinsky, R. (1988) Restructuring the capitalist labour process. *Cambridge Journal of Economics*, 12, 451-70.

Katz, H. and Sabel, C. (1985) Industrial relations and industrial adjustment in the car industry. *Industrial Relations*, 24(3), 295-315.

Kawanishi, H. (1986) The reality of enterprise unionism. In G. McCormack and Y. Sugimoto (eds), *Democracy in Contemporary Japan*. Armonk, NY: M.E. Sharpe.

Kenney, M. and Florida, R. (1988) Beyond mass production: production and the labor process in Japan. *Politics and Society*, 16(1), 121-58.

Kern, H. and Sabel, C. (1991) Trade unions and decentralised production. Discussion Paper/45/91, New Industrial Organisation Programme. Geneva: International Institute for Labour Studies.

Kern, H. and Schumann, M. (1984a) *Das Ende der Arbeitsteilung?* Munich: Verlag C H Beck.

Kern, H. and Schumann, M. (1984b) Work and social character: old and new contours. *Economic and Industrial Democracy*, 5, 51-71.

Kern, H. and Schumann, M. (1987) Limits of the division of labour: new production and employment concepts in West German industry. *Economic and Industrial Democracy*, 8, 151-70.

Kern, H. and Schumann, M. (1989) New concepts of production in West German plants. In P. J. Katzenstein (ed.), *Industry and Politics in West Germany: toward the Third Republic*. Ithaca: Cornell University Press.

Koike, K. (1987) Skill formation in the US and Japan: a comparative study. In M. Aoki (ed.), *The Economic Analysis of the Japanese Firm*. Amsterdam: Elsevier Science Publishers.

Koike, K. (1987) Human resource development and labor-management relations. In K. Yamamura and Y. Yasuba (eds), *The political economy of Japan: Volume 1: the Domestic Transformation*. Stanford, CA: Stanford University Press.

Kumazawa, M. and Yamada, Y. (1989) Jobs and skills under the lifelong *nenko* practice. In S. Wood (ed.), *The Transformation of Work?* London: Unwin Hyman.

Lane, C. (1988) Industrial change in Europe: the pursuit of flexible specialisation in Britain and West Germany? *Work, Employment and Society*, 2(2) 141-68.

Lazerson, M. (1990) Subcontracting in the Modena knitwear industry. In F. Pyke, G. Beccantini and W. Sengenberger (eds), *Industrial Districts and Interfirm Cooperation in Italy*. Geneva: International Institute for Labour Studies.

Leborgne, D. and Lipietz, A. (1988) New technologies, new modes of regulation: some spatial implications. *Environment and Planning D: Society and Space*, 6, 263–80.

Lipietz, A. (1987) Behind the crisis: the tendency of the rate of profit to fall – a regulation school perspective on some French empirical works, *Review of Radical Political Economy*, 18, 13–32.

Littler, G. (1982) *The Development of the Labour Process in Capitalist Societies*. London: Heinemann.

Littler, G. (1983) A history of 'new' technology. In G. Winch (ed.), *Information Technology in Manufacturing Processes*. London: Rossendale.

Malsch, T., Dohse, K. and Jürgens, U. (1984) Industrial robots in the automobile industry. A leap toward 'Automated Fordism'? LLVG/dp 84–222. Berlin: Wissenschaftszentrum.

Marx, K. (1973) *Grundrisse*. Harmondsworth: Penguin.

Marx, K. (1974a) *Capital, Vol. 1*. Harmondsworth: Penguin.

Marx, K. (1974b) *Capital, Vol. 3*. London: Lawrence and Wishart.

Marx, K. (1974c) Results of the immediate process of production. In *Capital, Vol. 1*. Harmondsworth: Penguin.

Moore, J. (1983) *Japanese Workers and the Struggle for Power, 1945–1947*. Madison, WI: University of Wisconsin Press.

Monden, Y. (1981) What makes the Toyota system really tick? *Industrial Engineering*, January, 36–46.

Morgan, K., Cooke, P. and Price, A. (1992) *The Challenge of Lean Production in German Industry*. Regional Industrial Research Report, No. 12. Cardiff: University of Wales.

Morroni, M. (1990) Production flexibility. Paper presented to the annual conference of the European Association for Evolutionary Political Economy, 15–17 November, Florence.

Murray, F. (1983) The decentralisation of production and the decline of the mass collective workers. *Capital and Class*, 19.

Muto, I. (1984) Class struggle on the shopfloor: the Japanese case, 1945–84. *AMPO: Japan-Asia Quarterly Review*, 16(4), 38–49.

Muto, I. (1986) Class struggle in post-war Japan. In G. McCormack and Y. Sugimoto (eds), *Democracy in Contemporary Japan*. Armonk, NY: M. E. Sharpe.

Naruse, T. (1991) Taylorism and Fordism in Japan. *International Journal of Political Economy*, 21(2), 31–48.

Palloix, C. (1976) The labour process from Fordism to neo-Fordism. In Conference of Socialist Economists, *The Labour Process and Class Strategies*. London: Stage One.

Papadimitriou, Z. (1986) Changing skill requirements and trade union bargaining. In O. Jacobi et al. (eds), *Technological Change, Rationalisation and Industrial Relations*. London: Croom Helm.

Piore, M. (1990) Work, labour and action: the experience of work in a flexible system of production. In F. Pyke, G. Beccatini and W. Sengenberger (eds), *Industrial Districts and Inter-firm Cooperation in Italy*. Geneva: International Institute for Labour Studies.

Piore, M. and Sabel, C. (1984) *The Second Industrial Divide*. New York: Basic Books.

Sabel, C. (1982) *Work and Politics. The Division of Labour in Society*. Cambridge: Cambridge University Press.

Sabel, C. (1989) The re-emergence of regional economies? In P. Hirst and J. Zeitlin (eds), *Reversing Industrial Decline*. Leamington Spa: Berg.

Sayer, A. (1986) New developments in manufacturing: the just in time system. *Capital and Class*, 30, 43–72.

Schonberger, R. J. (1982) *Japanese Manufacturing Techniques: Nine Hidden Lessons in Simplicity*. New York: Free Press.

Schüdlich, E. (1989) Between consensus and conflict: the development of industrial working time in the FRG. In J. Buber Agassi and S. Heycock (eds), *The Redesign of Working Time: Promise and Threat?* Berlin: Sigma Verlag.

Schumann, M. (1987) The future of work, training and innovation. In W. Wobbe (ed.), *Flexible Manufacturing in Europe: State of the Art Approaches and Diffusion Patterns* (FAST Occasional Papers No. 155). Brussels: European Commission.

Schumann, M. (1990) New forms of work organization in West German industrial enterprises. Unpublished paper, Soziologisches Forschungsinstitut Göttingen.

Shaiken, H., Herzenberg, S. and Kuhn, S. (1986) The work process under more flexible production. *Industrial Relations*, 25(2), 167–83.

Shirai, T. (1983) Japanese labor unions and politics. In T. Shirai (ed.), *Contemporary Industrial Relations In Japan*. Madison, WI: University of Wisconsin Press.

Smith, C. (1989) Flexible specialisation, automation and mass production. *Work, Employment and Society*, 3(2), 203–20.

Sohn Rethel, A. (1978) *Intellectual and Manual Labor*. Atlantic Highlands, NJ: Humanities Press.

Sorge, A. and Streeck, W. (1988) Industrial relations and technical change: the case for an extended perspective. In R. Hyman and W. Streeck (eds), *New Technology and Industrial Relations*. Oxford: Basil Blackwell.

Streeck, W. (1989) The uncertainties of management in the management of uncertainty. *Work, Employment and Society*, 1(3), 281–308.

Sugimori, Y., Kusunoki, K., Cho, F. and Uchikawa, S. (1977) Toyota production system and Kanban system: materialization of just-in-time and respect for human system. *International Journal for Production Research*, 15(6), 553–64.

Thompson, E. P. (1967) Time work-discipline and industrial capitalism. *Past and Present*, 38.

Thompson, P. (1989) *The Nature of Work*. London: Macmillan.

Tokunaga, S. (1983) A marxist interpretation of Japanese industrial relations, with special reference to large private enterprises. In T. Shirai (ed.), *Contemporary Industrial Relations in Japan*. Madison, WI: University of Wisconsin Press.

Tomaney, J. (1991) Technical Change and the Transformation of Work.

194 *John Tomaney*

Unpublished PhD thesis, University of Newcastle upon Tyne, Newcastle upon Tyne, UK.

Walker, R. (1989) Machinery, labour and location. In S. Wood (ed.), *The Transformation of Work?* London: Unwin Hyman.

Wiedermayer, M. (1989) New technology in West Germany: the employment debate. *New Technology, Work and Employment*, 4(1), 54–65.

Williams, K., Cutler, T., Williams, J. and Haslam, C. (1987) The end of mass production? *Economy and Society*, 16(3), 405–39.

Williams, K., Haslam, C., Williams, J., Cutler, T., Adcroft, A. and Sukdev, J. (1992) Against lean production. *Economy and Society*, 21(3), 321–354.

Windolf, P. (1985) Industrial robots in West German industry. *Politics and Society*, 14(4), 459–95.

Womack, J., Jones, D. and Roos, D. (1990) *The Machine that Changed the World*. New York: Rawson Associates.

Wood, S. (1989) From Braverman to Cyberman: a critique of the flexible specialisation thesis. In W. Buitelaar (ed.), *Technology and Work*. Aldershot: Avebury.

6

The Transition to Flexible Specialisation in the US Film Industry: External Economies, the Division of Labour and the Crossing of Industrial Divides

Michael Storper

FLEXIBLE SPECIALISATION AND POST-FORDIST INDUSTRIALISATION

Fordism as a type of production organisation appears to be losing its dominance in the advanced industrial economies. A wealth of industrial case studies has been amassed over the past decade documenting the appearance of new ways of organising production systems, labour markets, and labour–capital relations (Solinas, 1982; Scott, 1984a; Rubery and Wilkinson, 1981; Murray, 1983; Ikeda, 1979; Bagnasco, 1977; Berger, 1981; Christopherson, 1986; Brusco, 1982; Brusco and Sabel, 1983). Most especially, the recent evidence suggests that vertical integration, mass production, and stable oligopolistic market structures – the hallmarks of Fordist industries – are not the necessary culminations of sectoral development, as was often assumed in the early post-war years (Storper, 1985). Since Fordism refers not only to a type of production organisation but also a compatible form of macro-economic coordination (the welfare state and the mass consumption

This chapter is an abridged version of an article published in the *Cambridge Journal of Economics* (1989), vol. 13, no. 2, pp. 273–305.

society) these changes have implications for the political economy of industrial societies generally (Aglietta, 1976; Boyer and Coriat, 1986).

In this chapter I shall be concerned with the process of transition from mass production methods to a 'post-Fordist' form of production organisation. At the outset, it should be noted that we remain far from any consensus as to exactly what constitute post-Fordist modes of production organisation, labour processes, or macroeconomic arrangements (cf. Leborgne and Lipietz, 1987). Nonetheless, two broad interpretations of post-Fordist production organisation (each with inumerable variants) have surfaced in the case-study literature. These include neo-Fordism, whether of the neo-Taylorist variety in many labour-intensive industries, or the revival of Fordism itself but with the use of dedicated automatic technologies of production. Counterposed to neo-Fordism is *flexible production*, which includes everything ranging from flexible mass production to flexible specialisation (Piore, 1987). These are technologically dynamic production systems in which skilled workers use flexible capital equipment to produce a constantly changing variety of goods. Flexible specialisation typically occurs in smaller-scale industries with a greater variety of output than is possible in flexible mass production (Boyer, 1987; Leborgne, 1987; Piore, 1987). Henceforth, this discussion will concern itself with flexible specialisation.

Flexibly specialised industries have three defining characteristics (Piore and Sabel, 1984). First, they produce a wide range of products for highly differentiated markets and they constantly alter these goods in response to changing tastes and in order to expand their markets. The production system has the flexibility to do this because outputs can be changed by altering the mix of participating input suppliers or because these firms themselves are capable of changing their outputs. In more conventional parlance, the system is vertically disintegrated. Unlike the case of industrial dualism within Fordism, however, small firms are not simply shock absorbers for large firms (Berger and Piore, 1980). They occupy central roles in flexibly specialised sectors, participating in a sophisticated network of interfirm relations whereby firms share knowledge and thereby develop new products and production methods together.

Second, individual firms use flexible and widely applicable technologies: general-purpose machines rather than large, dedicated machine systems. Product innovation is not held back by massive capital investments in rigid technologies. Workers in these firms possess the skills to produce and develop a wide range of products because there is less separation of conception and execution than is required by the deep technical division of labour characteristic of Fordist production.

Finally, flexibly specialised industries balance competition and cooperation among firms. Competition encourages perpetual innovation, unlike traditional craft systems, which may use flexible equipment and skilled labour but are not technologically dynamic. Cooperation is accomplished through learned social practices as well as more formal rules which sustain local business communities and labour markets by socialising knowledge and controlling opportunistic behaviour (Storper and Scott, 1988). These practices and institutions tend to be highly regional in nature because flexibly specialised industries are often highly agglomerated in space owing to the existence of dense transactional relations between firms (Storper and Christopherson, 1987; Scott, 1986).

There are many famous nineteenth century industrial districts: Lyon's silk industry, the cutlery and tool sectors of Solingen and Sheffield, and the textile industries in Philadelphia and Pawtucket (Piore and Sabel, 1984; Scranton, 1983). A large case-study literature has also emerged on contemporary examples of flexible specialisation, most notably in the 'Third Italy' (Bagnasco, 1977; Brusco, 1982; Brusco and Sabel, 1981; Russo, 1986; Becattini, 1987; Fua, 1983), other areas of Europe (Scott, 1988; Sabel et al., 1987; Savy, 1986), Japan (Ikeda, 1979), and even in North America in such sectors as high technology, advanced producer services, publishing, clothing, and steel (Scott and Storper, 1987; Scott, 1984b).

History, destiny, and all that

Piore and Sabel (1984) advance a theory of 'industrial divides', which are shifts from one hegemonic technological–organisational model of production, such as Fordism, to another, such as a putative post-Fordism. They claim that these divides mark major periods in economic history and social organisation within industrial capitalism. Their story is a useful point of departure, and it can be summarised as follows.

In contrast to theories which hold that technologies and production organisation move along a 'narrow track' of history, economies are better characterised as 'gigantic collective experiments'. Very little about the evolution of technology and production organisation is historically predictable, because the precise contexts in which economic decisions are made are themselves actively constructed by agents wielding complex strategies; these agents in turn construct institutions to do their bidding and solidify their gains. As a result, technology and production organisation have histories like a 'branching tree'. The decisions made at certain critical points steer the future along a branch, and cut off other branches (Piore and Sabel, 1984; David, 1975; Nelson and Winter, 1982; Sabel and Zeitlin, 1985). The question is why, at certain junctures, one specific path is taken rather than another.

The first modern industrial divide was initiated in the mid-nineteenth century when circumstances in the USA allowed capitalists to put into place the means to enlarge and stabilise industrial markets. The famous 'American system' of mass production was not the necessary culmination of nineteenth-century industrialisation, but a creature of particular American circumstances that only later, and incorrectly, came to be described as the essential destiny of modern industry in general (Hounshell, 1984; Rosenberg, 1969; Urry, 1986; Braverman, 1974). In reality, Fordism originated as an historical particularity. The American circumstances that generated it included the erasure of European tastes for customised goods, a large number of independent farmers with the means to consume manufactured goods, and the development of the large corporation: all these created an environment favourable to the standardisation of products, the control of markets, and the rationalisation and mechanisation of production. Aided by the stagnation of productivity in a number of British industries, American methods triumphed internationally (Rothbarth, 1946). Once in place, mass production enjoyed powerful advantages over any competing approach. In the twentieth century, mass markets were enlarged by a virtuous circle of rising wages in the mass-production industries themselves, and then given a new lease of life in the post Second World War period by the welfare state, American international economic hegemony, and high levels of domestic market concentration in many countries.

Why, then, would we expect a 'second industrial divide' to bring the end of Fordism and the rise of flexible specialisation? Because the institutions that once held the Fordist system together – stabilising demand at high levels and with a high level of intertemporal certainty – have been broken down by the shocks suffered in the capitalist economies starting with the late 1960s. Principal among these is the breakdown of international macroeconomic coordination under American dominance (Boyer, 1986). It is argued by a number of people – from both historical and game-theoretic perspectives – that it is unlikely that internationally coordinated Keynesian macroeconomic stabilisation can be implemented and thus bring back Fordism (Elster, 1982; Mistral, 1986; Piore and Sabel, 1984). There is no single dominant power to provide the central coordination such a system would require. If one accepts this premise, it follows that flexible specialisation – along with flexible mass production – is one of the few workable possibilities at the level of production organisation to the current state of 'disorganised capitalism' (Piore and Sabel, 1984; Offe, 1985).

It is important to appreciate in what this analysis does, and does not, consist. The argument is that initial technological choices are not necessarily dictated by relative efficiencies, but once adopted they tend to persist until a major shock makes them inviable. It is, of course, an empirical question as to whether initial forms of Fordist production were, in static terms, more efficient than the existing competition, an issue which has generated considerable controversy in American and British economic historiography (Habbakuk, 1962; Rothbarth, 1946; David, 1975; Temin, 1966). The point is that mass production technologies were installed against a changing macroeconomic environment which provided the conditions for Fordism *to become* a superior technique. Thus, the analytical core of Piore and Sabel's claim to an historical *theory* of technology and production organisation is that macroeconomic and institutional conditions have a certain independence in history. Or, to put it more pedantically, if there is no general equilibrium, then the fates of industrial sectors are outcomes of a contingent history.

The argument does not, however, theorise the putative *transition* from Fordism to flexible specialisation. It simply reasons that if the first industrial divide was a contingent outcome of particular historical circumstances then a second divide is now possible due to changed circumstances. The argument is conspicuously silent as to the *process* by which initial organisational and technological experiments in response to changing circumstances might eventually cause a divide to be crossed, as the new technologies and organisational forms become superior to the old ones. Moreover, virtually all the existing literature on flexibly specialised industries is based on cases of transition from traditional craft production to flexible methods or on the rise of flexible production *ab initio* in new sectors such as high technology and producer services. None actually documents a transition from the use of mass-production methods to flexible specialisation. In this chapter, therefore, I document the transition from the use of mass-production principles to flexible specialisation in the post-war US film industry. Contrary to its glamorous and artisanal image, large firms once manufactured motion pictures via a production process organised along mass-production principles in stable, oligopolistic markets. The leading capitalists in the industry explicitly used Henry Ford as their role model. The detailed processes of competition, technical choice, and reorganisation which effected the transition are described at some length.

The film industry offers an unusually rich case study in support of the theory of flexible specialisation (related to but different from the original theory of Piore and Sabel – see section 3 of the original article published in the *Cambridge Journal of Economics* for my version). First, it is quite far along in the process of organisational change, having begun to abandon routinised batch production as early as 1948. Second, the whole industry, and not a specialised or marginal segment thereof, has experienced the transformation. Finally, it is an American industry of the twentieth century. It grew up in an environment lacking the artisanal and regional traditions of Europe, and without the nineteenth century antecedents of other industries. Because it emerged in the world centre and at the historical apex of mass production, it provides insight into the way flexible specialisation develops in the specific and important context of late twentieth century America.

THE RISE AND FALL OF MASS-PRODUCTION METHODS IN THE FILM INDUSTRY

From craft to mass-production methods: the Golden Age of Hollywood

The history of the film industry is similar to that of many other industries as they developed in the United States after the turn of the century. It began as a craft but, with the creation of a large, assured market, the product was standardised and the production process rationalised.[1]

The film industry that developed in New York shortly after the turn of the century closely replicated the craft production techniques of the theatre. Production was carried out by small crews in firms such as Lumiere, where artisans worked together to produce an unstandardised product. Despite artisanal production techniques, however, pressure was applied on the industry to adopt mass-production methods by the then-existing entertainment industry – nickelodeons and vaudeville – who provided the speculative capital to produce films. They intended to develop the mass market of new immigrants who populated American cities. Movies came to be an entertainment product rather than strictly an art form.

By the time film-making was established in California in the 1920s, it had become industrialised. While we now classify it as a 'service' industry, one of the earliest studios was named the Universal Film *Manufacturing* Company. Its artificially lighted stage was dedicated by the mass-production capitalist of the age, Henry Ford. Within a year of its establishment in 1918, this one plant had produced 250 films, a figure equal to the feature film production of the entire American film industry today. The other early studios in California, such as D. W. Griffiths' Fine Arts Studio, were established as full-service film production facilities intended to produce a standardised film product.

Films were sold by the foot rather than on the basis of content (Hampton, 1970).

Two other figures involved in building the film industry, Thomas Ince and Adolph Zukor, were also responsible for rationalising its production process. Zukor, founder of Paramount Pictures, integrated production and distribution through the use of contracted exhibitors nationwide. From his office in Times Square in New York City, Zukor contracted with 6000 theatres nationwide to provide three to four films per week. The US public supported Zukor's marketing network by going to the movies three to four times weekly. Weekly attendance in the USA eventually reached 90 million. The downtown theatres typical of that period had seating capacities of 2000, compared to today's average of 300–500 (and still declining owing to the spread of mini-theatres).

Paralleling Zukor's innovations in corporate structure were the production innovations of Thomas Ince. With an assured and stable theatrical market, the entire range of film-making activities could be integrated within one large factory, the studio. Ince set up the studio to fabricate and assemble batches of a semi-standardised product, the 'formula' picture (Storper and Christopherson, 1985). Ince developed a management-oriented model that strictly separated conception from execution. The vehicle for this production process was the 'continuity script', which fragmented the story of a motion picture and reordered it so that each bloc of scenes in a set or location could be filmed at the same time or, alternatively, so that a set of actors could film all the scenes in which they were to be involved in a continuous work session. The continuity script also impeded costly improvisation by giving the producer virtually complete control over film content. Scripts could be ordered from writers according to a desired formula, for a desired length, and producers could insure that directors would be faithful to them. This production management process was honed in 'Inceville', as it was known, under a schedule of two productions per week.

The production process established in this period consisted of: pre-production (selection and preparation of the script and shooting location); production (construction of sets, filming); and post-production (film processing, editing, sound track). Each of the three labour processes was organised according to mass-production principles. For example, the major studios had permanent staffs of writers and production planners who were assigned to produce formula scripts in volume and push them through the production system. Production crews and stars were assembled in teams charged with making as many as thirty films per year. Studios had large departments to make sets, operate sound stages and film labs, and carry out marketing and

Table 6.1   Films produced and re-issued in the USA, 1930–1977

Year	New	Re-issued	Total
1930	–	–	355
1935	388	3	391
1940	472	3	475
1941	497	7	504
1942	484	8	492
1943	426	6	432
1944	409	6	415
1945	367	8	375
1946	383	17	400
1947	371	55	426
1948	398	50	448
1949	406	85	491
1940–9 average	421	25	446
1950	425	48	473
1951	411	28	439
1952	353	33	386
1953	378	36	414
1954	294	75	369
1955	281	38	319
1956	311	35	346
1957	363	19	382
1958	327	25	352
1959	236	18	254
1950–9 average	338	36	374
1960	233	15	248
1961	225	15	240
1962	213	24	237
1963	203	20	223
1964	227	15	242
1965	257	22	279
1966	231	26	257
1967	229	35	264
1968	241	17	258
1969	241	10	251
1960–9 average	230	20	250
1970	267	39	306
1971	281	32	313
1972	279	39	318
1973	237	38	275
1974	229	45	274
1975	190	40	230
1976	187	30	217
1977	154	32	186
1970–7 average	228	37	265

Source: Motion Picture Association of America.

distribution. A product would move from department to department in assembly-line fashion. The studios endeavoured to maximise capacity utilisation and stabilise throughput.[2] As a result, the internal organisation – or technical division of labour – in each phase of the labour process became increasing similar to that of true mass production, where routinisation and task fragmentation were the guiding principles. This factory-like organisation and oligopolistic corporate structure, popularly known as the 'studio system', was well-established throughout Hollywood by the mid-1920s, and it prevailed until the late 1940s (Storper and Christopherson, 1985).

This period is viewed by many as the Golden Age of the industry because the volume of production permitted the establishment of something resembling a regional 'mass collective' workforce in Hollywood (cf. Murray, 1983). Workers had the expectation of stable work over a fairly long period of time. Apprenticeships within the patriarchal world of the studios represented admission to a restricted internal labour market. Entry barriers to someone not already in 'the industry' were enormous (Christopherson and Storper, 1989).

The studio system was a concentrated oligopoly: a small number of producers were responsible for the majority of the industry's output and they simultaneously controlled distribution and exhibition. In 1944, for example, the five major studios earned 73% of domestic cinema rentals and owned or had interests in 4424 theatres – 24% of the US total. The latter statistic, while impressive, understates the extent of the major studios' vertical interests, since their cinemas included 70% of the first-run cinemas in the 92 cities with populations greater than 100,000 and these same cinemas accounted for more than 50% of all US box office receipts. The extent of market concentration at smaller geographical scales was even greater: for example, RKO owned 100% of first-run capacity in Minneapolis and Cincinnati and Warner Brothers owned 90% in Philadelphia. In 46% of US markets, one distributor owned *all* cinemas (Waterman, 1982). It was the destruction of these assured market outlets that spelled the end of the studio system.

The crisis of the studio system

The studio system reached its zenith during the war years. The number of films released peaked in 1942 (Table 6.1). Direct studio employment in Los Angeles, by this time the centre of the US film industry, reached its high point in 1944, at 33,000. Attendance in US cinemas peaked in 1946, with over 90 million admissions per week.

Table 6.2 US box office receipts ($ million)

Year	Nominal $	1967 $
1945	1450.0	2690.0
1950	1376.0	1908.0
1955	1326.0	1653.0
1960	951.0	1072.0
1965	927.0	980.9
1970	1162.0	999.1
1975	2115.0	1312.0
1980	2899.0	1174.6
1982	3450.0	1193.0

Source: International Motion Picture Almanac, 1983.

In the late 1940s and early 1950s, the absolute size of the market for films began to shrink and the remaining market was much less stable. There were two main shocks to the studio system. The first, anti-trust action by the US Supreme Court, made the industry's market less certain. 'The Paramount Decision' (*US* v. *Paramount Pictures*, 334 US 131, 1948) forced the studios to divest their cinema chains. Since the assured market once enjoyed by the studios was now gone, average returns per picture declined and returns per film began to fluctuate wildly. The second shock to the studio system, the advent of television, altered the industry's market structure and overall growth prospects. Television's success was closely tied to demographic changes, such as the high rate of post-war family formation and, spatially, to the process of suburbanisation. With the diffusion of television ownership, what had been essentially a unified market for filmed entertainment, dominated by one medium, became a segmented market in which different products competed for the consumer's entertainment expenditures. The feature film audience declined by 50% between 1946 and 1956. The size of the box office as a whole declined by almost 40% in real terms between 1945 and 1955 and in 1960 was only 39% of its real level at the end of the War (Table 6.2). The result, in combination with the Parmount decision, was that the gross revenues of the ten leading companies in the industry fell by 26% in this same period, from $968 million to $717 million. Profits of the leading eight studios declined by more than 50% in real terms (Table 6.3).

Table 6.3 Profits in the film industry ($ million)

	Eight major studios[a]		Whole industry post-tax[b]	
Year	Nominal $	1967 $	Nominal $	1967 $
1945	57.2	106.1	99.0	183.6
1950	38.0	52.7	60.0	83.2
1955	37.4	46.6	61.0	76.0
1960	32.0	36.1	1.0	1.1
1965	72.5	76.7	39.0	41.2
1970	−57.2	−49.8	8.0	6.8
1975	262.0	162.5	131.0	81.2

Source: [a]*The Economist*, as quoted in Steinberg, C., *Film Facts*, 1980, pp. 85–87. [b]US Department of Commerce, Bureau of Economic Analysis, *Censur of Service Industries*, 1977.

Early flexibility strategies: vertical disintegration and product innovation

The studios responded to the crisis with two strategies designed to increase their flexibility. They initially reduced the number of films produced; later, as we shall see, they turned to vertical disintegration as a way to cut overheads and increase the quantitative and qualitative flexibility of output. The number of US-produced feature films declined by 28% in the ten years after 1946 (Table 6.1). The average number of films made per year in the USA during the 1950s was only 80% of the 1940s level and, by the end of the 1950s, stood at less than half the number produced in the peak production year of 1941 (Table 6.1).

The industry also began to increase qualitative flexibility to compensate for output reductions, by undertaking to differentiate their products through constant innovation. Initially, the most standardised categories of film-making, short subjects and newsreels, were completely eliminated from the major studios' product range. In turn, studios drew people back into the cinemas with an innovative type of film known as the 'spectacular', which recast the feature as a form of entertainment significantly different from television. Technical innovations were aimed at the 'look' of the film in an effort to make the image in motion pictures superior to that of television. Cinerama, Technicolor, and 3D – all innovations of the 1950s – were aimed at constituting the film as an event rather than an everyday experience. The increased attention to the individual film meant increased budgets for talent, marketing and advertising. As Table 6.4 indicates, individual production budgets rose rapidly along with the decline in volume of

Table 6.4   Production expenditures and production costs US

	Total industry production expenditures[a]		Average production cost per feature[b]	
	$	1967 $	$	1967 $
1941	NA	NA	400,000	950,000
1949	2,881,600,000	4,035,854,300	1,000,000	1,400,000
1955	2,738,700,000	3,414,837,900	NA	
1960	2,966,000,000	3,343,855,000	NA	
1965	2,917,000,000	3,086,772,400	NA	
1972	NA	NA	1,890,000	1,508,370
1974	NA	NA	2,500,000	1,550,868
1978	NA	NA	5,000,000	2,558,850
1980	NA	NA	8,500,000	3,444,084
1982	2,500,000,000[c]	NA	11,300,000	3,908,682

Source: [a]Standard and Poor's *Industry Survey*, 1961, p. A62, 1966, p. A72.
[b]*International Motion Picture Almanac*, 1983.
[c]Daily Variety.

total production in the immediate post-war period. The average cost per picture made by Metro-Goldwyn-Mayer rose from $1.3 million in 1952–3 to $1.8 million in 1954–5. For Paramount, the comparable figures are $1.7 million and $2.5 million.

This strategy of product differentiation increased the need for specialised inputs. The studios began to turn to independent producers to develop these differentiated film products. In the early 1950s, they established a putting-out system for pre-production work, in an effort to encourage innovative ideas. Warner Brothers made their first major advances to outside producers in 1951 to the tune of $6.4 million, and increased them rapidly to $25 million by 1956. As the decade progressed, additional aspects of the production process were split off from the studios' operations and moved to the external market. Eventually, this meant the end of the 'term contract', under which writers, actors, and skilled production technicians worked exclusively for one studio full-time for a guaranteed period. This strategy of reducing labour overheads necessitated changes in employment contracts. In the late 1950s, writers, actors, producers and directors were all put under project contracts, usually for just one film. The heavily unionised skilled craft-workers, on the other hand, were placed on seniority rosters, effectively shifting the old internal labour markets of the studios to an external, collectivised system. The unions came to serve as hiring halls (Christopherson and Storper, 1989).

Each round of overheads reduction in the face of a stagnant, more unstable and more segmented market created unanticipated new pressures for further disintegration, which the studios could not control. For example, the studio system had functioned as a star creation machine, placing individuals under long-term contracts at favourable prices and then making some of them into very valuable commodities, stars. Under the 'star system', as it was known, if an individual achieved star status, the studio reaped the benefits of having him or her under a long-term contract whose terms had been established prior to stardom. The studios thus obtained a monopoly over the actor's specific human capital by controlling access to training at the port of entry to the labour market for stars. Since the maturation of stardom necessitated long-term investments in specific human capital, the star system encouraged vertical integration (cf. Williamson, 1985).

With the end of long production runs came the end of long-term contracts. It not only became more difficult to control product markets long enough to produce stars, but in the short run stars became another form of the overheads the studios were attempting to shed. Thus, the need for asset specificity was overshadowed by scale, overheads, and other flexibility considerations in the studios' decision-making. Successful stars, however, were no longer bound to long-term contracts and could now demand much higher salaries or very lucrative profit-sharing arrangements in return for appearing in a film. In exercising their newly found market power, stars shifted distribution of the rents to specific assets in their favour.[3] According to industry sources, a significant proportion of the dramatic increase in production budgets in recent years is for steep increases in stars' salaries (Table 6.4; Storper and Christopherson, 1985). These increases have placed even greater pressure for cost reduction on other parts of the film budget which, in turn, encourages further vertical disintegration. Thus, the beginnings of vertical disintegration, intended to cut costs and achieve product differentiation and innovation, had in turn unforeseen consequences which promoted further vertical disintegration. The studios could not control the process they had started.

The 1960s: failed attempts at building stable markets

The 1960s opened with the studios' attempt to restabilise markets at a tolerable minimum size by increasing distribution of American pictures abroad through international integration of exhibition. The market for privatised entertainment products such as television had developed much more slowly in Europe than in the USA during the

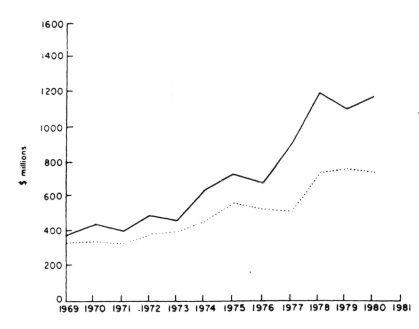

Figure 6.1   Domestic and foreign rentals of nine US companies (Allied Artists, Columbia, Disney, MGM, Paramount, Twentieth Century Fox, United Artists, Universal and Warner Bros).—: US and Canadian rentals, ... : foreign rentals.

Source: Wertheimer Associates.

1950s, and so the market for cinema films continued to grow there. The major studios bought cinema chains in Europe and even in Africa, attempting to replace the loss of their domestic market. Foreign markets accounted for 50% of total revenues at this time, primarily through pre-sales (Figure 6.1).

The most important strategy adopted by the major studios during this transition period was to attempt to dominate television markets. In 1965, television networks spent $115 million to commission made-for-television films (MFT). The average budget per MFT increased from $169,000 in 1961 to $290,000 in 1966 because of the depletion of film libraries. The studios hoped that capturing the market for MFTs, combined with their growing European cinema market, would enlarge and restabilise their markets. The television networks, however (as oligopsonistic consumers of MFTs), began to contract with smaller studios (so-called 'mini-majors') in order to force the major studios into

Table 6.5 Film releases in the USA, 1943–1978

Year	Imported	Total	Year	Imported	Total
1943	30	427	1960	233	387
1944	41	442	1961	331	462
1945	27	377	1962	280	427
1946	89	467	1963	299	420
1947	118	486	1964	361	502
1948	93	459	1965	299	452
1949	123	470	1966	295	451
			1967	284	462
1950	239	622	1968	274	454
1951	263	654	1969	180	412
1952	139	463			
1953	190	534	1970	181	367
1954	174	427	1971	199	432
1955	138	392	1972	147	376
1956	207	479	1973	168	463
1957	233	533	1974	270	550
1958	266	507	1975	242	604
1959	252	439	1976	222	575
			1977	240	560
			1978	137	354

Sources: Film Facts, 1980: Motion Picture Association of America

competitive bidding over the price of MFTs. Because the studios owned large physical plants ('back-lots', large studios) and because they were almost completely unionised, they were essentially forced out of these more cost-sensitive segments of the market, low-budget cinema films and MFTs, which were then taken over by the same independent production companies whose existence in the first place had been set into motion by subcontracting from the major studios. This blow was aggravated by the fact that European producers' presence in American markets grew dramatically in the early 1960s (Table 6.5). Thus, even though new sources of market growth arose in the 1960s, they could not be captured or controlled by the major studios.

The failure to reassert mass markets was reflected in a return of the industry's profitability crisis in 1970, when the eight major studios all suffered large losses, and almost no profits were made in the industry as a whole (Table 6.3). The studios still held large quantities of property (in sound stages, 'back-lots', and film libraries). With low profits but large assets, their stocks were undervalued and they became vulnerable to takeovers. Some studios, such as Paramount, responded by allowing friendly takeovers to occur, in their case by becoming a division of the conglomerate Gulf & Western. Most of the studios, however, began to trim their facilities and reduce overheads again. They redefined their production facilities as 'profit centres', requiring them to support themselves through rentals to independent producers making films with studio financing. In a number of cases, the studios simply sold their back-lots. Twentieth Century Fox, for example, sold the land which is now Century City on Los Angeles' Westside – a large office, commercial and residential development.

Increased filming on location also promoted the reduction in physical scale of the major studios. Initially, vertical disintegration encouraged location shooting as a cost-cutting move on the part of independent production companies, and as a product differentiation strategy in the case of some spectaculars. Location shooting, which is a type of change in production technique, began as a direct *consequence* of vertical disintegration; like many such practices, it seems to have reinforced itself in circular and cumulative fashion with the result that the studios can no longer control its use. The inital increase encouraged technological innovations designed to make location work easier. The Cinemobile (a mobile studio) and the panaflex camera (hand-held, but very quiet) make it possible to achieve technical quality on location equal to the studio or back-lot. Location shooting is now a genuine alternative to the studio in most situations, offering a more realistic 'look' and lower overhead costs. Localities, too, have begun to promote themselves by offering better services and, sometimes, considerable subsidies to production companies (Storper and Christopherson, 1985).

Location shooting also enables producers to avoid work rules in the industry centres, Los Angeles and New York. West Coast union work rules prevail within a radius of 300 miles from the corner of Beverly and La Cienega Boulevards in Hollywood. Since these rules limit the length of the working day, they can force a film to stay in production for more shooting days than would otherwise be the case, entailing the fixed costs associated with each day of production activity. Even skilled workers who go on location from Hollywood within the radius often waive work rules informally when they are on location. And non-unionised screen extras and construction workers can be secured on location. For all these reasons, the studios' stages and back-lots are now in many ways unable to compete – whether in quality or price terms – with locations.

By the 1970s most of the studios had, in effect, ended their roles as physical movie factories. Even though disintegration had begun with the limited objectives of cost-cutting and product differentiation, in the end specialised firms and non-studio locations proved superior to the studios, not only for low-budget films and MFTs, but for high-budget

Table 6.6 Number and percentage of productions by organisation type, selected years, 1960–1980

	1960	*1965*	*1970*	*1975*	*1980*
Independent	42 (28%)	40 (21%)	93 (44%)	138 (56%)	129 (58%)
Major	100 (66%)	130 (68%)	96 (46%)	81 (33%)	69 (31%)
Mini-major	9 (6%)	20 (11%)	18 (9%)	24 (10%)	24 (11%)
Totals	151	190	209	244	223

Source: Storper and Christopherson, 1985 (see also note 5)

and high-revenue productions as well. The studios could no longer compete against the independent production companies and specialised contractors they had helped to create, in the very market segments they had hoped to retain. Virtually none of the major studios today can offer the range of specialised services which are obtainable from independent firms; few can even carry out relatively routine tasks at lower costs than the independent supplier firms.[4]

The new structure of the film industry

After their initial experiment in contracting out writing in the 1950s, the studios developed a system of working jointly with independent production companies, also in order to encourage new ideas. Production costs per picture were already rising rapidly in the 1960s, so the studios also used the new system to share invesment risks with the independents. In the event of success, profits are divided; but in the case of failure, the studio's invesment exposure is minimised because the independent production company usually raises a substantial proportion of the initial investment using the major studio's capital as 'seed money'. Table 6.6 reports the changes in the types of organisations carrying out film production between 1960 and 1980.[5] The trend toward production by independent companies and away from the major studios is clear. In 1960, 28% of US films were produced by independents or independents combined with others, while 66% were made with the participation of major studios. By 1980, the 1960 proportions were almost reversed: independents produced 58% of films while majors participated in only 31%.

The increase in number of independent production companies, however, was only a small part of the organisational restructuring of the industry. The production system for various kinds of intermediate

Table 6.7 Number of Los Angeles area establishments: production firms

	1966	1974	1982
Production companies	563	709	1473
Rental stages	13	24	67
Properties	66	33	184
Editing	4	31	113
Lighting	2	16	23

Source: Storper and Christopherson, 1985 (see also note 5)

Table 6.8 Number of Los Angeles area establishments: post-production

	1966	1974	1982
Recording/sound	20	33	187
Film processing	43	76	55
Film effects	10	27	42

Source: Storper and Christopherson, 1985 (see also note 5)

inputs steadily grew and diversified. Both the studios and the independent production companies turned to specialised, independent supplier firms and subcontractors to carry out the whole range of pre-production functions. We examined the births and deaths of selected film-making services and facilities in Southern California. The facilities and services tabulated all increase in absolute numbers during the period (Tables 6.7 and 6.8).[6] Given that film output was stable for the index years, the magnitude of these increases provides convincing evidence of a trend toward vertical disintegration. In all categories of input-supplying firms, the major leap in the number of firms took place between 1974 and 1982, after the crisis of the early 1970s. We also looked in detail at the dates of establishment of a sample of 200 independent production companies in all segments of the industry, including commercials, industrial films, animation, special effects, television, and cinema films. Of these, 140 were established between 1971 and 1982 (*The Production Company*, 1984).

These statistics on organisational proliferation are confirmed in Table 6.9, which demonstrates the dramatic increases in total number of establishments in the film industry. Significantly, SIC 7819 (services allied to motion picture production), which covers virtually all the new,

Table 6.9   Establishments – USA

		1968	*1974*	*1981*
SIC 7813:	Motion pictures excluding TV	666	1279	1023
SIC 7814:	Motion pictures and tape production for TV	490	978	1420
SIC 7819:	Services allied to motion picture production	NA	716	1077
Total		1156	2973	3520

Source: US Dept of Commerce, *County Business Patterns*

specialised firms in the industry, was only created as a separate reporting category in the mid-1970s in response to the increasing visibility
of these enterprises.

The deepening of the social division of the labour in the motion
picture industry as a consequence of vertical disintegration should be
associated with increasing output specialisation on the part of the supplier firms, who should have a narrower *scope* of activity than the
integrated major studios they replace. The evidence for this comes from
interviews with firms in the industry, with most reporting exactly what
is expected theoretically: the smaller firms are generally specialised in
a particular type of intermediate output, but within that field, they have
a wider range of potential variations – because they are innovative –
than the independent firms which existed in the 1950s or the specialised
departments in the major studios which once carried out similar phases
of the production process. A film lab, for example, will no longer do
all kinds of film processing, but in turn will tend to have a much greater
variety of techniques it can apply within its specialised domain, and
it constantly interacts with production companies and equipment
manufacturers to develop new ways of processing film (Storper and
Christopherson, 1985; cf. Russo, 1986).

The changing division of labour should be reflected in declining firm
size in an industry such as this, where total output is not increasing;
in a growing industry, it would be reflected in slower growth in the
size of intermediate output producers than in the output of the industry
as a whole. Table 6.10 shows that the size of establishments in the
specialised supplier part of the industry (SIC 7819), measured by
number of workers, has indeed undergone a steady decline. This decline
differs markedly from the cyclical declines and recoveries observed
in other parts of the industry. Table 6.11 confirms the decrease in

Table 6.10   Employees per establishment

	1969	Change[a] 1974	1969–74	1981	Change[a] 1974–81
SIC 7813					
CA	38.98	15.89	40.76	45.42	285.94
NY	13.12	7.12	54.26	8.78	123.31
FL	16.08	4.75	29.53	7.78	163.78
TX	14.42	11.58	80.3	14.72	127.11
USA	23.21	11.19	48.2	25.04	223.77
SIC 7814					
CA	26.25	36.28	138.20	31.48	86.7
NY	23.15	11.18	48.29	21.72	194.2
FL	13.33	NA	NA	12.08	NA
TX	18.3	NA	NA	NA	NA
USA	21.2	20.82	98.2	24.10	115.75
SIC 7819					
CA	NA	34.02	NA	22.7	66.9
NY	NA	13.34	NA	10.8	81.3
FL	NA	14.7	NA	6.6	45.1
TX	NA	10.07	NA	15.60	154.9
USA	NA	21.33	NA	16.87	79.09

Source: County Business Patterns.
[a] First Year = 100.

Table 6.11   Receipts per establishment

Year	Norminal $	1967 $
1963	533,869	582,190
1967	642,792	642,792
1972	607,313	484,687
1977	971,033	535,004
1982	1,279,827	442,693

Sources: US Department of Commerce, Census of Service Industries Deflator; US Bureau of Labor Statistics, Consumer Price Index.

Table 6.12 Revenue mix for cinematic films, selected years 1978–1984

	1978(%)	1980(%)	1983(%)	1984(%)
Rentals	80	74	48	54
Pay TV	2	5	12	12
Cassettes	NM	1	15	22
Networks and syndication	14	14	19	8
Other	4	6	6	4
Total	100	100	100	100

Source. Wertheimer Associates; Metro Goldwyn Mayer.

establishment size by showing that it is also manifested in a decrease in revenues per establishment between 1963 and 1982.[7]

The recomposition of the entertainment industrial complex

The process of reorganisation does not end with the vertical disintegration of film production and creation of a flexibly specialised production system. Both the major studies and specialised production firms have spread the risk that comes with unstable markets and highly differentiated products by diversifying into related markets. The studios, for example, form financial alliances with firms in other areas of entertainment provision, playing the role of institutional investor. They also finance multiple production packages and advance capital for distribution in return for some intertemporal control over different marketing areas. The entertainment industries, including television, recording and video as well as motion pictures, are witnessing a wave of horizontal integration as new entertainment products are created, enjoying overlapping production processes and markets. A film, for example, has a profitable 'after-life' in outlets other than cinemas, including television, videocassettes, sound tracks, and related promotional devices. This is reflected very powerfully in the changing revenue mix for theatrical films (Table 6.12).

Input-supplying firms, on the other hand, increase the scale of their operations by specialising in certain generic functions (props and scenery; film editing; sound mixing) but working on a broad variety of final outputs and constantly innovating. In production, firms branch out to serve other final output sectors in the entertainment area, and by exploiting some of the advantages of specialisation. A typical story is that of Cinnabar, a firm established by two individuals to make sets for independent productions, essentially a specialised carpentry shop. Having successfully built sets, they began to work collaboratively with production companies in designing sets, and in so doing diversified into making the physical props for all kinds of *trompe l'oeil* effects. Currently a 100-person firm, they are now actually producing commercials which require special effects, and themselves subcontracting much of the more standardised carpentry and construction work of set-building because they have outgrown their own facilities. They now work in movies, television, and commercial markets.

This recomposition of the entertainment industries into an entertainment industrial complex is an attempt to reallocate and collectivise risk in the production process. Since demand from the whole complex is greater than that from any particular market, some of the uncertainty that exists in any particular output sector is offset, and greater scale and specialisation on the part of individual firms is supported. This is affirmed by the dramatic shift of the television production industry from New York to Los Angeles in the period under examination. With the exception of network news, the vast majority of television production shifted to the West Coast in the 1970s (Storper and Christopherson, 1987). Television has simultaneously gone through a process of vertical disintegration and it requires inputs similar to those used in films. The geographical consolidation of filmed entertainment production increases the potential throughput for Hollywood's specialised firms and enables them to trade better on their specialised skills (Marshall, 1919; Becattini, 1987; Bellandi, 1986).

New interindustrial relations, by increasing the variety of potential interconnections and markets to be served by a specialised firm, encourage innovational activity within the firm's specialised product domain. This switch from product *differentiation* in the motion picture industry to product *variety* in the entertainment industry thus has strong dynamic properties. Increases in product variety are typical of both flexible automation and flexible specialisation, whereas only product differentiation was typical of Fordist industries (Boyer and Coriat, 1986; Holmes, 1987). In the end, it can be said that the interindustrial redivision of social labour stems as much from endogenous innovation dynamics 'from below' as it does from corporate planning 'from above'.

CONCLUSIONS

The history recounted above is puzzling in certain respects. First, why did the studios not simply shed risk in the face of greater uncertainty or instability, and then arrest the of process of vertical disintegration at that point by limiting the role of production subcontractors and independent producers? In other words, we have no explanation of why the breakdown in Fordist regulatory institutions in the motion picture industry did not lead to industrial dualism, rather than flexible specialisation. Second, in the many well-documented cases of flexible specialisation in the revitalised craft industries of Western Europe, markets have been enlarged through internationalisation, and a well-developed set of marketing intermediaries now exists to smooth demand fluctuations and permit some production planning. Yet vertical disintegration seems to persist nonetheless. Our existing treatments of flexible specialisation are long on comparative statics, but short on theoretical explanations of its dynamic properties.

The original version of this chapter (section 3) theorizes the processes by which the divide between mass production and flexibilization may be crossed. It explains the transition in terms of a new form of production organization, which embodies external economies of scale as a result of the development of an industry's social division of labour. It develops its argument by emphasizing the role of vertical disintegration, external economies of scope and transaction costs in contexts of market volatility and uncertainty. It argues that once producers begin to adjust to increased intertemporal uncertainty through vertical disintegration, external economies can, at a certain point, be said to have overtaken economies of scale, in both production and transaction costs. The existence of strong external economies means that these outcomes need not be intended or planned by large firms; if new production techniques are superior, at a given moment, to what they replace, the path taken can be the outcome of short-term strategies or even accidents. Once taken, however, the path is not necessarily reversible.

The transition from Fordism to vertically disintegrated flexible specialisation might be accounted for as follows. Some initial shock – political, macroeconomic, institutional in nature – dramatically raises the level of uncertainty instability in an industry's markets. In their initial strategies of self-preservation, firms turn to subcontracting or outwork, thus creating a dualistic production system. They may, in the meantime, begin to search for production techniques which can function under increased uncertainty without a loss of control (as in today's search for flexible automation), and they may also explore avenues for reasserting control over markets. Still, their markets are subject to periodic shocks (overproduction, decline) and these large firms suffer rising costs or periodic losses. Subcontractors may begin by occupying specialised market niches. They proceed to develop new products or services and to diversify their marketing strategies. Horizontal inter-firm networks begin to grow: product variety begins to supplement product differentiation and horizontal inter-industry relations offset some of the risk faced by supplier firms and encourage specialisation. As the efficiency of these networks increases – manifested in higher quality, lower prices, or product innovation – the larger firms increasingly turn to them in crises. In the absence of opportunities to resynthesise labour processes, the internal economies of large firms continue to falter while external economies slowly increase in the production complex as a whole. With each round of crisis, large producers use vertical disintegration as a survival strategy. Each round of disintegration simultaneously strengthens external economies. A process of replacement of internal economies is set into motion, and beyond a certain point the large firms can no longer reverse it, because no single firm can assert enough control for a long enough period of time. Disintegration, in this manner, may begin with subcontracting, but it may end with the appearance of a network of independent supplier firms and a flexibly specialised system (Chaillou, 1977). Short-term events along the way are critical to the unfolding of the whole process. It holds, moreover, that the precise form that flexible specialisation takes is not necessarily the optimal one (in comparative static terms) from the starting point. The particular path of vertical disintegration that is taken, at a certain point, becomes self-confirming. History is produced.

In this chapter, a broad argument has been laid out concerning the process of transition from large batch or mass production to flexible specialisation. The argument has focused on the steady weakening of internal scale economies in favour of external economies, attributable to a shift toward a vertically disintegrated form of production organisation. Our intention is in no way to detract from the use of a rich method of historical political economy in explaining industrial divides, but rather to develop the analytics of transition processes. Responses to changed circumstances generate counter responses, and these processes have their own internal dynamics. In turn, these same processes may have effects upon the macroeconomic and institutional environments which set them into motion in the first place.

One implication of the reasoning advanced in this chapter is that the role of external economies in industrial development has – with only a few exceptions – been severely underestimated. This is true of the contemporary flexible production debate as well, where it is frequently argued that flexible specialisation is a system with few economies of scale and therefore offers little hope for contributing to a viable post-Fordist macroeconomic regime of accumulation (Boyer, 1987; Leborgne, 1987). However, scale economies are not created only by progressive lengthening of the production run, but can result from

different combinations of flexibility and specialisation and inter-
connection between activities. It is indeed theoretically possible that
reductions in both aggregate output and the size of particular production runs could still be accompanied by rapidly increasing returns
to scale.[8]

If we are correct in these claims, then there are general lessons for
the explanation of economic history. Most importantly, the organisation of production is not determined strictly by predictable responses
to given external circumstances, whether those of neo-classical choice
and substitution theories, classical models of heterogeneous capital, or
neo-Marxist models of labour control. Rather, in the presence of these
circumstances, the future is – in some significant measure – steered by
what is already cemented into a complex and highly externalised
system of economic relations and organisational forms and practices,
and choices made along the way are important to long-run outcomes;
they are not just part of the standard deviation around predictable and
externally determined trends (Nelson and Winter, 1982). By no means
does this then imply that evolution is everything, i.e. that the system
is closed to the possibility of industrial divides. It suggests, however,
that divides are not precipitated by marginal alterations in circumstances, but require major changes in institutions, markets, or technological possibilities, such that the basic possibilities for the division
of labour are altered. Once set into motion, these divides may be
self-perpetuating.

Because we know so little about the role of external economies in
industrial development their dynamic interaction with technological
innovation and choice and the structure of markets should be at the
centre of further efforts to extend our existing understanding of
industrial divides. For example, we need to know whether vertical
disintegration – and the dynamic processes of learning-by-doing and
development of externalised, embedded, social practices with which it
is associated – itself encourages continual diversification of product
markets and thus, after a certain point, whether it might therefore
impede the kind of technological or organisational innovations that
would be capable of resynthesising labour processes and restoring mass
or batch production or vertical integration.[9] Especially relevant to the
current conjuncture is the question of whether flexible automation
offers the potential to respond to current market configurations but
without the levels of vertical disintegration implied in the flexible
specialisation model (cf. Boyer and Coriat, 1986). Mass production
industries such as automobiles and steel have larger blocs of fixed
capital equipment than does the motion picture industry. Do greater
indivisibilities at each phase of the technical division of labour – even

if not inherently associated with economies of scope – limit the possibility that specialised firms could build up their capital stocks under conditions of market uncertainty? Do they therefore allow large firms to control the futures of those industries? Alternatively, will flexible *automation* become practical for a wide variety of production runs, reducing minimal optimal scales and reducing the differences between flexible specialisation and flexibly automated mass production? Does such a reduction lead back to vertical integration through increased economies of scope, or to specialisation and vertical disintegration? All these questions are concerned with whether the inter-firm relationships in flexibly specialised industrial sectors find stable reproductive schemes over the medium term, or whether they are simply temporary aberrations from higher levels of vertical integration.

These questions represent a minimum agenda for moving forward into a scientifically viable and politically relevant theory of industrial divides. They go to the very roots of contemporary industrialisation processes in the advanced capitalist countries. New experiments in the organisation of production systems, the development of productive labour, and the structuring of industrial communities are under way. How these experiments evolve and are given form in durable configurations of industrial systems has major implications for the future of industrial societies.

NOTES

1   This section draws upon Storper and Christopherson (1985).
2   The studio system was organised according to mass-production principles even though the number of films produced per year in a studio (between 30 and 200 or so) was small enough to count as batch production by the standards of most other industries. Analogous cases are airframe construction or tanker construction. These are not, as is commonly thought, 'one off' production methods. The latter are found in, for example, the construction of some aerospace or military hardware systems. In those cases, the large firm is a 'systems house', which engineers the final output and issues orders for the production of necessary components, and then assembles the final product, driving the whole system by final demand. The studios, on the other hand, took slightly customised versions of a technologically similar product and pushed them through the production process, with its well-defined division of labour. The system ran on the assumption of a stable demand and planned output. This is also what occurs in airframe construction once the product is designed and enters serial production. The systems house and mass-production firm organise their labour processes very differently, the latter being geared toward routinisation, the former toward flexibility.

3   Profit participation arrangements, by definition, are designed to shift distribution in favour of stars, because they are negotiated *in addition to* salaries, not as a replacement thereof. Rising salaries, even without profit participation, probably effected dramatic redistribution of the rents on stardom toward the stars themselves, thus reducing the profit shares of the studios because this was a period of declining market size and very limited demand elasticity. While some spectaculars could have very high earnings, average earnings per film were in decline, yet studios were forced to establish salaries by contract in advance of profit data. It follows that studios' shares were cut in favour of stars' shares.

4   Rigorous production cost analysis is virtually impossible in the film industry, precisely because production has become so much less standardised than it used to be. It is equally difficult to supply data on minimum efficient dimensions of the different phases of the production process. Note, too, that it is not being claimed here that today's independent firms can carry out their activities at lower unit cost than could be done by very specialised departments under the old studio system, but rather that they can produce more specialised outputs at lower costs than the studios are able to do at their *current* output levels.

5   Information on film-making services and facilities in the Los Angeles region was obtained by using service directories for the industry, including the *Hollywood Blu-Book*, the *International Motion Picture Almanac*, and *The Production Company*. While the firms listed in the *Blu-Book* and the *Almanac* are not necessarily a complete listing of services and facilities, they come closest to sampling the whole industry. In establishing the numbers of firms in each category, we assumed that a firm not listed in the previous period had been established in the interim. We were careful, also, to eliminate any duplication in directory listings, so as to minimise the possibility of double-counting. The production companies for films were obtained by following the 'Production Charts' in *Daily Variety* and *The Hollywood Reporter* each week for the entire year of each year tabulated. We then classified the companies as major studios, mini-majors, independents, and so on.

6   It is irrelevant whether concentration in final markets changes or does not. Vertical disintegration is measured in terms of whether the number of intermediate input producers changes for given levels of final output.

7   In passing, it should be noted that vertical disintegration has been accompanied by a dramatic change in the industry's labour demand. The low point in total employment was reached in 1963, reflecting the decline of workforces at the major studios. Beginning with the last and most dramatic stage of vertical disintegration in the early 1970s, the industry's workforce grew very rapidly, so that in 1982 it was 259% of its 1963 level in a period of stable output and declining total production expenditures. Nonetheless, the aggregate quantity of work available (i.e. the total hours of work available) has not increased. Thus, a much larger pool of individuals is competing for the available work, and most of them are now employed intermittently and on a part-time basis. The Writers' Guild is a typical

case: membership has increased from approximately 800 in 1970 to 8000 today, but the quantity of scripts commissioned has not risen appreciably. A complete shift in the nature of employment relations in the industry has occurred, characterised by new forms of employment instability and qualitatively new forms of labour market segmentation (Christopherson and Storper, 1989). In fact, the total amount of *work* available in these firms has decreased dramatically, even as the number of workers has grown. This is consistent with their decreasing participation in production.

8   The attention given to the size of the production run is, in our view, something of an analytical hangover from the practices of economists trained in observing Fordist industries. The argument that *only* flexible automation – with its more limited product variety and its longer discrete production runs – has even the theoretical possibility of achieving the productivity gains which would be required to form the basis of a new regime of accumulation in the advanced capitalist economies seems highly questionable in light of the arguments presented in this chapter. In the medium and long runs, productivity and innovation are very likely going to depend on maximising the ability to shift between different product ranges – what we used to call 'retooling' and now call 'dynamic flexibility'. This is precisely why the new modal form of organisation of the large, capital-intensive industries is the *systems house* rather than the vertically integrated manufacturing firm. Even in flexibly automated mass-production industries, the sources of productivity will be not only in internal economies of scale but in the organisation of the production system as a whole so as to maximise convertibility – an external economy.

9   At present the major studios (and the mini-majors) give orders in the film industry. They are capable of advancing funding for a project, whether internally or to an independent production company under contract. They also typically finance the distribution of a film, which for a major cinematic production averages more than $5 million today. As such, final market concentration remains very high and studios retain an enormous influence over the industry's output. In 1987, output of the US industry rose 17% over the previous year, attaining its mid-1970s levels and resulting in a shortage of exhibition screens in major US markets such as New York and Los Angeles. Major distributors such as Paramount or Warner Brothers have formed strategic alliances in the 1980s (i.e. forms of quasi-integration which remained legal after 1948 according to the interpretation of the Reagan antitrust lawyers), permitting them exclusive access to the most coveted cinemas, while independent producers have a much more difficult time securing screens, especially at certain times of year. The combination of greater output and shortage of screens will most likely lead to the weakening of some of the smaller studios and a new wave of mergers between major studios and mini-majors and independents. Oligopoly is thus securely installed, even in the flexibly specialised film industry. The structure is something like Benetton in the Italian clothing industry, or the US machine tool industry after its most recent wave of mergers and

acquisitions. Nonetheless, this continuing and vigorously reasserted financial centralisation in the industry has not led to reintegration of production activity. The latter suggests that the current organisation of production continues to be reproduced by very strong external economies.

REFERENCES

Aglietta, M. (1976) *A Theory of Capitalist Regulation*, London, New Left Books.

Bagnasco, A. (1977) *Tre Italie: La Problematica dello Svillupo*, Bologna, Il Mulino.

Becattini, G. (ed.) (1987) *Mercato e Forze Locali: il Distretto Industriale*, Bologna, Il Mulino.

Bellandi, M. (1986) 'The Marshallian Industrial District', Florence: Università degli Studi di Firenze, Dipartamento di Scienze Economiche, Studi e Discussioni no. 42.

Berger, S. and Piore, M. J. (1980) *Dualism and Discontinuity in Industrial Societies*, Cambridge, CUP.

Berger, S. (1981) 'The Uses of the Traditional Sector in Italy', in S.Bechofer and B. Elliot (eds), *The Petite Bourgeoisie*, London, Macmillan.

Boyer, R. (1986) 'Les Crises ne sont plus ce qu'elles etaient . . .', in R. Boyer (ed.), *Capitalismes Fin de Siècle*, Paris, Presses Universitaires de France.

Boyer, R. (1987) 'What is the Next Socio-Technical System Made of?' Berkeley, CA: Paper presented at BRIE Conference on Skills and Automation, September.

Boyer, R. and Coriat, B. (1986) 'Technical Flexibility and Macro Stabilisation', Paper presented to the Conference on Innovation Diffusion, Venice, March.

Braverman, H. (1974) *Labour and Monopoly Capital*, New York, Monthly Review Press.

Brusco, S. (1982) The Emilian model: productive decentralisation and social integration, *Cambridge Journal of Economics*, vol. 6, no. 2.

Brusco, S. and Sabel, C. (1981) Artisanal production and economic growth, in: F. Wilkinson (ed.), *The Dynamics of Labor Market Segmentation*, London, Academic Press.

Chaillou, B. (1977) Definition et Typologie de la Sous Traitance, *Revue Economique*, vol. 28, no. 2.

Christopherson, S. (1986) 'Peak Time, Slack Time: Trends Toward Labor Flexibility in the Reported and Unreported Economy', Washington, DC: Report to the US Congress, Office of Technology Assessment.

Christopherson, S. and Storper, M. (1989) New forms of labor segmentation and production politics in flexibly specialized industries, *Industrial and Labor Relations Review*, vol. 42, no. 3, 331–347.

David, P. A. (1975) *Technical Choice, Innovation, and Economic Growth*, New York, Cambridge University Press.

Elster, J. (1982) *Ulysses and the Sirens*, Cambridge, CUP.

Fua, G. (1983) Rural industrialization in later developed countries: the case of Northeast and Central Italy, *Banco Nazionale del Lavoro Quarterly Review*, December, 351–377.

Habakkuk, H. J. (1962) *American and British Technology in the Nineteenth Century*, Cambridge, CUP.

Hampton, B. (1970) *History of the American Film Industry: From Its Beginnings to 1931*, New York, Dover.

Hollywood Reporter annual. *Studio Blu-Book Directory*. Los Angeles, *Hollywood Reporter*.

Holmes, J. (1987) The impact of technological change on the organization and locational structure of automobile production in Canada, in K. Chapman and G. Humphrys (eds), *Technological Change and Industrial Policy*, Oxford, Basil Blackwell.

Hounshell, D. (1984) *From the American System to Mass Production, 1800–1932: The Development of Manufacturing Technology in the United States*, Baltimore, Johns Hopkins University Press.

Ikeda, M. (1979) The subcontracting system in the Japanese electronic industry, *Engineering Industries of Japan*, vol. 19, 43–71.

International Motion Picture Almanac, 1933–1985, annual. New York, Quigley Publications.

Kuznets, S. (1930) *Secular Movements in Production and Prices*, Boston, Houghton-Mifflin.

Leborgne, D. (1987) 'Equipements Flexibles et Organisation Productive: les Relations Industrielle au Coeur da la Modernisation–Elements de Comparaison Internationale', Paris: CEPREMAP, Couverture Orange.

Leborgne, D. and Lipietz, A. (1987) 'New Technologies, New Modes of Regulation: Some Spatial Implications', paper presented to the Conference on Changing Labour Processes and New Forms of Urbanization, Samos, Greece, Paris, CEPREMAP, Couverture Orange No. 8726.

Marshall, A. (1919) *Industry and Trade*, London, Macmillan.

Mistral, J. (1986) Régime Internationale et Trajectoires Nationales, in R. Boyer (ed.), *Capitalismes Fin de Siècle*, Paris, Presses Universitaires de France.

Murray, F. (1983) The decentralisation of production: the decline of the mass collective worker, *Capital and Class*, vol. 19, 74–99.

Nelson, R. and Winter, S. (1982) *An Evolutionary Theory of Economic Change*, Cambridge, Mass., Harvard University Press.

Offe, C. (1985) *Disorganized Capitalism*, Cambridge, CUP.

Piore, M. (1987) 'Corporate Reform in America and the Challenge to Economic Theory', paper presented to the Industrial Relations Seminar, MIT, February.

Piore, M. and Sabel, C. (1984) *The Second Industrial Divide*, New York, Basic Books.

The Production Company: The Complete Guide to Commercial and Industrial Production Companies in Los Angeles (1984 edn.) Edited by Louis Nicolaides, Los Angeles, Parmorand Publications.

Rosenberg, N. (1969) *The American System of Manufactures*, Edinburgh, Edinburgh University Press.

Rothbarth, E. (1946) Causes of superior efficiency of USA industry as compared with British industry, *The Economic Journal*, vol. 56, 383–390.

Rubery, J. and Wilkinson, F. (1981) Outwork and segmented labour markets, in F. Wilkinson (ed.) *The Dynamic of Labour Market Segmentation*, London, Academic Press.

Russo, M. (1986) Technical change and the industrial district: the role of interfirm relations in the growth and transformation of ceramic tile production in Italy, *Research Policy*, vol. 14, 329–343.

Sabel, C. and Zeitlin, J. (1985) Historical alternatives to mass production: politics, markets, and technology in nineteenth century industrialization, *Past and Present*, vol. 108, 133–176.

Sabel, C. F., Herrigel, G., Kazis, R., Deeg, R. (1987) How to keep mature industries innovative, *Technology Review*, April.

Savy, M. (1986) Les Territoires de l'Innovation: Technopoles et Aménagement, l'Expérience Française, *Revue d'Economie Régionale et Urbaine*, vol. 1, 41–60.

Scott, A. J. (1984a) Territorial reproduction and transformation in a local labor market: The animated film workers of Los Angeles, *Environment and Planning D: Society and Space*, vol. 2, 277–307.

Scott, A. J. (1984b) Industrial organization and the logic of intrametropolitan location III: A case study of the women's dress industry in the Greater Los Angeles region, *Economic Geography*, vol. 60, 3–27.

Scott, A. J. (1986) Industrial organization and location: division of labor, the firm, and spatial process, *Economic Geography*, vol. 62, 215–231.

Scott, A. J. (1988) *New Industrial Spaces: Flexible Production Organization and Regional Development in North America and Western Europpe*, London, Pion.

Scott, A. J. and Storper, M. (1987) High Technology Industry and Regional Development: A Theoretical Critique and Reconstruction, *International Social Science Review*, vol. 1, no. 12, 215–232.

Scranton, P. (1983) *Proprietary Capitalism*, Philadelphia, Temple University Press.

Solinas, G. (1982) Labour market segmentation and workers' careers: the case of the Italian knitwear industry, *Cambridge Journal of Economics*, vol. 6, no. 4.

Storper, M. (1985) Oligopoly and the product cycle, *Economic Geography*, vol. 61, no. 3.

Storper, M. and Christopherson, S. (1985) *The Changing Location and Organization of the Motion Picture Industry*, Los Angeles, UCLA Graduate School of Architecture and Urban Planning, Research Monograph No. 127.

Storper, M. and Christopherson, S. (1987) Flexible specialization and regional industrial agglomerations. *Annals of the Association of American Geographers*, vol. 77, no. 1.

Storper, M. and Scott, A. J. (1988) The geographical foundations and social regulation of flexible production complexes, in J. Wolch and M. Dear (eds), *Territory and Social Reproduction*, London, George Allen & Unwin.

Temin, P. (1966) Labor scarcity and the problem of American industrial efficiency in the 1850s, *Journal of Economic History*, vol. 26, 272–298.

Urry, J. (1986) Capitalist production, scientific management, and the service class, Scott, A. J. and Storper M. (eds), *Production, Work, Territory*, London, George Allen & Unwin.

Waterman, D. (1982) The structural development of the motion picture industry, *American Economist* vol. XXVI, no. 1.

Wiliamson, O. (1985) *The Economic Institutions of Capitalism*, New York, The Free Press.

7

Competing Structural and Institutional Influences on the Geography of Production in Europe

Ash Amin and Anders Malmberg

INTRODUCTION

These are times of momentous change in Europe, particularly in the geography of production, in which a number of major political and structural transformations are converging to establish the foundations of a new spatial division of labour. The transformations, at one level, are related to developments such as the creation of the Single European Market and the opening up of the East European economies to market forces. Both imply new opportunities for the location of economic activity as well as greater competition between places in an increasingly borderless economic landscape. But, change can be anticipated also in the very nature and organisational characteristics of production itself. Among different schools of thought on the dynamics of structural economic change – neo-Schumpeterians, regulationists, theorists of flexible specialisation – the present is often characterised as a period of epochal, systemwide, change.

These scholars write of the end of the hitherto dominant Fordist system of mass production, characterised by the urban agglomeration of production, and later, by the functional division of tasks between cities and regions which are hierarchically linked to each other. Against

This chapter is a reprint of an article published in *Environment and Planning A* (1992), vol. 24, pp. 401-16.

or overlaid on this Fordist scenario is anticipated a new age of more flexible production, characterised by a greater emphasis on the vertical disintegration of the division of labour and decentralised decision-making. The geography of post-Fordist production is said to be, at once, local and global. The new organisational networks, involving foreign direct investment and alliances, are transnational in their operational structure. But, in contrast to Fordism, production in individual localities, it is argued, is neither footloose nor reliant predominantly on nonlocal linkages. This is because the achievement of flexibility and new economies through the decentralisation of management and production is said to favour the establishment of strong ties and linkages at a local level: the global integration of production, thus, could unleash powerful decentralising tendencies and raise the potential for greater local embeddedness of the division of labour. Such a scenario, suggestive as it is of a 'Europe of the regions', stands in sharp contrast to the more familiar, Fordist, landscape of a small number of metropolitan regions and giant corporations dominating and controlling the development of the remaining majority of cities and regions.

In this chapter, we examine the changing balance between localising and globalising tendencies in the production system. We focus on developments of a structural rather than contingent nature, which are likely to exert a significant influence on both the location of economic activity and the potential for local economic development in the Europe of the 1990s. The chapter is conceptual in its orientation. The aim is not to provide a real map of changing geographies of production in Europe but simply an outline of some of the influencing tendencies. Furthermore, although accepting the notion of the present as a period of profound change, it should be emphasised that we reject the vision of an epochal transition from one all-embracing geography of production under Fordism to another singular geography characteristic of a new age of flexible production. This is because of a number of factors, including an appreciation of: the mosaic of varied corporate and sectoral geographies which may coexist in any one historical period; the persistence of strong organisational continuities from one period to another, both as influences on new developments and trends in their own right; and the equivocal nature of the present, as a period of experimentation and transition, rather than one of achieved and identifiable changes in the geography of production. The discussion, therefore, in this chapter of the geography of key aspects of change in the production system is deliberately contradictory and open-ended, reflecting as it does such tendencies in the reality of contemporary structural change.

To write a comprehensive account of the major influences on the changing geography of production in Europe is beyond the scope of this chapter, not least because the number of such influences is not small. This problem is compounded by difficulties associated with selecting the criteria for deciding which influences qualify to be of 'structural' significance. We have tended to circumvent this issue by focusing on four processes of change recognised in the contemporary literature on structural change to be of major importance. Two of the processes concern the locational effects of change in the organisational strategies of firms, and the remaining two focus on the impact of institutional and policy transformations at national and European level affecting the uneven regional distribution of production and local economic development prospects. Beginning with an assessment of the significance of new tendencies towards the local agglomeration of production, we go on to examine the geography of new forms of internationalisation in corporate activity. In the third section, we examine the implications of the rules governing the Single European Market on the question of regional economic convergence and cohesion in the European Community. In the final section we assess the implications for local economic development associated with the general shift in emphasis at national policy level, from the philosophy of interventionism to entrepreneurialism.

A LOCALISED EUROPE?

The most powerful case for the possibility of a 'Europe of the regions' comes from a group of writers speculating over the rise of locally agglomerated production systems out of the crisis of Fordism. Envisaged is a sort of a return to a Smithian division of labour between self-contained, product-specialist regional economies. This is a thesis which draws upon the work of Piore and Sabel (Piore and Sabel, 1984; Sabel, this reader), Scott and Storper (Scott, 1988; Storper, this reader; Storper and Scott, 1989), Hirst and Zeitlin (1989; 1991), and others deploying the concepts of flexible specialisation or flexible accumulation to describe the new times of vertically disintegrated and locationally fixed production.

Their key argument is that the irreversible growth in recent decades of consumer sovereignty, market volatility and fragmentation, and shortened life-cycles for products requires production to be organised on an extremely flexible basis. Size, scale, hierarchy, vertical integration, and task dedication on the part of machinery and employees are said to be too inflexible to turn out short runs of better quality and differentiated goods with the minimum of time and effort. Instead, what the market is said to require is decentralised coordination and control, the 'deverticalisation' of the division of labour between independent but interlinked units, numerical and task flexibility among the work force, greater reliance on innovation, ingenuity, and skills, the deployment of multipurpose and flexible tools and machinery, and the elimination of surplus time and wastage in supply and delivery. Such a change is said to be particularly pertinent to consumer commodities facing pronounced volatility and product specialisation in their markets. Examples include electronics, designer clothing, craft goods, and other light industrial products. New market circumstances require, it is proposed, a radical transformation of the production system towards flexible intrafirm and interfirm arrangements which can combine the economies of scope and versatility.

Such a transformation, it is argued, implies a return to place; a dependence on locational proximity between different agents involved in any production *filière*. Agglomeration is said to offer a series of Marshallian (Alfred) benefits which a system of vertically disintegrated and 'knowledge-based' production can draw upon. This includes: a reduction in transaction and transport costs; the buildup of a local pool of expertise and know-how; a social structure and culture which encourages labour flexibility and social cooperation as a result of face-to-face contact and the build-up of communal ties; and the growth of a local infrastructure of specialised services, distribution networks, and supply structures. Via the consolidation of particular product specialisms in different areas a federation of self-contained regional economies is anticipated, each economy with its own 'Myrdalian' cumulative causation effects, drawing upon the external economies of agglomeration.

The empirical basis of this thesis is the observation that over the last few decades the most dynamic and competitive examples of restructuring have been Marshallian in their spatial dynamics. The examples which are quoted have now become only too familiar. They include high technology and innovation intensive areas such as Silicon Valley, Boston, Cambridgeshire, the M4 corridor, Grenoble, Montpellier, and other technopoles which have launched new products. They also include industrial districts, both in semi-rural contexts (such as those in the Third Italy regions) and in inner-city environments (for example, motion pictures in Los Angeles and the furniture industry in inner London), in which networks of small firms produce craft or better quality consumer goods. Last, also cited is the example of areas such as Baden-Württemberg in Germany, where leading-edge large engineering companies (for example, Bosch) are said to rely on local subcontracting and supply networks for their flexibility and innovative excellence.

The significance of this thesis should not be underestimated, equating, as it does, industrial renovation with territorial development. The examples given are very real cases of success, and the experiences of such areas could well be emulated by other areas with similar economic, social, and institutional milieux. The interesting aspect of this new approach is the (re)discovery of the locational importance of patterns of linkages and the formation of interfirm relationships, notably in relation to the exchange of information between buyer and seller and its influence on linkage costs through the imposition of different kinds of transaction costs. The new literature makes the proposition that negotiations involved in purchasing and selling certain types of commodity are less conveniently carried on at a distance.

Fredriksson and Lindmark (1979), for instance, distinguish between standardised supplies and customer-specific supplies. Standardised supplies have in general little information associated with them and may therefore be exchanged nationally or even globally. Customer-specific supplies, on the other hand, are often based on extensive technical cooperation between the seller and the buyer. Therefore, such cooperation requires reliable and rapid communication, which is still usually conveyed through personal contacts. Distance-sensitive contacts limit the geographical area in which possible contractors should be located, if production with them is to be profitable (Fredriksson and Lindmark, 1979).

A similar distinction is suggested by Scott in accounting for the simultaneous presence of agglomerating and deglomerating tendencies in the location of manufacturing industry. Scott distinguishes two contrasting forms of production: plants with unstandardised and constantly changing output, characterised by small-scale, labour-intensive activities, and plants which are able to standardise their output and utilise large-scale, capital-intensive activities (Scott, 1983). For Scott, each form of production is associated with a different type of linkage. In the first case, linkages tend to vary in form and spatial pattern. Small-scale production also implies that the volume of each linkage will be small, and because linkages associated with this form of production are often highly specialised they are likely to be mediated by face-to-face contact. Linkages in the second case are, on the other hand, predicted to be invariant in content, stability, and volume. For these types of activities, orders can be refilled without costly renegotiations of specifications.

Differences in linkage characteristics have obvious locational implications. For small-scale activities, transport and communication costs on linkages will be high and sensitive to increasing distance. They will therefore encourage spatial agglomeration. For large-scale, highly-standardised, and capital-intensive plants, however, linkage costs will be less sensitive to increasing distances because of low transport rates and low spatially determinate transaction costs. Such plants can take advantage of the lower costs of labour and land outside the large agglomerations, and may be thus expected to have a more decentralised location.

This approach provides a basis for the analysis of the kind of economic activities that can be expected to centralise or decentralise spatially, and the kind of linkages which might be formed locally or globally. Production of customised goods and services under conditions of 'dynamic' competition will tend to bring with it agglomeration and local integration and may thus promote the formation of industrial districts. Production of standardised goods under conditions of price competition will, on the other hand, tend to encourage the decentralisation of production and the globalisation of linkages.

The problem of this new approach, however, is the extension of its theoretical formulations to unreserved and generalised claims about the direction of contemporary change in the production system (for example, see Scott, 1988). To anticipate a pervasive, perhaps even total, transition to local production complexes in the post-Fordist economy makes little sense, for a number of reasons.

First, it is inaccurate to refer to the areas cited by this thesis as the only examples of success. Others in Europe must include: the reconsolidation of large metropolitan areas such as London, Milan, Frankfurt, and Paris as major centres of growth through their command over finance, management, innovation, business services, and infrastructure; the resurgence of major provincial cities such as Birmingham, Turin, and Manchester through new combinations of industry, office relocation, and their intermediate roles in the financial and service sectors; and the growing wealth of certain rural areas through new combinations including further capital intensification in agriculture, the development of light industry, and in-migration by wealthier commuters looking for a pleasant life-style. These additions to the geography of 'success' have little in common with the logic of flexible specialisation and the reaffirmation of Marshallian tendencies.

Second, the perspective offered on the new Marshallian districts and production complexes is static and short-term. These areas, too, are likely to evolve, and, perhaps, fragment internally in much the same way as did Alfred Marshall's textiles and cutlery districts in Yorkshire in the course of the twentieth century. Evidence of such change is already apparent in 'mature' production complexes such as Silicon

Valley, which is being drawn into a wider spatial division of labour because of intensive inward investment by non-US multinationals and the export of labour-intensive and intermediate production functions, respectively, to areas of cheap labour and burgeoning markets. The Italian industrial districts, too, are undergoing change as they begin to substitute external linkages for local ones owing to the threat of takeover of local banks by foreign financial institutions, the rise in power of local industrial consortia seeking to integrate vertically or export capacity and know-how overseas, and the threat of competition from the newly industrialising countries which is forcing firms to rethink their organisational strategies (Amin, 1989; Bianchini, 1990; Harrison, 1990).

Third, and most significant in terms of policy, the 'spread' of localised production complexes is severely restricted by the fact that many of the conditions for success are not readily transferable (Amin and Robins, 1990). Localisation of the division of labour requires a gradual build-up of know-how and skills, cooperative traditions, local institutional support, and specialist services and infrastructure. These not only take time to consolidate, but also escape the traditional instruments of policy intervention owing to their ephemeral and composite nature. In addition, there remains the problem that 'new' growth cannot, as on a tabula rasa, sweep aside local traditions which might resist such change in the areas of policy intervention. The dismal failure of strategies to promote technopoles in different European localities, as well as efforts to encourage within depressed regions greater local networking between small firms and better local purchasing practices by large firms, bear witness to this difficulty.

Fourth, there is no conclusive evidence of the demise of Fordist principles of mass production and consumption and of the multitude of labour processes which coexist under Fordism (for instance, customisation, batch production, mass assembly, continuous flow). The idea of a clean break between one macrosystem dominated by one · way of doing things, and another regime with its own distinctive organisational structure, is too simple a caricature of historical change and a denial of the ebb and flow, the continuity and discontinuity, and the diversity and contradiction, that such change normally suggests (Sayer, 1989). The 'new Europe' will continue to be composed of many dominant and secondary production systems.

Sensitivity to diversity is particularly essential for the analysis of the geography of production. Depending on the labour process in an industry, the organisational cultures of the players involved, the nature of the areas in which activity is located, and the market circumstances surrounding individual sectors, a diversity of geographies could be produced, each offering different options on the spectrum between locational fixity and global mobility. Viewed purely in locational terms (rather than in terms of the development prospects of areas), it may well be that 'post-Fordist' Europe will see an *increase* in the range of possible spatial divisions of labour. This will occur not only because of the increase in number of old and new ways of 'doing things', but also because of the great expansion of locational options resulting from the availability of distance-shrinking new technologies and the erosion of trade barriers within and between the post-Communist and EC countries.

The emergence of new localised production complexes in Europe should, to conclude this section, be noted seriously. But, this should not become a basis for assuming, as two observers do, that 'the mode of production has, in a sense, gone back to the future,' with 'local economies . . . already on the march' (Cooke and Imrie, 1989, p. 326). If localities are on the march, it is, if anything, as argued next, to the tune of globalising forces in the organisation of production; a process in which local economic sustainability is far from guaranteed.

THE GEOGRAPHY OF GLOBALISED CORPORATE NETWORKS

Against the trend towards localisation stands another, more powerful, globalising trend associated primarily with the growing influence of transnational corporations (TNCs) over national and local economic development prospects. There are, of course, important variations in the degree of direct and indirect TNC influence over different nations, localities, and sectors in Europe. However, aggregate evidence of the growth of TNC influence in the course of the 1980s, at the level of the EC as a whole, tends to imply a gradual erosion of these variations in years to come.

A few indicators suffice to illustrate the growing economic reach of the TNCs. The 1980s saw a massive 25% per annum increase in the number of industrial mergers across a wide range of sectors within the EC. These were dominated by giant mergers, across both EC and non-EC borders, rather than within individual countries. It appears that much of this merger boom, which has continued into the 1990s, was driven by the desire of market leaders to strengthen their position in different national markets and to expand capacity in both their original and related sectors of expertise (Jacquemin et al., 1989). One consequence is that seller concentration levels for the top 100 firms (in the manufacturing and energy sectors) rose from 14.8% in 1982 to 20%

in 1988 of total market share within the EC as a whole. The study reveals a similar pattern of mergers and market concentration within the service sectors (distribution, banking, and insurance), albeit at a lower scale of intensity and internationalisation than in manufacturing.

The 1980s also witnessed a substantial increase, in real value, of large-firm-led foreign direct investment both in services and in manufacturing (acquisitions and new investment) between the EC countries, as well as active investment by US and Japanese companies into the Community (United Nations, 1988). This is a trend which is likely to be intensified as a result of the market opportunities offered by the economic and monetary union of the EC (Julius, 1990). As a consequence of this process, TNC control over employment, output, and trade within, especially, the most developed economies of the EC appears to have intensified and expanded in terms of the geographical reach of individual companies (United Nations, 1988).

Questions concerning the impact of this process of continuing concentration and centralisation of capital on an international scale, upon national economic development, are well rehearsed, through debates on the influence of TNCs on issues such as technology transfer, balance of payments, transfer pricing, national economic sovereignty, government policy priorities, fair competition, employment, and so on. But what of the geography of this process and its implications for local economic development prospects in Europe? Perhaps the most obvious point, but one which the localisation thesis forces to be made, is that corporate activity is increasingly being articulated on a Europe-wide scale, with local fortunes more or less tightly locked into this process of economic integration. Put differently, the meaning of place is becoming increasingly defined within the hyperspace of corporate activity (Swyngedouw, 1989).

To say this is not, of course, a denial of the possibility of development at the local level. It is, rather, an assertion of the growing dependence of such development upon events and decisions within a wider corporate division of labour. The actual form of development in individual cities and regions is a matter of the nature of this division of labour and the position or status of different places within it. And, on this point, there appears to be no conclusive evidence of change in any one particular direction today as far as the functional and operational status of divisional sections and branch plants are concerned.

Despite claims for the opposite (for example, Walker, 1989), there are still good grounds for assuming that divisional sections and branch plants have a functional and operational status which is different from that of independent firms or establishments located close to the headquarter sites of a multilocational organization (Malmberg, 1990). The difference derives from the cost attached to establishing and controlling the performance of an economic activity at a distance. The existence of such a decentralisation cost means that a branch plant will be established only if some locational advantage will compensate for this cost, and, theoretically, that it will be closed down as soon as this advantage, for some reason, disappears.

It is, from the point of view of transaction costs, reasonable to argue that the decentralisation cost will produce a functional differentiation between branch plants and headquarter plants. There are differences between the costs of decentralisation of various types of activities. Unstandardised and complex operations (such as R&D) are more difficult to control and to coordinate at a distance than routinised and simple operations (for example, the assembly of standardised goods), and thus, other things being equal, branch plants are likely to be dominated by the simpler activities.

Of course, it may well be that individual companies, for reasons of contingency, find it more profitable to raise the functional profile of individual plants, thus offering greater scope for 'territorial integration' at individual sites within the intrafirm hierarchy. But equally there is an abundance of examples which show continuity with older functional spatial hierarchies, characterised, at one end, by the location of headquarter and strategic corporate functions within metropolitan areas and, at the other end, task-specific 'screwdriver' plants in peripheral regions.

Massey's work on the multiplicity of possible corporate spatial hierarchies (Massey, 1984) is a useful reminder of the futility of absolutising from particular locational forms. But, and this is the point, one generalisation which can be made is that, as a result of the widening reach of the TNCs, the functional status and development prospects of more and more localities in Europe are becoming tied to their role within these international corporate geographies rather than to their status as self-contained and independent economies. Increasingly, the metaphor of 'dependent development', capturing, as it once did, the problems of partial industrialisation, task specificity, failure of local linkage formation, and hypermobility of investment in peripheral regions, has to be applied to a wider range of localities in Europe – urban and rural, developed and developing, core and peripheral – as they are drawn into an internationally integrated production system.

What, however, of the post-Fordist argument that today the organisational arrangements of large corporations are less hierarchical and more loosely structured and decentralised than before? Is it not the case that new corporate production systems are, in the pursuit of greater flexibility, composed of loose networks of intrafirm and interfirm alliances? Do these networks not offer greater scope for local proactivity and territorial integrity? There can be no doubt about the growing significance of networking as a form of organisation and governance which combines elements of 'market' and 'hierarchy' within the field of corporate activity. The proliferation of literature on such subjects as 'hollowing out', new forms of subcontracting relations, 'just-in-time' delivery, new forms of joint venture, and 'strategic alliances' confirms this significance. However, on two critical questions affecting local possibilities, namely the geographical scale at which corporate networking is occurring and the locus of control and command within these networks, the answers are far from clear.

In the case of 'hollowing out', the experience of even the most celebrated example of Benetton – the Italian clothing giant – does not extend beyond the putting out of only production tasks to small companies within the regional economy. There is no decentralisation of control or strategic functions. Links with suppliers and subcontractors remain extremely hierarchical, and, as a consequence, the terms for local economic development are set at the apex of the production *filière*. Furthermore, in other cases, 'hollowing out' is far from being a local phenomenon, as companies scan the world for subcontractors, taking benefit of the cost-reducing effects of advanced transport and communication systems. It is also worth noting that new opportunities offered locally or globally to firms as a result of this process are double-edged, as often an accompanying development is forward vertical integration by the firms in order to gain strategic control over markets and distribution networks.

Similar contradictions are apparent also in another area of networking, which concerns changes in buyer–supplier relations. Much is made at present of the moves made by the largest and most progressive firms, in especially multicomponent industries such as motor vehicles, towards greater partnership and collaboration with suppliers. Contracts are now said to be more stable and long-term, involving joint design work, sole-sourcing agreements, respect for mutual areas of expertise, and a high premium on 'total service and quality'. Less trumpeted in the literature, however, is that such contracts are, more often than not, the privilege of only a minority of 'preferred-status' suppliers. Viewed from the perspective of the many more secondary status or excluded suppliers, these are exclusive partnerships representing a form of quasi-integration between dominant actors along the value-added chain in an industry, which threatens their survival and growth. 'Partnership' thus does not imply any simple erosion of oligopolistic or centralising tendencies in the production *filière*, and, as a consequence, as in the past, these tendencies will continue to determine who benefits in the supplier chain.

Nowhere could this be more true than in the case of 'strategic alliances' – another oft-cited example in the post-Fordist literature of corporate decentralisation. Strategic alliances proliferated in the 1980s in notably the research-intensive and volatile-market industries such as semiconductors, computers, aerospace, and machine tools. In contrast to other forms of alliance such as joint ventures, they appear to be long-term and multidimensional, involving joint R&D, technology transfer, licensing agreements, collaborative marketing, and coproduction as an attempt by firms to spread risks and costs and prevent market failure. But, as far as spatial questions are concerned, it has to be noted that these alliances are not local or small-firm based but global partnerships between the major actors in the same or a related industry. Add to this observation the fact that the proliferation in recent years of more orthodox forms of joint venture has also been increasingly across national boundaries (Jacquemin et al., 1989) and the scenario of net-working being a local phenomenon becomes unsustainable.

These various examples of blurring of corporate boundaries across territorial and ownership borders represent a new form of flexible integration rather than disintegration of the production system. Networking is a process of collaboration between large competitors, leading to the creation of global oligarchies dominated by the TNCs, with their 'loose–tight' webs of partners and subcontractors (Amin and Dietrich, 1991). As such, it is also a process of *geographical* integration, as more and more places come to be included in or excluded by these networks. The functional status of individual localities within these global networks may well be more complex and less hierarchical than that of cities and regions linked together purely in relation to their respective roles within an intrafirm division of labour. But, as far as the direction of development of these 'networked' localities is con-cerned, they too, and it seems strange to have to say this, are not masters of their own destiny, subject as they are to the authority and influence of the prime movers within the networks. In contrast, however, to the centres of control within intracorporate hierarchies, which are visibly clustered around the major European cities, it could be that the locus of control within the new global networks is more dif-fuse and less readily identifiable, thus making the task of situating the source of uneven development more difficult.

ECONOMIC AND MONETARY UNION AND THE REGIONS OF EUROPE

Thus far, issues concerning the restructuring of the production system have been discussed in terms of the implications of structural change in the economy itself. In this section, we examine the implications of major institutional changes proposed at a cross-European level on the geography of production and on prospects for local economic development. The discussion is focused on the implications of the emerging rules governing the Economic and Monetary Union (EMU) of the EC.

One of the meanings attached to the term 'Europe of the Regions' by the European Commission itself is the possibility, elucidated within the regional policy proposals attached to EMU, to reduce disparities within the EC via the introduction of various policies designed to improve industrial competitiveness in the less-favoured regions (LFRs). The Commission, contrary to popular opinion, does not share the neoliberal view that economic and monetary union will bring automatic efficiency and scale gains to all parties, including the LFRs. The latter is a view which anticipates regional economic convergence as a natural outcome of EMU, either as a result of the automatic 'trickle-down' of EC-wide growth to the LFRs, or because of the added scope which free competition and perfect factor mobility is supposed to provide for developing regional comparative advantage through product specialisation. The Commission, in contrast, agrees with the critics of this view who argue that integration left to the market only could well increase regional disparities by strengthening the hand of the strongest firms and the core regions.

The critique of the neo-Smithian view of Europe goes beyond a simple rejection of its neoclassical assumptions regarding the benign nature and rational allocative powers of the free market. It is argued that monetary union could severely damage the national and regional economies of countries with weaker currencies entering into the mechanism of permanent fixed exchange rates. In sacrificing monetary adjustment as a means of boosting exports or controlling imports, such economies will be forced to adjust or fall through the painful route of unemployment and an enforced fall in real wages and revenue (Begg, 1989). Monetary union could also threaten the successful industrialising regions if the impending liberalisation of financial markets facilitates predator behaviour by the larger institutions over the smaller banks which, in areas such as the Italian industrial districts, have played a critical role in the financing of growth. Last, monetary union, in implying a move towards the harmonisation of tax levels between member states, could curtail the differential use of fiscal incentives which, in some countries, have been an important tool for attracting investment into the less-favoured regions.

Market rather than monetary integration is perhaps the issue which has received most attention in the analysis of the economic prospects of the different regions of Europe. Two of the most common arguments, actively debated within the Commission itself (for example, Delors, 1989; Doyle, 1989), are, first, that higher transport and communication costs in the geographically peripheral regions will put the industries of such regions at a disadvantage and, second, that integration will automatically favour larger firms in the strongest regions as they will benefit most from the scale advantages offered by market expansion. The centralisation of production in the major metropolitan and provincial cities is anticipated also because of their proximity to markets and the agglomeration economies deriving from access to qualified labour, finance, business services, and so on (Begg, 1989). This tendency could be further encouraged, so the argument goes, by the removal of previous incentives to cross-border investments resulting from the existence of national trade barriers prior to 1992. The regional divergence thesis also draws attention to the possible loss of entrepreneurial potential within the LFRs owing to the migration of the most skilled and employable towards the fast-growing or core regions.

Brussels recognises the danger of polarised regional development after 1992, but it is not alarmed by this prospect, because of its faith in the ability of its reforms to regional policy to vitalise the competitive potential of the LFRs. Its optimism, however, is unwarranted. The institutional aspects of the reforms are undoubtedly innovative and positive in proposing more direct interaction between Brussels and the LFRs, more political autonomy to the regions (through the recognition of independent regional assemblies, and the initiatives of independent development agencies), and commitment to multiannual and programmatic finance for targeted projects in the LFRs.

But the substance of the reforms falls far short of achieving the objective of making the LFRs more competitive. The proposed doubling of real expenditure on the structural funds (regional policy, the social fund, and the guidance section of agricultural funds) will still amount to only 3% of the GDP of the Community. This, in the context of declining national government expenditure on the regions, is not enough to even begin to achieve the Commission's stated objectives, which are to develop the structurally backward regions, convert regions in industrial decline, combat long-term unemployment, increase youth employment, and secure the development of the rural areas. Furthermore, the major policy focus of the reforms on improvements in transport and communications infrastructure, training, and, to a lesser extent, the technological capability of the LFRs falls far short of enabling a successful supply-side solution for restoring regional competitiveness.

Much more is needed, particularly in the regions requiring improvements in the efficiency of manufacturing industry and related services; both sectors in which the established supremacy of the core regions will be further consolidated by the cumulative effects unleashed by EMU. In contrast, for regions with specific geophysical advantages the focus of the EC reforms on developing agriculture, related sectors, and tourism in the rural communities could provide a major stimulus for development. However, here too, there are threats to the weakest of such regions resulting from growing interregional competition in the tourism industry and the almost inevitable lowering of subsidies provided by the common agricultural policy.

The concentration of growth in the economically most advanced cities and regions, therefore, remains a distinct possibility, despite the proposed reforms to the structural funds. But what will be the precise cause of this process? In our opinion, the regional divergence model is not entirely accurate in assuming the regions to be coherent and self-contained economies pitted against each other, with resources flowing in one direction as a result of imbalanced interregional competition. Earlier in this chapter, it has been argued that through the internationalisation of business hierarchies and networks the European regions are becoming more and more integrated with each other on a functional basis within a transnational corporate division of labour. As a result, uneven spatial development is less a matter of interregional competition than a question concerning the impact on local economies of the uneven spatial distribution of tasks within a Europe-wide integrated corporate production system. The consequence of this process is the sacrifice of local territorial integrity as regions come to play fragmented roles in a global system. Implicit in this is also the narrowing of locally led development capability, as power and control become centralised in the diminishing number of headquarter locations of the most powerful firms.

These are the spatial tendencies which, in our opinion, EMU is most likely to further, as it strengthens the position of the core regions and the most powerful firms. The Commission, ironically, accepts the need to develop firms with a global presence in order to survive North American and Japanese competition. Indeed, big firms, by design or effect, are the major beneficiaries both of the various programmes which constitute the Commission's technology policy (Roobeek, 1990) and of the relaxed stance of EC competition policy towards the market behaviour of large firms. The spatial effects of these two major arms of EC policy remain unmonitored and unregulated, thus rendering less effective the underfunded instruments of regional policy to improve local entrepreneurship. This spatial paradox could well be exacerbated by the further stimulus to economic concentration which EMU will provide by attracting non-EC multinationals to establish a foothold in 'fortress Europe' and to join other multinational corporations to reap the scale benefits of EMU.

For the moment, then, it looks as though the Brussels dream of a 'Europe of the Regions' could well be sacrificed. This is an unfortunate outcome, because in many ways Brussels is the most appropriate locus for effective action over the spatial allocation of tasks within the Community's division of labour in production. The consolidation of global firms as major shapers and shakers of local economies in Europe, and the productive integration of cities and regions on a European scale, necessitate intervention at this spatial scale. With sufficient funding for the LFRs, appropriate reforms to the structural funds and the 'regionalisation' of other Community policies the Commission could become the guarantor of progress towards regional convergence.

THE TRANSITION TO THE ENTREPRENEURIAL STATE AND LOCAL ECONOMIC DEVELOPMENT PROSPECTS

Significant changes to the uneven spatial distribution of development prospects are implicit also in a major change in thinking and practice, at national level, in the arena of urban and regional policy in the course of the 1980s. Harvey has described this period as a phase of transition from 'managerialist' to 'entrepreneurial' models of spatial governance (Harvey, 1989). The managerialist model refers to a form of centralised intervention relying largely upon the modernisation of infrastructure and industrial relocation in the LFRs through active regional policy within an overall context of Keynesian macroeconomic management of the national economy. Entrepreneurialism, in contrast, refers to greater state reliance upon private-sector-led efforts to develop local entrepreneurial potential as the mainstay of urban and regional growth rather than the redistribution policies of central government.

Depending on geographical and political context, the entrepreneurial solution has drawn on a range of strategies, including: reduced expenditure on regional policy; the provision of financial, fiscal, and other incentives such as premises and advice and training to boost the formation and growth of new firms; the creation of 'technopoles' and 'science parks' and other forms of support to improve local technological capability and innovation potential; and the funding of public and private-sector 'partnerships' to regenerate urban areas through flagship property redevelopment projects and high-visibility initiatives such as theme parks, leisure centres, and popular cultural events. The entrepreneurial model is a novel response to the problem of uneven development which draws upon locally based efforts to improve the competitive potential of weaker and less-favoured cities and regions. It is also a model which is distinctly synoptic in its approach, venturing as it does from the provision of direct support to manufacturing industry, to targeted aid for new sectors such as the leisure and cultural industries, and upgrading of the general social, technical, and physical infrastructure for future entrepreneurship.

The transition to entrepreneurship has not been, by any means, total or identical in Europe. The New Right, antistatist version has been most pronounced in Britain, whereas more orthodox forms of regional support from central government continue to remain important in France and Italy, and entrepreneurship in Germany continues to involve active state participation at both federal and *Länder* level. But, set against the context of the previous and very different Keynesian model of public intervention, and the new language today of most policy-makers across Europe which celebrates the virtues of local entrepreneurship, the argument for seeing the above differences as simply shades of a new policy model of general significance is not without foundation.

What, then, are the implications of this model for the geography of local economic development prospects? The new local 'boosterism', where it has been accompanied by financial generosity on the part of the central state as well as a genuine desire to involve local authorities, the business community and other collective bodies such as the trades unions, is undoubtedly a step in the direction of identifying collective solutions for the problems of individual local economies. There is much to be commended in the attempt to develop a more comprehensive approach to local problems which widens the field of policy coverage, and experiments with different factors on the supply side in order to boost entrepreneurial potential. Thus, in its most imaginative and democratic guise the new localism can be seen as a genuine attempt to broaden the definition of what constitutes the local productive economy and of the ingredients necessary for its development; an exercise which may well free new local 'entrepreneurial' potential.

This new strategy to turn localities into self-promoting islands of entrepreneurship, however, faces some major difficulties if it is to become a universally viable strategy for local economic regeneration. At the simplest level, the synoptic nature of its approach runs the risk of losing focus as money comes to be spread thinly across a wide number of ventures (usually with short-term appeal) as has been the case with efforts in the 1980s to develop science parks, enterprise zones, waterfront redevelopment schemes, retail complexes, garden festivals, and so on. This fetish with diversity and continual change in policy priorities has, in many instances, amounted to simply a lack of clarity in vision about the purpose and scope of local economic development policy; an outcome in which the significance of the term 'local economic development' has become diffuse enough to include policies to promote factories, retail complexes, leisure centres, property redevelopment, infrastructural renovation, cultural spectacles, and so on.

The commitment to a strategy of multipronged intervention also considerably extends the prospect of failure, because, in practice, one necessary condition for success, namely effective coordination across the different tiers and areas of intervention, is readily sacrificed in all but the very few localities in which a central authority capable of fulfilling such a role can be identified. In the entrepreneurial model, relinquishing, as it does, control over the development process to a multitude of agencies, such failure is highly likely. In the event of failure, the principal achievement of the model will be that of sacrificing any obligation to develop a coherent or consistent approach to local economic regeneration, thereby exposing local communities to the horrifying prospect of becoming the playing field for a thousand-and-one different and fragmenting entrepreneurial ventures, bound together by nothing more than the profit-seeking adventurism of the private sector.

For weaker regions, this horror could well turn into a nightmare greater than the fragmentation of economic development priorities and the inevitable sectionalism associated with private-sector-led governance of the local economy. Entrepreneurship also represents the abandonment of such regions to less-regulated macroeconomic forces. At one level, this may mean the reduction of direct central state support for the LFRs through the erosion of regional policy incentives and it may also lead to deleterious consequences resulting from the privatisation or restructuring of state-owned industry or the deregulation of the public utilities and services.

At another level, the efflorescence, in a multitude of localities, of identical 'post-industrial' growth strategies, all without any central coordination, may have the effect of intensifying interregional competition. There are limits, for instance, to the number of local heritage centres which a national tourism industry can tolerate, and the risk of failure is even higher once places are forced to copy each other, as the barrel of new ideas becomes depleted. The implication, then, is that the first-comer areas or those with significant resources or market-size will have a competitive advantage over other areas, which, over the longer term, could lead to a recentralisation of economic activity.

A third consequence of the transition to an entrepreneurial model of governance could be the impairment of locally based growth strategies as a result of the anti-interventionist macroeconomic policies of the central state. Many of the characteristic features of neo-liberalism, such as free trade, tight monetary control, stringency in public-sector borrowing, reduced subsidisation of industry by the state, the removal of restrictions on corporate behaviour, and so on, have effectively removed any form of protective framework for less-efficient industry. The impact of this may be that of not only wiping out large sections of industry in the less-favoured cities and regions, but also endangering the new and fragile entrepreneurship which the state itself has sought to promote in such areas.

CONCLUSION

The major processes of economic and political restructuring in Europe today are, as proposed in this chapter, characterised by contradictory spatial tendencies. There are numerous indications of an increasing globalisation of the production system, but also evidence of localisation in particular industries and spatial contexts. The global reach and influence of the large TNCs appear to be ever increasing as a consequence of the process of international capital concentration and centralisation. At the same time, however, the TNCs are also adopting less-hierarchical modes of operation, combining local and global forms of industrial networking. We observe that some firms are tending towards intensification of their relations with suppliers, customers, and other actors in the immediate surroundings. We are also witnessing, albeit on a limited scale, the emergence in Europe as well as in the USA of new Marshallian industrial agglomerations, as an outcome of the need for constant and rapid interaction between firms in a world of fluctuating markets. Simultaneously, as the examples of TNC restructuring have illustrated only too clearly, these business alliances are by no means primarily a local phenomenon.

Contradictions prevail also in the arena of regional and industrial policy. At the level of the nation state, the transition towards locally based entrepreneuralism as a mainstay for urban and regional regeneration is at once a boost to local proactivity and a legitimation of a blurring in focus and direction of development priorities. Local 'boosterism', on the other side of the coin, is becoming accompanied by an intensification of interregional competition for investment and initiatives as national governments reduce their commitment to the principle of central coordination or regulation of the space economy.

The European Commission's vision of a 'Europe of the Regions' corresponds to a degree with the managerialist model that previously dominated spatial and industrial policy at the national level. The ambition seems to be that a central authority – in this case at a supranational level – should assume the responsibility of formulating a comprehensive strategy for the development of European cities and regions. This is mirrored in the proposed reforms to EC regional policy towards reconstructing the development capability of regions within a centrally regulated framework of resource allocation and monitoring of corporate industrial location patterns.

As things stand, the prospects for the weaker region – old industrial and newly industrialising – do not appear to be promising. The greater demand for organisational flexibility in the post-Fordist marketplace is not, as the localisation theorists would want it, leading to a generalised return to the region as the basic unit of economic development. If there is a certain tendency for the resurgence of Marshallian industrial districts, not only is this tendency of limited empirical significance, but it is also one which is focused in particular kinds of localities, the characteristics of which (craft traditions, informal networks and commonality of purpose, 'intact' local financial and institutional structures, and so on) are not readily transferable to or easily created within fragmented or externally integrated peripheral regions.

The implications, of institutional reform at both national and EC level, for weaker regions – more precisely, those in which development in the region is failing to produce development of the region – are equally unpromising. These regions might be sacrificed to the intensified interregional competition in Europe which is implied by both the erosion of trade barriers after the completion of the Single European Market and the loss of central responsibility towards the regions within those nation states pursuing neoliberal policies. If not this, they will almost certainly fall prey to the Europe-wide corporate geographies unfolding today, and likely to be enhanced by the '1992' agenda. On this issue, it is not clear whether the local commitment of TNC investment in the less-favoured regions has improved significantly in recent years. The central item for debate concerns whether the functional status of the branch plants and local divisions of the TNCs has changed so much that they can now act as growth poles for regional development. For this to occur, at least two basic conditions would need to be met: first, a significant improvement in local buyer–supplier linkages and, second, a genuine transfer of functional and strategic authority to local management. For the moment, there is no conclusive evidence of change in this direction.

REFERENCES

Amin, A. (1989) 'Flexible specialisation and small firms in Italy: myths and realities'. *Antipode*, 21(1), 13–34.

Amin, A., Dietrich, M. (1991) 'From hierarchy to "hierarchy": the dynamics of contemporary corporate restructuring in Europe', in *Towards a New Europe*, eds A. Amin, M. Dietrich (Edward Elgar, Aldershot, Hants) pp. 49–73.

Amin, A., Robins, K. (1990) 'The re-emergence of regional economies? The mythical geography of flexible accumulation'. *Environment and Planning D: Society and Space*, 8, 7–34.

Begg, I. (1989) 'European integration and regional policy'. *Oxford Review of Economic Policy*, 5(2), 90–104.

Bianchini, F. (1990) 'The "Third Italy": model or myth?', mimeograph, Centre for Urban Studies, University of Liverpool, Liverpool.

Cooke, P., Imrie, R. (1989) "Little victories: local economic development in European regions'. *Entrepreneurship and Regional Development*, 1, 313–327.

Delors, J. (1989) 'Regional implications of economic and monetary integration', in *Report on Economic and Monetary Union in the European Community*. Committee for the Study of Economic and Monetary Union (European Communities Commission, Luxembourg).

Doyle, M. (1989) 'Regional policy and European economic integration', in *Report on Economic and Monetary Union in the European Community*. Committee for the Study of Economic and Monetary Union (European Communities Commission, Luxembourg).

Fredriksson, C., Lindmark, L. (1979) 'From firms to systems of firms: a study of interregional dependence in a dynamic society', in *Spatial Analysis, Industry and the Industrial Environment–Progress in Research and Application: Volume 1, Industrial System*, eds F. E. I. Hamilton, G. J. R. Linge (John Wiley, Chichester, Sussex) pp. 115–138.

Harrison, B. (1990) 'Industrial districts: old wine in new bottles?' WP-90-35. School of Urban and Public Affairs, Carnegie Mellon University, Pittsburgh, PA.

Harvey, D. (1989) 'From managerialism to entrepreneurialism: the transformation of urban governance in late capitalism'. *Geografiska Annaler*, 71, 3–17.

Hirst, P., Zeitlin, J. (1989) 'Flexible specialisation and the competitive failure of UK manufacturing'. *Political Quarterly*, 60(3), 164–178.

Hirst, P., Zeitlin, J. (1991) 'Flexible specialisation vs post-Fordism: theory, evidence, and policy implications'. *Economy and Society*, 20, 1–56.

Jacquemin, A., Bulges, P., Ilkovitz, F. (1989) *European Economy 40. Horizontal Mergers and Competition Policy in the European Community* (Directorate-General for Economic and Financial Affairs, Commission for the Europe Communities, Luxembourg).

Julius, D. (1990) *Global Companies and Public Policy: The Growing Challenge of Foreign Direct Investment* (Frances Pinter, London).

Malmberg, B. (1990) 'The effects of external ownership. A study of linkages and branch plant location'. *Geografiska Regionstudier No. 24*, Kulturgeografiska Institutionen, Uppsala Universitet, Uppsala.

Piore, M., Sabel, C. F. (1984) *The Second Industrial Divide* (Basic Books, New York).

Roobeek, A. (1990) 'The technological debacle: European technology policy from a future perspective'. *Futures*, 904–912.

Sayer, A. (1989) 'Post-Fordism in question'. *International Journal of Urban and Regional Research*, 13, 666–695.

Scott, A. (1983) 'Industrial organisation and the logic of intra-metropolitan location. 1. Theoretical considerations'. *Economic Geography*, 59(3), 233–250.

Scott, A. J. (1988) *Studies in Society and Space 3. New Industrial Spaces: Flexible Production Organisation and Regional Development in North America and Western Europe* (Pion, London).

Storper, M., Scott, A. J. (1989) 'The geographical foundations and social regulation of flexible production complexes', in *The Power of Geography: How Territory Shapes Social Life*, eds, J. Wolch, M. Dear (Unwin Hyman, Winchester, MA) pp. 21–40.

Swyngedouw, E. (1989) 'The heart of the place: the resurrection of locality in an age of hyperspace'. *Geografiska Annaler*, 71(1), 31–42.

United Nations (1988) *Transnational Corporations in World Development* (United Nations Centre on Transnational Corporations, New York).

Walker, R. (1989) 'A require for corporate geography: new directions in industrial organisation, the production of place and uneven development'. *Geografiska Annaler*, 71(1), 43–68.

Part III
Policy and Politics Beyond Fordism

8

Post-Fordism and the State

Bob Jessop

Movement from Fordism to post-Fordism involves a complex and interrelated series of changes in the labour process and the overall dynamic of macroeconomic growth. It also involves changes both in the social mode of economic regulation which guides and governs the prevailing mode of growth and in the overall character of the political and social order associated with it. It is the implications of these changes for the form and functions of the state that concern me here. I argue that the state is undergoing a fundamental restructuring and strategic reorientation in two key respects. First, there is a tendential shift from the Keynesian welfare state appropriate to the Fordist mode of growth to a Schumpeterian workfare state more suited in form and function to an emerging post-Fordism. And, second, there is also a tendential 'hollowing out' of the national state, with state capacities, new and old alike, being reorganized on supranational, national, regional or local, and translocal levels.[1] It would be wrong, of course, to attribute these changes exclusively to the impact of the transition from Fordism to post-Fordism. But I do hope to show how this transition can be related to current changes in the state and its activities.

FORDISM AND POST-FORDISM

As the other chapters in this reader amply reveal, there are huge disparities in how Fordism and post-Fordism are interpreted. Since the transition between them plays a crucial role in my argument, it is important to define my own use of the terms. I begin with the nature of Fordism and its ideal-typical form of state. This will prepare the ground for defining post-Fordism and the post-Fordist state and thereby provide firmer foundations for my arguments about the hollowing out of the Schumpeterian workfare state.

The nature of Fordism

Drawing on the regulation approach, some order can be introduced into studies of Fordism and post-Fordism by distinguishing five alternative referents for these terms: (a) the labour (or production) process considered as a particular configuration of technical and social relations of production; (b) an accumulation regime, i.e. a macroeconomic regime sustaining growth in capitalist production and consumption; (c) a social mode of economic regulation, i.e. an ensemble of norms, institutions, organizational forms, social networks and patterns of conduct which guide and govern a given accumulation regime;[2] (d) a mode of societalization, i.e. a pattern of institutional integration and social cohesion which complements the dominant accumulation regime and its social mode of economic regulation and thereby secures the conditions for its dominance within the wider society; and (e) a social formation characterized by the contingent correspondence of all four of the preceding features (see Jessop 1992a, b).

It should be noted here that there is no consensus among regulationists as to whether the first four referents are simply so many different sites or levels on which Fordism or post-Fordism might arise (without regard to their presence elsewhere), successively emergent levels of organization (originating in the labour process) or potentially complementary forms of (post-)Fordism whose contingent co-presence helps to stabilize the corresponding social relations on any given site. This is not the place to address this set of questions in detail. Instead I will simply assume that a given labour process can exist independently of the corresponding accumulation regime; that an autocentric (relatively closed and self-sustaining) accumulation regime of a given type can be associated with various labour processes as long as these are organized under the dominance of the corresponding labour-process; that the stability of an accumulation regime, autocentric or not, depends on the contingent and often precarious co-presence of an appropriate social mode of economic regulation; and that a given mode of societalization results from the dominance of an accumulation regime and its mode of regulation in conjunction with various social routines that successfully cope with the social conflicts and perturbations originating in the dominance of that regime.

With all due regard to these qualifications, it remains the case, as noted above, that Fordism and post-Fordism can be defined in various ways. First, it can be seen as a distinctive type of labour process. In this context it can be considered either at the level of a specific production process independent of any wider linkages or in terms of its articulation to other types of labour process in an enterprise, branch, region or wider economic space. Seen in the latter sense, as a distinctive combination of labour processes, Fordism involves mass production of complex consumer durables based on moving assembly line techniques operated with the semi-skilled labour of the mass worker. Not all branches or workers will be directly involved in mass production in a Fordist economy, of course: the important point is that mass production is the main source of its dynamism.

Second, as a stable mode of macroeconomic growth, Fordism in its strict, ideal-typical sense should involve a virtuous circle of growth in relatively closed economies. This would be based on mass production, rising productivity based on economies of scale, rising incomes linked to productivity, increased mass demand owing to rising wages, increased profits based on full utilization of capacity and increased investment in improved mass production equipment and techniques.[3] However, it is also common to describe as Fordist, economies in which such a pattern of growth tends to be dominant. The term is also used even more loosely to describe modes of growth in more open economies in which rising wages and increasing mass consumption are premised on exports of other goods or services to pay for imports of mass-produced consumer durables.

Third, as a social mode of economic regulation, Fordism involves several key features. These comprise: the separation of ownership and control in large corporations with a distinctive multidivisional, decentralized organization subject to central controls; monopoly pricing; union recognition and collective bargaining; wages indexed to productivity growth and retail price inflation; monetary emission and credit policies oriented to securing effective aggregate demand; state-sponsored social reproduction oriented to the generalization of norms of mass consumption and the provision of infrastructure and means of collective consumption suitable to a Fordist mode of growth; and state involvement in managing the conflicts between capital and labour over both the individual and the social wage so that the virtuous circle of Fordist growth can be maintained. In this context the key wage bargains will be struck in the mass production industries: the going rate will then spread through comparability claims among the employed and through the indexation of welfare benefits financed through progressive taxation for those not economically active. This pattern need not mean the demise of dual labour markets or non-unionized firms or sectors as long as mass demand rises in line with productivity.

Fourth, Fordism can be seen as a general pattern of social organization involving the consumption of standardized, mass commodities in nuclear family households and the provision of standardized, collective goods and services by the bureaucratic state. This typically implies that Fordist society is an urban-industrial, 'middle mass', wage-earning society.[4] Finally, as indicated above, Fordism sometimes refers to the co-presence, structural coupling, co-evolution and strategic coordination of all four possible Fordist phenomena.

Even when the first four possible referents can be separated for analytical purposes, real problems still remain in operationalizing the concept of Fordism, for it is not always clear whether Fordism refers to actually existing structural forms and dynamics or simply to the presence of modes of calculation and/or strategies which aim to implement them. It is perfectly possible, for example, that corporate managers, economic policy-makers or state managers more generally operate on Fordist assumptions in the short-run at least, even though the labour process, accumulation regime or social mode of economic regulation actually correspond to some other pattern (e.g. Kristensen, 1990). In this sense there is considerable scope for discongruence between the structural forms of Fordism and their expression in strategic paradigms, as well as for significant local and national variations. This is possible, of course, for each of its dimensions. This in turn requires that specific theoretical choices are made so that, whatever the general problems involved in defining Fordism (and, *a fortiori*, post-Fordism), its denotation and connotations in any given study are clear. For present purposes, at least, the distinctiveness of Fordism as a phase of capital accumulation is grounded in its basic features as a social mode of economic regulation.

The Keynesian welfare state

Given these remarks and cautions, we can now consider the links between Fordism and the Keynesian welfare state. All four aspects of Fordism are relevant here, for the dynamic of Fordism is closely related to the form and function of the Keynesian welfare state and it in turn has important implications for the dynamic of Fordism. This can be seen both in the heyday of Fordism and in its later crisis-ridden stages.

Several aspects are worth noting. First, given the key role of economies of scale in the Fordist labour process and the supply-driven ('just-in-case') character of production, the state acquired an important role in compensating for the rather limited forms of microeconomic flexibility in Fordist production. In managing the wage relation and labour market policies, and guiding aggregate demand, it helped to balance supply and demand without the violent cyclical swings characteristic of competitive markets. Moreover, by holding out the promise of smoothing economic fluctuations and securing stable, calculable growth, it also permitted Fordist firms to secure increasing returns to scale and encouraged them to invest.

Second, given the potential virtuous circle of expansion rooted in rising productivity, rising wages, rising demand, rising profits and rising investment that was made possible by the Fordist mode of growth, the state acquired a key role in integrating the capital and consumer goods industries and managing the wage relation to this end.[5] It invested in infrastructural projects, promoted economies of scale through nationalization or merger policies, encouraged Fordist mass consumption through its housing and transport policies, and generalized norms of mass consumption through intervention in labour markets and collective bargaining and through its provisions for collective consumption.

Third, many of these activities are also closely tied to the nature of the Fordist mode of regulation. Particularly important here was state support for responsible trade unionism, collective bargaining, the consolidation of big business and social partnership. At the same time it was the dominance of the Fordist mode of growth that enabled the state to link the interests of organized capital and labour in a programme of full employment and social welfare. Fourth, as the societalization pattern associated with Fordism was consolidated, it created and/or intensified 'social problems' for which welfare state solutions could be sought. Many of the welfare policies pursued by the state in the 1960s and 1970s (the era of massive expansion in welfare employment) were prompted by the growth of the Fordist regime, with its commodification, urbanization and bureaucratism (see especially Hirsch and Roth, 1986).

The expansion of the Keynesian welfare state was in turn strongly shaped by the development of the Fordist mode of growth; for, although full employment is often cited as a major policy objective during this period and its attainment is often attributed to state intervention, success in this regard was actually rooted much more in the basic dynamic of Fordist expansion than in fine-tuning through government employment policy. But the continuing expansion of the post-war boom did help to legitimate Keynesian welfare policies and to consolidate a social basis for the Fordist accumulation regime. The real test of the policy commitment to full employment came only with the collapse of the post-war boom, the emerging crisis of Fordism and such contingent events as the 'oil price shocks'. In this context, although the policy commitment was maintained for some time, it proved much harder for the state to secure full employment and yet avoid inflation (see Therborn, 1986; Scharpf, 1987).

The apparent success of the welfare state during this period was also grounded in the nature of the post-war boom. The Fordist upswing generated the tax revenues to finance welfare expansion and also provided the material basis for a class compromise between capital and labour. Moreover, insofar as full employment was achieved in a labour market which was relatively unified rather than segmented, it also reduced the volume of primary poverty among working families.[6] This in turn created room for more generous income maintenance programmes for other groups (thereby sustaining and generalizing mass consumption) and/or for welfare expansion into other areas (often tied to the changing social reproduction requirements involved in Fordism). In short, if the Keynesian welfare state helped to secure the conditions for Fordist economic expansion, the latter helped in turn to secure the conditions for the expansion of the Keynesian welfare state.

It must be noted, of course, that the expansion of the welfare state also came to undermine some of the conditions which had sustained Fordist accumulation. It altered the balance of class forces in favour of organized labour in the economic sphere – a shift which only became critical as the crisis of Fordism emerged, and capital tried to restructure the labour process and restrain labour costs. It institutionalized a social wage whose downward rigidity (if not its upward momentum) could act as a brake on profits and capital accumulation. In addition, the welfare state acquired its own expansionary drive, with major structural as well as resource implications for the Fordist regime. Thus, alongside the well-known increase in the social welfare budget (with its consequences for the restructuring of the tax and credit systems), the welfare state also underwent changes in its basic structural forms, associated social policy communities and its political bases of support.

These changes in turn threatened the Fordist regime through their adverse impact on both sides of the capital–labour relation (in terms of the balance of forces as well as the basic incentive to invest and/or work) and the overall pattern of societalization (notably in terms of the relative decoupling of welfare policies from the circuit of capital). This was especially significant in those liberal welfare regimes which separated economic and social policy areas and treated them as distinct. The crisis was less severe in smaller, open economies which modified social and economic policy in the light of how trade relations affected full employment (Mishra, 1985). In all cases, however, the crisis of the Keynesian welfare state provided capital with an opportunity forcibly to reimpose the unity of economic and social policy in the interests of renewed accumulation. Insofar as this was successful, it would help promote the transition to post-Fordism and a post-Fordist state.

THE NATURE OF POST-FORDISM

A satisfactory account of post-Fordism would treat it like Fordism – distinguishing its various levels as well as their structural and strategic moments. Before attempting this, however, we should justify 'posting' Fordism in this way. A minimum condition for referring to post-Fordism is to establish the nature of the continuity in discontinuity which justifies the claim that it is not just a variant form of Fordism but does actually succeed Fordism. Without significant discontinuity, it would not be *post*-Fordism; without significant continuity, it would not be post-*Fordism*. This double condition is satisfied where: (a) post-Fordism has demonstrably emerged from tendencies originating within Fordism but still marks a decisive break with it; or (b) the ensemble of old and new elements in post-Fordism demonstrably displaces or resolves basic contradictions and crises in Fordism – even if it is also associated with its own contradictions and crisis tendencies in turn (Jessop, 1992b). In this context post-Fordism could be related to the continuity in discontinuity found in one or more of the dimensions of Fordism, namely the labour process, accumulation regimes, social modes of economic regulation or modes of societalization. And this in turn would give a basis for defining a typical post-Fordist state analogous to the Fordist state discussed above.

Key features of post-Fordism

Let us now briefly review possible features of a consolidated post-Fordism. These can be considered in terms of the same four (or five) dimensions used earlier to specify Fordism. Thus, as a labour process, post-Fordism can be defined as a flexible production process based on flexible machines or systems and an appropriately flexible workforce. Its crucial hardware is microelectronics-based information and communications technologies. This pattern could properly be labelled post-Fordist insofar as it emerges from the Fordist labour process itself and/or helps resolve the crisis of Fordism. Indeed, by looking at how post-Fordism operates from the latter viewpoint, we can include process and product innovations which emerge outside any immediate Fordist context. Flexible specialization complexes, which have long coexisted with Fordist mass production and now seem to have won a new lease of life both materially and ideologically, can be included here; so can the new technologies (such as microelectronics, biotechnology and new materials) which have a key role in overcoming some of the problems of Fordist control or materials-intensive production (Roobeek, 1987; Altvater, 1991). In seizing on these new or recharged sources of flexibility, capitalists hope to overcome the alienation and resistance of the mass worker, the relative stagnation of Taylorism and mass production, competitive threats from low-cost exporters in the Third World (or, indeed, from domestic or foreign competitors already using post-Fordist production techniques) and the relative saturation of markets for standardized mass produced goods; and/or to meet the growing demand for more differentiated products, action to brake the rising costs of non-Fordist service sectors (notably in the public sector) and measures to boost productivity and profits in manufacturing.

Second, as a stable mode of macroeconomic growth, post-Fordism would be based on the dominance of a flexible and permanently innovative pattern of accumulation.[7] As such its virtuous circle would be based on flexible production, growing productivity based on economies of scope (i.e. diversified production rather than long runs of identical products) and/or process innovations, rising incomes for polyvalent skilled workers and the service class, increased demand for new differentiated goods and services favoured by the growing discretionary element in these incomes, increased profits based on technological and other innovation rents and the full utilization of flexible capacity, reinvestment in more flexible production equipment and processes and/or new sets of products and/or new organizational forms, and a further boost to productivity owing to economies of scope and constant innovation. In contrast to the core Atlantic Fordist economies (the USA, the UK, France, Germany, Benelux and Sweden), post-Fordist growth need not generalize core workers' rising incomes to other workers and/or the economically inactive. Indeed, as post-Fordist accumulation will be more oriented to worldwide demand, global competition could further limit the scope for general prosperity and encourage market-led polarization of incomes. Besides its emergence from, and organization around, genuinely post-Fordist labour processes, this new accumulation regime could also be treated as post-Fordist in so far as it resolves (or is held to do so) crisis tendencies in its Fordist predecessor. These were the relative exhaustion of the growth potential which came from extending mass production into firms, branches or sectors it had not previously penetrated, the relative saturation of markets for mass consumer durables and the disruption of the virtuous circle of Fordist accumulation owing to internationalization and the problems this created for national regulation.[8] In these respects post-Fordism is important because it transforms mass production and goes beyond it (especially as its productivity-enhancing techniques can be applied to more sectors), segments old markets and opens new ones and, insofar as it is demand- rather than supply-driven, is less constrained by national demand conditions.

Third, as a social mode of economic regulation, post-Fordism would involve supply-side innovation and flexibility in each of the main areas of regulation. Thus the wage relation would be recomposed with a polarization between skilled and unskilled workers; there would be greater emphasis on flexibility in internal and external labour markets; a shift would occur towards enterprise- or plant-level collective bargaining; and new forms of social wage would develop. The enterprise system could see a shift from the primacy of the hierarchical, well-staffed, bureaucratic 'Sloanist' (after Albert Sloan, pioneer manager of General Motors) form of corporate structure towards flatter, leaner, more flexible forms of organization. Forms of organization between hierarchy and market will become more important in managing strategic interdependencies, both within and among firms, and in responding quickly to changing demands. Profits of enterprise will depend on: the capacity to engineer flexible production systems (or to design flexible service delivery systems) and to accelerate process and product innovation; the search for technological rents based on continuous innovation in products and processes; and economies of scope. In turn competition will turn on non-price factors such as improved quality and performance for individual products, responsiveness to customers and customization, and rapid response to changing market conditions. The money form will probably be dominated by private, rootless bank credit which circulates internationally, and state credit will be subject to limits set by the logic of international money and currency markets. Moreover, with the growing emphasis on differentiated forms of consumption, commercial capital will be reorganized to create and serve increasingly segmented markets. Finally, state intervention will shift in the ways noted above and described more fully below.

Together these forms seem to comprise a distinctive social mode of economic regulation. They also appear to emerge from tendencies inherent in Fordism and to resolve at least some of its crisis tendencies. Thus some of the new structural forms and regulatory practices arose from attempts to manage the crisis of Fordism, others from attempts to escape it; some are primarily defensive, others offensive. Among the problems they help to solve are the breakdown in Fordist incomes policies and the crisis of Fordist labour market institutions, the contradiction between Fordist wage forms and the post-Fordist need to promote responsible worker autonomy in the workplace, rising R&D costs, rapidly changing and shortening product life cycles, greater risks of market failure, the availability of technologies permitting greater task integration and easier communication between divisions, and so on. Politically, the new forms of state intervention respond to Keynesian stagflation, the fiscal crisis of the state, slower productivity growth in the welfare state compared to the private sector, the rigidities and dysfunctions of bureaucratic administration and planning, the growing resistance shown by class forces and new social movements toward the forms and effects of the Fordist state, and so on.

Fourth, with regard to a post-Fordist 'mode of societalization', it is too soon to anticipate what this would involve. As yet there is no obvious predominant post-Fordist mode of 'societalization' comparable to Americanization in the Fordist era. Instead we find an unresolved competition which involves at least the Japanese, German, and American models – each of which is, in any case, encountering mounting problems on its home ground. Certainly, the neo-liberal euphoria of Reaganism and Thatcherism in the 1980s has been rudely deflated by the crisis-prone 1990s. At best we could describe, on a case to case basis, the societalization effects of the uneven transition toward post-Fordism. And this means, fifth, that a well-developed and relatively stable post-Fordist social formation remains an as yet unrealized possibility.

Forces behind the transition to a post-Fordist state

The preceding section presented some features of post-Fordism with regard to its possible sites of emergence and consolidation. This somewhat static account took for granted the accomplishment of a transition to post-Fordism without trying to explain it. Clearly the crisis of Fordism does not in itself guarantee such a transition and it is therefore worth noting three general driving forces behind the emergence of post-Fordism in the labour process, accumulation regimes and modes of regulation. These three forces are: (a) the rise of new technologies; (b) internationalization; (c) the paradigm shift from Fordism to post-Fordism.[9] Each of them is partly rooted in the crisis tendencies of Fordism, but each also has other roots in other economic and political processes with only tangential links to Fordism.

Each in turn has major consequences for the continued viability of Fordist structures on each of its possible sites. In discussing them I will focus on how they have helped to undermine the structural and strategic congruence between Fordism and the Keynesian welfare state in the current phase of capitalist development and thereby created pressures for the development of a new state form.

First, given the growing competitive pressures from newly industrialized countries (NICs) in low cost, low tech production and, indeed, in simple high tech goods and services, the advanced capitalist economies must move up the technological hierarchy and specialize in the new core technologies if they are to maintain employment and growth. States have a key role here, in technological intelligence gathering, creating independent technological capacities, promoting innovative capacities and transferring technology and technical competence so that as many firms and sectors as possible benefit from the new technological opportunities created by R&D activities undertaken in specific parts of the economy (Chesnais, 1986, p. 86). Moreover, given the budgetary and fiscal pressures on states as national economies become more open, states must shift industrial support away from efforts to maintain declining sectors and towards promoting new sectors. Alternatively, given that the new core technologies are generic and applicable to many different fields of production, states should at least intervene to restructure declining sectors so that they can apply new processes, upgrade existing products and launch new ones. In all cases the crucial point is that state action is required to encourage the development of new core technologies and their application to as wide a range of activities as possible to promote competitiveness.

Second, as internationalization proceeds apace, states can no longer act as if national economies were effectively closed and their growth dynamic were autocentric. Small open economies had already faced this problem during the post-war boom, of course; now even large, relatively closed economies have been integrated into the global circuits of capital. Thus key macroeconomic policy instruments associated with the Keynesian welfare state lose their efficacy with growing internationalization and must be replaced or buttressed by other measures if post-war policy objectives such as full employment, economic growth, stable prices and sound balance of payments are still to be secured. Moreover, as the national character of money is subordinated to the flows of international currencies, and as internationalization emphasizes the character of wages as costs of production rather than sources of home demand, the basic domestic premises of Keynesian welfarism are called into question. Consequently almost all states have become more involved in managing the process of internationalization itself in the hope of minimizing its harmful domestic repercussions and/or of securing maximum benefit to its own home-based transnational firms and banks. They must get involved in managing the process of internationalization and creating the most appropriate frameworks for it to proceed. Among the many activities included here are introducing new legal forms for cross-national cooperation and strategic alliances, reforming international currency and credit systems, promoting technology transfer, managing trade disputes, developing a new international intellectual property regime or developing new forms of regulation for labour migration. This leads to the paradox that, as states lose control over the national economy, they are forced to enter the fray on behalf of their own multinationals.

Third, as the dominant techno-economic paradigm shifts from Fordism to post-Fordism, the primary economic functions of states are redefined. Fordism was typically associated with a primary concern with demand management within national economies and with the generalization of mass consumption norms. This reflected the belief that Fordist mass production was supply-driven and could only be profitable when high levels of demand were maintained and markets for mass consumer durables expanded. The class compromise supporting the Fordist Keynesian welfare state also encouraged this pattern of economic intervention. But the transition to a post-Fordist paradigm is prompting a reorientation of the state's primary economic functions. For the combination of the late Fordist trend towards internationalization and the post-Fordist stress on flexible production has encouraged states to focus on the supply-side problem of international competitiveness and to attempt to subordinate welfare policy to the demands of flexibility.

THE NATURE OF THE CONSOLIDATED POST-FORDIST STATE

Given these remarks on post-Fordism and the driving forces behind its development and their implications for state functions, we can now attempt to define the character of the post-Fordist state. This requires due regard to the discontinuity in continuity which links Fordism and post-Fordism. In this context we should note that the initial response to the crisis of Fordism and its state did not lead at once to anything like a post-Fordist state. Instead it typically involved intensifying the features of the Fordist state, reinforcing and complementing them. This was reflected in some circumstances in efforts to promote full employment despite growing stagflationary tendencies and to maintain welfare commitments despite tendencies towards a fiscal crisis; and, in others, in increasing emphasis on economic austerity and social retrenchment to squeeze out inflation and reduce public spending. Which of these tendencies predominated depended on state capacities and the prevailing balance of forces from case to case (Keman et al., 1987; Scharpf, 1987). In all cases we could refer to a conjunctural transformation of the Fordist state rooted in its attempts to manage Fordist crises and limit their repercussions on its own organization and unity.

When such measures could not restore conditions for Fordist accumulation and precipitated a crisis of (and not merely in) the Fordist Keynesian welfare state, economic and political forces alike stepped up the search for a new state form that they hoped would be able to solve the deepening contradictions and crises of Fordist accumulation and restabilize the state system. This search process is associated with extensive trial-and-error experimentation and various transitional political forms and policy measures (on some issues involved in analysing transitional post-Fordist regimes, see Jessop, 1993). None the less, I argue that what is gradually emerging from this search process is a structural transformation and fundamental strategic reorientation of the capitalist state. The tendential product of this continuing search process can be described as a 'hollowed-out Schumpeterian workfare state'. I will deal with its features in two stages.

The Schumpeterian workfare state

Insofar as the restructuring and reorientation of the economic and social functions of the Keynesian welfare state system succeed, they tend to produce a new state form which could be termed a 'Schumpeterian workfare state'. In abstract terms, its distinctive objectives in economic and social reproduction are: to promote product, process, organizational and market innovation in open economies in order to strengthen as far as possible the structural competitiveness of the national economy by intervening on the supply side; and to subordinate social policy to the needs of labour market flexibility and/or the constraints of international competition. In this sense it marks a clear break with the Keynesian welfare state as domestic full employment is downplayed in favour of international competitiveness and redistributive welfare rights take second place to a productivist reordering of social policy. In this sense its new functions would also seem to correspond to the emerging dynamic of global capitalism as discussed earlier. Indeed, as the description of the driving forces should have brought out, the current shifts in the world economy seem to require just such a transformation of the state. None the less, just as there were different forms of Keynesian welfare state, we can expect to find differences across societies in this new form of state.

The 'hollowing out' of the national state

The national state is now subject to various changes which result in its 'hollowing out'. This involves two contradictory trends, for, while the national state still remains politically important and even retains much of its national sovereignty (albeit as an ever more ineffective, primarily juridical fiction reproduced through mutual recognition in the international community of nations), its capacities to project its power even within its own national borders are decisively weakened both by the shift towards internationalized, flexible (but also regionalized) production systems and by the growing challenge posed by risks emanating from the global environment. This loss of autonomy creates in turn both the need for supranational coordination and the space for subnational resurgence. Some state capacities are transferred to a growing number of pan-regional, plurinational, or international bodies with a widening range of powers; others are devolved to restructured local or regional levels of governance in the national state; and yet others are being usurped by emerging horizontal networks of power – local and regional – which by-pass central states and connect localities or regions in several nations. Often these changes are closely linked to the reorientation of these capacities to Schumpeterian workfare measures.

Why the 'hollowed out' Schumpeterian workfare state might be seen as post-Fordist

The Schumpeterian workfare state briefly sketched above could be seen as post-Fordist in one or both of two different respects: (a) because it helps to resolve significant crisis tendencies within Fordism in general or the Fordist state in particular; and (b) because it helps to consolidate the emerging dynamic of a post-Fordist accumulation regime. In the first respect, the Schumpeterian workfare state may be seen as having a post-Fordist nature to the extent that its emerging functions resolve (or are held so to do) crisis tendencies in Fordism or the Keynesian welfare state. Among the relevant crisis tendencies in this regard we might note the stagflationary impact of the Keynesian welfare state on the Fordist growth dynamic (especially where state economic intervention is too concerned with maintaining employment in sunset sectors) and its growing fiscal crisis rooted in the ratchet-like expansion of social consumption expenditure. The Schumpeterian workfare state would seem to address both problems. Not only does it adopt supply-side intervention to promote innovation and structural competitiveness, it also goes beyond the mere retrenchment of social welfare to restructure and subordinate it to market forces. Both functions not only help to resolve Keynesian welfare state crisis tendencies but also seem to match the dynamic of the post-Fordist regime.

This remark brings us to the second way in which the Schumpeterian workfare state might be seen as post-Fordist, i.e. its potential role in consolidating an emergent post-Fordist regime. In this regard we could mention the following three factors. Its strategic orientation to innovation takes account of the enormous ramifications of new technologies; its concern with structural competitiveness recognizes the changing terms and conditions of international competition as well as its increased significance; and its restructuring and reorientation of social reproduction towards flexibility and retrenchment signifies its awareness of the post-Fordist paradigm shift as well as the impact of internationalization on the primary functions of money and wages. Thus it seems that the Schumpeterian workfare state could prove both structurally congruent and functionally adequate to post-Fordist accumulation regimes.

A similar approach can be adopted in dealing with the 'hollowing out' of the national state which accompanies the development of the Schumpeterian workfare state. This process can also be seen as having a post-Fordist nature both with regard to how it helps to resolve crisis-tendencies in Fordism and with regard to how it helps to consolidate an emerging post-Fordism. Thus 'hollowing out' could be regarded as a response to the various 'state failures' (especially those concerning the effectiveness and legitimacy of state action) which accompany the crisis in the Fordist accumulation regime and its social mode of regulation, for it tends to relocate responsibility for accumulation (value creation and reproduction) as well as important legitimacy functions to levels of political organization which are deemed to be able to cope more effectively with the symptoms of Fordist crisis. This is especially important for those problems which are either too small or too large in scale for the national state to handle effectively (Bell, 1988). But 'hollowing out' can also be seen as a process that helps to consolidate the emerging post-Fordist economic order. Here its key contribution is to bring supply-side intervention closer than was possible for a national state to the inherently localized sites of structural competitiveness in local or regional innovation systems (see chapter 4 by Sabel) and local or regional labour markets, as well as to develop new state organizations and policies which are structurally and strategically better adapted to the emerging international economic order.

VARIANTS OF THE SCHUMPETERIAN WORKFARE STATE

It would be wrong to suggest that there is one dominant form of Schumpeterian workfare state that will sweep the world before it. Just as there were variant forms of the Keynesian welfare state in the Atlantic Fordist period, so can we expect to find variant forms of the Schumpeterian workfare state. This is especially likely because the newly emerging economic order is more global in scope than Atlantic Fordism and is associated with the struggle for hegemony of several alternative models of capitalism rather than with the hegemony (at least after 1945) of the American Fordist model. Rather than trying to present a full typology of actually existing (or currently emerging) Schumpeterian workfare state regimes, the following remarks will specify some basic tendencies around which specific forms of Schumpeterian workfare state may well be articulated. After alternative Schumpeterian workfare state strategies have been presented in this section of the chapter, I will explore various dimensions of the 'hollowing out' of the state.

Alternative Schumpeterian workfare state strategies

There is still much improvisation and trial-and-error involved in the current transition as well as a continuing need to adjust policies to the changing balance of forces and new structural and/or conjunctural problems. Having regard to the current diversity of political regimes, an emerging Schumpeterian workfare state could well take neo-liberal, neo-corporatist and neo-statist forms depending on institutional legacies and the balance of political forces in specific social formations. One or other line will tend to be dominant in specific countries and other strategic elements will come to be aligned to it.

Neo-liberalism is primarily concerned to promote a market-guided transition towards the new economic regime (e.g. Reaganism in the USA and Thatcherism in the UK). For the public sector, it involves a mixture of privatization, liberalization and the adoption of commercial criteria in the residual state sector; for the private sector, it involves deregulation and a new legal and political framework providing passive support for market solutions. In particular neo-liberalism leads to:

government promotion of 'hire-and-fire', flexi-time and flexi-wage labour markets; the growth of tax expenditures steered by private initiatives based on fiscal subsidies for favoured economic activities; and the reorientation of state activities to the needs of the private sector. Coupled with this is a rejection of social partnership arrangements in favour of managerial prerogatives, market forces and a strong state. It involves a cosmopolitan approach which welcomes internationalization even if this conflicts with the creation and/or maintenance of a coherent national industrial core that can provide the basis for international competitiveness. In this context innovation is expected to occur spontaneously through the liberation of the animal spirits of entrepreneurs as they take advantage of the new market orientation and incentives. Although it is sometimes said to involve a return to the free market and the liberal state, the neo-liberal strategy not only involves strong state action during the transition for the purpose of restructuring markets but will also reinforce monopolistic regulation, and requires continuing state intervention once the transition is completed.

Neo-corporatism, along with corporatism, relies on the *ex ante* concentation of the economic decisions and activities of private economic agents oriented to their own economic interests. But this strategy also involves significant differences from the pattern of Fordist corporatism: the latter may not permit a smooth transition to neo-corporatism; nor is it necessary that a neo-corporatist road be built on corporatist foundations. Neo-corporatist arrangements must instead reflect the expansion of relevant interests in policy communities as well as the increasing heterogeneity of the labour force and labour markets. Moreover, while earlier Keynesian welfare state corporatist arrangements grew out of concern with full employment and worries about stagflation, neo-corporatist arrangements in an emerging Schumpeterian workfare system will be more directly and explicitly oriented to innovation and structural competitiveness. One effect of this will be that neo-corporatist concertation could extend beyond the organizations of capital and labour to include other policy communities representing distinct functional systems (e.g. science, health, education) which bear on innovation and competitiveness. Likewise, policy implementation could be made more flexible through the extension of 'regulated self-regulation' and private interest government so that greater freedom exists on the 'supply-side' (Streeck and Schmitter, 1983). In the field of industrial and incomes policies, corporatist arrangements could become more selective (e.g. excluding some previously entrenched industrial interests and more peripheral or marginal workers, integrating some 'sunrise' interests and giving more weight to core workers); and, reflecting the more flexible forms of the post-Fordist economy, the centre of corporatist gravity will shift to the microlevel away from macroeconomic concertation. The state is involved in neo-corporatist strategies as in the neo-liberal and neo-statist approaches. But its actions are more concerned to back or support the decisions reached through corporatist negotiation than to pursue neo-liberal disengagement and/or to resort to active state initiatives along neo-statist lines; and compliance with state measures is voluntary and/or depends on actions taken by self-regulating corporatist organizations endowed with public status.

Neo-statism is primarily concerned to promote a state-guided approach to economic reorganization through intervention from outside and above market mechanisms. There is little or no consultation with organized economic interests and intervention is based on the state's powers of imperium (imperative coordination) and/or dominium (its own economic resources and/or activities as one economic actor among others) (on imperium and dominium, see Daintith, 1985). It involves a mixture of decommodification, state-sponsored flexibility and state activities concerned to secure the dynamic efficiency of an industrial core. In particular this is associated with an active structural policy in which the state sets strategic targets for flexible accumulation, continuous innovation and the promotion of the overall structural competitiveness of the national economy. It pursues an active labour market policy to reskill the labour force and ensure a flexi-skill rather than flexi-price labour market; it intervenes directly and openly to restructure declining industries and to promote sunrise sectors; and it engages in societal guidance strategies to promote specific objectives through concerted action within varied policy communities which embrace public, mixed and private interests. These activities aim to move the economy up the technological hierarchy by maintaining a coherent and competitive industrial core and pursuing a strategy of flexible specialization in specific high technology sectors. The state must become flexible because of the openness of post-Fordist economies and the rapid changes involved in flexible accumulation.

Mixed Schumpeterian workfare state strategies

Elements of these strategies can certainly be combined within and across different levels of political organization. This can be seen at all levels of political intervention. In the European Union (EU), for example, we find: (a) the single market strategy premised on a neo-liberal approach to competitiveness, creating a Europe-wide market through liberalization, deregulation and internationalization; (b) a neo-statist strategy through which the EU coordinates cross-territorial networks[10] across different levels of government in different states as well as various semi-public and private agencies including educational institutions, research institutes, enterprises and banks in order to promote new technologies, technology transfer, etc.; and (c) a neo-corporatist strategy oriented to a Social Charter which will prevent 'social dumping' and thereby underpin attempts to reskill and retrain workers in the interests of more flexible, responsible work (see Grahl and Teague, 1990). These may not be inconsistent. Indeed, the European Commission has argued (perhaps with an element of special pleading or political fudging) that the neo-liberal elements of its strategy for structural competitiveness can be seen as catalysts and the neo-statist elements as its accelerators. It also suggests that some aspects of the neo-corporatist project could be seen as prerequisites of structural adjustment and enhanced competitiveness insofar as they help to secure economic and social cohesion (European Commission, 1991: p. 23).[11]

Different strategies are also found inside each European state. Thatcherism clearly involves the dominance of a neo-liberal strategy, for example, but it has not totally rejected other strategies. Thus central government programmes (admittedly on a small scale) have been oriented to technology transfer and research into generic technologies; and, notwithstanding blanket hostility to tripartite corporatism and national-level social partnership, it has promoted enterprise corporatism and a 'new realism' on the shop floor. Moreover, while central government has been in retreat, there has been a real proliferation of regional and local economic development initiatives along Schumpeterian workfare lines. Under Labour-led local authorities in Britain these have often been run on neo-corporatist or neo-statist lines; while Conservative authorities incline more to neo-liberalism or a neo-corporatism without organized labour. In all cases, however, lack of effective central government support causes problems in pursuing more local strategies for economic regeneration.

MORE ON THE HOLLOWING OUT OF THE NATIONAL STATE

It is a key part of my argument here that the Fordist state has not only been undergoing a reorientation towards Schumpeterian workfare functions but has also been subject to a structural transformation. In part this involves the reordering of the relations among state apparatuses on each level of political organization considered in its own terms (for a British case study, see Jessop, 1993). But it also involves the reordering of relations among different levels of political organization along lines sketched out above in terms of the 'hollowing out' of the national state. It is this particular aspect of the current transformation of the state that I want to consider here.

The growth of supranational regimes

First, the role of supranational state apparatuses or systems and of international political regimes is expanding. This holds not only for bodies such as the European Union but also for various other supranational regional and transnational bodies. Such bodies are not new in themselves: they have a long history. What is significant today is the sheer increase in their number, the growth in their territorial scope and their acquisition of important new functions. One of the most significant areas of functional expansion is supranational bodies' concern with structural competitiveness in the economic spaces they manage. This goes well beyond concern with managing international monetary relations, foreign investment or trade to include a wide range of supply-side factors, both economic and extra-economic in character.

These changes concern not only the emergence of new international economic and political regimes governing and guiding the dynamic of the world economy as a whole. They are also actively shaping its structure. In particular we can note the impact of supranational and transnational regimes on the three growth poles of an emerging 'triadic' world economy, i.e. the Asian Pacific region, an emerging European Economic Space and North America. Among the key features of these triadic regions is that foreign direct investment and international trade still tend to be 'localized' within them. For there is a greater degree of cross-national investment and trade within each triadic region (especially from the lesser economic powers within a region) than there is between regions. While this can sometimes involve an actual or potential triad-wide strategy, there are many examples (notably in the European and East Asian regions, with their greater number of national states) of more localized (but still cross-national) regional growth strategies. None the less, regardless of their scope, this means that, whereas national economic spaces are typically becoming more penetrated by foreign investment and trade as well as becoming more extraverted through the investment and trading activities of their home-based firms, the triadic regions to which they belong remain relatively more closed because this mutual penetration–extraversion process still tends to be confined within each region. This could provide the basis for broadening and deepening of complementarities among national, regional or local economies within each triad and for the emergence of crisis-management policies coordinated by the dominant economy (Japan, Germany or the USA) in each of the three regions. At the same time it can provide the basis for regional rivalries and demands for neo-mercantilist protection against other triadic blocs.

This shift is particularly clear in the European Union. Thus, following a series of relatively ineffective attempts at concerted crisis management in various declining industries in the late 1960s and early 1970s, attention has turned to supply-side issues in new products and processes bearing above all on key aspects of what has come to be seen as structural competitiveness. The EU is attempting to create world-class competitors in R&D-intensive, high value-added and high growth sectors, not only by establishing the basis for the emergence of Eurofirms but also by encouraging strategic alliances of various kinds. Key areas targeted for intervention include information technology, manufacturing technology, telecommunications, biotechnology, new materials and marine science and technology. Such policies have complex 'multiplier' and 'inhibitor' effects at national, regional and local level. They can have significant demonstration effects and promote technological and institutional learning throughout the EU. But they can also pre-empt or over-shadow national or local initiatives and/or fail because adequate transmission belts are lacking at national, regional or local level.

The resurgence of regional and local governance

The second aspect of 'hollowing out' concerns the fact that, in tandem with the rise of these international state apparatuses, we find a stronger role for regional or local states (see chapter 10 by Mayer). This is as much a reflection of growing internationalization as it is of the economic retreat of the national state. Globalization of the world economy means that 'the local economy can only be seen as a node within a global economic network [with] no meaningful existence outside this context' (Amin and Robins, 1990, p. 28). During the Fordist era, local states operated as extensions of the central Keynesian welfare state and regional policy was primarily oriented to the (re-)location of industry in the interests of spreading full employment and reducing inflationary pressures owing to localized overheating within a largely autocentric economy. Thus local states provided local infrastructure to support Fordist mass production, promoted collective consumption and local welfare state policies and, in some cases (especially as the crisis of Fordism unfolded), engaged in competitive subsidies to attract new jobs or prevent the loss of established jobs. Today we are seeing a reorientation of local economic activities, however, with an increasing emphasis placed on economic regeneration and on how best to make local or regional economies more competitive in the new world economy (see, on the US–American case, Fosler, 1988, p. 5). This involves more than a simple 'technical fix' and requires local states to engage in other fields of public policy, ranging from basic infrastructural provision to cultural policy (see Nijkamp and Stöhr, 1988, p. 351; Mayer, chapter 10 in this volume). In this sense we can find a growing interest among local states in regional labour market policies, education and training, technology transfer, local venture capital, innovation centres, science parks and so forth. It is this shift which led van Hoogstraten (1983, p. 17) to claim that the state, 'although badly challenged at the national level because of its Fordist involvement with crisis management, seems to have risen from the ashes at the regional and local level' (cf. Moulaert et al., 1988, p. 12). Whether these new local efforts can be treated as a main plank of post-Fordist governance structures is not straightforward, as illustrated in chapter 9 of this book, by Peck and Tickell, who question their strength and paradigmatic character.

This shift in functions 'downwards' is none the less linked in turn with the reorganization of the local state as new forms of local partnership emerge to guide and promote the development of local resources. In this sense we can talk of a shift from local government to local governance. Thus local unions, local chambers of commerce, local venture capital, local education bodies, local research centres and local states may enter into arrangements to regenerate the local economy. This trend is also reinforced by the central state's inability to pursue sufficiently differentiated and sensitive programmes to tackle the specific problems of particular localities. It therefore devolves such tasks to local states and provides the latter with general support and resources (Dyson, 1989, p. 118). More optimistic accounts of this trend envisage it leading to a confederation of job-creating, risk-sharing local states rooted in strong regional economies which provide reciprocal support in the ongoing struggle to retain a competitive edge (e.g. Sabel, 1989). But there are also more pessimistic scenarios which anticipate growing polarization within localities (including the rise of an urban underclass occupying inner-city ghettoes) as well as increased regional inequalities.

One effect of this shift towards the regional or local level is a growing variety of forms and strategies of state intervention. This is related to the shift to words Schumpeterian workfare state functions as well as to differing local supply-side conditions, which are best dealt with close to the ground. But it is important that central government coordinates and supports these efforts. Effective political 'decentralization on a territorial basis requires an adequate allocation of responsibilities between communal, regional and national authorities as well as a proper coordination of their actions' (Perrin; 1988, p. 422). This is especially important where economic initiatives involve not only different tiers of government but also business associations and private bodies. Thus it is essential to establish new institutional arrangements and allocate specific roles and complementary competences across different spatial scales and/or types of actor, and thereby to ensure that the dominant strategic line is translated into effective action (see Przeworski, 1986, p. 428; Kawashima and Stöhr, 1988; Perrin, 1988, p. 423).[12] Without such coordination top-down policies can lead to implementation failure and bottom-up policies to wasteful and ineffective 'municipal mercantilism' (see Young 1986, p. 446; Fosler, 1988).

This second feature of 'hollowing out' can also be seen on a world scale. At the same time that the triadic growth poles are emerging, we can see renewed interest in the promotion of subnational regional and local economies at the expense of concern with the national economy as such. This is occurring for both economic and political reasons. On the one hand, as the supply side is increasingly seen as a vital element in national competitiveness, policies are demanded that are oriented to improving the infrastructure, human resources and innovation systems relevant to local or regional firms, sectors or clusters. Since the supply-side conditions making for structural competitiveness vary among firms, sectors and clusters, it is deemed important that these be identified at the appropriate level and implemented locally. On the other hand, as the national state loses effective powers on the international stage and proves less capable of delivering full employment and growth on a national scale, the political pressures also mount for more effective local or regional government to satisfy economic demands.

An emerging trend towards translocal linkages

Closely linked to the first two changes, but as yet rather less pronounced, there are also growing links among local states. Indeed, Dyson (1989, p. 1) writes that 'one of the most interesting political developments since the 1970s has been the erratic but gradual shift of ever more local authorities from an identification of their role in purely national terms towards a new interest in trans-national relationships.' In the European context this involves both vertical links with EU institutions, especially the European Commission, and direct links among local and regional authorities in member states. The search for cross-border support is reinforced to the extent that the central state pursues a more neo-liberal strategy but it can be found in other countries too (see the studies presented in Dyson, 1989). Similar trends are discernible in North America with cooperation among local states in Canada and the USA (especially following the signing of the Free Trade Agreement), as well as among city governments in different provinces or states. There are also growing links between cities in the growing number of transborder metropolitan regions between Mexico and the USA. Likewise, in Japan regional authorities are being encouraged to set up transnational links with subnational regions elsewhere in East Asia as part of a more general diversification and decentralization policy.

Is there still a role for the national state?

Despite these various upward, downward and outward shifts in political organization, a key role still remains for the national state as the most significant site of struggle among competing global, triadic, supranational, national, regional and local forces. It is for this reason that I have written of the 'hollowing out' of the national state rather than its simple demise. Just as the 'hollow corporation' retains its core command, control and communication functions within the home economy while transferring production activities abroad, so the 'hollowed out' national state retains crucial political functions despite the transfer of other activities to other levels of political organization. In particular the national state has a continuing role in managing the political linkages across different territorial scales and is expected to do so in the interests of its citizens. As Ziebura has argued, globalization and transnational regionalization tendencies provoke a counter-tendency in a popular search for transparency, democratic accountability and proximity. He adds that the desire for local, regional or (at most) national identity reflects powerful drives, especially in small national states, to compensate for threats from powerful neighbouring states and/or from the rise of supranational institutions which lack any democratic accountability (Ziebura, 1992). This point is reinforced when we consider that the national state is currently still best placed to deal with social conflicts and redistributive policies, for, while supranational bodies seem preoccupied with the internationalization of capital and promoting (or limiting) the structural competitiveness of triadic regions and their constituent national economies, they are less concerned about more social conflicts and redistributive policies. These are mainly confined within national frameworks and it is national states which have the potential fiscal base to effect significant change in this regard. Indeed, without central government support, it is difficult for most local or regional states to achieve much in this regard. This presents the national state with a dilemma: on the one hand, as noted above, it must become actively engaged in managing the process of internationalization; and, on the other, it is the only political instance which has much chance of preventing a growing divergence between global market dynamics and the conditions for institutional integration and social cohesion (Ziebura, 1992).

In this sense, then, there remains a central political role for the national state. But it is a role which is redefined as a result of the more general rearticulation of the local, regional, national and supranational levels of economic and political organization. Unless or until supranational political organization acquires not only governmental powers but also some measure of popular-democratic legitimacy, the national state will remain a key political factor as the highest instance of democratic political accountability. How it fulfils this role will depend not only on the changing institutional matrix and shifts in the balance of forces as globalization, triadization, regionalization and the resurgence of local governance proceed apace.

At this point it would be prudent to register a final theoretical caution concerning the dangers of functionalism. To avoid the dangers of falling into a teleological analysis of the hollowed out Schumpeterian workfare state as the functionally necessitated complement to an emergent post-Fordist labour process, accumulation regime or social mode of economic regulation, the arguments presented above must be qualified by more concrete and complex analyses of Fordist modes of growth as well as by more substantive work on the crisis mechanisms of the Keynesian welfare state considered as a political regime (for an example of the latter analysis in this context, see Jessop, 1992c). Thus a more detailed analysis of the Schumpeterian workfare state would need to explore: the structural coupling between each type of Fordism and the character of the nation state and the problems this creates; the complexities of the capital relation in each regime type and its implications for economic and political struggles over crisis resolution; the path dependency of the trajectory out of crisis which emerges in and through such struggles; and the problems that arise when the pre-Schumpeterian workfare state lacks the capacities to manage the transition.

CONCLUSION

Since we are still living through a phase of transition, experimentation and strategic intervention, caution is called for in dealing with the likely form and functions of the post-Fordist state. Its final form will only become apparent later and will certainly vary from society to society. One general conclusion is justified, however, even if it seems banal. If the wage form (even in its new, more flexible guise) continues to be the dominant social relation in capitalism, then there will still be a role for the welfare state (suitably flexibilized) in securing the reproduction of wage labour and the wage form. Thus the crucial question is how the welfare state will be restructured and within what limits its role can be reduced (from a neo-liberal viewpoint) or expanded (from a neo-statist or neo-corporatist viewpoint) without seriously undermining structural competitiveness or restraining the transition to post-Fordism. It is in this context that I suggest that the Keynesian welfare state will be replaced with a Schumpeterian workfare state. This will continue to exercise a crucial role in the social reproduction of wage labour but this role will be linked to the economic issues confronting the state in open economies rather than the relatively closed, quasi-autocentric economies of Atlantic Fordism.

NOTES

1   In this text regional and local are used interchangeably to refer to subnational economic or political spaces unless it is important to distinguish between them. The context makes the exact usage clear.

2   I prefer the term 'social mode of economic regulation' to both the usual French regulationist label (mode of regulation) and that suggested by Peck and Tickell in this volume (social mode of regulation) on the grounds that only the first highlights both the manner of regulation and its object. Peck and Tickell's usage conflates the mode of regulation of the economy in its integral sense and the mode of regulation of the wider society in which a specific integral economic order is dominant (see also Tickell and Peck, 1992).

3   A complication occurs here regarding modes of growth of regions or national economies which are complementary to the dominant global dynamic but not themselves based on the dominance of the matching labour process in the domestic economy: thus the mode of regulation in Denmark involved a Fordist consumption pattern and welfare state which was made possible by a mode of growth based on the complementarity between its own flexibly specialized labour process in manufacturing and the global dynamic of Atlantic Fordism.

4   Fordist and post-Fordist societalization effects will be ignored below. In

general they can be seen as derived effects of the dominance of an 'accumulating regime in regulation' and/or as contributing to that dominance.

5 The relative weight of the two sectors obviously varies across national economies and this is reflected in different patterns of export- and import-dependence for these sectors; thus the state's role in integrating them also extends to exchange and foreign economic policies.

6 The Fordist mode of regulation and the Keynesian welfare state were both premised on stable nuclear and patriarchal families in which the male breadwinner received a family wage and was held responsible for maintaining his wife and other dependants. One of the factors contributing to the crisis of the Keynesian welfare state has been the decomposition of this family form.

7 Flexibility alone is insufficient to define post-Fordism: all accumulation regimes contain elements of flexibility and, indeed, flexible specialization regimes also predated Fordism (Piore and Sabel, 1984). The novel element in post-Fordism is the way flexibility is shaped and enhanced by a new techno-economic paradigm which institutionalized the search for permanent innovation.

8 The argument that there was a relative saturation of markets for mass consumer durables has been strongly contested by Williams et al. (1987).

9 In earlier work I suggested that four trends were important for the genesis of post-Fordism and the Schumpeterian workfare state; subsequent discussions with Ash Amin and Klaus Nielsen have led me to conclude that regionalization might better be seen as an economic and/or political response to the three trends identified here.

10 The term 'cross-territorial' derives from Perrin; it does not refer to interurban or interregional coordination but to a hierarchy of territorial sites from locality to supranational (Perrin, 1988, p. 422).

11 The labels attached to these elements are mine: the EC Bulletin referred to here simply lists a range of policies and describes their respective roles.

12 An interesting example of this can be found in Japan. Here MITI has developed a three-tier technology policy comprising: (a) a national Tsukuba Science City, established in 1970, with various ten-year national R&D projects in new technologies; (b) 19 technopoles dispersed over strategic locations throughout the archipelago, established under a law passed in 1983; and (c) a more dispersed set of 28 research cores serving mainly as incubators or small a medium high tech firms, established under a law passed in 1986 (Kawashima and Stöhr, 1988, p. 427–39).

REFERENCES

Altvater, E. (1991) *Die Zukunft des Marktes*. Münster: Westfälisches Dampfboot.

Amin, A. and Robbins, K. (1990) The Re-emergence of regional economies? The mythical geography of flexible accumulation. *Environment and Planning, D: Society and Space*, 8, 7–34.

Bell, D. (1988) The World and the United States in 2013. *Daedalus*, Summer.

Chesnais, F. (1986) Science, technology and competitiveness. *STI Review*, 1 (Autumn), 86–129.

Daintith, T. (1985) The executive power today: bargaining and economic control. In J. Jowell and D. Oliver (eds), *The Changing Constitution*. Oxford: Clarendon, 174–97.

Dyson, K. (ed.) (1988) *Local Authorities and New Technologies: the European Dimension*. London: Croom Helm.

European Commission (1991) European industrial policy for the 1990s. *Bulletin of the European Communities*, Supplement 3/91.

Fosler, R. S. (ed.) (1988) *The New Economic Role of American States*. New York: Oxford University Press.

Grahl, J. and Teague, P. (1990) *1992: the Big Market*. London: Lawrence and Wishart.

Hirsch, J. and Roth, R. (1986) *Das neue Gesicht des Kapitalismus*. Frankfurt: EVA.

Jessop, B. (1992a) Post-Fordism and flexible specialization: incommensurable, contradictory, complementary, or just plain different perspectives? In H. Ernste and V. Meyer (eds), *Flexible Specialization and the New Regionalism*. London: Pinter, 25–44.

Jessop, B. (1992b) Fordism and post-Fordism: critique and reformulation. In A. J. Scott and M. J. Storper (eds), *Pathways to Regionalism and Industrial Development*. London: Routledge, 43–65.

Jessop, B. (1992c) Regulation und Politik: Integrale Ökonomie und Integraler Staat. In A. Demirovic et al. (eds), *Akkumulation, Hegemonie und Staat*. Münster: Westfälisches Dampfboot.

Jessop, B. (1993) From the Keynesian welfare to the Schumpeterian workfare state. In R. Burrows and B. Loader (eds), *Towards a Post-Fordist Welfare State?* London: Routledge, 13–37.

Kawashima, T. and Stöhr, W. B. (1988) Decentralized technology policy: the case of Japan. *Environment and Planning, C: Government and Policy*, 6(4), 427–40.

Keman, H., Paloheimo, H. and Whitely, P. F. (eds) (1987) *Coping with the Economic Crisis: Alternative Responses to Economic Recession in Advanced Industrial Societies*. London: Sage.

Kristensen, P. H. (1990) Denmark's concealed production culture, its sociohistorical construction and dynamics at work. In F. Borum and P. H. Kristensen (eds), *Technological Innovation and Organizational Change – Danish Patterns of Knowledge, Networks, and Culture*. Copenhagen: Copenhagen Business School New Social Science Monographs, 165–88.

Mishra, R. (1985) *The Welfare State in Crisis*. Brighton: Harvester.

Moulaert, F., Swyngedouw, E. and Wilson, P. (1988) Spatial responses to Fordist and post-Fordist accumulation and regulation. *Papers of the Regional Science Association*, 64(1), 11–23.

Nijkamp, P. and Stöhr, W. B. (1988) Technology policy at the crossroads of economic policy and physical planning. *Environment and Planning, C: Government and Policy*, 6(4), 371–5.

Perrin, J.-C. (1988) New technologies, local synergies and regional policies in Europe. In P. Aydelot and D. Keeble (eds), *High Technology Industry and Innovative Environments*. London: Routledge, 139-62.

Piore, M. J. and Sabel, C. F. (1984) *The Second Industrial Divide*. New York: Basic Books.

Przeworski, J. F. (1986) Changing intergovernmental relations and urban economic development. *Environment and Planning, C: Government and Policy*, 4, 423-38.

Roobeek, A. J. M. (1987) The crisis in Fordism and the rise of a new technological paradigm. *Futures*, 19(2), 129-54.

Sabel, C. F. (1989) Flexible specialization and the re-emergence of regional economies. In P. Q. Hirst and J. Zeitlin (eds), *Reversing Industrial Decline? Industrial Structure and Policy in Britain and Her Competitors*. Oxford: Berg, 17-70.

Scharpf, F. (1987) *Sozialdemokratische Krisenpolitik in Europa*, Frankfurt: Campus Verlag.

Stöhr, W. (1989) Regional policy at the cross-roads: an overview. In L. Albrechts et al. (eds), *Regional Policy at the Cross-Roads: European Perspectives*. London: Jessica Kingsley.

Streeck, W. and Schmitter, P. C. (1983) Community, market, state - and associations? The prospective contribution of interest governance to social order. In W. Streeck and P. C. Schmitter (eds), *Private Interest Government*. London: Sage.

Therborn, G. (1986) *Why Some Peoples Are More Unemployed than Others*. London: Verso.

Tickell, A. and Peck, J. (1992) Accumulation regimes and the geographies of post-Fordism: missing links in regulationist theory. *Progress in Human Geography*, 16(2), 190-218.

Van Hoogstraten, P. (1983) *De ontwikkeling van het regionaal beleid in Nederland 1949-1977*. Nijmegen: Stichting Politiek en Ruimte.

Williams, K., Cutler, A., Williams, J. and Haslam, C. (1987) The end of mass production? *Economy and Society*, 16(3), 405-39.

Young, K. (1986) Economic development in Britain: a vacuum in central-local government relations. *Environment and Planning, C: Government and Policy*, 4(4), 440-50.

Ziebura, G. (1992) Über den Nationalstaat. *Leviathan*, 4, 467-89.

9

Searching for a New Institutional Fix: the *After*-Fordist Crisis and the Global–Local Disorder

Jamie Peck and Adam Tickell

INTRODUCTION

It has become commonplace to portray the period since the crisis of Fordism as *new times*, characterized by the emergence of new political forms, new social movements, new systems of production and the like. Already, some have argued, these new structures are beginning to coalesce around a flexible or post-Fordist regime of accumulation. We want to suggest in this chapter that such claims are premature, based as they are on a fundamental misreading of the contemporary situation. This, we argue, is more accurately portrayed as *hard times*: the crisis of Fordism remains, as yet, unresolved. This is because a *demonstrably reproducible* replacement has yet to stabilize. Certainly, there is no shortage of intriguing local experiments – such as the widely documented examples from the Third Italy and Baden-Württemberg – some of which may indeed be lighting the way beyond the protracted Fordist crisis. But local solutions alone are not enough. Our argument in this chapter is that the feverish search for local solutions is a symptom of the crisis itself, a reflection of continuing global political-economic disorder. In the scramble for jobs and investment, all these local experiments are liable to regulatory undercutting by other localities willing to do what is necessary to get a piece of the action.

Localities in the *after*-Fordist crisis have, to borrow a phrase from Marx, become 'hostile brothers', flinging themselves into the competitive process of attracting jobs and investment by bargaining away living standards and regulatory controls. Needless to say, not all localities can be victorious in this competition, the losers ending up with more than their share of global unemployment. While Mayer (1992, and in chapter 10 in this reader) has sought to argue that progressive and liberatory possibilities exist in this new local politics of post-Fordism – as space for new political movements is seen to open up at the local level – such an interpretation is misleading. As the financial system has internationalized, as production and trade have globalized and as transnational corporations have progressively extended their reach, localities have been left with precious little bargaining power. The consequences of these developments are more likely to be politically and socially regressive than progressive (Dunford and Kafkalas, 1992; Swyngedouw, 1992). This is not to say that local strategies are irrelevant or that they have no constructive role to play (see Cox, 1993), but that such strategies will only fuel further instability if they perpetuate competitive relations between the 'hostile brothers'.

What is striking about local strategies at the present is just how *un*local they are. Workforce training, the erosion of social protection, the construction of science and business parks, the vigorous marketing of place and the ritual incantation of the virtues of international competitiveness and public–private partnership seem now to have become almost universal features of so-called 'local' strategies. In this sense, the local really has gone global. The explanation for the staggering lack of originality in local strategies does not lie in these localities themselves, with some shortfall in wit and imagination on the part of local actors. Rather, it is a reflection of the *global context* within which these strategies are being formulated. In a situation of continuing global crisis and deregulation, in which there is not enough investment to go around, localities are resorting to beggar-thy-neighbour strategies. The prevailing orthodoxy of neo-liberal economic policy – pioneered by Reagan and Thatcher and enforced by powerful global financial institutions – provides a political rationalization (of sorts) for these strategies through the faith which it places in the immutability of global economic forces and the virtues of competition. Neo-liberalism, then, is most certainly not part of the solution to the crisis, but on the contrary is the political essence of the problem. Neo-liberalism is the politics of the crisis, a kind of 'jungle law' which tends to break out – along with financial instability, accelerated labour exploitation and the self-destructive dynamic of the unfettered market – when economic growth slows and when social compromises collapse. It is this process which regulation theorists are describing when they talk of the breakdown of the 'golden age' of Fordist mass production and with it the social compromise enshrined in the Keynesian welfare state (see Jessop, chapter 8 in this volume).

The search for a new social compromise, which we characterize here as the search for a new institutional fix, must – of necessity – begin with the overthrowing of neo-liberalism. Without this, a resolution to the crisis will prove elusive. What regulationists call a post-Fordist 'mode of social regulation' – a new institutionalized compromise capable of restoring *sustainable* growth – requires the reining in of the destructive processes of deregulated competition. Essential to this process of establishing new regulatory rules is the requirement that relations *between* localities are reconstituted. The crisis politics of neo-liberalism are as a result inextricably linked to the current crisis of uneven development. One of the fundamental regulatory problems of the *after*-Fordist crisis, then, is the re-establishment of a set of *supralocal* regulatory rules: as Dunford and Kafkalas (1992, p. 29) have observed, 'the shape and success of Europe and its cities and regions depends . . . on the degree of supra-local solidarity'.

It is in this sense that the crisis of Fordism and the search for a new institutional fix are both intrinsically geographical problems. The collapse of Fordism–Keynesianism led to a crisis in which the nation state was decentred and its capacity to intervene eroded. In the vacuum created by the weakening of the nation state, a new set of global–local relations have emerged, though these remain profoundly asymmetrical, and almost by definition unstable. This alignment of global–local relations – which Swyngedouw (1992) has termed 'glocalization' – is not so much a new spatial order as a continuing spatial *dis*order. It is the geography of the unresolved crisis. Resolving this crisis, is, first and foremost, a supralocal matter: it is about overthrowing the 'jungle rule' of neo-liberalism at the level of the global economy and international political relations (see Altvater, 1992, 1993).

In this chapter, we take up the issue of the search for a new institutional fix. Questions of social regulation will be emphasized, in contradistinction to the focus, in the majority of the post-Fordist literature, on changing conditions in the productive sphere. We begin by briefly sketching our position on the post-Fordist debate, within which, we maintain, regulation theory continues to have some utility. This is followed by an examination of regulation under Fordism and the search for a new institutional fix which has accompanied its breakdown. The final section of the chapter considers the changing nature of global–local relations during this period of crisis and institutional searching.

REGULATION AND THE POST-FORDIST DEBATE

The debate around post-Fordism has usefully highlighted a host of innovatory developments in the organization of production and work. It has, however, been a truncated, 'productionist' debate in that it is not until recently that analysts have begun seriously to explore how this putative post-Fordist economy might be regulated (see Jessop, chapter 8 in this volume). In other words, in contrast to the comprehensive cataloguing of production innovations, work on emergent political structures and state forms has only just begun. This means that our understanding of post-Fordism is lopsided and underdeveloped: the crisis of Fordism was a crisis of Fordist accumulation (based on mass production and mass consumption) *and* Keynesian regulation (based on the welfare state and demand management). According to regulation theory, the crisis in *both* spheres must be resolved, and the two successfully recoupled, if sustainable growth is to return. Leborgne and Lipietz (1992, p. 333) have recently voiced the concern that 'most participants in the post-Fordist debate reduce it to a debate about new production systems and, contrary to most French regulationists, hold that there is already a solution, whether neo-Fordist or post-Fordist, to replace Fordism.' The detailed work which has been carried out into the dynamics of flexible production systems – at the level of both the firm and the regional production complex (see, for example, Scott, 1988) – constitutes an important (though still controversial) part of the post-Fordist jigsaw, but it does not add up to a comprehensive picture of post-Fordism. Neither does it satisfy the requirements of a regulationist analysis.

Yet what is at stake here is not just a defence of the integrity of a particular theoretical position, but the much broader question of how we interpret, theorize and respond politically to the present politicaleconomic disjuncture.

On the ruins of Fordism and Stalinism, humankind is at the crossroads. No technological determinism will light the way. *The present industrial divide is first and foremost a political divide.* The search for social compromise, around ecological constraints, macroeconomic consistency, gender and ethnic equality, all mediated by the nature and degree of political mobilization will decide the outcome. . . . The macroeconomics of the future may be based on a downward spiral of social and ecological competition, leading to recurrent financial, business and environmental crises, or an ecologically sustainable and macroeconomically stable model. . . . Radical economists and geographers may be part of finding the better pathway, both by identifying the possibilities for prosperity and by criticizing unrealistic optimism for flexibility as a panacea. *(Leborgne and Lipietz, 1992, pp. 347-8, emphasis added)*

There are alternatives to the way in which regulation theory has been deployed in the post-Fordist literature, as the theory provides a conceptual framework for interpreting and evaluating the current plethora of political and economic experiments. Rather than legitimating post-Fordist claims, regulation theory can be used critically to assess these claims.

Our proposition here is that much post-Fordist speculation is based on a series of generalizations from changing conditions in *production*. For all its use of regulationist jargon, a great deal of the post-Fordist literature falls considerably short of the requirements of a regulation approach in failing to specify either how the post-Fordist economy might be socially or politically regulated or how it might be pieced together in macroeconomic terms. Critical emphasis in regulation theory is placed on the 'structural coupling' between the system of accumulation (a macroeconomically coherent production–distribution–consumption relationship) and the ensemble of state forms, social norms, political practices and institutional networks which regulationists term the mode of social regulation. We cannot yet, therefore, speak of a post-Fordist *regime of accumulation* because such a system has yet to be comprehensively identified. Regimes of accumulation refer to particular couplings of systems of accumulation and modes of social regulation, or in other words to institutionally specific development paths – defined in terms of historical phases and patterns of development – which are characterized by economic growth and under which (immanent) crisis tendencies are contained, mediated or at least postponed. Modes of social regulation represent temporary institutional 'fixes', they do not neutralize crisis tendencies completely. Eventually, the ability of the mode of social regulation to mediate, accommodate and absorb these crisis tendencies is exceeded – through a process which might be characterized as 'institutional exhaustion' – and the regime of accumulation will break down (this is explored further in Tickell and Peck, 1992). Regulation theory, then, confronts the paradox that capitalism has proved rather more durable than envisaged in classical Marxian theory, that crises may not only be way-stations on the path of terminal decline, but that – in terms of the actualities of capitalist development – they may also play a rejuvenating role, 'brutally restoring the contradictory unity' of the accumulation process (Boyer, 1990, p. 35; see also Dunford, 1990). Central to this entire process, for regulation theorists, is the role played by the mode of social regulation.

In order to understand capitalist reproduction in an integral sense, it is necessary to grasp the wider social and institutional context within which accumulation takes place. For regulationists, it is the mode of social regulation which defines 'the social context in which expanded economic reproduction occurs' (Jessop, 1992a, p. 50). The mode of social regulation, which comprises a complex ensemble of social norms and habits, state forms, structures and practices, customs and networks, and institutionalised compromises, rules of conduct and enforceable laws, represents a set of codified social relations which have the effect of guiding and sustaining the accumulation process (Aglietta, 1979, p. 382). According to Jessop, it provides the most sound basis on which a regime of accumulation should be determined (rather than the labour process or the pattern of accumulation) because it specifies

> the institutional and organizational conditions which secure[d] Fordism as a national accumulation regime and is especially helpful in defining the peculiarities of different Fordist regimes. But it should not be divorced from work on the more general dynamics of capitalism. For the latter defines the basic tendencies and counter-tendencies, structural contradictions, strategic dilemmas, and overall constraints which inevitably shape modes of regulation, which find provisional, partial and unstable resolution in the latter. . . . [Modes of social regulation] cannot be properly understood without considering how [they] modify and yet remain subject to the general laws of capital accumulation. *(Jessop, 1992a, p. 50)*

Following this logic, the mode of social regulation and the accumulation process exist in a dynamic relationship: the former is defined in the context of political–economic parameters, but also plays a part in shaping the course of accumulation itself (see Boyer, 1988). Thus while it may be possible to make both abstract claims and empirical generalizations about globally hegemonic regimes of accumulation, regulationist accounts have pointed to a considerable degree of institutional (and geographical) variability *within* individual regimes. So while global Fordism could be characterized in general terms as a global system, the building blocks from which this system was constructed were in effect a whole series of interconnected and institutionally specific *national Fordisms*. More precisely, these national variants of Fordism effectively comprised a range of geographically specific couplings between Fordist accumulation systems and Keynesian welfare modes of regulation, the specificities of which are sketched out on a country-by-country basis in Table 9.1.

Given these concerns, it should not perhaps be surprising that

Table 9.1 Variants of Fordism

Type of Fordist regime	Characteristics of coupling	Examples
'Classic Fordism'	Mass production and consumption underwritten by social democratic welfare state.	USA
'Flex-Fordism'	Decentralized, federalized state. Close cooperation between financial and industrial capital, including facilitation of inter-firm cooperation.	West Germany
'Blocked Fordism'	Inadequate integration of financial and productive capital at the level of the nation state. Archaic and obstructive character of working class politics.	Great Britain
'State Fordism'	State plays leading role in creation of conditions of mass production, including state control of industry. *L'état entrepreneur.*	France
'Delayed Fordism'	Cheap labour immediately adjacent to Fordist core. State intervention played key role in rapid industrialization in the 1960s.	Spain, Italy

'Peripheral Fordism'	Local assembly followed by export of Fordist goods. Heavy indebtedness. Authoritarian state structures coupled with movement for democracy, attempts to emulate Fordist accumulation system in absence of corresponding MSR.	Mexico, Brazil
'Racial Fordism'	Dualistic workforce. Privileged minority has North American-style working conditions and remuneration levels. This relies upon authoritarian state structures and the 'super-exploitation' of majority population.	South Africa under apartheid
'Primitive Taylorization'	Taylorist labour process with almost endless supply of labour. Bloody exploitation, huge extraction of surplus value. Dictatorial states and high social tension.	Malaysia, Bangladesh, the Philippines
'Hybrid Fordism'	Profit-driven expansion based upon modified Taylorism. Truncated internal market, societal segmentation and under-developed welfare state. Indirect wage indexation.	Japan

Source: updated from Tickell and Peck, 1992

regulation theory has been deployed not only in retrospective analyses of capitalist development, but also – since the breakdown of the Fordist growth pattern – in *prospective* work on the determination of the successor regime. Although the theory itself is not predictive, it certainly begs questions of *if*, how, when and where growth will be restored *after* Fordism. Speculative work on the shape of post-Fordism, it is probably fair to say, has generated more heat than light. Particular problems have been encountered where crude or partial readings of regulation theory have been deployed to shore up the premature claim that a post-Fordist or flexible regime of accumulation is already in evidence. Invariably, these are based on generalizations from developments in the production system (many of which are themselves contentious) and as such they fall considerably short of the regulationist requirement for an integrated analysis of the wider process of accumulation and its associated regulatory forms (Tickell and Peck, 1992). This has stimulated calls from regulation theorists for a more restrained and critical approach to post-Fordism (Jessop, 1992a; Leborgne and Lipietz, 1992).

The regulationist framework we have outlined above provides a basis for critically interpreting (or reinterpreting) the host of contemporary political–economic features which are typically cited in evidence for post-Fordist claims. The uncertainties created by the breakdown of Fordism–Keynesianism are bound to stimulate critiques of existing production systems and institutional structures, as well as experimental searches for new solutions. In the process, mistakes will be made. Capitalism develops, of course, by getting things wrong as well as by getting them right. Some experiments will succeed while others will fail. Others will thrive on the very uncertainty itself. Needless to say, such conditions pose immense interpretative problems for social scientists, particularly those concerned with separating the durable wheat from the ephemeral chaff. More broadly, there are real analytical dangers in attempting to read regime-wide and predictive conclusions from the flux of crisis. According to Altvater, the crisis both

> destroys traditional social forms and social and economic regulation and it generates new forms of regulation. Whereas the process of destruction is more or less obvious and identifiable, it is much more difficult to deduce the generation of new social forms of regulation. Social stability can only be achieved by means of a complex set of complementary, compatible, and cohesive institutions. Since there is no single directing agent which defines and creates these new institutions ... a new mode of regulation or a new accumulation regime can only emerge as the

outcome of conflicting tendencies of progressive acts and regressive setbacks. *(Altvater, 1992, p. 22)*

In trying to deduce the significance of contemporary developments, such as flexible specialization, neo-liberal labour regulation or forms of elite consumption, it is worth recalling then that 'the history of capitalism is full of experiments which led nowhere, aborted revolutions, abandoned prototypes and all sorts of monstrosities' (Lipietz, 1987, p. 15). Weeding out such monstrosities is an intrinsically political process. Regulation theory, we want to argue, has a positive role to play in this process, not in prematurely defining a single, post-Fordist development path (Graham, 1992), but in raising macrolevel and critical questions about the *sustainability* – social, ecological, economic – of different development options. The theory has a positive role to play in the development of a progressive agenda. It has to mean more than bundling together a host of (regressive and progressive) contemporary developments, then conferring upon these the status and legitimacy of a post-Fordist or flexible regime of accumulation (see Peck and Miyamachi, 1995). It need not lamely endorse a neo-liberal or neo-competitive agenda because that is the one – perhaps by default – which happens to be dominant at the moment. On the contrary it can *and must* be deployed directly to challenge this agenda. Out of this, the pragmatic objective for the left, as Lipietz argues in this volume and elsewhere (1992), is the definition of a new (admittedly capitalist) compromise.

REGULATION UNDER FORDISM

The pretext for examining institutional experimentation *after* Fordism must of course be a consideration of regulation under Fordism and its subsequent rupture. This helps to define much of the 'problem' to which post-Fordist 'solutions' must respond. The process of social regulation under Fordism was anchored in the Keynesian welfare state, under which collective bargaining and monopoly pricing were institutionalized, policy instruments were deployed to maintain and manage aggregate demand, and norms of mass consumption and 'American ways of life' were generalized (see Jessop, 1992a, b). By implication, these processes of social regulation were rooted, first and foremost, in and around the *nation* state. One of the fundamental tensions of the Fordist regime was the uneasy interface between *national* forms of regulation and the *globalizing* dynamic of accumulation. Altvater, for example, characterizes the Keynesian state in these terms:

> The state supports rationalization [in the labour process] via the increase of effective demand which helps to resolve the always threatening realization problem. The economic interventions of the state under the pressure of international competition are effective impulses for the dynamization and modernization of the system, for an increase in growth rates. And the welfare state is a very efficient vehicle for the mobilization of monetary funds for the compensation of unemployment, health problems, environmental damage, etc. But even within this comprehensive structure the Keynesian state has limits. ... [The] rationalizing dynamics of the capitalist labor process go far beyond national frontiers and have a global reach. The Keynesian state is by its very definition a national state and is therefore limited to the national space in the exercise of its regulatory functions. *(Altvater, 1992, p. 25)*

The regulatory 'logic' of the Fordist system may have been rooted in the nationally constituted Keynesian welfare state, but this regulatory system was itself predicated on a specifically configured international order. In an important sense, then, regulation under Fordism was primarily articulated at the interface of the national and the global.

Essential to the viability of Keynesian welfare states in core Fordist countries was the institutionalization of international economic and political relations under the *Pax Americana*. The establishment of the USA as global financial hegemon – backed by the country's military, economic and political might and institutionalized under Bretton Woods – provided a means of regulating the international system in a way compatible with the requirements of Keynesian regulation at the level of the nation state (Corbridge, 1988; Altvater, 1992). As with all such institutional fixes, this was a fragile one, most significantly because it fostered a state of dynamic interdependency between the US economy and the global economy, between the dollar as national currency and the dollar as world currency (see Cooper, 1987; Leyshon, 1992). The hegemonic position of the USA consequently posed the constant threat of crisis tendencies being transmitted from the domestic US economy to the world economy and vice versa. Leyshon (1992, p. 258) argues that this resulted from the USA's ability 'to pursue a policy of expansionary growth over a long period that served to significantly increase the volume of credit circulating within the international financial system.' However, the degree of control exercised by Bretton Woods over *monetary* circulation could not be exerted over the emerging global *credit* system. Lubricated by the growth of TNCs and with the development of unregulated 'Euromarkets' in money, the global credit system became, in effect, a privatized system, beyond the reach of political–institutional control (Gilpin, 1987; Walter, 1991; Swyngedouw, 1992). As private capital began increasingly to circuit globally on a deregulated basis, Keynesian nation states progressively lost control of one of the most important macroeconomic levers – the setting of interest rates. The loss of interest rate sovereignty was a significant contributor to the breakdown of the fragile international order established under Fordism (Glyn et al., 1991). 'Unregulated global credit was [consequently] a factor of erosion of the (political institutional) regulation of the whole Fordist system' (Altvater, 1992, p. 37).

Global Fordism was, then, ultimately undermined by the evolution of those international financial institutions which had initially underwritten it. Yet it was not solely in terms of macroeconomic policy that the *Pax Americana* proved contradictory. Global Fordism stimulated an internationalization of both trade and production, which enervated those national economies that provided the system with its strength. Along with the International Monetary Fund and the International Bank for Reconstruction and Development (the 'World Bank'), the General Agreement on Tariffs and Trade (GATT) constituted one of the central pillars of the Fordist world economy. The GATT was set up in 1947 in order to facilitate trade, initially between developed countries, through the multilateral removal of tariff and non-tariff barriers (Dicken, 1992a). Like the two Bretton Woods institutions, the GATT was maintained by the strong support provided by the United States in its role as Fordist hegemon. As the GATT expanded during the 1960s, however, it began to undermine accumulation in some sectors in the Fordist countries, as cheaper or technologically more sophisticated imports successfully competed with indigenous industries which were reaching the limits of the Taylorist division of labour. Tensions within the United States between nationally and internationally oriented capital contributed to a retreat from multilateralism in the 1970s and concomitant growth in bilateralism and protectionism (Dicken, 1992a, b; Leyshon, 1992). Problems within the Fordist countries triggered the further internationalization of production. Keynesianism became discredited and monetarism increasingly influential. The internationalization of production and the growth of the export sector meant that wages were increasingly seen as a drag on economic competitiveness rather than a contributor to consumption. Consequently, real wages began to slow and then decline, compounding the problems of stagnating consumer demand. The virtuous cycle of Fordism had turned vicious.

There is an important sense, then, in which Fordism was undermined by its emergent geographical contradictions or, alternatively, the contradictions of Fordism took on a geographical form. Central to this was the contradiction between globalizing accumulation and national regulation, or more particularly between the emerging unregulated global credit system and the fiscal integrity of the Keynesian welfare state. The erosion of interest rate sovereignty undermined the basis for the regulation of aggregate demand at the nation state level. In the absence of effective demand management, the system of Fordist regulation was itself ruptured. The continuing process of globalization, moreover, implies that the current crisis is *qualitatively* different to earlier crises (see Martin, 1994). The recourse to monetarism and supply-side strategies on the part of nation states following the breakdown of Fordism might represent a *tactical response* to these new global economic realities, but it would be a mistake to represent these developments as a putative regulatory 'solution'. As variants of the 'jungle law' of liberal ideology, they represent a regulatory vacuum, not a regulatory fix. They do not provide the basis for the restoration of generalized and sustainable economic growth. 'Growth rates approaching the golden age [or Fordist] levels will only be feasible *and sustainable* with low inflation, on the basis of new domestic rules of co-ordination, and a rather different international order. However, this will *require the abandonment* of the fledgling [neo-liberalist] economic regime of the 1980s' (Glyn et al., 1991, p. 118, emphasis added).

The search for a new institutional fix continues. It may be fruitless, because a crucial component – perhaps *the* crucial component – must be the construction of a new *global* regulatory order. One thing we can be fairly certain of, however, is that neo-liberalism is part of the problem, not part of the solution.

SEARCHING FOR A NEW INSTITUTIONAL FIX

Perhaps the greatest controversy in terms of *after*-Fordist institutional searching concerns the conceptual and political status of neo-liberalism which, along with Jessop (chapter 8 in this volume), we define as a political project concerned with the liberalization (or constitution) of competitive market forces, the abandonment of demand-side intervention in favour of supply-side policy measures and the rejection of both social partnership and welfarism. Because the rise of neo-liberalism in the 1970s and 1980s coincided with the breakdown of Fordism and the apparently terminal collapse of Keynesian social regulation, it has in some accounts been afforded the status of a mode of social regulation in-waiting. This issue has been confronted most explicitly by Jessop (1992b, pp. 31–2), who defines the 'emerging post-Fordist mode of regulation', based on the twin principles of flexibility and supply-side innovation, in the following way.

- The wage relation: a recomposition of the collective labourer and a resegmentation of the labour market, involving skill polarization, flexibilization in internal and external labour markets, decentralized pay bargaining, new forms of social wage.
- The enterprise system: a shift towards flatter, leaner and more flexible forms of corporate organization, involving increased contracting out of functions, greater intra-corporate competition, emphasis on continual innovation, a search for economies of scope, non-price based competition.
- The money form: dominated by private, globalized bank credit, involving the emergence of more flexible forms of credit, innovation in financial services, subordination of state credit to imperatives of international money and credit markets.
- The consumption sphere: emphasis on differentiation and niche marketing, combination of global sourcing with customized production for elite markets.
- The state form: displacement of Keynesian welfare statism with Schumpeterian workfare statism, involving the promotion of competition and supply-side innovation (at all levels of the production system and between social institutions), use of social policy instruments not to generalize norms of mass consumption but to encourage flexibility, 'hollowing out' of the nation state as powers are displaced upwards (to global and pan-regional bodies) and downwards (to local and regional states, which also begin to integrate with one another in ways that by-pass the nation state).

For Jessop (1992b, p. 32) these developments 'could create a distinctive ensemble of regulatory practices which is reproducible in the medium term'. Not to be confused, Jessop argues, with the neo-liberal assault on Keynesian welfare state institutions, this nascent post-Fordist mode of social regulation represents a response both to the contradictions of the Keynesian mode of social regulation and to the imperatives of globalized accumulation. More recently, he has gone as far as to say that the Schumpeterian workfare state (see chapter 8 in this volume for details) constitutes the 'best possible political shell for post-Fordism' (Jessop, 1993, p. 7). He argues that this state form will meet the regulatory needs of post-Fordism by strengthening national economic competitiveness and by subordinating social to economic policy. With his eye firmly on the *forms* of the emergent Schumpeterian workfare state, Jessop argues that its particular shape will vary from country to country according to the institutional and political context in which it emerges. While some countries are developing neo-liberal state forms, others are moving towards neo-corporatism (which remains at least partially consensual) or neo-statism (with policies of active intervention). This typology, with its emphasis on actually existing economic and state structures, provides a useful reminder that the form of the post-Fordist state is not predetermined.

These remain, however, contentious claims. While Jessop is at pains to dissociate the Schumpeterian workfare state from pure neo-liberalism, the two certainly share many common features: an emphasis on supposedly immutable global economic forces, a reliance on supply-side instruments, advocacy of the virtues of the market and of competitive pressures. The deployment of these neo-liberal devices, coupled with the fact that the 'jungle law' of neo-liberalism continues to prevail at the global scale despite its inability to offer a way out of the long-term recession marking the end of Fordism, raises questions about the ability of the Schumpeterian workfare state to sustain economic growth (although neo-liberal devices *may*, perhaps through their failure, have a role to play in illuminating the path towards *non*-liberal institutional fixes). All three variants of the Schumpeterian workfare state must face the problem of coping with a deregulated global financial system, one which is likely to continue to encourage regulatory undercutting and capital switching, and which therefore has the potential to undermine both neo-statist and neo-corporatist experiments. Ironically, neo-liberal states may be seen to be winning this 'race to the bottom' (as the strategy of undercutting wage levels and other social standards proves attractive, in the short term, to mobile capital), but as the experience of Britain and the USA in the 1980s suggests, these approaches are *internally* contradictory and crisis-prone. In the context of continuing global disorder, neo-liberal variants of the Schumpeterian workfare state may be able to undermine the (more progressive) alternatives, while at the same time being incapable of providing a *sustainable* model in their own right.

It may consequently be inappropriate to label this particular market-led ensemble of regulatory practices as an emergent mode of social regulation because it is internally crisis-prone and therefore unstable. Lipietz (1992) has suggested that four flaws exist in the neo-liberal model developed under the Reagan and Thatcher administrations during the 1980s, but also adopted in different ways by other nation states (e.g. Spain, Brazil, New Zealand), by supranational institutions (e.g. the European Union's desire for a single market) and by global institutions (e.g. the World Bank, the IMF, the OECD). First, neo-liberalism is associated with a tendency for social polarization, with the attendant possibility of either disruptive collective action or social breakdown. Second, neo-liberalism does not resolve the contradictions of the Taylorist labour process central to the breakdown of Fordism: namely, growing social alienation from the rigidly fragmented and rigidly policed production process, and the collapse of the social framework around which productivity gains could be shared with and between workers. Third, neo-liberalism tends to exaggerate, rather than contain, swings in the business cycle, with the result that macroeconomic crashes are a constant threat and, we would add, the internationalization of neo-liberalism has meant that cyclical crises are rapidly transmitted from one nation state to another. Fourth, the neo-liberal deregulation of international trade does not lead unproblematically to structural adjustment but to the exacerbation of structural imbalances and to forced deflations, as nation states respond to global competition by adopting beggar-thy-neighbour policies.

These contradictory tendencies in neo-liberal regulation are already becoming manifest, as evidence mounts of the fragility of 1980s growth patterns and/or their incompatibility with neo-liberalism. The pattern of regionalized growth which is so often held up as the paradigmatic post-Fordist accumulation dynamic, flexible specialization, has been shown to be dependent upon a *high-trust* regulatory environment, with its associated cooperative relations between economic actors and with its extensive utilization of collective services and institutions (Lorenz, 1992). Such regulatory requirements, Hirst and Zeitlin (1992, p. 76) argue, are 'incompatible with a neo-liberal regime of unregulated markets and cut-throat competition'. Although it is often argued that high-trust regulatory practices can be constructed (and maintained) in localized enclaves such as Emilia-Romagna, these regulatory systems are being challenged as they come into contact with the harshly competitive global environment (Amin and Robins, 1990; Peck, 1994).

Perhaps more significantly, neo-liberalism also seems to be failing in its own backyard. The patterns of growth exhibited in regions such as Britain's M4 corridor and the Californian technopoles, and for which so much is claimed by proponents of (and apologists for) neo-liberalism, faltered badly in the recession of the early 1990s. Predictable market failures had already become apparent at the peak of the cycle in labour markets, for example, as deregulation in saturated labour markets led to crises of skill formation, labour poaching and wage inflation (Scott and Paul, 1990; Peck and Tickell, 1992). In the South East of England, chronic and simultaneous overheating in labour, housing, finance and commercial property markets contributed to the suffocation, in the late 1980s, of the regional growth pattern. This was subsequently to push Britain as a whole into a deflationary spiral which led to the deepest recession of the post-war period. Meanwhile, the downturn in California triggered a state-level fiscal crisis. Interestingly – and in stark contrast to the ideology of neo-liberalism – the mode of growth exhibited during the 1980s in both California and the M4 corridor was significantly underwritten by state defence expenditure (Lovering, 1991; Markusen, 1991). These areas were consequently the beneficiaries of what was in effect a repackaged version of regional Keynesianism (coupled with regressive income redistribution), presented through the neo-liberal rhetoric of enterprise and individualism.

It is no coincidence, though, that a rash of neo-liberal projects should have emerged *after* Fordism – in the crisis period following a stable regime. This is because neo-liberalism reflects a deeper set of currents in capitalist development. There are essentially two ways of interpreting the current grip of neo-liberalism. One interpretation is that because there are so many neo-liberal projects (and so few functioning alternatives), they must be part of a post-Keynesian institutional fix. Here, neo-liberalism is portrayed as a regulatory solution. Another interpretation – and the one which we favour – is that the ascendancy of neo-liberalism represents a regulatory vacuum, the *absence* of a new institutional fix. Here, neo-liberalism is seen as a symptom of, and contributor to, the crisis. Neo-liberalism, we have argued, is capitalism's 'law of the jungle'. As such it has a massive destructive capacity. *Non*-liberal regulatory projects, in order to be durable, must be capable of fending off these destructive tendencies. They must be capable of preventing the breakout of 'jungle law'.

In summary, then, we have suggested that far from providing the basis for a new regulatory fix, neo-liberalism represents one of the sources of the problem. It is accordingly tautological to argue that neo-liberalism is 'concerned to promote a market-led transition towards the new economic regime' (Jessop, 1993, p. 29), because the path defined by neo-liberalism is one which leads off the precipice. Neo-liberalism is now, as ever, the politics of crisis. Even if the regressive social effects are set aside, there are very real doubts over whether neo-liberalism can *sustain* economic growth. While neo-liberalism is able to 'release' (often state-subsidized and unevenly distributed) growth, as a political–economic programme it seems incapable of securing the medium-term reproduction of that growth, given its susceptibility to cyclical imbalances and short-term plundering, and given the absence of a framework of policies, institutions and economic norms necessary for ensuring continuous reinvestment in skills, technologies and innovations. As the experience of the 1980s so clearly shows, neo-liberalism tends to promote systemic instability, both temporarily and geographically: business cycles swing ever more violently, while localized growth is increasingly fragile and short-lived. The remainder of this chapter addresses the geographical implications of this continuing crisis. Has a 'new spatial order' been established – based on reconstituted global–local relations and a 'hollowed out' nation state – or are we still witnessing the geography of crisis, a 'spatial *dis*order'?

A GLOBAL-LOCAL ORDER OR GLOBAL-LOCAL DISORDER?

The period since the breakdown of Fordism has been characterized by flux and transformation, not least in the geographical sphere. National economic fortunes have ebbed and flowed, a new set of highly productive regions – Orange County, the Third Italy, Baden-Württemberg – have risen to international prominence, and globalization in finance, trade and production has accelerated. In terms of regulatory changes, supranational institutions such as the European Commission are apparently assuming greater significance, while nation states seem to be losing control over their economic destinies. Meanwhile, local regulatory fixes – such as those in the aforementioned growth regions – appear increasingly seductive, though in practice difficult to emulate. What should we make of these geographical shifts? Are they emblematic of a new geographical order, a first sight of the spatial logic of post-Fordism? Or are they geographies of crisis and turbulence?

The developments have recently been conceptualized through the related notions of 'hollowing out' and 'glocalization', each of which is summarized as follows:

> Over the last decade or so the relative dominance of the nation state as a scale level has changed to give way to new configurations in which both the local/regional and the transnational/global scale have risen to prominence. Global corporations, global financial movements and global politics play deciding roles in the structuring of daily life, while simultaneously more attention is paid to local and regional responses and restructuring processes. There is, in other words, a double movement of globalisation on the one hand and devolution, decentralisation or localisation on the other [which has been termed] 'glocalisation'. This concept also suggests that the local/global interplay of contemporary capitalist restructuring processes should be thought of as a single, combined process with two inherently related, albeit contradictory movements and as a process which involves a *de facto* recomposition of the articulation of the geographical scales of economic and social life. *(Swyngedouw, 1992, p. 40)*

> [The nation-state's] capacities to project power even within its own national borders are becoming ever more limited due to a complex triple displacement of powers upward, downward, and, to some extent, outward. *(Jessop, 1993, p. 10)*

In this reading, then, nation states have lost much of their *raison d'être*, as economic changes have increased the importance of both global and local political sites. While pointing to the contradictory nature of the global–local realignment, these analyses imply that an emerging global–local *order* may be in evidence. While these conceptions may reflect some of the current geographical realities (Gertler, 1992), the crucial issue is how far it is possible to project forward from the present crisis period.

Given present conditions, the *symmetry* that is implied in the terminology of the global–local nexus is rather misleading. The global–local nexus is, we would argue, a lopsided concept, comprised on the one hand of powerful processes of global *disorder* and on the other hand of largely reactive, and typically shallow, local *responses*. Local regulatory experiments, to be sure, have a role to play, but they have to be understood for what they are. First, their global prominence and ideological significance stem to a certain extent from their straightforward rarity: there seem to be just a handful of genuinely innovative local experiments and a raft of pale imitations. Second, their 'visibility' is also a reflection of the fact that they have been sucked into the political vacuum left by the breakdown of national regulation *after* Fordism–Keynesianism: against the systemic significance attributed to them by Mayer in chapter 10 in this volume, we would argue that they are unlikely to fill the regulatory 'space' left by the collapse of Fordism–Keynesianism. They seem, however, to be all that we have. Third, in the context of neo-liberal hegemony and a generalized shortage of global investment, it is difficult to see how local strategies can do anything other than bend to the will of global competition: progressive local social contracts are likely to be difficult to sustain in the face of 'jungle law' at the global level. The basic difficulty, then, lies in trying to establish local order in the face of global disorder.

Our argument here is that, while some localities may be successful for some of the time, their success in the current global climate is only being achieved at the expense of failure elsewhere. Local successes, moreover, are likely only to be transitory. The current configuration of global–local relations, as Table 9.2 shows, is chronically unstable and contradictory. The table illustrates the spatial contradictions of Fordism and the ways in which they contributed to the crisis of the Fordist regime of accumulation. It also indicates some of the spatial relations which characterize the unstable period since Fordism's demise. This new geography is not, of course, the polar opposite of its predecessor, although there are fundamental differences between them. Global disorder seems to be intrinsically connected to local disorder.

Global disorder . . .

Restructuring in the international financial system has been a key stimulus for change at the supranational scale. These changes have not only led to a structural shift in accumulation, where the returns on the fictitious churning of financial capital can now far outstrip the potential returns from material production (Walter, 1991; Altvater, 1992), they have also *destabilized global production*. This can be seen in the disruptive effects on the spatial strategies of transnational corporations: 'Monetary chaos makes integrated global sourcing strategies extremely vulnerable as costs . . . cannot be easily established *a priori*. Offshore direct investment strategies are becoming increasingly risky ventures in a volatile international monetary environment' (Swyngedouw, 1992, p. 54). This instability has strengthened pressures to expand the role of supranational state institutions, such as the European Union. Although such bodies are not new, Jessop (1993, and chapter 8 in this volume), for example, claims that they have massively increased in number, scope and function. To characterize these developments as part of a new, *supranational*, mode of social regulation would be to misinterpret their role. As currently constituted, they remain part of the regulatory problem.

While we would not wish to deny the importance of supranational regulatory bodies, we would question their ability to promote sustainable growth. On the one hand, some crucial international institutions seem powerless in the face of the prevailing 'jungle law'. The GATT, for example, has seen its influence wane, as bilateral trade negotiations proliferated against the backcloth of the Uruguay renegotiations, which took almost a decade to reach a resolution, and which remain highly fragile. The fledgling European Monetary System has also faltered badly. It may be the case that powerful international institutions require the backing of a hegemonic power, without which the 'agreement' and enforcement of rules becomes problematic. It is surely significant that those emergent supranational and international institutions which *have* seen their role enhanced are pursuing (or lamely endorsing) a neo-liberal agenda which, we would argue, is a recipe for continued global economic *instability*. Rather than providing the bedrock for sustained accumulation, such regulatory bodies are likely to prove to be a destabilizing force (Hübner, 1991). In this vein, Walter (1991, pp. 209, 215) argues that

> the allocation of global capital is highly sensitive to shifts in expectations, which may result in considerable volatility in capital flows. . . . It is also possible that the size and volatility of capital flows and asset prices

Table 9.2 Spatial constitution of regulatory relations under and after Fordism

Spatial Scale	Fordism		After Fordism	
	Characteristics	Contradictions	Characteristics	Contradictions
Global system	Bretton Woods financial system and GATT underwrite financial stability and global trade, acting as mechanisms which 'transmit' Fordist features internationally. An international 'regulated space'.	USA acts as governor and guarantor of regulatory order at same time as exploiting the system for its own economic interests. US ideology of market undermines efficacy of international regulatory discourse.	New international financial system operates outwith control of regulators, while 'market logic' dominates negotiations over the GATT. Creation of 24 hour global markets enable capital to engage in 'regulatory arbitrage', further undermining regulation.	Financial system increasingly volatile and unstable. Economic cycles rapidly transmitted through system, accentuating both growth and decline and undermining basis for stable development.

Global–national relations	Nation states have the capacity to set independent monetary policy within the context of US hegemony.	In later stages of Fordism, progressive internationalization of capital undermines economic self-sufficiency of nation states. Transmission of US 'domestic' problems through global economy.	Nation states cede powers to emergent supranational bodies which attempt to control internationalisation of financial and productive capital (e.g. BIS, European Union). TNCs engage in regulatory arbitrage.	National economies become further absorbed into global circuits of capital – necessitating further supranationalization of power. This further undermines both nation state and relatively weak supranational regulatory structures.
National scale	Central regulatory functions dispensed by Keynesian welfare state which secures conditions for mass production and consumption.	Fiscal crisis of nation state triggered by deindustrialization, rise of mass unemployment and loss of interest rate sovereignty.	'Hollowing out' of nation state, as national governments cede power to supranational and local bodies.	State loses some control over accumulation process and becomes more responsive to the demands of capital. Less able to meet social welfare objectives, further undermining cohesion of the national social formation.

Table 9.2 *Continued*

Spatial Scale	Fordism		After Fordism	
	Characteristics	*Contradictions*	*Characteristics*	*Contradictions*
National–local relations	Centralization and consolidation of nation state powers as governments attempt to control national economies and introduce social welfare systems. Nation states seek to ameliorate the worst effects of uneven development via regional policy.	Political and economic contradictions of uneven development within nation state. Failure of regional policy following deepening peripheralization.	Unstable. Geographically specific political responses. Targeted local interventionism replaced by selectivity based on market criteria.	Increasing competition between local states fosters 'regulatory undercutting'. Zero-sum local–local competition. Spatial inequalities exacerbated.
Local scale	Key regulatory functions around social reproduction dispensed through local welfare states.	Fiscal crisis of national state transmitted to the local state, undermining local welfarism.	Some argue local states have enhanced economic role. Supply-side local state managing, for example, training policy.	Local states powerless in global economy, reacting to external economic forces. Few degrees of local freedom.

(including exchange rates) in recent years has hampered adjustment to domestic and international imbalances. Is it entirely plausible, for example, to view the coincidence of a strong dollar and a massive deterioration in the US current account in the early 1980s as an efficient outcome, other than in a purely technical sense? . . . In summary, the economic consequences of the global financial revolution have probably been an increasing volatility of world interest rates, exchange rates and business cycles, while the innovation associated with it raises serious questions about world financial fragility.

That the internationalization of accumulation has eroded the power of nation states is hardly contentious (although see Hirst and Thompson, 1992; Glyn and Sutcliffe, 1992). A new global system has yet to stabilize. Fuelled by neo-liberalism, the system seems still to be unravelling. Set against this context, tendentious shifts in local-level regulatory practices are perhaps even more fragile.

. . . And local disorder

What is the role for localities in this global disorder? In some variants of the localization thesis, local states are seen to have an enhanced role in the world economy because they have been able to by-pass national states. Mayer, for example, argues that nation states have devolved significant, material powers to cities and regions, which

> have become direct players in the world economy. The particular location of a place within the international division of labour under conditions of heightened inter-urban competition thus not only sets certain constraints, but itself becomes an asset to be exploited *on the basis of locally-determined priorities.* . . . By identifying the particular strengths and assets a city or region has to offer (to investors etc.), *local political actors can exact payments and concessions, and can exert leverage over supra-local actors.* (Mayer, 1992, pp. 263, 269, emphasis added; see also Stoker, 1990; Stoker and Mossberger, 1992, for similar sentiments)

Such claims are, to say the least, debatable. While cities and regions *may* be competing with each other, it is difficult to see that, in so doing, they are wielding significantly greater *power* than during the Fordist period. If *nation* states are insufficiently powerful to set their economic policy or to prevent transnational companies from engaging in regulatory arbitrage, local states will surely have even less success. To claim otherwise is to deproblematize uneven development as a process endemic to capitalism, and perhaps also to legitimate contemporary increases in spatial inequality (see Dunford and Kafkalas, 1992). In fact, for the vast majority of cities and regions, the scope for local economic intervention is limited to the creation of a so-called 'good business environment' which bends to the will of mobile capital in its search for a new spatial fix. While this may ultimately prove beneficial to a few regions, the competition engendered is at best a zero-sum game and at worst destructive (Schoenberger, 1991; Swyngedouw, 1992; Tickell and Dicken, 1993). A few privileged growth regions *may* be able to exact concessions from 'supralocal actors' but the overall effect has been to *reduce* the power of local and regional states – in terms of economic intervention and the maintenance of progressive social welfare systems (see, for example, Davis, 1993). Furthermore, the process of competition between regions for pieces of global capital raises the constant spectre of 'regulatory undercutting' (see Table 9.2), while the speeding up of turnover times alluded to by Swyngedouw (1992; see also Harvey, 1989) makes even the strongest growth regions vulnerable to devalorization and crisis. In other words, the more vigorously localities compete with one another, the more pronounced their subordination to supralocal forces becomes.

In contrast to such theorizations of the enhanced power of local states, Swyngedouw (1992, p. 57) conceives a narrower role for local regulatory innovation, arguing that the collapse of the national (Fordist) social contract means that structures of social regulation now have to be constructed at the local level. Swyngedouw is surely right in framing localization as a *regulatory problem*, an interpretation that contrasts with Mayer's tendency in this book to see it as portentous of a new, post-Fordist mode of social regulation. There are serious doubts about whether it will prove possible to forge *local* social contracts in any but the most successful regions. The regions privileged by 1980s neo-liberalism, for example, proved to be incapable of containing the contradictions of their own growth (Peck and Tickell, 1994). As Harvey (1985) demonstrated some years ago in his analysis of urban 'structured coherence', local communities of interest are difficult to sustain, not least because different factions of the community have different material interests. Furthermore, if nation states, with their relatively greater control over ideological devices, are instigating neo-liberal agendas which positively eschew social contracts, this is a harsh climate indeed to seek to establish local *non*-liberal regulatory projects. Viewed from the northern reaches of Britain, the situation certainly looks bleak. As Paddison (1993, p. 167) argues, 'as much as a federal or other "solution" may be only feasible through concerted action between "coalitions of the excluded", the scenarios for future spatial restructuring, the deepening of regional decline and the intensifying of competition for the re-valorization of local and regional economies, is hardly the base from which to build such coalition.'

The internationalization of the world economy, and the weakened power of nation states, present a profound regulatory problem. As Jessop (1993) argues, in many ways the most significant change over the past twenty years has been the collapse of the Keynesian welfare state and its regulatory infrastructure. This poses questions about the *significance* of the process of glocalization described above. There clearly have been some formal increases in local economic intervention and, certainly, *local social responsibility* across both Europe and North America (see Moulaert et al., 1988; Davis, 1993). These have, however, surely been the result of the vacuum which has emerged at the level of the nation state following the breakdown of Fordism-Keynesianism, rather than the appropriation of *new powers* by the local state. As *nation states* are losing the capacity for economic intervention, it is difficult to see what significant levers are available at the local level *vis-à-vis* the more powerful process of globalization (but see Lipietz's defence of the local in chapter 11 of this volume).

Towards a resolution?

We have argued here that glocalization is an inherently unstable process, which not only undermines local economies, but reflects some of the underlying contradictions of capitalism. There is as yet no mechanism in place for regulating (uneven development in) global capitalism. Without such a mechanism there can be no basis for the formation of a new regime of accumulation. While some attempts to create supranational institutions are under way, and even though some of these institutions (such as the Bank for International Settlements) are attempting to grapple with the demands of a financial system which is largely out of control, it is our argument that as long as these institutions continue to adhere to neo-liberal ideologies, the global economy will remain in crisis. It is, furthermore, difficult to see how a new local order can precede a new global order. The geographies of *after*-Fordism sketched in Table 9.2, then, are intrinsically unstable. They are geographies of crisis.

If we are sceptical about the possibility for economic stability engendered by processes of glocalization, it remains incumbent upon us to develop some sort of understanding about the preconditions for economic renewal. The depth of the current economic and environmental crises facing the world may preclude the development of a new global regime of accumulation (Altvater, 1993, although see Tylecote, 1992). However, if regulation theory has achieved anything, it has reminded us that capitalism has a remarkable capacity for self-transformations. A new institutional fix, should it emerge, must be capable of sustaining accumulation on at least a medium term basis. In so doing, it must provide an alternative to the prevalent 'jungle law' of unfettered competition. The associated regulatory undercutting is rendering national and regional economies vulnerable to the vagaries of mobile capital, and is undermining the social contract upon which sustainable accumulation must rest.

As Table 9.3 suggests, the emergent regulatory problems of *after*-Fordism will call for putative solutions based at different spatial scales. Many of these will require regional, national and supranational cooperation. Local strategies may well have a role, but this must be within a supportive national and supranational framework. While localized labour market overheating during periods of endemic unemployment, for example, may require locally sensitive workforce programmes, these must be embedded within wider national policies which underwrite, rather than undermine, regional employment strategies (see Peck and Jones, 1994). Similarly, the loss of interest and exchange rate sovereignty at the national level means that multilateral approaches to money have become an essential precondition for renewed accumulation (see Tickell, 1992). Local strategies will never, of course, realize their potential if they are reduced to self-destructive beggar-thy-neighbour competition. The essence of the *after*-Fordist regulatory problem, then, is the age-old one of countering the destructive effects of competition. In a globalized economy, however, there is a need to regulate competition not only between workers and between capitals, but also between *places*. The 'hostile brothers' must be made to get back on friendly (or at least friendlier) terms.

Nevertheless, while the 'solutions' tentatively suggested in Table 9.3 may form a *prerequisite* for the emergence from crisis, we remain sceptical about the prospects for doing so. There will, undoubtedly, be temporary 'winners', just as the post-1973 crisis has spawned success in parts of South East Asia and in parts of the hitherto Fordist economies (see Peck and Miyamachi, 1995). However, we would maintain that a *general solution* remains elusive, and will do so for the foreseeable future. This is because two fundamental barriers to an institutionalized solution remain: first, as stressed above, the international monetary form has become predominantly credit-based, rather than reflecting commercial activities. For authors such as Altvater (1992) this creates an intractable regulatory problem because the global credit system is inherently at odds with the regulatory competence of the international monetary regime. While Altvater's position may be over-stated, in that it is *theoretically* possible to reassert regulatory control over credit capital (through rules which insist that financial institutions retain core capital reserves in relatively stable forms), he does point to the crux of the problem. Second, there are doubts about whether further accumulation is ecologically and economically sustainable. Based as it is on the transformation of nature, capitalism requires that nature is, effectively, an infinite resource. Yet as environmental resources are progressively degraded and as the end is in sight for oil (the commodity which both literally and metaphorically fuelled Fordism), it is becoming increasingly clear that capitalism has perilously transformed all of nature (although see Lipietz, chapter 11 in this volume, for a possible, ecologically sound alternative). Economically, too, growth appears unsustainable. Turnover times for cities, regions and products seem to have shortened. While economic 'success' remains elusive for most, it is increasingly fragile for those that have it. As long as neo-liberalism prevails – with its emphasis on competitive relations, individualism and the fast buck – socially, economically and ecologically sustainable growth will be difficult to attain. In the continuing disorder of the *after*-Fordist crisis, then, the place of localities in the sun is likely to be increasingly short-lived: attracting growth may be difficult, *keeping it* will prove harder still.

CONCLUSION

We have argued in this chapter that it is premature to talk about a post-Fordist regime of accumulation because, while some significant experiments are under way in the production sphere, a coherent post-Keynesian mode of social regulation has yet to stabilize. Thus, it is only possible at present to talk about post-Fordism in the negative sense (Altvater, 1992). The institutional and political conditions for a renewed period of sustained economic growth remain elusive. Given the existence of severe reservations about the sustainability of flexible accumulation (see Gertler, 1988; Pollert, 1988; Tickell and Peck, 1992), it is impossible to make any conclusive statements about the spatial logics of post-Fordism. There are, to be sure, substantial shifts in the spatial ordering of the world economy under way at present. But rather than in terms of the language of a new global–local order, they are perhaps best understood in terms of accelerating uneven development.

The geographies of glocalization and 'hollowing out' are, we

Table 9.3 Geographies of 'jungle law'

Spatial scale	Regulatory 'problem'	Putative solution
International	Unstable and volatile financial system, neo-liberal in orientation, undermines national economic intervention and global stability.	A new hegemon? Unlikely to emerge. Triadic hegemony? Potential in European Union, North American Free Trade Area and Japan/ASEAN.
		Supranational institutions which reassert control over money/finance? Potential in Bank for International Settlements or World Bank but must be realized by democratization and eschewing of neo-liberalism. Financial cooperation and common currencies (i.e. European moves to single currency) diminish advantages of speculative global financial system, but render weak countries more vulnerable to external economic conditions.
	Neo-mercantilism and worsening terms of trade for Third World induces significant risk in trading system. Uruguay round of GATT heralds neo-liberal trading regime, while maintaining relative protection of Anglo-Saxon financial sector.	Enhanced role for GATT, as the International Trade Organization originally envisaged by Keynes? Unlikely to emerge.
		Formation and enhancement of regional trading blocs? Provide some protection for those within strong blocs, but detrimental impact on poorer and weaker states.
	Regional trading and political blocs organized along neo-liberal lines. Creates supranational instability and exacerbates uneven development.	Spatial redistributive policies to ameliorate worst effects of uneven development (at nation state and supranational levels).

'Regulatory arbitrage', where corporations pressurize states to develop minimal restrictions, and 'regulatory undercutting', where states attempt to woo capital by imposing low standards (e.g. the British 'opt-out' of the European Social Chapter).

Supranational institutions to assert common minimum standards across a range of areas (i.e. European Commission on 48 hour working week; minimal capital adequacy standards).
Development of high-skill rather than low labour-cost national base.

National

Mass unemployment.

Renewed national Fordism-Keynesianisms? Unlikely to emerge and changed international and productive environments mean that unable to form basis for new period of sustained growth.
Supranational Keynesianism allied to 'flexible production system'?

Neo-liberal regulation at national level unable to contain its geographical contradictions.

Policies to stimulate growth in lagging regions and contain growth in core. Regional policy organized at national or supranational level?

'Hollowing out' of the nation state, undermines legitimacy of nation states unable to meet social welfare objectives.

Supranational regulation to prevent pressures to minimize standards'? International neo-liberalism stimulates 'regulatory undercutting' and therefore needs to be overcome.
Progressive fiscal structures to forge new social compromise?

Table 9.3 Geographies of 'jungle law'

Spatial scale	Regulatory 'problem'	Putative solution
Local	Zero-sum competition between localities and regions encourages geographically uneven undermining of social standards and fragmentation.	Embedding of capital within localities to stimulate a spatial fix, perhaps through provision of training or technological infrastructures. National and supranational state activities to limit wasteful competition?
	Local growth coalitions are inherently unstable and short-termist.	Democratization of growth, emphasizing growth which benefits all inhabitants of region. Reduced emphasis on growth coalitions as conduit for development. Enhanced power for local and regional governments.
	Local state increasingly seen as central to economic regeneration but powers of intervention are limited.	Increased local political autonomy and power within wider structural frameworks.
	Growing links among successful local states detrimental to weaker areas.	National and supranational stimulation of regional development to enhance position of less developed regions.
	'Flexible' labour markets unable to contain contradictions.	New, interfirm modes of skill formation and labour regulation, reformed state regulation.

maintain, the geographies of the *after-*Fordist crisis, not the geographies of stable post-Fordism. Such stability cannot be attained until the 'jungle law' of aggressive competition and regulatory undercutting, manifest in the practices and discourses of neo-liberalism, is overcome. We have argued that, first, the construction of a new compromise under a new mode of social regulation must invoke a central commitment to economic, ecological and social sustainability, and, second, the establishment of such a 'positive' programme must imply a fundamental critique of *and response to* neo-liberalism. As we continue to be faced by conditions of *systemic instability* at the level of the global economy, claims that a new global–local order has emerged seem premature. The nation state *may* have been eroded from above and from below, but the nature of this erosion has been different in each case. Below the nation state, local regulatory systems (particularly local states) have been conferred *responsibility without power*: regulatory responsibilities have been handed (or have drifted, as they have been shunned by nation states) down from the nation state level, but localities can wield little in the way of political–economic power in the context of globalizing accumulation and global deregulation. Above the nation state, supranational regulatory systems have inherited *power without responsibility*: remaining wedded to a neo-liberal agenda, they continue to fuel global economic instability with apparent disregard for its damaging effects on national and local economies and its pernicious ecological and social consequences.

Workable *after-*Fordist regulatory 'solutions' at the national or local scales are unlikely to stabilize until there is a truce between the 'hostile brothers', until a new institutional fix is found at the global scale. The pressing need, then, is for a new *supralocal* regulatory framework based, perhaps, on emergent politico-trading blocks, such as the European Union. The global financial institutions in particular must be harnessed and reformed, a process which will doubtless require concerted action through nation states. It is consequently important that the nation state is not written off as a key site in this regulatory struggle, for this is likely to remain the principal scale at which democratic control and political power can be (re)coupled. True, the nation state may have become 'hollowed out' during the *after-*Fordist crisis, but a resolution to this crisis may involve some degree of 'filling in' of the nation state in order to effect a stabilization of local–local and local–global regulatory relations. Solutions to the crisis of uneven development in *after-*Fordism are unlikely to come from the bottom – *through local competition* – but instead must begin with action from above – *through national and global coordination*.

NOTES

We would like to thank Ash Amin, Colin Hay and Bob Jessop for helpful comments on an earlier draft of this chapter. The usual disclaimers apply.

REFERENCES

Aglietta, M. (1979) *A Theory of Capitalist Regulation: the US Experience*. London: New Left Books.

Altvater, E. (1992) Fordist and post-Fordist international division of labor and monetary regimes. In M. Storper and A. J. Scott (eds), *Pathways to Industrialization and Regional Development*. London: Routledge, 21–45.

Altvater, E. (1993) *The Future of the Market: an Essay on the Regulation of Money and Nature after the Collapse of 'Actually Existing Socialism'*. London: Verso.

Amin, A. and Robins, K. (1990) The re-emergence of regional economies? The mythical geography of flexible accumulation. *Environment and Planning, D: Society and Space*, 8, 7–34.

Boyer, R. (1988) Formalizing with growth regimes. In G. Dosi, C. Freeman, R. Nelson, G. Silverberg and L. Soete (eds), *Technical Change and Economic Theory*. London: Pinter, 608–30.

Boyer, R. (1990) *The Regulation School: a Critical Introduction*. New York: Columbia University Press.

Cooper, R. N. (1987) *The International Monetary System*. Cambridge, MA: MIT Press.

Corbridge, S. (1988) The asymmetry of interdependence: the United States and the geopolitics of international financial relations. *Studies in Comparative International Development*, 23, 3–29.

Cox, K. (1993) The local and the global in the new urban politics. *Environment and Planning, D: Society and Space*, 11, 433–48.

Davis, M. (1993) Who killed LA? A political autopsy. *New Left Review*, 197, 3–28.

Dicken, P. (1992a) *Global Shift: the Internationalisation of Economic Activity*, 2nd edn. London: Paul Chapman.

Dicken, P. (1992b) International production in a volatile regulatory environment: the influence of national regulatory policies on the spatial strategies of transnational corporations. *Geoforum*, 23, 303–16.

Dunford, M. (1990) Theories of regulation. *Environment and Planning, D: Society and Space*, 8, 297–322.

Dunford, M. and Kafkalas, G. (1992) The global–local interplay, corporate geographies and spatial development strategies in Europe. In M. Dunford and G. Kafkalas (eds), *Cities and Regions in the New Europe: the Global–Local Interplay and Spatial Development Strategies*. London: Belhaven, 3–38.

Gertler, M. (1988) The limits to flexibility: comments on the post-Fordist vision of production and its geography. *Transactions, Institute of British Geographers*, 13, 419–32.

Gertler, M. (1992) Flexibility revisited: districts, nation-states, and the forces of production. *Transactions, Institute of British Geographers*, 17, 259–78.

Gilpin, R. (1987) *The Political Economy of International Relations*. Princeton, NJ: Princeton University Press.

Glyn, A., Hughes, A., Lipietz, A. and Singh, A. (1991) The rise and fall of the Golden Age. In S. Marglin and J. B. Schor (eds), *The Golden Age of Capitalism*. Oxford: Clarendon Press, 39–125.

Glyn, A. and Sutcliffe, B. (1992) Global but leaderless? The new capitalist order. In R. Miliband and L. Panitch (eds), *New World Order? Socialist Register 1992*. New York: Monthly Review Press.

Graham, J. (1992) Post-Fordism as politics: the political consequences of narratives on the left. *Environment and Planning, D: Society and Space*, 10, 393–410.

Harvey, D. (1985) *The Urbanization of Capital*. Oxford: Blackwell.

Harvey, D. (1989) *The Condition of Post-modernity: an Enquiry into the Origins of Cultural Change*. Oxford: Blackwell.

Hirst, P. and Thompson, G. (1992) The problem of 'globalisation': international economic relations, national economic management and the formation of trading blocs. *Economy and Society*, 21, 355–96.

Hirst, P. and Zeitlin, J. (1992) Flexible specialization versus post-Fordism: theory, evidence, and policy implications. In M. Storper and A. J. Scott (eds), *Pathways to Industrialization and Regional Development*. London: Routledge, 70–115.

Hübner, K. (1991) Flexibilization and autonomization of world money markets: obstacles for a new expansion? In B. Jessop, H. Kasendiek, K. Nielsen and O. Pedersen (eds), *The Politics of Flexibility: Restructuring State and Industry in Britain, Germany and Scandinavia*. Aldershot: Edward Elgar, 50–66.

Jessop, B. (1992a) Fordism and post-Fordism: a critical reformulation. In M. Storper and A. J. Scott (eds), *Pathways to Industrialization and Regional Development*. London: Routledge, 46–69.

Jessop, B. (1992b) Post-Fordism and flexible specialisation: incommensurable, contradictory, complementary, or just plain different perspectives? In H. Ernste and V. Meier (eds), *Regional Development and Contemporary Response: Extending Flexible Specialisation*. London: Belhaven Press, 25–44.

Jessop, B. (1993) Towards a Schumpeterian workfare state? Preliminary remarks on post-Fordist political economy. *Studies in Political Economy*, 40, 7–39.

Leborgne, D. and Lipietz, A. (1992) Conceptual fallacies and open questions on post-Fordism. In M. Storper and A. J. Scott (eds), *Pathways to Industrialization and Regional Development*. London: Routledge, 332–48.

Leyshon, A. (1992) The transformation of regulatory order: regulating the global economy and environment. *Geoforum*, 23, 249–68.

Lipietz, A. (1987) *Mirages and Miracles: the Crises of Global Fordism*. London: Verso.

Lipietz, A. (1992) The regulation approach and capitalist crisis: an alternative compromise for the 1990s. In M. Dunford and G. Kafkalas (eds), *Cities and Regions in the New Europe: the Global–Local Interplay and Spatial Development Strategies*. London: Belhaven, 309–34.

Lorenz, E. H. (1992) Trust, community, and cooperation: toward a theory of industrial districts. In M. Storper and A. J. Scott (eds), *Pathways to Industrialization and Regional Development*. London: Routledge, 195–204.

Lovering, J. (1991) The changing geography of the military industry in Britain. *Regional Studies*, 25, 279–94.

Markusen, A. (1991) The military–industrial divide. *Environment and Planning, D: Society and Space*, 9, 391–416.

Martin, R. (1994) The economy, economics and economic geography. In D. Gregory, R. Martin and G. E. Smith (eds), *Human Geography: Society, Space and Social Science*. London: Macmillan.

Mayer, M. (1992) The shifting local political system in European cities. In M. Dunford and G. Kafkalas (eds), *Cities and Regions in the New Europe: the Global–Local Interplay and Spatial Development Strategies*. London: Belhaven, 255–78.

Moulaert, F., Swyngedouw, E. A. and Wilson, P. (1988) Spatial Responses to Fordist and post-Fordist accumulation and regulation. *Papers of the Regional Science Association*, 64, 11–23.

Paddison, R. (1993) Scotland, the Other and the British state. *Political Geography*, 12, 165–8.

Peck, J. A. (1994) Regulating Labour: the social regulation and reproduction of local labour markets. In A. Amin and N. Thrift (eds), *Globalisation, Institutions and Regional Development in Europe*. Oxford: Oxford University Press.

Peck, J. A. and Jones, M. (1994) Training and Enterprise Councils: Schumpeterian workfare state, or what? *Environment and Planning A*, in the press.

Peck, J. A. and Miyamachi, Y. (1995) Regulating Japan? Regulation theory versus the Japanese experience. *Environment and Planning, D: Society and Space*, in the press.

Peck, J. A. and Tickell, A. (1992) Local modes of social regulation? Regulation theory, Thatcherism and uneven development. *Geoforum*, 23, 347–64.

Peck, J. A. and Tickell, A. (1994) The social regulation of uneven development: 'regulatory deficit', England's South East and the collapse of Thatcherism. *Environment and Planning, A*, in the press.

Pollert, A. (1988) Dismantling flexibility. *Capital and Class*, 34, 42–75.

Schoenberger, E. (1991) Globalization and regionalization: new problems of time, distance and control in the multinational firm. Paper presented to the Annual Meeting of the Association of American Geographers, Miami.

Scott, A. J. (1988) *New Industrial Spaces*. London: Pion.

Scott, A. J. and Paul, A. (1990) Collective order and economic coordination in industrial agglomerations: the technopoles of southern California. *Environment and Planning, C: Government and Policy*, 8, 179–93.

Stoker, G. (1990) Regulation theory, local government and the transition from Fordism. In D. S. King and J. Pierre (eds), *Challenges to Local Government*. London: Sage, 242–64.

Stoker, G. and Mossberger, K. (1992) The post-Fordist local state: the dynamics of its development. Paper presented at the conference Towards a Post-Fordist Welfare State?, University of Teesside, 17–18 September.

Swyngedouw, E. A. (1992) The Mammon quest. 'Glocalisation', interspatial competition and the monetary order: the construction of new spatial scales. In M. Dunford and G. Kafkalas (eds), *Cities and Regions in the New Europe: the Global–Local Interplay and Spatial Development Strategies*. London: Belhaven, 39–67.

Tickell, A. (1992) The social regulation of banking: restructuring foreign banks in Manchester and London. Unpublished PhD thesis, School of Geography, University of Manchester.

Tickell, A. and Dicken, P. (1993) The role of inward investment promotion in economic development strategies: the case of northern England. *Local Economy*, 8, 197–208.

Tickell, A. and Peck, J. A. (1992) Accumulation, regulation and the geographies of post-Fordism: missing links in regulationist research. *Progress in Human Geography*, 16, 190–218.

Tylecote, A. (1992) *The Long Wave in the World Economy: the Present Crisis in Historical Perspective*. London: Routledge.

Walter, A. (1991) *World Power and World Money: the Role of Hegemony and International Monetary Order*. Brighton: Wheatsheaf.

10

Post-Fordist City Politics

Margit Mayer

This chapter looks at local (urban) institutions and politics under post-Fordism. It first identifies the new practices and forms of urban governance observable in most Western European nations as well as in the United States over the past two decades. It assumes that we are in a transitional period of experimenting with ways that might resolve the current economic and welfare state crisis, to screen the changes that have occurred in the context of urban governance in order to examine whether they contribute to resolving the current dilemmas of urban politics in consistency with the logic of a new 'growth model'. This approach echoes the regulationist analysis embraced by other chapters in this book, which assumes that there is more than one way out of the crisis of Fordism. For example, in terms of the organization of capital–labour relations, some countries have developed more negotiated involvement, while others have adopted less consensual flexibility strategies.[1] Applying such a regulationist analysis to urban politics therefore points to strategic implications (spelled out in the final section of this chapter) for the social movements and actors working to develop democratic concepts for local politics and management.

CHANGES IN URBAN GOVERNMENT

Many changes have affected local politics over the past two decades, some of which have congealed into patterns common across national and regional particularities. At least three parallel trends have been identified in the recent literature on urban politics.

First, in all advanced Western nations local politics have gained in importance as a focus for proactive economic development strategies. The background for these developments is changes in capital mobility and shifts in the technological and social organization of production, which are described elsewhere in this book. One of the effects relevant for the local level has been that the changes have made it increasingly impossible for particular (re)production conditions to be organized or coordinated by the central state. While under Fordism local modes of regulation played a minor and subordinate role in assuring the coherence of the overall regime (the central state and other larger-scale modes of regulation played the crucial roles), efforts to respond to the crises of Fordism have involved a shift in this 'division of labour'. The specific local conditions of production and reproduction required by globally mobile capital cannot be orchestrated by the central state. Hence local political organizations, their skills in negotiating with supraregional and multinational capital, and the effectiveness with which they tailor the particular set of local conditions of production have become decisive factors in shaping a city's profile as well as its place in the international urban hierarchy.

Second, there has been an increasing mobilization of local politics in support of economic development and a concomitant subordination of social policies to economic and labour market policies. This shift in emphasis between different policy fields has often been labelled as a shift towards the 'entrepreneurial' city, and it goes hand in hand with a restructuring of the provision of social services. Both in the local economic interventionism and in the reorganization of public services the local state now involves other, non-governmental, actors in key roles.

This constitutes the third novel trend in urban governance, namely the expansion of the sphere of local political action to involve not only the local authority but a range of private and semi-public actors. To coordinate these various policy fields and functional interests, new bargaining systems have emerged, and new forms of public–private collaboration, in which the role of the local authority in respect of business and real estate interests, and the voluntary sector and community groups, is becoming redefined.

The first trend, the development of a 'perforated sovereignty' whereby nations become more open to trans-sovereign contacts by subnational governments, and regional/local forces become more active in advancing their own locational policy strategies oriented directly to the world market, is seen by many observers to contribute to a greater salience of the local state (as well as other local institutions of governance and economic relations – see chapter 8 by Bob Jessop). 'Greater salience' does not mean greater strength, autonomy or a shift in the balance of central–local relations; in fact, local authorities have extended their strategic and active intervention at a time when they have been under increasing political pressure – in the UK there is even a question mark over their very survival (see Page, 1993). Despite or because of this, there is a resurgence of local politics, which provides the basis for the other two changes in urban governance, which I will present in some more detail.

Shifts in emphasis between different policy fields

Increased engagement of the local authority in economic development

With central government grants decreasing since the mid-1970s, local authorities have sought to respond to whatever restructuring problems were manifest in their region. In the declining old industrial areas, anti-unemployment programmes and local labour market policies were put into place (e.g. Maier and Wollmann, 1986; Bullmann, 1991; Getimis, 1992): diverse strategies were explored to foster a more favourable business climate; many cities increased spending on culture and leisure facilities, or implemented strategies to upgrade the 'image' or the ambiance of a town (see Logan and Swanstrom, 1990; Stöhr 1990; Mayer, 1992). Some local governments seem to be aware of the increasingly polarized occupational and class structure of their cities and seek to counteract the attendant social disintegration with consciously chosen strategies to stimulate growth (Heinelt and Mayer, 1993). From case studies we can gather that the urban leaders engaged in diverse local economic development activities were often far from certain as to how precisely an improvement in the course of urban development might be brought about, except in agreeing that 'industry and employment matters should be important' (Cochrane, 1992, p. 122). Gradually, these activities have consolidated into a more systematic economic development policy strategy oriented explicitly towards nurturing 'growth' and, supposedly, employment.

This increased local economic interventionism is expressed not merely in the quantitative growth of local government spending for economic development, but, more importantly, in qualitatively different approaches to economic intervention, which seek to make use of indigenous skills and entrepreneurship, which emphasize innovation and new technologies, and which involve non-state actors in the organization of conditions for local economic development. While traditionally the economic development measures of local authorities would focus on attracting mobile capital (with conventional location inducements such as financial and tax incentives, infrastructure improvement or assistance with site selection), a shift in the approach of local economic development offices is now obvious. Subsidies are now targeted to industries promising innovation and growth; more public resources are focused on stimulating research, consulting and technology transfer, as well as on building alliances embracing universities, polytechnics, chambers of commerce and unions; land is no longer a cheap resource to be offered generously, but a precious one to be developed strategically (Dyson, 1988; Parkinson et al., 1988; Cooke and Imrie, 1989; Bennett et al., 1990). Instead of seeking to attract capital from elsewhere, strategies focus on new business formation and small business expansion; thus, instead of competing with other jurisdictions for the same investment, cities make efforts to strengthen existing and potential indigenous resources (Moore, 1983; Eisinger, 1988; Robinson, 1989). Going beyond traditional booster campaigns used by development officials to publicize the virtues of their respective business climate, cities increasingly 'market' themselves in the global economy. Finally, the new development strategies frequently include employment strategies involving the so-called 'third' or 'alternative' sector (Ashworth and Vogel, 1989; Lasser, 1990; Mayer, 1990).

These diverse efforts to mobilize and coordinate local potential for economic growth together have produced the effect of gradually undermining the traditional sharp distinctions between different policy areas. This is particularly true in the case of labour market and social policy domains, but equally, educational, environmental and cultural policies have become more integrated with, and are often part and parcel of, economic development measures. In addition, the new efforts have introduced institutional changes: new departments and inter-agency networks have been created within the administration, and new institutions which contribute in significant ways to the shaping of local politics have been established and/or supported outside of the local authority (e.g. urban development corporations, training and enterprise councils, technology centres, growth alliances, local 'round tables').[2]

Restructuring and subordination of social consumption

In addition to the mobilization of local politics for economic development, whereby the local state seeks to organize private capital accumulation by including relevant private actors, the local state has also been significantly restructured in its public services and welfare functions (social consumption). The pressures exerted by economic restructuring and mass unemployment on the one hand and by shrinking subsidies from central government on the other and the willingness to accord priority to economic development policies have pushed into the background one of the formerly central functions of local state politics, namely the provision of social consumption goods and welfare services. Not only has local government spending for social consumption declined as a proportion of overall expenditure, but a qualitative restructuring has taken place involving an increase in the importance of non-state (private and voluntary sector) organizations or of public agencies directed by market criteria (quasi-governmental agencies) in the provision of public services. In various policy fields where the local state used to be the exclusive provider of a service, non-governmental agencies have been upgraded or private markets have emerged (e.g. in waste disposal). In urban renewal, environmental and social policies local authorities cooperate more and more frequently with neighbourhood initiatives, self-help or other social movement organizations (Blanke et al., 1987; von Hauff, 1989; Evers, 1991).

As in the sphere of economic development, in the sphere of social reproduction once public sector led forms of service provision and management have been scaled down and complemented or replaced by a variety of private, voluntary and semi-public agencies and initiatives, and parallel coordinating structures have begun to emerge. What is more, the traditional redistributive policies of the welfare state have been supplemented by employment and labour market policies designed to promote labour force flexibility. For example, in many cities attempts are being made to switch from unemployment compensation to job creation and retraining programmes, and to generate employment opportunities for specific social groups (which directly supplement or replace traditional welfare policy). A plethora of municipally funded programmes have been established in social, environmental and urban renewal policy domains, which tend to be hybrid programmes emphasizing workfare and job creation while burdening non-profit (third sector) organizations with the delivery and implementation of urban repair or social service functions.[3] Though they are quantitatively rather insignificant, municipal employment and training programmes have served to mobilize and integrate the job-creating potentials from different policy areas. Active labour market policy measures of this kind therefore imply a blurring of the traditional distinction between economic and social policies, as they create a real link between the local economy and the local operation of the welfare state: welfare becomes increasingly redefined in the direction of the economic success of a local area.

This means that social welfare measures which used to be relatively universal and guaranteed by the national welfare state (but delivered by the local state) are now an arena of struggle, and are implemented in a fragmented fashion. This shift away from service provision through unitary and elected authorities towards more fragmented structures with increased involvement of local business, as well as of other private and voluntary sector agencies, has turned local government into merely one part – though perhaps the 'enabling' part – of broader 'growth coalitions'. Further, the new mix of unpaid self-service labour and private and public sector paid labour contributes to the development of a new consumption norm which supports the commodification and/or the self-servicing of welfare functions (Jessop, 1991b, p. 101).

Thus, the new public–private forms of cooperation in the area of social consumption are also part of structural changes in the repertoire of municipal action. Whether the local struggles and bargaining processes will result in more egalitarian and accountable models responsive to broad local needs, or in divisive models enforcing processes of polarization and marginalization, one of the certain new characteristics of the emerging local 'welfare state' that distinguishes it from the past is its role in enabling negotiation with, and initiating activities by, 'outside' actors.

Expansion of the sphere of local political action: new bargaining systems and public–private partnerships

The strategies developed to mobilize local potential for economic growth involve actors way beyond those of classical municipal politics. Labour market policy, for example, now involves not only the local authority, but also federal or national employment offices, individual state programmes (and their local participants), social welfare associations, churches, unions and in many cases individual companies and newly created consultancies. Urban development policy now involves private actors as early as the planning stage, while the local authority also has a say in implementation processes. And urban social programmes, emphasizing self-organized and community-based forms of social service provision, and relying on funds from diverse state and other sources, require novel types of cooperation between different municipal actors as well as between municipal and private agencies.

In these novel cooperation processes, spanning different policy fields and bringing together actors from very different backgrounds, bargaining systems have emerged which exhibit round-table structures and are characterized by a cooperative style of policy-making where, instead of giving orders, the local authority moderates or initiates cooperation. Such a non-hierarchical style seems to have been recognized as essential for identifying and acting on the intersecting areas of interest of the different actors (Hesse, 1987, p. 72; Scharpf, 1991). The novelty consists in the fact that bargaining and decision-making processes increasingly take place outside of traditional local government structures, and that urban governance becomes based on the explicit representation and coordination of functional interests active at the local level (compare the new 'alternative' politics of post-Fordist democracy espoused by Lipietz in chapter 11 in this volume).

The actors participating in the definition and implementation of economic development and technological modernization programmes tend to be business associations, chambers of commerce, local companies, banks, research institutes, universities and unions. The restructuring of the local welfare state, on the other hand, has expanded the sphere of local political action to include an additional set of actors: welfare associations, churches and frequently grassroots initiatives and community organizations.[4] Given the new employment structures, the growth of precarious and casualized job relations and structural long-term unemployment, the traditional distinction between these 'soft' and 'hard' policy spheres, however, has been eroded as municipal programmes seek to address 'social' problems in the context of economic development and labour market policies.

Alongside the new forms of public–private collaboration in economic development and in social service provision, explicit public–private partnerships have also emerged in urban renewal and urban physical development programmes. Faced with both tight budgets and increasing redevelopment tasks many city governments have explored new ways of planning and financing urban redevelopment. In order to upgrade their central business districts, to refashion old industrial sites and to develop attractive new projects, they have entered into partnerships with large investors, developers and consortia of private firms.

There is no 'typical' public–private partnership, but more or less intensive forms of cooperation and more or less traditional forms of partnership. The new partnership embraces a range of forms of collaboration, from mere transfer of subsidy from the local authority to particular firms, in which local government plays the role of a 'junior partner', to joint ventures where state and firms share risks and equity interests on a relatively equal footing. Partnership projects most frequently focus on the physical upgrading of a large area near the central business district (Frieden and Sagalyn, 1989; Dekker, 1992), but increasingly they involve development planning and implementation in more neglected neighbourhoods, which include community development corporations and other neighbourhood-based groups (Simmons et al., 1985, pp. 35 ff, 49 ff; Costonis, 1990; Selle, 1991).

In any event, the partnership rests on a 'deal' between the public and the private participants: in exchange for the local authority's subsidy, use of governmental powers (planning, assembling of properties, tax concessions), interpretation of government regulations (zoning, land usage) etc., the private partner is expected to meet certain project goals and to take on later management tasks. The private partner also has to share project returns with the local authority. This may occur through later lease or tax payments, through the provision of public infrastructure (e.g. subway stations), or through the hiring of local (often minority) workforces in project construction or maintenance (Smith, 1989; Molotch, 1990).

Private investors gain from such a deal because the local authority's resources offer them attractive ways to expand their activities. In areas with intense physical development pressures, urban redevelopment provides highly profitable opportunities for private developers, who need access to promising real estate as well as land titles (Wollmann, 1992). Large investors, such as banks, insurance companies and construction contractors, have recognized the potential of this municipal market for some time.

City governments gain from this deal because it allows them to attract more financial resources into urban development and to increase their effectiveness in achieving development goals. By combining public powers with entrepreneurial flexibility, organizational capacity and additional private (venture) capital, complex urban development tasks can be carried out more quickly and efficiently. Further, city governments can decrease their dependency on the national government and are able to tailor development more directly to particular local needs. Pressure on limited municipal administrative capacities is relieved and partnerships often work to increase the qualification and flexibilization of public administrations. In contrast to the total privatization of public tasks, the city retains, despite limited finances, some control and influence (Kirlin and Kirlin, 1983; Heinz, 1993). In fact, over the years, public negotiators have become more skilled in obtaining concessions from developers and in holding private partners responsible for meeting performance obligations (Fainstein and Fainstein, 1993, p. 102).

Nevertheless, this 'deal' between the public and private sectors contains a high level of ambiguity, as partnership schemes remain sites of continuing political and economic renegotiation: 'In effect, what is "going on" in partnerships is a version of the broader conflict over the future organisation and scope of the public sector' (Mackintosh, 1992, p. 221). Precisely this ambiguous character, however, leaves space for a strategic role for local government and other 'public interest' organizations.

Both community-oriented partnerships and redevelopment partnerships in growth-promising central areas vary greatly in terms of their openness and responsiveness to affected interests, depending on local political traditions and prevailing balances of power. The more horizontal style of the new bargaining systems and project-specific partnerships does not necessarily imply greater openness to democratic influence or accountability to local social or environmental needs (see Lipietz, chapter 11 in this volume, in contrast). On the contrary, the participants may form an exclusive group representing only selected interests. While there remain significant differences in the relative power of business, unions and community groups, as well as between 'established' community groups and more marginalized, unorganized interests, and while new bargaining systems and partnerships continue to vary in their inclusiveness, the new institutional relations and arenas of urban management have altered the political terrain and opportunities for *all* local political actors. Politics in the sense of arriving at and implementing binding decisions occurs more and more via *negotiation* and *renegotiation* between different public and private actors, both of whom are affected by the process of bargaining, as the partners try to 'move the objectives and culture of the other towards their own ideas' (Macintosh, 1992, p. 216).

In these partnerships, the distinction between urban (re)development projects and economic development strategies, as described earlier, is increasingly blurry, especially in the case of community development projects or corporations, which now are typically as concerned with industrial and commercial development objectives as with housing and physical renewal. Such partnerships, which usually include some form of community representation, may offer services and technical assistance to local (small) businesses, run job placement services or help with developing export programmes for local businesses. They seek to tap whatever local economic development potential exists, thus contributing to the municipal strategy of mobilizing indigenous potential for economic growth and regeneration (National Congress for Community Economic Development, 1989; Wievel and Weintraub, 1990).[5]

On the other hand, the expansion of development corporations concerned with improving housing and social conditions and the quality of life in neglected neighbourhoods may also be considered as part of the restructuring of the local welfare state along the lines described earlier. In the past, municipalities have used non-profit organizations to different degrees in different nations, primarily for the *delivery* of services. But since public funds for community development have dried up everywhere, broader partnerships have been forged, involving banks, investors and voluntary association – with community development corporations (CDCs) as catalytic actors within them. Now, they are involved in the planning as well as implementation of (social and physical) renewal of urban communities (Selle, 1991); their intermediary organizations and renewal agents combine social, environmental and revitalization work while also performing lobbying and political functions (Schnepf-Orth and Staubach, 1989; Froessler and Selle, 1991).

In addition to private (market) actors and public (state) actors, these partnerships importantly involve the so-called voluntary or third sector. A boom of 'third sector' literature reflects the 'discovery' of this sector at a time when politicians began to reconsider the division of labour between public and private sectors, and to examine ways of reducing state responsibility (Anheier and Seibel, 1990, p. 8; Anheier and Salamon, 1992). However, while research identifies an explosive growth in the non-market, non-government organizations and activities lumped together under this label, less attention has been paid to the parallel penetration of this sector by the logic of the state and/or the market. Simultaneously, while traditional third sector organizations (previously dominated by the Fordist welfare state) tend increasingly to be run for profit like capitalist enterprises, newer organizations also function as elements in an alternative economy, which, in turn, is tied increasingly to municipal programmes (Mayer, 1993). Both cases, while serving to make the welfare state more flexible through less rigid bureaucratic forms and more competition, also enlarge and restructure the sphere of local political action. In this expanded system of local politics the public sector reduces its functions, yet plays a more activist role in its interaction with the non-state sectors. No longer the centre of decision-making, as bargaining and decision-making processes occur outside traditional, local government structures, local government takes on the role of a moderator, managing the intersecting areas of interest and – in successful cases[6] – exerting more leadership and control as it provides its resources on a *conditional* basis.

While, in the more traditional collaboration between the public and the private sector, cities would seek to attract investors with cheap land, low taxes and capital subsidies (without expecting to influence the firms' future behaviour and decisions), the recent urban economic development programmes focus public resources on firms and industries that promise growth, and they hold the private partner responsible for meeting contractual and other obligations (Eisinger, 1988, p. 23). While in traditional urban development the redevelopment process was subject to approval by federal bureaucrats, now things are 'entirely up to the locality, where communities are mobilized or have gained access to City Hall, they have the potential to influence programs' (Fainstein and Fainstein, 1993, p. 119).

Thus, the role of the municipality has changed from being the (more or less redistributive) local 'arm' of the welfare state to acting as the catalyst of processes of innovation and cooperation, which it seeks to steer in the direction of improving the city's (or community's) economic and social situation. These forms of cooperation are increasingly replacing state-provided functions to ensure social reproduction. In order to win the resources and competences of various private actors, the local authority has to respect to some degree the peculiar character and particular functional conditions of these non-state organizations.

REGULATIONIST ANALYSIS: IDENTIFYING THE CONSTRAINTS AND OPTIONS FOR LOCAL POLITICS

A regulationist analysis helps in disentangling the implications of the identified changes in the forms and institutions of urban governance for political action. However, there has been a lot of confusion over 'post-Fordism' because the theoretical language of the regulationist framework, as originally developed by French political economists during the 1970s, has been adopted and redefined by many other writers. The British debate, in particular, has been massively influenced by a version put forth by the journal *Marxism Today*, which sees the breakdown of the monolithic methods of production under Fordism leading inevitably to the success of 'post-Fordist' political and social aims. This variant seeks to replace the old debate between the Left and Right by a new opposition between past and future (hence its use of the term *New Times*): the reorganization of production around new methods of flexible specialization is supposed to bear greater individual freedom and the end of centralized bureaucracies; post-Fordism is seen as a preordained successor to Fordism (Murray, 1988).[7]

Against such a 'mistranslation' (Barbrook, 1990) of the regulationist approach, which has influenced the debate concerning local state restructuring in Britain (Stoker, 1990; Lovering, 1991; Tickell and Peck, 1992; Cochrane, 1993, pp. 81 ff), this chapter draws on the original French analysis of post-Fordism, which offers a framework for assessing the possibility of *different* compromises under the conditions thrown up by a new accumulation regime and new social modes of regulation (Hirsch and Roth, 1986; Hirsch, 1988, 1991; Boyer, 1990; Jessop, 1991a, b; Lipietz, 1992a, b). While there are different theoretical explanations within the regulation approach,[8] it is generally assumed that the Fordist regime of accumulation has been in crisis since the mid-1970s and that – without major restructuring and new modes of regulation – the crisis cannot be transformed into a new constellation of prosperity. By focusing on the correspondence between the system of accumulation and modes of social regulation,[9] and by seeing the latter playing a crucial role in securing (temporary) stability and coherence in the capitalist system which is highly dynamic and in principle unstable, the regulation approach provides the opportunity to explore whether emerging elements of regulation are helping to resolve crisis tendencies and address the limits of the Fordist models[10] and whether they contribute to securing the conditions for a post-Fordist 'virtuous circle' to operate. Further, by identifying the compatibility requirements of a new mode of regulation, the regulation approach allows us to explore the variety of options and scenarios theoretically possible within this mode and to recognize the conditions under which more progressive/democratic or more conservative/ exclusionary models would emerge. The issue of compatibility and the issue of versions of post-Fordist models of regulation are discussed in turn below.

Compatibility

Can the new entrepreneurial local state outlined in the previous section be described as post-Fordist? If it can be shown that both the new forms of state intervention and the new institutional relations at the local level described in the first half of this chapter address the limits and solve the crises of the traditional model, and contribute to securing the conditions for a new growth model, then they may indeed be said to prefigure forms of urban governance capable of delivering a new coherent framework for urban management rather than being mere transitional forms of crisis management.

As we have seen, the new *forms of economic intervention*, which focus on competitiveness, seek to promote primarily technological innovation, new sectors, or new processes in established or restructured sectors, and thereby do address the problem of insufficient productivity; they move away from the traditional (Keynesian, central government led) interventionism designed to maintain levels of aggregate demand compatible with full employment (seeking, even, to maintain employment in declining sectors), which contributed to the stagflation of the 1970s and to disrupting the Fordist growth dynamic. Further, with its restructuring of social welfare in the direction of subordinating welfare policy to the demands of flexible labour markets and structural competitiveness, and of promoting more flexible and innovative provision of collective consumption, the entrepreneurial local state not only reduces social consumption expenditure (which had triggered the fiscal crisis of the Keynesian welfare state), but also reorients social policy away from generalizing the norms of mass consumption and the forms of collective consumption that supported the Fordist growth dynamic. Instead, a fragmented and potentially highly uneven provision of social consumption – tied to economic performance – is established, depending on the skills, political priorities and mobilization of local political actors.

The new *institutional relations* also contribute to resolving crisis tendencies of the traditional local state by replacing the overbearing, hierarchical state with a more pluralistic and, in some ways, more egalitarian version. This reorganization of the local political system reflects the new requirement to make connections between different policy areas, in particular between economic and technology policies, and policies on education, manpower training, infrastructural provision and so on. The sphere of local political action has been expanded: local unions, chambers of commerce, investors, education bodies and research centres have entered into partnership arrangements of different kinds with the local state to regenerate the local economy, and new bargaining systems based on negotiation have evolved. These local networks and bargaining systems address the limits of the centralized, hierachical, bureaucratic–corporative structures that were characteristic of the Fordist state and that ended up producing huge costs, inefficiency and waste, as well as protest by new social movements. Further, the distribution of territorial management activities among a *range* of private and semi-public agencies as well as local government might prove more capable of contributing to stable reproduction under the new conditions of sharpened interregional and intercity competition.

Identifying these features of compatibility in the local mode of regulation implies that we can equate the requirements for 'local economic integrity' or for 'success' more widely than with mere institutional capacity (i.e. the presence of many institutions of different kinds, with high levels of interaction and an awareness of a common enterprise: Amin and Thrift, 1994). 'Institutional thickness' would be the condition for success, but *specific* institutions compatible with and oriented towards supporting the emerging regime of accumulation must be present. The examples of the North of England or the Ruhr Valley illustrate that the presence of countless regeneration-oriented institutions (*and* national government subsidies) do not bring about successful regional restructuring (Grabher, 1990, p. 11; Lehner, 1993). It appears that the persistence of 'old-fashioned' unions, strong Keynesian welfare institutions and long-entrenched social-democratic labour coalitions is blocking rather than aiding the generation of a local institutional framework conducive to successful restructuring. Thus, the 'new mechanisms for attaining some form of local economic integrity' may be captured more adequately than in terms of institutional thickness by focusing on, as regulation theory does, the necessary correspondence between the mode of social regulation and the structures of an emerging post-Fordist accumulation regime.

However, even though this new pattern of urban entrepreneurialism and partnership is on the agenda of all post-Fordist scenarios (liberal, progressive, conservative), it is quite another question whether social and political conflict will allow the actual establishment of these new arrangements as elements of a *dominant* mode of social regulation. The entrenched habits of those in power, routinized forms of party political competition, occasional powerful political support for declining sectors (where these are strong, the need for new products and processes does not get fully articulated) and institutional inertia are renowned as stumbling blocks to the actual implementation of strategies that are meanwhile widely applauded in political discourse. But institutions and policy interventions which *do not* take into account the constraints of the emerging accumulation regime and the elements of the new mode of regulation face the likelihood of failure and the huge costs associated with such failure.

Possible versions of post-Fordist modes of regulation

As indicated above, a variety of political platforms pursue this post-Fordist scenario: whether dominated by the Left or by the Right, city governments now commonly give priority to economic development policies (via the entrepreneurial mobilization of indigenous potential), thereby pushing one of the formerly central functions of local state politics, namely the provision of collective consumption goods and welfare services, into the background. This devolution or privatization of the local (welfare) state and its increased engagement in the arena of economic development tends to occur via new forms of negotiation and implementation privileging non-governmental (intermediary) organizations.

We find this basic model experimented everywhere, long-held political traditions notwithstanding. Subnational state intervention to encourage growth and employment is pursued even in the most liberal, so-called non-interventionist, environments,[11] and the post-Fordist welfare–workfare state is present on the most diverse political agendas: the Right finds it attractive because it involves voluntary action and workfare, allowing state shrinkage; the Left because it is 'enabling' people to exercise power for themselves; and the liberals because it emphasizes local community action. Furthermore, as we have seen, new bargaining structures have become a reality in many different cities even if they contrast starkly in terms of their inclusiveness and responsiveness with regard to interests outside those in the central business district, real estate and the large investor sector. In addition, cleavages have become apparent not just between neighbourhoods and large developers or large firms, but also between newly included community interests and groups peripheral to the new arrangements. In any event, city governments *can* play a more initiating and more active role than in the past, and local state activity is bound to reflect the power struggles and political conflicts within a locality.

In other words, more or less democratic versions of this basic model are possible – without seriously restraining the transition to post-Fordism. Indeed, it is not a requirement that the new institutions, in order to contribute to a new temporary stability, must prefigure political empowerment within localities (as Amin and Thrift, 1994, indicate), nor is it the case that the new bargaining structures *per se* are more biased towards private business than the old form of urban governance, which emphasized the separation between public benefit and private profit. Concrete developments and the degree of responsiveness and openness of versions will depend on how actors at the local level seize and struggle over the opportunities and forms provided within this basic model.

So what should the (environmental and democratic) movements be arguing for as key elements and practices of urban management? Different proposals have been put on the table: Lipietz in chapter 11 in this volume, for instance, argues for the creation of a new sector dedicated to socially useful tasks of the kind which are provided expensively by the welfare state, by unpaid female work or not at all. Others argue for a strengthening of national redistributive policies and for challenging the political ideology 'that eschews state ownership of housing and industry' (Fainstein and Fainstein, 1993, p. 119).

Our analysis, however, shows that the situation has already become more complicated. The 'new alternative sector' envisioned by Lipietz to be the way forward is already a widespread practice within many of the municipal programmes which are tying third sector groups and their polyvalent work[12] to state employment policies. It has already differentiated into a multilayered, conflictual set of arrangements, subject to the pressures of both market and public sector demands, and characterized by internal tensions and cleavages.[13] The task for movements, then, is not to *create* such an 'alternative sector', but to make it accessible to and resourceful for marginalized groups threatened by the powerful polarization processes of post-Fordism. Social movements need to use the new channels and forums provided by the new bargaining systems to challenge the powerful post-Fordist trend towards inequality and to attack its social divisions and its political forms of exclusion in order to strengthen the democratic potential of the new forms of urban governance.

On the other hand, while one may conceive of national strategies that redistribute resources from wealthy to poor areas or groups as a prop for democratic movements, demands for such national projects are improbable today, given the national welfare state's overbearing form (which contributed to the crisis of Fordism) and the disappearance of the preconditions for a Fordist 'deal' embracing the big social blocks (unions, employers, the state). In any case, such demands have to confront the erosion ('hollowing out') of the nation state form, 'especially in its Keynesian welfare state guise' (Hirsch, 1991, p. 73; Jessop, 1992, p. 3, and chapter 8 in this volume). These trends have to be taken into account, so a more appropriate strategy might be to make use of the forms and structures that have become available at the subnational level.

Instead of hanging on to 'old-fashioned' large-scale, nationally oriented strategies, instead of demanding unspecified third sector or community representation, social movements will need to use their own card within the structure of the new bargaining systems. Since urban governance has become based on the representation of functional interests active at the local level, and since the local authority has to respect to some degree the particular functional characteristics of the other actors involved in the new 'partnerships', and since *all* the involved participants control resources that are necessary for the policies to be effective, even social movement groups have a real basis for negotiation.

But 'negotiation' may be a mild term for the struggle at hand. The emerging post-Fordist regime, with the new social modes of regulation including the new forms of urban governance described in this chapter, may function with some temporary stability, but it poses enormous long-term problems of social disintegration. The emphasis on economic innovation and competition, and the subordination of all social programmes to these economic priorities, will tend to produce deep divisions in society and threaten the decay of civil society (which, of course, in the long run causes difficulty for economic stability). Given emerging increasingly polarized class relations and the fragmented local situations, social movements need to mobilize to create pressure on the local authority, first, to develop strategic plans that make every effort to avoid social segregation and marginalization, and, second, to use the resources of large private investors to meet local social and environmental needs. If they manage to seize the opportunities and spaces provided by the new, fragmented political arrangements, they may yet influence the concrete shape of the post-Fordist development path.

NOTES

This chapter is based on a paper prepared for the 'Challenges in Urban Management Conference' held at the University of Newcastle upon Tyne, UK, in March 1993. The redraft has benefited from the comments of the conference organizers, especially Patsy Healey, and participants. The chapter closely resembles my contribution to the publication resulting from the conference, edited by Healey et al. (1994). I am grateful to the editors for consenting to this publication.

1   The USA and UK would be located on the 'flexible-liberal-productivist' end of the spectrum, whereas Sweden and to some extent other Scandinavian countries, Germany and Japan have developed 'negotiated involvement' models. See Lipietz (1992a, p. 318), as well as chapter 11 in this reader.

2   The UK and the USA, having been first among the OECD countries to experience severe urban economic decline, were also the first to shape national programmes directed specifically towards encouraging economic activities in urban areas, and established distinct national agencies to administer them (see Fox Przeworski, 1986).

3   The controversial and painful process of institutionalization of alternative local politics, which turned movement participation into interest group politics and co-production of services, has been variously described (Dackweiler et al., 1990; Roth, 1990; Mayer, 1993). Though under pressure, these projects and intermediary organizations are now an integral part of the urban political landscape and the local modes of social

regulation. They serve to cushion the labour market and manpower policies which are to flexibilize the labour force, while they are themselves part of a more flexible and innovative provision of collective consumption.

4 While established welfare associations and churches have long been involved in the provision of social services, community organizations, alternative groups and movement organizations active around health, women, immigrant and youth issues, for example, have been screened by municipal governments since the early 1980s for their usefulness in dealing with long-term unemployment and marginalization problems – policy fields in which the traditional welfare state mechanisms apparently no longer function effectively (Offe and Heinze, 1992).

5 Unlike the central business district oriented partnerships, the community-oriented ones usually suffer, however, from limited staff and financial resources as well as diversion of staff time to fund-raising rather than project implementation.

6 Mackintosh (1992, pp. 221–2) lists some of the elements that joint ventures need to contain for them to be 'successful' and for local authorities to establish an active strategic role within them.

7 Those who disagree with the magazine's celebratory reading of the ongoing transformation processes and its politics of cross-party coalition often also reject the determinist explanation of its inevitable triumph (e.g. Clarke, 1988, and earlier chapters in this volume).

8 For a summary of the disagreements among regulationists see Jessop (1990b).

9 'A mode of social regulation comprises an ensemble of norms, institutions, organizational forms, social networks, and patterns of conduct which sustain and "guide" an accumulation regime' (Lipietz, 1985, p. 121). 'Modes of regulation reinforce and underpin these regimes [of accumulation] by institutionalizing class struggle and confining it within certain parameters compatible with continuing accumulation' (Jessop, 1990a, p. 309).

10 Any 'feasible reorganization of the welfare state must resolve not only the problems rooted in its own dynamic but also those rooted in its regulatory role in relation to accumulation' (Jessop, 1991b, p. 103).

11 A typical example is the United States, which is described as a 'weak state' model where investment and production decisions are left almost entirely to the private sector and government does not pursue a conscious development strategy (Zysman, 1983, p. 19).

12 For instance, via the simultaneous delivery of the urban repair, social, lobbying and political functions described earlier.

13 The cleavages, for example, between 'established' community groups and newer, 'outsider' protest groups are a reflection of the intensifying social polarization which the post-Fordist economy entails. Newly marginalized groups and their advocates frequently attack the work of community development and alternative renewal organizations that are (meagrely) funded by municipal programmes.

REFERENCES

Amin, A. and Thrift, N. (1994) The local in the global. In A. Amin and N. Thrift (eds), *Globalisation, Institutions, and Regional Development in Europe*. Oxford: Oxford University Press.

Anheier, H. K. and Salamon, L. M. (1992) Genese und Schwerpunkte internationaler Forschung zum Nonprofit-Sektor. *Forschunqsjournal Neue Soziale Bewegungen*, 5(4), 40–8.

Anheier, H. K. and Seibel, W. (eds) (1990) *The Third Sector. Comparative Studies of Nonprofit Organizations*. Berlin/New York: de Gruyter.

Ashworth, C. J. and Vogel, H. (1989) *Selling the City*. New York: Pinter Publ.

Barbrook, R. (1990) Mistranslations. Lipietz in London and Paris. *Science as Culture*, 8, 80–117.

Bennett, R., Krebs, G. and Zimmermann, H. (eds) (1990) *Local Economic Development in Britain and Germany*. London: Anglo-German Foundation.

Blanke, B., Heinelt, H. and Macke, C. W. (eds) (1987) *Großstadt und Arbeitslosigkeit: ein Problemsyndrom im Netz lokaler Sozialpolitik*. Opladen: Westdeutscher Verlag.

Boyer, R. (1990) *The Regulation School: A Critical Introduction*. New York: Columbia University Press.

Bullmann, U. (1991) *Kommunale Strategien gegen Massenarbeitslosigkeit*. Opladen: Leske & Budrich.

Clarke, Simon (1988) overaccumulation, class struggle and the regulation approach. *Capital and Class*, 36, 59–92.

Cochrane, A. (1992) Das veränderte Gesicht der städtischer Politik in Sheffield: vom 'municipal labourism' zu 'public-private partnership'. In H. Heinelt and M. Mayer (eds), *Politik in europäischen Städten. Fallstudien zur Bedeutung lokaler Politik*. Basel: Birkhäuser, 119–36.

Cochrane, A. (1993) *Whatever Happened to Local Government?* Buckingham: Open University Press.

Cooke, P. and Imrie, R. (1989) Little victories: local economic development in European regions. *Entrepreneurship and Regional Development*, 1, 313–27.

Costonis, J. J. (1990) Tinker to Evers to Chance: community groups as the third player in the development game. In T. J. Lasser (ed.), *City Deal Making*. Washington, DC: The Urban Land Institute, 155–66.

Dackweiler, R., Poppenhusen, M., Grottian, P. and Roth, R. (1990) *Struktur und Entwicklungsdynamik lokaler Bewegungsnetzwerke in der Bundesrepublik. Eine empirische Untersuchung an drei Orten*. Unpublished DFG Research Project Report, Free University Berlin.

Dekker, A. M. (1992) Cross-national comparison of large scale entrepreneurial city renewal: building a theoretical framework. University of Amsterdam.

Dyson, K. (1988) *Local Authorities and New Technologies: the European Dimension*. New York: Croom Helm.

Elsinger, P.K. (1988) *The Rise of the Entrepreneurial State. State and Local Economic Development Policy in the United States*. Madison: University of Wisconsin Press.

Evers, A. (1991) Pluralismus, Fragmentierung und Vermittlungsfähigkeit. Zur Aktualität intermediärer Aufgaben und Instanzen im Bereich der Sozial- und Gesundheitspolitik. In H. Heinelt and H. Wollmann (eds), *Brennpunkt Stadt*. Basel: Birkhäuser, 221–40.

Fainstein, S. and Fainstein, N. (1993). Public–private partnerships for urban (re)development in the United States. In W. Heinz (ed.), *Public Private Partnership – ein neuer Weg zur Stadtentwicklung?* Stuttgart: W. Kohlhammer.

Fox Przeworski, J. (1986) National government responses to structural changes in urban economies. In H.J. Ewers et al. (eds), *The Future of the Metropolis*. Berlin: de Gruyter.

Frieden, B. J. and Sagalyn, L. B. (1989) *Downtown, Inc. How America Rebuilds Cities*. Cambridge, MA: MIT Press.

Froessler, R. and Selle, K. (1991) *Auf dem Weg zur sozial und ökologisch orientierten Erneuerung? Der Beitrag intermediärer Organisationen zur Entwicklung städtischer Quartiere in der BRD*. Dortmund: Dortmunder Vertrieb f.Bau- und Planungsliteratur.

Getimis, P. (1992) Dezentralisierungspolitik und Handlungsmöglichkeiten des lokalen Staates in Griechenland – am Beispiel der örtlichen Arbeitsmarktpolitik in Athen. In H. Heineilt and M. Mayer (eds), *Politik in europäischen Städten. Fallstudien zur Bedeutung lokaler Politik*. Basel: Birkhäuser, 213–38.

Grabber, G. (1990) *On the Weakness of Strong Ties. The Ambivalent Role of Inter-Firm Relations in the Decline and Reorganization of the Ruhr*. Discussion Paper FS I 90-4, Wissenschaftszentrum Berlin.

Hauff, M. von (1989) *Neue Selbsthilfebewegung und staatliche Sozialpolitik*. Wiesbaden: Deutscher Universitätsverlag.

Healey, P., Cameron, S., Davoudi, S., Graham, S. and Madani Pour (eds) (1994) *Managing Cities: the New Urban Context*. Chichester: John Wiley.

Heinelt, H. and Mayer, M. (eds) (1993) *Politik in europäischen Städten. Fallstudien zur Bedeutung lokaler Politik*. Basel: Birkhäuser.

Heinz, W. (1993) *Public Private Partnership – ein neuer Weg zur Stadtentwicklung?*. Stuttgart: W. Kohlhammer (Schriften des Deutschen Instituts für Urbanistik, Bd 87).

Hesse, J. J. (1987) Aufgaben einer Staatslehre heute. In Th. Ellwein et al. (eds), *Jahrbuch zur Staats- und Verwaltungswissenschaft*, volume. 1. Baden-Baden: Nomos.

Hirsch, J. (1988) The crisis of Fordism, transformations of the 'Keynesian' security state, and new social movements. *Research in Social Movements, Conflicts and Chance*, 10, 43–55.

Hirsch, J. (1991) From the Fordist to the post-Fordist state, In B. Jessop et al. (eds), *The Politics of Flexibility*. Aldershot: Edward Elgar, 67–81.

Hirsch, J. and Roth, R. (1986) *Das neue Gesicht des Kapitalismus. Vom Fordismus zum Post-Fordismus*. Hamburg: VSA.

Jessop, B. (1990a) *State Theory. Putting Capitalist States in Their Place*. Cambridge: Polity Press.

Jessop, B. (1990b) Regulation theory in retrospect and prospect. *Economy and Society* 19(2), 153–216.

Jessop, B. (1991a) 'Thatcherism: the British road to post-Fordism. In B. Jessop, H. Kastendiek, K. Nielsen and O. K. Pedersen (eds), *The Politics of Flexibility*. Aldershot: Edward Elgar.

Jessop, B. (1991b) The welfare state in the transition from Fordism to post-Fordism. In B. Jessop et al. (eds), *The Politics of Flexibility*. Aldershot: Edward Elgar, 82–105.

Jessop, B. (1992) From the Keynesian welfare to the Schumpeterian workfare state. Lancaster Regionalism Group, Working Paper 45.

Kirlin, J. J. and Kirlin, A. M. (1983) Public/private bargaining in local development. In B. H. Moore (ed.), *The Entrepreneur in Local Government*. Washington, DC: International City Management Ass., 151–67.

Lasser, T. J. (ed.) (1990) *City Deal Making*. Washington, DC: The Urban Land Institute.

Lehner, F. (1993) Die Politik kann verflucht wenig tun. Interview with F. Lehner on the steel crisis and restructuring in the Ruhr Valley. *Die Tageszeitung*, 5 March.

Lipietz, A. (1985) Akkumulation, Krisen und Auswege aus der Krise: Einige methodische Überlegungen zum Begriff 'Regulation'. *Prokla* 15(1), 109–37.

Lipietz, A. (1992a) The regulation approach and capitalist crisis: an alternative compromise for the 1990s. In M. Dunford and G. Kafkalas (eds), *Cities and Regions in the New Europe*. London, Belhaven Press, 309–34.

Lipietz, A. (1992b) *Towards a New Economic Order. Postfordism, Ecology and Democracy*. New York: Oxford University Press.

Logan, J. and Swanstrom, T. (eds) (1990) *Beyond the City Limits. Urban Policy and Economic Restructuring in Comparative Perspective*. Philadelphia: Temple University Press.

Lovering, J. (1991) Theorising postFordism: why contingency matters. *International Journal of Urban and Regional Research* 15(2), 298–301.

Mackintosh, M. (1992) Partnership: issues of policy and negotiation. *Local Economy*, 7(3), 210–24.

Maier, H. E. and Wollmann, H. (eds) (1986) *Lokale Beschäftigungspolitik*. Basel: Birkhäuser.

Mayer, M. (1990) Lokale Politik in der unternehmerischen Stadt. In R. Borst et al. (eds), *Das neue Gesicht der Städte*. Basel: Birkhäuser, 190–208.

Mayer, M. (1992) The shifting local political system in European cities. In M. Dunford and G. Kafkalas (eds), *Cities and Regions in the New Europe*. London: Belhaven, 255–74.

Mayer, M. (1993) The role of urban social movement organizations in innovative urban policies and institutions. *Topos Review of Urban and Regional Studies*, Special Issue, 209–26.

Molotch, H. (1990) Urban deals in comparative perspective. In J. Logan and T. Swanstrom (eds), *Beyond the City Limits. Urban Policy and Economic Restructuring in Comparative Perspective*. Philadelphia: Temple University Press.

Moore, B. H. (1983) *The Entrepreneur in Local Government*. Washington, DC: International City Management Association.

Murray, R. (1988) Life after Henry (Ford). *Marxism Today*, October, 8–13.

National Congress for Community Economic Development (1989) *Against All Odds: Achievements of Community-based Organizations*. Washington, DC.

Offe, C. and Heinze, R. G. (1992) *Beyond Employment*. Cambridge, Polity Press.

Page, E. C. (1993) The future of local government in Britain. In U. Bullman (ed.), *Die Politik der dritten Ebene*. Regionen im EG-Integrationsprozess. Baden-Baden: Nomos.

Parkinson, M., Foley, B. and Judd, D. J. (eds) (1988) *Regenerating the Cities. The UK Crisis and the US Experience*. Manchester: Manchester University Press.

Robinson, C. J. (1989) Municipal approaches to economic development: growth and distribution policy. *American Planning Association Journal*, 55(3), 283–95.

Roth, R. (1990) Stadtentwicklung und soziale Bewegungen in der Bundesrepublik. In R. Borst et al. (eds), *Das neue Gesicht der Stadt*. Basel: Birkhäuser, 209–34.

Scharpf, F. (1991) Die Handlungsfähigkeit des Staates am Ende des 20. Jahrhunderts. *Politische Vierteljahresschrift*, 32(4), 621–34.

Schnepf-Orth, M. and Staubach, R. (1989) *Bewohnerorientierte Stadterneuerung. Erfahrungen aus Beispielfällen ortsnaher Beratungs- und Kommunikationsstellen*. Dortmund: ILS.

Selle, K. (1991) *Mit den Bewohnern die Stadt erneuern. Der Beitrag intermediärer Organisationen zur Entwicklung städtischer Quartiere. Beobachtungen aus sechs Ländern*. Dortmund: Dortmunder Vertrieb f. Bau- und Planungsliteratur.

Simmons, J. M., d. Kelleher, W. and Duckworth, R. P. (1985) *Business and the Entrepreneurial American City*. Washington, DC: US Chamber of Commerce.

Smith, M. P. (1989) The uses of linked-development policies in US cities. In M. Parkinson, B. Foley and D. Judd (eds), *Regenerating the cities*. Manchester: Manchester University Press, 93–109.

Stöhr, W. B. (ed) (1990) *Global Challenge and Local Response. Initiatives for Economic Regeneration in Contemporary Europe*. London: Mansell.

Stoker, G. (1990) Regulation theory, local government and the transition from Fordism. In D. S. King and J. Pierre (eds), *Challenges to Local Government*. Newbury Park, CA: Sage.

Tickell, A. and Peck, J. A. (1992) Accumulation, regulation and the geographies of post-Fordism: missing links in regulationist research. *Progress in Human Geography*, 16(2), 190–218.

Wievel, W. and Weintraub, J. (1990) Community development corporations as a tool for economic development finance. In R. Bingham, E. Hill and S. White (eds), *Financing Economic Development. An Institutional Response*. Newbury Park, CA: Sage, 160–76.

Wollmann, H. (1992) Neue Wege der privaten Finanzierung von Stadterneuerungs- und Stadtentwicklungsaufgaben. Discussion paper for Workshop of the Federal Ministery of Housing and Urban Development (BmBau). Bonn, October 1992.

Zysman, J. (1983) *Governments, Markets, and Growth*. Ithaca, NY: Cornell University Press.

11

Post-Fordism and Democracy

Alain Lipietz

In a series of stimulating essays, C. B. Macpherson (1962, 1977) proposed a variety of different 'models' highlighting the connection between conceptions of democracy and socio-economic realities. The exercise was open to the charge of a certain reductionism. At any rate, if it usefully illuminated certain past political–economic configurations, it would be risky to extend its analysis to the future. Yet Macpherson's intuition, continuing a tradition that stretches back, beyond Marx, to Montesquieu, seems perfectly sound. There is indeed a 'common principle' which appears to govern both socio-economic realities and forms of democracy. No doubt this principle brings neither the one nor the other into being. Let us rather say that the evolution of these different processes is marked by a reciprocal influence, with moments of 'harmony' when a common principle of social identification seems to prevail. We shall call this principle (or rather, bundle of principles) a 'societal paradigm'.

When we turn to the future, it is no longer a question of 'discovering' this paradigm, but of promoting it, in the case of the political activist, and identifying competing paradigms, in the case of the researcher. In this chapter, we must first identify the paradigms which are currently

This chapter is a translation, by Gregory Elliott, of an article originally published in French as Après-fordisme et démocratie, in *Les Temps Modernes* (1990), vol. 524, pp. 97–121.

in conflict (let us name them straight away: 'liberal-productivist' and 'alternative'), and then sketch some of the economic bases which might correspond to the conception of democracy compatible with the principles of the alternative.

The first section will briefly summarize how thought derived from the 'regulation approach'[1] helps to illuminate the correspondence between the economy and the 'societal paradigm', thus underlining the relativism of conceptions of 'democracy'. The second section will, with equal brevity, summarize the 'correspondence' peculiar to the Fordist model of development, today in crisis. The third section will outline the 'liberal-productivist' paradigm, while the fourth will be devoted to the alternative paradigm. In the fifth section we shall emphasize a particular aspect of social identification in the alternative paradigm: the importance it accords to concrete, territorialized communities.

SOCIETAL PARADIGM AND MODEL OF DEVELOPMENT

The reproduction of a capitalist market economy via its transformations is far from self-evident. Nevertheless, its transformations remain regular for extended periods, and accumulation and economic growth experience no major disruption. This kind of conjoint and compatible mode of transformation of the norms of production, distribution and exchange is called a *regime of accumulation*. This regime rests upon general principles of labour organization and utilization of techniques, which might be called a *technological paradigm*.

A regime of accumulation thus refers to an observed macroeconomic regularity. This regularity is a precious guide for economic agents. But their initiatives are nevertheless threatened by radical uncertainty as regards their aggregate coherence in the future. Regulatory mechanisms must therefore intervene. We shall call the set of norms (implicit or explicit) and institutions, which continuously adjust individual anticipations and behaviours to the general logic of the regime of accumulation, the *mode of regulation*. We might say that the mode of regulation constitutes the 'scenery', the practical world, the superficial 'map' by which individual agents orient themselves so that the conditions necessary for balanced economic reproduction and accumulation are met in full (Lipietz, 1985). The establishment of a mode of regulation, like its consolidation, largely depends upon the political sphere. Here we are in the domain of socio-political struggles and 'armistices', institutionalized compromises.

These struggles, armistices and compromises are the equivalent in the political domain of competition, labour conflicts and the regime of accumulation in the economic sphere. Defined by their daily conditions of existence, and in particular by their place in economic relations, social groups do not engage in a struggle without end. *Social bloc* is the term to delineate a stable system of relations of domination, alliances and concessions between different social groups (dominant and subordinate). A social bloc is *hegemonic* when its interests correspond with those of a whole nation. In any hegemonic bloc the proportion of the nation whose interests are discounted has to be very small.

The fit between 'hegemonic bloc', 'regime of accumulation' and 'mode of regulation' becomes visible as long as the interests constituting the consensus on which the hegemonic bloc is built and reproduced are economic interests. But how are the 'interests' which legitimately demand satisfaction to be defined? How is the validity of, and respect for, the compromises which solder the hegemonic bloc to be measured? In the name of what do the conflicting groups within the bloc demand 'justice'? A 'universe of political representations and discourses' must be assumed, in which individuals and groups can recognize one another and express their identity, their interests and divergences (Jenson, 1989a). The very possibility of the hegemonic bloc depends upon the formation of this universe.

Societal paradigm is the name we shall give to a mode of structuration of the identities and legitimately defensible interests within the 'universe of political discourses and representations'. The regime of accumulation, mode of regulation, hegemonic bloc and societal paradigm are all four the result of a process of conflictual historical evolution. Each is a historic find, while their mutual compatibility within what we might call a model of socio-economic development is itself a quasi-miracle. Once discovered, however, this coherence certainly tends to be consolidated. But it is also undermined, on the one hand, by contradictions specific to the model and, on the other hand, by what has remained or developed 'outside' the model, ignored or repressed by it.

Thus we see two forms of struggle emerge. The first form concerns struggle, within the same paradigm, over differences about the equity or even the reality of the distribution of mutual benefits that are supposed to be guaranteed by the hegemonic bloc within the regime of accumulation. These struggles are directed against what are perceived as 'encroachments', 'anomalies', even 'overdue payments', and they aim at the implementation or improvement of regulatory mechanisms. The second involves struggle against the hegemonic paradigm in the name of another paradigm, alternative identities or other interests, that is, in the name of a different conception, past or future, of social life, involving another regime of accumulation, other forms of regulation and a different social bloc.

It is here that we encounter the ambiguity of the word 'democracy'. It manifestly refers to a procedural form of political regulation of these two types of conflict: the participation of citizens in the improvement of a paradigm or in arbitration within a paradigm; but, equally, the sovereignty of citizens over the choice of a model of socio-economic development. Now these are not the same thing, since the definition of 'citizens' itself, for example, depends upon the existing paradigm: do women, proletarians or slaves figure among the 'citizens'? The field of democratic regulation is likewise dependent upon the existing paradigm: is the organization of work, or the distribution of the fruits of growth, accountable to democratic sovereignty?

Now we see a different meaning slip in behind the word 'democracy', alluding to a graduated scale of substantive difference *between* paradigms and models of development. A model which enhanced the range of citizenship and the rights of citizens would be considered 'more democratic'. This is the traditional meaning of the 'Right/Left' opposition. Unfortunately, the list of the rights '*recognized*' within the 'universe of political discourses' precisely depends upon ... the reigning paradigm. Athens can regard itself as democratic despite the exclusion of women and slaves; the United States of America can in all good conscience exclude sexual equality from its Constitution and proclaim respect for 'managerial privileges' in companies; the Communist parties can declare themselves 'democratic' while accepting Taylorism (i.e. rigid and alienating rules of work).

The birth of a new paradigm, expanding democracy by rendering visible new identities which demand consideration of their aspirations, is the concern of radical social movements. Even in the second sense ('upgrading' between paradigms) democracy is not a sphere to be managed or enlarged. It is a continent to be discovered, from one century to the next. As an example, we shall start with the conception of democracy prevalent in the model of development which the regulation approach terms 'Fordism'.[2]

FORDISM AND ITS CRISIS

This model of development, hegemonic in the developed capitalist countries after 1945, stood on a tripod. One leg was a dominant form of labour organization, structured around the Taylorist separation of conception and execution and the systematic incorporation of the know-how of technical workers in the automatic operation of machines. These Taylorist principles theoretically excluded the direct producers from any involvement in the intellectual aspect of labour, but in reality implied a certain 'good will', a 'paradoxical involvement' disclaimed on both sides (by management and workers). The second leg was a regime of accumulation, involving growth in popular consumption, and hence 'outlets', commensurate with productivity gains. The third leg was a set of forms of regulation inducing the conformity of employers and wage-earners alike to the model. In particular, the Fordist mode of regulation drew upon collection agreements and the welfare state, which guaranteed the great majority of wage-earners a regularly rising income (thus helping to sustain the levels of demand required by the mass production norm under Fordism).

The Fordist societal paradigm offered a conception of progress which itself rested upon three pillars: technical progress (conceived as technological progress unconditionally driven by 'intellectual workers'); social progress (conceived as progress in purchasing power while respecting the constraint of full employment); and state progress (the state conceived as guarantor of the general interest against the 'encroachments' of individual interests). And this triple progress was supposed to weld together society, by advancing goals worthy of collective pursuit.

From Rooseveltian intellectuals to West European Communists, this progressivist paradigm was dubbed 'democratic'; not so much in the first sense of the term (pre-war liberalism was often just as democratic – except that the right to vote was still denied to women), but precisely because of its 'progressive' character. The primacy of science and technology flattered a certain humanism built around technical progress – and all the more so since the regime of accumulation ensured a general redistribution of the 'fruits of progress'. Finally, through the role assigned to the state or other collective forms of non-market regulation, this paradigm appeared to limit the distortions to democracy introduced by the unequal distribution of wealth (democracy defined in the first sense of the term, i.e. the capacity of all to participate in the settlement of disputes). The progress of Fordist democracy could thus be defended by 'the forces of labour and culture'.

In retrospect, however, the term 'hierarchical organicism' is much more appropriate for this 'democratic' conception of social progress. It is 'organicist' in the sense that it does not, in principle, exclude anyone from a 'share in the fruits of progress' (in practice, there are, of course, always some exceptions). On the other hand, it systematically deprives poorly qualified producers of control over their activities, it excludes citizens from decisions about what is to count as progress (*vis-à-vis* consumption, public services, town planning and, more generally, the ecological consequences of progress) and so forth. Organised by the welfare state, solidarity assumes a strictly distributive and administrative form: a hierarchical, market solidarity.

This model entered into crisis throughout the entire advanced capitalist world in which it was established. It was certainly an economic crisis: a crisis of the model of labour organization based upon the fragmentation of tasks, the division between 'conception' and 'execution' and ever costly mechanization; it was a crisis of the 'welfare state', and it was a crisis of the nation state, incapable of regulating an increasingly internationalized economy.

But in France, for example, this crisis was exacerbated by another one which preceded the economic crisis: a crisis of the societal paradigm, in its adherence to the dominant conception of progress. While the common programme of the Left merely took Fordism's ideal of democratization (from above!) to extremes, new working-class and popular struggles (workers, peasants, employees) and the new social movements – regionalist, feminist and ecological – which flourished after May 1968 rejected the very model. A new star shone forth above the old tripolar progressivist constellation, expressing an ideal at once very old and very new: the desire for autonomy and initiative, individual and collective; and the ambition to 'take control' of one's own affairs, to 'see things through'. This 'fourth pole' contributed to breaking up the old triangle where modernists of the Right and Left met, and it posed new fundamental questions. Technical progress? Perhaps, but not at the cost of the impoverishment of work. Social solidarity? Perhaps, but not in the anonymous, bureaucratic mould in which the welfare state cast it. A state synthesizing social aspirations and obligations? Perhaps, but not a state of technocrats imposing their conception of the good and the beautiful, including sending in the army to enforce 'progress'.

It is thus scarcely surprising that the first two years of the Mitterand presidency, when the parties of the Left worked to death trying to revive a model of development in crisis without gaining the support of the popular masses or intellectuals who no longer expected much from it, ended in virtually total failure.

LIBERAL-PRODUCTIVISM

When the state abandons its ambitions, when the money and the willingness to contribute to social solidarity run out, when one clings on to technological modernization and when one continues to rely on the initiatives of those used to taking them, what is left? Economic liberalism. On the ruins of the old model and the old ideals of the Left, the rebirth of initiative becomes the cult of the enterprise: the enterprise as it is, with one leader (or ten) who decides, while the rest obey – in accordance with the interests of the firm, if not the collective interest.

The clarion call of the Western intelligentsia in the first half of the 1980s was: we must be competitive! And to that end the initiative of entrepreneurs must be freed. And if the social consequences are unfavourable? Too bad. We must be competitive! To what end? Because free enterprise dictates that we be competitive. And so the story unfolded.

Previously, technical progress had been justified by social progress. Free enterprise was supposed to ensure universal well-being automatically. But 'liberal-productivism' is a law unto itself; it no longer requires social justification. 'Accumulate! Innovate! And look at Silicon Valley!' People look; but they do not see everything. They often ignore the fact that Silicon Valley is hardly the 'spontaneous' product of individual initiative, but was created forty years ago by Stanford University for its former students, and has essentially always lived off public military orders. But even so we observe that executives and technicians live there alongside female employees and refugee workers from Central America – female Martians serving men from Venus – at the two poles of a society without a middle class, with no hope of transferring from one planet to the other. This is an economy shaped like an hourglass, where those at the bottom survive on left-overs from the luxury of those above. The towns of the USA are being 'Brazilianized', and this 'hourglass' society is becoming global: at one end the overconsumption (on credit) of the rich; at the other the industrial gulags of the free enterprise zones. It is one possible future for capitalism.

However, no technological determinism ensures the final triumph of liberal-productivism on the ruins of Fordism. On the contrary, conceptual and empirical analysis of the outlines of possible new models of development (Leborgne and Lipietz, 1987) reveals their weaknesses in three respects: as technological paradigm, regime of accumulation and mode of regulation. The 'historical opportunity' for liberal-productivism was the breakdown of the Fordist paradigm at the end of the 1970s. Despite the economic and ecological problems that have become increasingly apparent since the 1980s, liberal-productivism is still sustained through the weakness of its competitor paradigms.

The liberal-productivist paradigm can be summarized thus:

- Intensification of the productivist technico-economic imperative – now rendered 'categoric', with the hollowing out of the idea of society as a democratic prerogative (we invest because we must export; we export because we must invest).
- Fragmentation of social identification, with the enterprise directly playing the role formerly allocated to the country (we must stick together against competitors).

- A great variety of forms of integration of the individual into the enterprise, ranging from sheer discipline to negotiated involvement, but always on an individual basis, to replace a previously class-based social individuality.
- A general decline of forms of solidarity of the administrative kind linked to membership of a national collectivity; 'civil society' (now, quite simply, the family) is supposed to assume responsibility for what the welfare state can no longer guarantee.

In other words, liberal-productivism deliberately and explicitly rejects the organicism of the Fordist model. But it accentuates its 'hierarchical' character, albeit a decentralized hierarchy. The entrepreneur is master of his[3] own domain; the 'winners' are masters of the market; if possible, the father of the family is master at home. 'Democracy' in both senses of the term thus retreats on every front. Debate and the vote are emptied of purpose by the omnipotence of the forces of the world market. The fraction of humanity in a position to influence its own existence is reduced.

The decline of organicism, that is, society's capacity to regard itself as a living whole, is immediately expressed in the development of social exclusions and the accumulation of ecological tensions and international imbalances. There is, however, a glimmer of hope: amid the imbalances, those nations and regions which have remained the most 'organicist' manage to extricate themselves. The machine-tool industry of Emilia-Romagna in Italy, the enduring strength of Germany and Sweden, the industrial hegemony of Japan, all demonstrate that, *even from a capitalist perspective*, the best course is to negotiate, to organize, to multiply the cooperative links between firms, local and regional collectivities and universities, and to mobilize workers through participation and union agreements. The superiority of organicism over liberalism is obviously insufficient to induce an alternative paradigm, since the *rewards* which citizens can extract *in return* from this superiority remain to be seen. (Japan and Sweden are manifestly not going in the same direction!) Thus, we must turn from observation to mapping out an alternative project to Fordism and liberal-productivism.

THE ALTERNATIVE

An alternative can be traced to the social movements which have been demanding change since the late 1960s – from the French May in 1968 to the German Greens in more recent years. What does the alternative counterpose to the old Fordist paradigm that is dying, and to a liberal-productivist paradigm that is trying to be born? Certainly not a rejection of technical progress, but a refusal to accept it as a value in its own right. Three themes provide the yardstick for the alternative by which to measure any 'progress' and any policy: the autonomy of individuals and groups; solidarity between individuals and groups; and ecology as a principle binding the relations between society, the product of its activity and its environment. In sum, it represents a non-hierarchical organicism.

The alternative responds as follows to the crisis of the Fordist paradigm:

- Transformation of the relations between people in work, towards a greater control by the producers over their activity.
- Reduction of the amount of time devoted to wage labour, and hence a reduction of market relations in consumption and leisure in favour of free creativity.
- Systematic selection of the most ecological technologies (i.e. the least predatory *vis-à-vis* natural resources), the fullest possible recycling of the by-products of human activity, restoration of industrial and urban derelict land, etc.
- Transformation of social relations in the direction of a reduction of hierarchies, and respect for quality in difference – especially between the genders and between races.
- Transformation of the forms of solidarity within the national collectivity, from purely monetary distribution to subsidies for activities which are self-organized and of agreed social usefulness.
- Evolution towards forms of grass-roots democracy, which are more 'organic' and less delegated.
- Reopening of the whole question of unegalitarian relations between different national collectivities, and evolution towards mutually beneficial relations between self-determining communities.

As a new paradigm, the alternative paradigm is not located along the Right–Left polarization characteristic of the Fordist paradigm (when more or less democratic means 'more or less welfare state'). If the alternative attains the position of 'hegemonic paradigm' with respect to the political forces which might establish themselves twenty or thirty years hence, it will then have its own Right, Centre and Left, which will 'democratically' (in the first sense) settle differences. Yet as a new model of 'progress', the alternative takes over from the former 'democratic' movements. More significantly, its social foundation would gather the oppressed, the abused and the exploited, in revolt against alienating social relations, bringing together, thus, women, workers adversely affected by economic restructuring or degrading technologies, the unemployed and precariously employed, the multicultural youth of the conurbations, indebted or non-industrialized peasants, and so on. It thus succeeds and embraces all emancipatory movements. In this sense (i.e. the historic sense), the alternative is a 'new Left', a 'democratic alternative': it discovers a wider scope to democracy.

What would be the economic foundation of the democratic alternative? What sort of technological paradigm, regime of accumulation, mode of regulation would it have? It is not enough simply to introduce 'some democracy' (in the first or second sense) into each dimension of the model of development. This new democracy must be 'constructed'. Further, the alternative needs to respond to the economic impasse of the old Fordism, now in crisis.

Let us recall that Fordism entered into crisis for two kinds of reason. On the one hand, the internationalization of production and markets came to disrupt the possibility of *national* regulation of the Fordist model of development. On the other hand, the dominant form of labour organization reached its limits. 'Paradoxical involvement' yielded only declining productivity gains for rising per capita investment. The results were a fall in profitability, a crisis of investment, a crisis of employment and a crisis of the welfare state.

Downward spirals in the international economy currently occupy centre-stage. But we shall not deal with them here. Assuming that there might be positive solutions to these problems, it remains to be seen whether there exists a 'democratic' way out of Fordism with respect to its internal spirals, which extend from the crisis of labour to that of the welfare state.[4]

For a new social compromise on productivity

At the root of the current economic crisis of labour is a crisis of Taylorism as a form of 'paradoxical non-involvement' of the direct worker. In themselves information technologies do not represent a solution to this crisis. This is why Japanese employers, the Dalle and Riboud reports on industrial relations in France, the theoreticians of the Harvard Business School and the initiators of General Motors' Saturn car project in the United States concur in condemning Taylorist principles. Direct operators should be able to involve themselves, with all their imagination, their capacity for innovation, qualifications and the know-how acquired in routine production, not only to refine the operation of the productive process, but also to socialize and collectivize their acquired practical knowledge: a task which Taylor reserved for the office of methods.

To put it bluntly, the workers' movement and all other democratic movements should take up the challenge to occupy the terrain of an anti-Taylorist revolution. Not only by way of compromise, but as a first step towards historic goals: a more democratic, more 'self-managed' society, a step towards the 'humanization of humankind'. Fine, but it will *also* be a compromise. Doubtless any boss would be delighted to have employees working with enthusiasm, with all their intellectual abilities, for the greater glory of the enterprise! If Taylorism opted to forgo such possibilities, it was for political reasons – for micropolitical reasons to do with control of the factories, but also for macropolitical reasons, reasons of state. Indeed, a highly qualified and enterprising group of workers, proud of so being, risks challenging Taylorist managerial control over the intensity of labour, the sharing out of productivity gains and the usefulness of products. And a working class conscious of its managerial abilities might harbour ambitions as regards its capacity for political and social leadership.

If management seeks to reunite what Taylor separated (that is, intellectual and routine aspects of labour), what can it offer and, in turn, what might wage-earners demand in return? With regard to the latter, a first demand is obvious: *maximum stability of employment*. No wage-earner is prepared to display a cooperative spirit in pursuit of productivity gains which entail his or her own redundancy! The problem, of course, is that a firm cannot guarantee employment of the same kind beyond the medium term. Job security must therefore be a *dynamic* guarantee, involving both aspects internal to the firm and social aspects. This immediately raises the question of job 'mobility' and productive 'restructuring'.

Most wage-earners are unwilling to accept mobility between kinds of work and between regions. They are right. Work is only one aspect of individual and social life. Emotional and familial relations are the main component in the conditions for human development and happiness, and they require material conditions: stability of communities, linked to territories. The compromise should therefore embrace not only the 'right to work', but also the 'right to live and work in one's own region'. This implies the unions' collective involvement in the local dynamic of new job creation, as and when redundant jobs disappear.

The involvement of wage-earners in the issue of 'how to produce' leads on to the second question: 'what to produce'. Two imperatives must consistently guide the alternative's position on the restructuring of the productive apparatus. First and foremost is the *preservation and enrichment of know-how*. It is as humiliating as it is irrational not to acknowledge the acquired know-how of workers. This is why wage-earners must be involved in decisions about restructuring. They contribute their know-how and can demand retraining in return. This right to retraining and control over the objectives of restructuring must form part of the compromise over dynamic restructuring.

The second imperative is the *democratic definition of the social needs to be satisfied*. A temptation for unions is to defend the existing jobs of their members. However, these jobs might be dangerous for the community (e.g. nuclear complexes), or of dubious social usefulness (e.g. old mines, the arms industry). This is why control over what is to be produced is a matter not only for existing workers, but for the whole of society. New forms of democratic planning, preceding any 'judgement of the market', must be invented. This can probably be done at the regional level, at the level of local labour markets. We shall return to this question later.

Sharing the benefits

First we must specify another aspect of the compromise. Assuming that the establishment of new professional relations, allied to the 'information revolution', entails a return to high productivity increases, who should benefit from them? At the very least, wage-earners should benefit as much as enterprises. If not, sluggish demand, contrasting with 'soaring' productivity, would result in overproduction and rising unemployment. However, the new model of development can resolve this problem either through an increase in the purchasing power of wage-earners (via salaries or the welfare state), or through an extension in their free time. In my view (and this is the essential point) the *compromise should bear mainly on an expansion of free time*, and less on an increase in purchasing power over communities. There are good arguments in favour of this option.

In the first place, a massive reduction in the length of the working week is the principal effective weapon for a rapid reduction in unemployment. Next, in our advanced capitalist countries (the situation is different in the Third World), the majority of the population has achieved, in quantitative terms, a standard of living in which the right to well-being is restricted more by a 'lack of quality of life' than a 'lack of possessions'. Even before the economic crisis, around 1968, the post-war model of mass consumption began to reveal its existential deficiencies. People need time to live with what they have; they need to experiment with new social relations and independent creative activities. Even the new commodities offered by the electronics revolution – hi-fi, video, home computers – take up time, whereas the typical Fordist commodities (cars, washing machines) were supposed to be time-saving. In addition, logic suggests that, in the long term, wage-earners who are actively involved at work should also be active citizens in democratic life, with enough free time for cultural activity and improvement of educational levels.

Further, the generalization in advanced industrial countries of a new model based on high rates of growth of material consumption would imply a near unsustainable pressure on natural resources and on global 'sinks' for waste. As the Rio conference has shown, we have reached a situation where ecological constraints have become a determinant parameter for the choice of regimes of accumulation. Thus, while new technology may permit more growth with less consumption of energy, and a reduced greenhouse effect, it might be wiser to reserve these margins of material growth to less advanced countries.

Finally, a model of development in which full employment is based upon a slower growth of market relations and the expansion of free time, that is, of non-market relations, is less subject to the economic disruptions which derive from international competition. The 'consumption of free time' does not suck in imports, and protectionism is not required to ensure the possibility of making music or theatre, reading novels or making love. 'Accumulating in happiness' permits a more balanced growth and enhances the capacity for democratic regulation of national economies.

Now, a model of this kind most definitely involves other compromises on the part of wage-earners. Since there are minorities who are currently far from enjoying an acceptable standard of living in the society in which they live, compensation in wages for the reduction of labour time will, of necessity, have to be unequal. In other words, the range of the wages hierarchy will have to be reduced. Although new work practices based upon worker involvement could be less demanding in terms of per capita investment, fixed capital investment will still be required to create jobs. A large-scale creation of jobs through a reduction of the working week would thus be impossible in the short term, unless more wage-earners come to work in existing plants. To put it another way, the reduction of human labour time must proceed in tandem with an extension of mechanized labour time, and hence of shift-work. In the case of services, such work might be desirable to users, who are themselves essentially wage-earners.

In short, the 'new compromise' is not only between those 'above' and those 'below', between management and workers. It is also a compromise within the ranks of wage earners: an issue that raises the problem of solidarity, which, in the Fordist model, was embodied by the welfare state.

Resolving the crisis of the welfare state

In the form that it took as a result of union struggles, the victories of social democracy in Europe and the recognition of macroeconomic and social demands by conservative or social-Christian governments, the welfare state appeared as a powerful, but very particular, form of solidarity.[5] Basically, it is a form of compromise between capital and labour, in the form of a compromise between citizens. A proportion of income is subtracted from the purchasing power directly allocated to individuals and assigned to a reserve fund. This reserve pays a monetary income to those who, for 'legitimate' reasons, cannot 'earn their living normally by working'. This 'norm' entails some schizophrenic, even Kafkaesque, consequences for the economically active and inactive alike.

The active – employers as well as employees – pay taxes and contributions to the welfare state to feed into 'reserves'. When this deduction of income becomes too heavy, they begin to protest that they are paying for 'layabouts', for people who do not wish to work. The reality is that such people would like to work, but cannot do so in exchange for a wage, and do not have the right to do so while in receipt of benefits. And they bear the psychological cost of this illogicality. If they have no occupation, they feel socially rejected, they feel like dependent children. If they have an activity (helping out neighbours, moonlighting) while collecting their benefits, then they are considered to be scroungers, swindlers; they can be prosecuted and deprived of their benefits.

The double schizophrenia of the Fordist welfare state can be avoided. This would involve the creation of a *new sector of activity*, restricted in its scope (to something like 10 per cent of the active population, or the prevailing rate of unemployment). Its workers, or rather the agencies which would have to pay them (let us call them 'intermediate agencies of socially useful work'), would continue to receive subsidies from the welfare state of equivalent value to unemployment benefit (which should, in any case, be consolidated into a genuinely universal benefit).[6] Neither the agency nor the employees would have to pay any more in tax contributions than the unemployed: the cost of the operation would thus be neutral for the welfare state. Employees in this sector would receive a normal wage from the agencies and be covered by the normal social legislation. The difference lies in the fact that the cost of labour would be very low for the agencies. Their activity would be devoted to socially useful work, such as:

- activities currently provided at a high cost (since unsubsidized) by certain sectors of the welfare state itself (e.g. care for the sick, assistance to convalescents);

- activities currently provided by the unpaid labour of women;
- activities not performed at all currently because they are too costly (improvement of the environment, especially in poorer districts, etc.).

Given that this sector would be subsidized and exempt from taxes, its services would be inexpensive; and new activities might also be generated. It would not be in competition with other sectors (e.g. the private sector, government organizations), since the latter do not (or only marginally) take on these activities, either because they perceive no effective demand or because they dare not raise taxes to finance them. In fact the sector would only come into competition with the unpaid labour of women and with moonlighting: an excellent thing! And it would weigh no more heavily upon the welfare state than does unemployment, which in fact it will help reduce – on condition, obviously, that the size of the 'third sector' does not exceed the prevailing level of unemployment.

As can be seen, the development of this 'third sector of social utility' eliminates most of the faults of the Fordist welfare state. The critique of 'schizophrenia' disappears. The active contributors of the first two sectors would know what they were paying for: socially useful work. Those in the third sector would have a job which was more socially recognized and more rewarding for their self-esteem than moonlighting or precarious casual work. The microeconomy would be preserved by the development of jobs that were inexpensive for the remunerative bodies, but ensured a stable income for workers who would not come into competition with others.

But there is more. New 'democratic' social relations could be experimented with in this new economic sector. It could be organized into small, self-managed cooperatives, which could combine training and work, with the help of social psychologists and trainers. In addition, in its relations with 'users', it could innovate by searching for new contractual relations (not market, or patriarchal, or administrative) for the performance of services, with continuous audit by the recipients (municipalities, environmental protection agencies, health insurance funds, etc.) of the effective 'social usefulness' of the cooperatives.

Thus, this new 'alternative' sector could be a school for self-management, gender equality and democracy in the definition of tasks. Although immersed in the market and in wage relations (albeit protected by its connection with the welfare state), it could be a new step in the democratization of economic relations.

INITIATIVE AND SOLIDARITY: THE COMMUNITARIAN SYNTHESIS

Compared with the alternative, the Fordist paradigm scarcely seems democratic (in the substantive sense), even in its left-wing versions! Indeed, it quite simply ignores the essential dimensions of democracy. Just as the economism of the account which I have just given neglects certain crucial components (such as the ethics of sexual difference – and not simple equality). In Fordism worker initiative was repressed equally by Taylorist management and a trade unionism hostile to 'self-management'. The redistribution of the benefits of the welfare state was abstract, anonymous, formal and bureaucratic, and union participation in the management of social security agencies did not improve matters. This 'abstract welfare' gradually became a sour and constricting provider for contributors and recipients alike.

With the advent of Mrs Thatcher, Great Britain, mother of social security, became the first country to bring to power a fanatical adherent of individualism. The Fordist Left has died because it did not know how to impart the spirit of initiative, or human warmth, to solidarity. For a long time it believed that it would impose solidarity upon capitalism solely via the state, from on high. It neglected the importance of direct initiative on the part of workers and citizens. And it has rediscovered a taste for autonomy only to make a present of it to enterprise. Out of the ashes, is it possible today to image a form of solidarity that would transcend the administrative kind? Can initiative be conceived in a form other than that of free enterprise?

Thinking through a new alliance between initiative and solidarity is no easy matter. The connection even seems contradictory. It presupposes face-to-face contact and negotiation at the base. In short, it privileges the local[7] as the site of democratic regulation in the first (procedural) sense of the term: a direct encounter between, on the one hand, resources, know-how, spirit of initiative, imagination and, on the other hand, the inventory of unsatisfied needs, the necessary compromises. This implies people sitting around a table on which sometimes divergent interests are put, but no longer merely as a matter of paying or making pay. It is known on whom each sacrifice will fall; the mutual benefits are also calculated. The fact that a factory which discharges waste creates jobs but pollutes a river, that a better-trimmed hedge yields more than a direct path for a tractor, can no longer be ignored. Behind monetary fluctuations, material and human realities are weighed up. An overall ecology replaces a financial economy, in rural and urban milieux alike. The welfare state becomes the welfare community.

Caution! Local development and local democracy are not a paradise where all are sisters and brothers. Oppositions persist. But mutual interest in advancement is no longer drowned in the hollow rhetoric of the 'collective interest'. The struggle for equality and justice is conducted more sharply: 'today you gain more than me, but I gain as well, and tomorrow I will remind you that you need me.' There is no longer an 'external force' (the central state) whose role is to settle all accounts. Each party becomes conscious that contempt for the other does not pay. Gradually, there is a transition from pure self-interest to genuine solidarity: a consciousness that one's own freedom of action, one's own well-being, depends upon advancement of the freedom, the success and the well-being of the person opposite.

We first came across the local, or the regional, when we evoked the new social pact (the dynamic guarantee of employment), when we emphasized the decisive role of partnership between unions, employers, local government and a system of local training. To the network of enterprises helping one another locally, sustained by a population which in return demands jobs and observance of ecological standards, we then added 'intermediate agencies' in the collective service of the local population. There should be no Chinese wall between these agencies and local private enterprises, set up with the aid of the collectivity: individuals may change sector; agencies of socially useful work which have become profitable in a particular 'niche' may become private, unsubsidized enterprises.

But who is going to define social usefulness? Who is going to assign it its domain, so as to avoid enterprises in the third sector 'eating into' unsubsidized activities? Who else, if not the users and the local authorities elected by them? Radical reform of the welfare state will thus involve radical decentralization as regards its management, even if financing it must remain largely national and even continental.[8]

But the risks of a local solution remain: a patchwork of subsistence activities; an inability to release funds to promote initiatives; the competition of other regions; the temptation to revert to the status of assisted consumer. Solidarity and local initiative will only be able to blossom by expanding their horizon to the whole world – and, in the first instance, to that site of the social contract where the rules of the game are decided, namely the national state, even if the latter is extended to operate at a continental level (without forgetting co-development agreements with the Third World). Without supraregional authorities which decide the rules of the game, the regions, the 'countries', risk finding themselves in a situation of 'free competition', one pitted against another to the detriment of the least well-off. There can be no local development without national and international solidarity. It is reasonable to assume that for the foreseeable future the regulation of the rules of the game and the equalization of interregional finances will remain the preserve of representative (electoral) democracy – doubtless extended to a European scale – and that the establishment of a non-aggressive international order will remain the business of state power relationships and diplomacy.

But hierarchies are overturned. We no longer expect change below to come from change on high. Rather, people demand change above in order to consolidate and develop the results of initiative from below. In the words of an organizer of local initiatives for the regeneration of the 'Rustbelt' of the north-eastern USA, 'perhaps in ten years time we will be considered pioneers. Perhaps we will be swept aside by macroeconomic forces outside our control. But in any case, what we are trying to do seems to me to be the only honourable course in the current situation' (Jack Russel, quoted in Messine, 1987, p. 41).

CONCLUSION

On closer examination, democracy proves to be a notion with two distinct registers. Within a given societal paradigm it takes the form of popular participation in the regulation of differences over supposedly established rights. Between paradigms it seems like a scale of value measuring the enlargement of real rights. Given that the scope of these 'rights' can be extended to spheres which were inconceivable within previous paradigms, democracy in this sense is an invention of each century.

The Fordist compromise, which was the summit of the success of the working class movement in Western Europe in the second half of the twentieth century, guaranteed a right to the 'organicist' redistribution of the fruits of technical progress. But it reinforced the hierarchical character of labour organization and society, by delegating power to technocratic castes. The crisis of Fordism opens the way to a regression which is just as hierarchical, but a lot less organicist: liberal-productivism.

This is not the only path possible at the crossroads of the twenty-first century. A democratic alternative remains viable, reconciling organicism and the reduction of hierarchies, extending the scope of democracy to labour organization and social solidarity. It is based upon the collectively negotiated involvement of the producers, the dynamic guarantee of employment and the enhancement of free time. It implies a profound transformation of the 'welfare state' into the 'welfare community'. The forms of direct, and hence local, demographic regulation will play a determining role. With his concept of 'participatory democracy', Macpherson (1977) came close to the same idea in the late 1970s.

But such an alternative could not be stabilized outside the context of a 'non-aggressive' global economic order, whose definition and character exceed the scope of this chapter and also, regrettably, the known framework of democracy.

NOTES

1   The work of the 'regulation school' initially focused on the economy (CEPREMAP, 1977; Aglietta, 1979). An international conference in Barcelona in 1988 indicated the possible extension of the approach to other disciplines in the social sciences (e.g. Lipietz, 1988a). Here I shall be presenting the methodology developed jointly with Jane Jenson in the sphere of political science (Jenson, 1987, 1989a, b; Lipietz, 1988b, 1991).
2   For a brief account of Fordism and its crisis see, for example, Lipietz (1985).
3   Since the entrepreneur is usually a man, it makes no sense here to stick to gender-neutral formulations. The reality is *not* gender-neutral.
4   For a fuller presentation of the democratic alternative, including its international and globally ecological dimensions, see Lipietz (1989, 1993).
5   On the welfare state and the critique of it (left- and right-wing), see Rowbotham et al. (1979), Gough (1983) and Lipietz (1983).
6   On universal allocation (or basic income), see the debates in *Cahier du Movement Anti-Utilitariste dans les Sciences Sociales*, no. 23, 1987.
7   For the renewed importance of the 'local', see Chassagne and de Romefort (1987).
8   On these 'contractual' relations, see Eme and Laville (1988).

REFERENCES

Aglietta, M. (1979) *A Theory of Capitalist Regulation: the US Experience*. London: New Left Books.

CEPREMAP (1977) Approches de l'inflation: l'exemple français. Mimeo, Paris.

Chassagne, M. and de Romefort, A. (1987) *Initiative et solidarité: l'affaire de tous*. Paris: Syros.

Eme, B. and Laville, J.-L. (1988) *Les 'petits boulots' en question*. Paris: Syros.

Gough, I. (1983) Thatcherism, the New Right and the welfare state. *Cahiers de l'Association Canadienne-Française pour l'Avancement de les Sciences*, no. 16.

Jenson, J. (1987) Gender and reproduction or, babies and the state, *Studies in Political Economy*, 20, 9–46.

Jenson, J. (1989a) Paradigms and political discourse: protective legislation in the USA and France before 1914. *Canadian Journal of Political Science*, 22, 235–58.

Jenson, J. (1989b) Different but not 'exceptional': Canada's permeable Fordism. *Canadian Review of Sociology and Anthropology*, special issue on comparative macrosociology, Winter, 69–97.

Leborgne, D. and Lipietz, A. (1987) L'après-Fordism et son espace. *Les Temps Modernes*, 501, 73–114.

Lipietz, A. (1983) Crise de l'état-providence. *Les Temps Modernes*, 448.

Lipietz, A. (1985) *Mirages et Miracles*. Paris: La Découverte (translated into English as *Mirages and Miracles. The Crisis of Global Fordism*. London: Verso).

Lipietz, A. (1988a) Reflections on a tale: the Marxist foundations of the concepts of regulation and accumulation. *Studies in Political Economy*, 27, 7–36.

Lipietz, A. (1988b) La trame, la chaîne et la régulation: outils pour les sciences sociales. Paper presented at the Colloque international sur la théorie de la régulation, Barcelona 16–18 June (translated into English in G. Benko and U. Strumayer (eds), *Space and Social Theory*. Oxford: Blackwell).

Lipietz, A. (1988c) Building an alternative movement in France. *Rethinking Marxism*, 1, 8–99.

Lipietz, A. (1989) *Cholsir l'audace. Une alternative pour le xxie siècle*. Paris: Le Découverte (translated into English as *Towards a New Economic Order. Postfordism, Ecology and Democracy*. Oxford: Oxford University Press).

Lipietz, A. (1991) Governing the economy in the face of international challenge: from national developmentalism to national crisis. In J. F. Hollifield and G. Ross (eds), *Searching for the New France*. New York: Routledge.

Lipietz, A. (1993) *Vert-Espérance*. Paris: La Découverte.

Macpherson, C. B. (1962) *The Political Theory of Possessive Individualism*. Oxford: Oxford University Press.

Macpherson, C. B. (1977) *The Life and Times of Liberal Democracy*. Oxford: Oxford University Press.

Messine, P. (1987) *Les Saturniens*. Paris: La Découverte.

Rowbotham, S., Segal, L. and Wainwright, H. (1979) *Beyond the Fragments*. London: Merlin Press.

Part IV
Post-Fordist City Lives and Lifestyles

12

Flexible Accumulation through Urbanization: Reflections on 'Post-modernism' in the American City

David Harvey

Proletarian revolution is the critique of human geography through which individuals and communities have to create places and events suitable for their own appropriation, no longer just of their labour, but of their total history. (Guy Debord, *Society of the Spectacle*)

Times are hard, but (post) modern. (Adaptation of an Italian saying)

INTRODUCTION

Christopher Jencks (1984: 9) dates the symbolic end of modernist architecture and the passage to the post-modern as 3.32 p.m. on 15 July 1972, when the Pruitt-Igoe Housing development (a version of Le Corbusier's 'machine for modern living') was dynamited as an unlivable environment for the low-income people it housed. Shortly thereafter, President Nixon officially declared the urban crisis over.

1972 is not a bad date for symbolizing all kinds of other transitions in the political economy of advanced capitalism. It is roughly since then that the capitalist world, shaken out of the suffocating torpor of the stagflation that brought the long post-war boom to a wimpering end, has begun to evolve a seemingly new and quite different regime of capital

This chapter is a reprint of an article published in *Antipode* (1987), vol. 19, no. 3, pp. 260–86.

accumulation. Set in motion during the severe recession of 1973–5 and further consolidated during the equally savage deflation of 1981–2 (the 'Reagan' recession) the new regime is marked by a startling flexibility with respect to labour processes, labour markets, products, and patterns of consumption (see Armstrong et al., 1984; Aglietta, 1974; Piore and Sabel, 1984; Scott and Storper, 1986; Harvey, 1987). It has, at the same time, entrained rapid shifts in the patterning of uneven development, between both sectors and geographical regions – a process aided by the rapid evolution of entirely new financial systems and markets. These enhanced powers of flexibility and mobility have permitted the new regime to be imposed upon a labour force already weakened by two savage bouts of deflation that saw unemployment rise to unprecedented post-war levels in all the advanced capitalist countries (save, perhaps, Japan). Rapid displacements, for example, from the advanced capitalist countries to the newly industrializing countries or from skilled manufacturing to unskilled service jobs hammered home the weakness of labour and its inability to resist sustained levels of high unemployment, rapid destruction and reconstruction of skills, and modest (if any) increases in the real wage. Political economic circumstances also undermined the power of the state to protect the social wage, even in those countries with governments seriously committed to defence of the welfare state. Though the politics of resistance may have varied, austerity and fiscal retrenchment, sometimes accompanied by the resurgence of a virulent neo-conservatism, have become widespread in the advanced capitalist world.

What is remarkable about cultural and intellectual life since 1972 is how it, too, has been radically transformed in ways that appear to parallel these political-economic transformations. Consider, for example, the practices of 'high modernity of the international style' as practised in 1972. Modernism had by then lost all semblance of social critique. The protopolitical or Utopian programme (the transformation of all of social life by way of the transformation of space) had failed (Jameson, 1984a) and modernism had become closely linked to capital accumulation through a project of Fordist modernization characterized by rationality, functionality and efficiency. By 1972, modernist architecture was as stifling and torporous as the corporate power it represented. Stagflation in architectural practice paralleled the stagflation of capitalism (perhaps it was no accident that Venturi, Scott Brown and Izenour published *Learning from Las Vegas* in 1972). Critics of modernity had been around for a very long time (think of Jane Jacobs's *Life and Death of Great American Cities*, published in 1961) and there was a sense, of course, in which the revolutionary cultural movement of the 1960s was fashioned as a critical response to rationality, functionality and efficiency in everything. But it took the 1973 crisis sufficiently to shake up the relationship between art and society to allow post-modernism to become both accepted and institutionalized.

'Post-modernism' is, however, a most contentious term. Most agree that it entails some kind of reaction to 'modernism'. But since the meaning of that term is a muddle, the reactions to it are doubly so. There appears, however, to be some kind of consensus 'that the typical post-modernist artefact is playful, pluralist, self-ironizing and even schizoid; and that it reacts to the austere autonomy of high modernism by impudently embracing the language of commerce and the commodity.' Furthermore, 'its stance towards cultural tradition is one of irreverent pastiche, and its contrived depthlessness undermines all metaphysical solemnities, sometimes by a brutal aesthetics of squalor and shock' (Eagleton, 1987). But even in a field like architecture, where the 'artefact' is clearly in view and writers like Jencks (1984) have sought to define what post-modernism is about, the meaning and definition of the term still remains in contention. In other fields, where post-modernism has become intertwined with post-structuralism, deconstruction and the like, matters have become even more obscure (see Huyssen, 1984). In the urban context, therefore, I shall simply characterize post-modernism as signifying a break with the idea that planning and development should focus on large-scale, technologically rational, austere and functionally efficient 'international style' design and that vernacular traditions, local history and specialized spatial designs ranging from functions to intimacy to grand spectacle should be approached with a much greater eclecticism of style.

This kind of post-modernism, it seems to me, seeks some kind of accommodation with the more flexible regime of accumulation that has emerged since 1973. It has sought a creative and active rather than a passive role in the promotion of new cultural attitudes and practices consistent with flexible accumulation, even though some of its defenders, such as Frampton (1985), see it as containing potentialities for resistance as well as conformity to capitalist imperatives. The institutionalization and hegemony of 'post-modernism' rests, therefore, upon the creation of a distinctive 'cultural logic' in late capitalism (Jameson, 1984b).

One other element to the picture must be considered. Not only have capitalism and its associated cultural and ideological practices together undergone a sea change, but our 'discourses' (to use the current buzz-word) have likewise shifted. The deconstruction of structuralist interpretations, the abandonment of theory for empiricism in much of social science, the general backing away from Marxism (for both political and intellectual reasons) and the sense of futility in the realm of real representation (the impenetrability of 'the other' and the reduction of all meaning to a 'text') make it very difficult to preserve any sense of continuity to our understanding of that transformation that set in around 1972. We talked about the world in a different way, used a different language then, compared to now. Yet here, too, I think a case can be made that the political–economic transformations achieved through a succession of economic crises and working class defeats have affected discourses as well as cultural and ideological practices (see Harvey and Scott, 1989). That sounds like, and is, old-fashioned Marxian argument. But I cannot help but be impressed at the way in which a whole world of thought and cultural practice, of economy and institutions, of politics and ways of relating, began to crumble as we watched the dust explode upwards and the walls of Pruitt-Igoe come crashing down.

FLEXIBLE ACCUMULATION THROUGH URBANIZATION

An understanding of urbanization, I have argued elsewhere (Harvey, 1985a, b) is critical for understanding the historical geography of capitalism. It has partly been through shifts in the urban process that the new systems of flexible accumulation have been so successfully implanted. But also, as various historians of the rise of modernism have pointed out, there is an intimate connection between aesthetic and cultural movement and the changing nature of the urban experience (Berman, 1982; Bradbury and McFarlane, 1976; Clark, 1984; Frisby, 1986). It seems reasonable, therefore, to look at transitions in the urban process as a key point of integration of the political–economic move towards flexible accumulation and the cultural–aesthetic trend towards post-modernism.

Urbanization has, like everything else, dramatically changed its spots in the United States since 1972. The global deflation of 1973–5 put incredible pressure on the employment base of many urban regions. A combination of shrinking markets, unemployment, rapid shifts in spatial constraints and the global division of labour, capital flight, plant closings, technological and financial reorganization, lay at the root of that pressure. The geographical dispersal was not only to other regions and nations. It included yet another phase of urban deconcentration of populations and production beyond the suburbs and into rural and small-town America in a way that almost seemed like the fulfilment of Marx's prediction of the 'urbanization of the countryside'. Fixed capital investments and physical infrastructures in existing locations were consequently threatened with massive devaluation, thus undermining the property tax base and fiscal capacity of many urban governments at a time of increasing social need. To the degree that federal redistributions also became harder to capture (this was the import of Nixon's declaration in 1973), so social consumption was reduced forcing more and more governments to a political economy of retrenchment and disciplinary action against municipal employees and the local real wage. It was exactly in such a context that New York City went into technical bankruptcy in 1975, presaging a wave of fiscal distress and radical restructuring for many US cities (Szelenyi, 1984; Clavel et al., 1980; Fainstein et al., 1986; Tabb, 1982).

Ruling class alliances in urban regions were willy-nilly forced (no matter what their composition) to adopt a much more competitive posture. Managerialism, so characteristic of urban governance in the 1960s, was replaced by entrepreneurialism as the main motif of urban action (Hanson, 1983; Bouinot, 1987). The rise of the 'entrepreneurial city' meant increased inter-urban competition across a number of dimensions. I have elsewhere argued (Harvey, 1985a, chapter 8) that the competition can best be broken down into four different forms: (a) competition for position in the international division of labour; (b) competition for position as centres of consumption; (c) competition for control and command functions (financial and administrative powers in particular); and (d) competition for governmental redistributions (which in the United States, as Markusen (1986) has shown, focused heavily these last few years on military expenditures). These four options are not mutually exclusive and the uneven fortunes of urban regions have depended upon the mix and timing of strategies pursued in relation to global shifts.

It was in part through this heightened inter-urban competition that flexible accumulation took such a firm hold. The result has been, however, rapid oscillations in urban fortunes and in the patterning of uneven geographical development (see Smith, 1984). Houston and Denver, both boom towns in the mid-1970s, are suddenly caught short in the collapse of oil prices after 1981, Silicon Valley, the high-tech wonder of new products and new employment in the 1970s, suddenly loses its competitive edge, while New York and the once-jaded economies of New England rebound vigorously in the 1980s on the basis of expanding command and control functions and even new-found manufacturing strength. Two other more general effects have then followed.

First, inter-urban competition has opened spaces within which the new and more flexible labour processes could be more easily implanted and opened the way to much more flexible currents of geographical mobility than was the case before 1973. Concern for a favourable 'business climate', for example, has pushed urban governments to all kinds of measures (from wage-disciplining to public investments) in order to attract economic development, but in the process has lessened the cost of change of location to the enterprise. Much of the vaunted 'public–private partnership' of today amounts to a subsidy for affluent consumers, corporations and powerful command functions to stay in town at the expense of local collective consumption for the working class and the impoverished. Second, urban governments have been forced into innovation and investment to make their cities more attractive as consumer and cultural centers. Such innovations and investments (convention centres, sports stadia, Disney Worlds, downtown consumer paradises, etc.) have quickly been imitated elsewhere. Inter-urban competition has thus generated leap-frogging urban innovations in life-styles, cultural forms, products and even political and consumer based innovation, all of which has actively promoted the transition to flexible accumulation. And herein, I shall argue, lies part of the secret of the passage to post-modernity in urban culture.

This connection can be seen in the radical reorganization of the interior spaces of the contemporary US city under the impulsions of inter-urban competition. I preface the account, however, with some general remarks on the class content of spatial practices in urban settings.

THE CLASS CONTENT OF SPATIAL PRACTICES IN URBAN SETTINGS

Spatial practices in any society abound in subtleties and complexities. Since they are not innocent with respect to the accumulation of capital and the reproduction of class relations under capitalism, they are a permanent arena for social conflict and struggle. Those who have the power to command and produce space possess a vital instrumentality for the reproduction and enhancement of their own power. Any project to transform society must, therefore, grasp the complex nettle of the transformation of spatial practices.

I shall try to capture some of the complexity through construction of a 'grid' of spatial practices (Figure 12.1). Down the left hand side I range three dimensions identified in Lefebvre's *The Production of Space*:

1 *Material spatial practices* refer to the physical and material flows, transfers and interactions that occur in and across space in such a way as to assure production and social reproduction.
2 *Representations of space* encompass all the signs and significations, codes and knowledge, that allow such material practices to be talked about and understood, no matter whether in terms of everyday common sense or

through the sometimes arcane jargon of the academic disciplines that deal with spatial practices (engineering, architecture, geography, planning, social ecology and the like).

3 *Spaces of representation* are social inventions (codes, signs and even material constructs such as symbolic spaces, particular built environments, paintings, museums and the like) that seek to generate new meanings or possibilities for spatial practices.

Lefebvre characterizes these three dimensions as the *experienced*, the *perceived* and the *imagined*. He regards the dialectical relations between them as the fulcrum of a dramatic tension through which the history of spatial practices can be read. The relations are, however, problematic. A 'vulgar Marxist' position would presumably hold that material spatial practices directly determine both the representations of space and the spaces of representation. Marx (1967, 1973) did not hold such a view. He depicts knowledge as a material productive force in the *Grundrisse* (pp. 699–701) and writes in a justly famous passage in *Capital* (vol. 1: 178): 'What distinguishes the worst of architects from the best of bees is this, that the architect raises his structure in imagination before he erects it in reality.' The spaces of representation, therefore, have the potential not only to affect representation of space but also to act as a material productive force with respect to spatial practices.

But to argue that the relations between the experienced, the perceived and the imagined are dialectically rather than causally determined leaves things much too vague. Bourdieu (1977) provides a clarification. He explains how 'a matrix of perceptions, appreciations, and actions' can at one and the same time be put to work flexibly to 'achieve infinitely diversified tasks' while at the same time being 'in the last instance' (Engels's famous phrase) engendered out of the material experience of 'objective structures' and therefore 'out of the economic basis of the social formation in question'. Bourdieu accepts the 'well-founded primacy of objective relations' without, however, making the false inference that the objective structures are themselves endowed with a power of autonomous development independent of human agency.

The mediating link is provided by the concept of 'habitus' – a 'durably installed generative principle of regulated improvisations' which 'produces practices' that in turn tend to reproduce the objective conditions which produced the generative principle of habitus in the first place. The circular (even cumulative?) causation is obvious. Bourdieu's conclusion is, however, a very striking depiction of the constraints to the power of the imagined over the experienced:

> Because the habitus is an endless capacity to engender products –
> thoughts, perceptions, expressions, actions – whose limits are set by the

Figure 12.1 A 'grid' of spatial practices

	ACCESSIBILITY AND DISTANCIATION	APPROPRIATION AND USE OF SPACE	DOMINATION AND CONTROL OF SPACE
MATERIAL SPATIAL PRACTICES (EXPERIENCE)	Flows of goods, money, people, labour power, information, etc.; transport and communications systems; market and urban hierarchies; agglomeration	Urban built environments social spaces of the city and other 'turf' designations; social networks of communication and mutual aid	Private property in land, state and administrative divisions of space; exclusive communities and neighbourhoods; exclusionary zoning and other forms of social control (policing and surveillance)
REPRESENTATIONS OF SPACE (PERCEPTION)	Social psychological and physical measures of distance; map-making; theories of the 'friction of distance' (principle of least effort, social physics, range of a good, central place and other forms of location theory)	Personal space; mental maps of occupied space; spatial hierarchies; symbolic representation of spaces	Forbidden spaces, 'territorial imperatives'; community; regional culture; nationalism; geopolitics; hierarchies
SPACES OF REPRESENTATION (IMAGINATION)	'Media is the message'; new modes of spatial transaction (radio, TV, film, photography, painting etc.); diffusion of 'taste'	Popular spectacles; street demonstrations, riots; places of popular spectacle (streets, squares, markets); iconography and graffiti	Organized spectacles; monumentality and constructed spaces of ritual; symbolic barriers and signals of symbols capital

historically and socially situated conditions of its production, the conditioning and conditional freedom it secures is as remote from a creation of unpredictable novelty as it is from a simple mechanical reproduction of the initial conditionings. *(Bourdieu, 1977: 95)*

I accept that theorization and will later make considerable use of it. Across the top of the grid (Figure 12.1) I list three other aspects to spatial practice drawn from more conventional understandings:

1 *Accessibility and distanciation* speaks to the role of the 'friction of distance' in human affairs. Distance is both a barrier to and a defence against human interaction. It imposes transaction costs upon any system of production and reproduction (particularly those based on any elaborate social division of labour, trade and social differentiation of reproductive functions). Distanciation (cf. Giddens, 1984: 258–9) is simply a measure of the degree to which the friction of space has been overcome to accommodate social interaction.

2 The *appropriation of space* examines the way in which space is used and occupied by individuals, classes or other social groupings. Systematized and institutionalized appropriation may entail the production of territorially bounded forms of social solidarity.

3 The *domination of space* reflects how individuals or powerful groups dominate the organization and production of space so as to exercise a greater degree of control either over the friction of distance or over the manner in which space is appropriated by themselves or others.

These three dimensions to spatial practice are not independent of each other. The friction of distance is implicit in any understanding of the domination and appropriation of space, while the persistent appropriation of a space by a particular group (say the gang that hangs out on the street corner) amounts to a *de facto* domination of that space. Furthermore, the attempt to dominate space, insofar as it requires reductions in the friction of distance (capitalism's 'annihilation of space through time', for example) alters distanciation.

This grid of spatial practices tells us nothing important in itself. Spatial practices derive their efficacy in social life only through the structure of social relations within which they come into play. Under the social relations of capitalism, the spatial practices become imbued with class meanings. To put it this way is not, however, to argue that spatial practices are derivative of capitalism. The spatial practices take on specific meanings and these meanings are put into motion and spaces used in a particular way through the agency of class, gender or other social practices.[1] When placed in the context of capitalist social relations and imperatives (the accumulation of capital), therefore, the grid can help us unravel some of the complexity that prevails in the field of contemporary spatial practices.

My purpose in setting up the grid was not, however, to set about a systematic exploration of the positions within it, though such an examination would be of considerable interest (and I have penned in a few controversial positionings within the grid for purposes of illustration). My purpose is to find a way to characterize the radical shifts in the class content and the nature of spatial practices that have occurred over the last two decades. The pressure to reorganize the interior space of the city, for example, has been considerable under conditions of flexible accumulation. The vitality of the central city core has been re-emphasized, themes such as the quality of urban living (gentrification, consumption palaces and sophisticated entertainment) and enhanced social control over both public and private spaces within the city have been of widespread significance. But the urban process has also had to cope with increasing impoverishment and unemployment, under conditions where the social wage could not be increased. Here, too, spatial practices have shifted in part towards an increasing control through a return to ghettoization (a practice that was never, of course, severely dented let alone overcome) and the rise of new spaces where the homeless wander, the schizophrenics and discharged mental patients hang out, and the impoverished practise both new and well-tried survival strategies. How, then, are we to make sense of all this shifting and conflict prone spatialization of class polarities? Are there ways, furthermore, to address the question of spatial enpowerment of the segregated, oppressed and impoverished populations increasingly to be found in all urban areas?

CLASS PRACTICES AND THE CONSTRUCTION OF COMMUNITY[2]

Different classes construct their sense of territory and community in radically different ways. This elemental fact is often overlooked by those theorists who presume *a priori* that there is some ideal-typical and universal tendency for all human beings to construct a human community of roughly similar sort, no matter what the political or economic circumstances. A study of class agency with respect to community construction under conditions of contemporary urbanization illustrates how essentially similar spatial practices can have radically different class contents.

Let us look, more closely, for example, at the class practices through which communities are typically constructed in urban settings. We here encounter all the flexibility and adaptability of perceptions, appreciations and actions that Bourdieu insists upon. But the contrast between community construction in low income and disempowered strata and in affluent and empowered strata of the population is indeed striking.

Low income populations, usually lacking the means to overcome and hence command space, find themselves for the most part trapped in space. Since ownership of even basic means of reproduction (such as housing) is restricted, the main way to dominate space is through continuous appropriation. Exchange values are scarce, and so the pursuit of use values for daily survival is central to social action. This means frequent material and interpersonal transactions and the formation of very small scale communities. Within the community space, use values get shared through some mix of mutual aid and mutual predation, creating tight but often highly conflictual interpersonal social bonding in both private and public spaces. The result is an often intense attachment to place and 'turf' and an exact sense of boundaries because it is only through active appropriation that control over space is assured.

Successful control presumes a power to exclude unwanted elements. Fine-tuned ethnic, religious, racial and status discriminations are frequently called into play within such a process of community construction. Furthermore, political organization takes a special form, generally expressive of a culture of political resistance and hostility to normal channels of political incorporation. The state is largely experienced as an agency of repressive control (in police, education, etc.) rather than as an agency that can be controlled by and bring benefits to them (see, Willis, 1977). Political organizations of a participatory sort are, as Crenson (1983) observes, weakly developed and politics of the bourgeois sort understood as irrelevant to the procuring of the use values necessary for daily survival. Nevertheless, the state intervenes in such communities since they are vital preserves of the reserve army of the unemployed, spaces of such deprivation that all sorts of contagious social ills (from prostitution to tuberculosis) can flourish, and spaces that appear dangerous precisely because they lie outside of the normal processes of social incorporation.

Contrast this with the practices of affluent groups, who can command space through spatial mobility and ownership of basic means of reproduction (houses, cars, etc.). Already blessed with abundant exchange values with which to sustain life, they are in no way dependent upon community-provided use values for survival. The construction of community is then mainly geared to the preservation or enhancement of exchange values. Use values relate to matters of accessibility, taste, tone, aesthetic appreciation, and the symbolic and cultural capital that goes with possession of a certain kind of 'valued' built environment. Interpersonal relations are unnecessary at the street level and the command over space does not have to be assured through continuous appropriation. Money provides access to the community, making it less exclusionary on other grounds (residential segregation by ethnicity and even race tends to weaken the further up the income scale one goes). Boundaries are diffuse and flexible, mainly dependent upon the spatial field of externality effects that can affect individual property values. Community organizations form to take care of externality effects and maintain the 'tone' of the community space. The state is seen as basically beneficial and controllable, assuring security and helping keep undesirables out, except in unusual circumstances (the location of 'noxious' facilities, the construction of highways, etc.)

Distinctive spatial practices and processes of community construction – coupled with distinctive cultural practices and ideological predispositions – arise out of different material circumstances. Conditions of economic oppression and socio-political domination generate quite different kinds of spatial practices and styles of community formation than will typically be found under other class circumstances.

INFORMALIZATION, THE PRODUCTION OF SYMBOLIC CAPITAL, AND THE MOBILIZATION OF THE SPECTACLE

Flexible accumulation has deeply affected class structures and political-economic possibilities so as to modify the processes of community production, while re-emphasizing the importance of the class content of spatial practices. I will look briefly at three aspects of this transformation.

Impoverishment and informalization

The United States has experienced an increase in the sheer numbers of the urban poor since 1972. The composition of this poverty population has also changed. Unemployed blue-collar workers thrown on the street by de-industrialization and the flood of displaced people out of depressed rural or regional economies or from Third World countries have been piled on top of what Marx called the 'hospital' of the working class, left to fend for itself in the cities. In some cases, particular urban communities tied to a dominant local employment source have been plunged as a whole into a condition of impoverishment by a single plant closing. In other instances, particularly vulnerable groups, such as female-headed households, have been plunged deeper into the mire of poverty, thus creating zones where phenomena like the feminization of poverty become dominant. Fiscal constraints, of which neo-conservativism has made a political virtue rather than an economic necessity, have at the same time undercut the flow of public services and hence the life-support mechanisms for the mass of the unemployed and the poor.

Learning to cope and survive in urban settings on almost no income is an art that takes a while to learn. The balance between competition, mutual predation and mutual aid has consequently shifted within low income populations. The growth of impoverishment has, paradoxically, led to a diminution of the power of some of the more positive mechanisms to cope with it. But there has also been one other dramatic response – the rise of what is known as the 'informal sector' in American cities (focusing on illegal practices such as drug-trafficking and prostitution, and legal production and trading of services). Most observers (see Castells and Portes, 1987) agree that these practices expanded in scope and form after 1972. Furthermore, the same phenomena were observed in European cities, thus bringing the urban process in the advanced capitalist countries as a whole much closer to the Third World urban experience (Redclift and Mingione, 1985).

The nature and form of informalization varies greatly, depending upon the opportunities to find local markets for goods and services, the qualities of the reserve army of labour power (its skills and aptitudes), gender relations (for women play a very conspicuous role in organizing informal economies), the presence of small-scale entrepreneurial skills and the willingness of the authorities (regulatory and oversight powers like the unions) to tolerate practices that are often outside the law.

Low income communities present, in the first place, a vast reserve of labour power under strong pressure in these times to find a living of almost any sort.

Under conditions of government laxness and trade union weakness, new kinds of production of goods and services can arise, sometimes organized from outside the community but in other instances organized by entrepreneurs within the low income community itself. Homework has become much more prominent, allowing women, for example, to combine the tasks of child-rearing and productive labour in the same space, while saving entrepreneurs the costs of overhead (plant, lighting, etc.). Sweatshops and the informal provision of services began to emerge as vital aspects of the New York and Los Angeles economies in the 1970s and by now have become important throughout the US urban system. These have been paralleled by an increasing commodification of traditional mutual aid systems within low income communities. Baby-sitting, laundering, cleaning, fixing up and odd jobs, which used to be swapped more as favours, are now bought and sold, sometimes on an entrepreneurial basis.

Social relations within many low income communities have, as a consequence, become much more entrepreneurial, with all of the consequences of excessive and often extraordinary exploitation (particularly of women) in the labour process. The flow of incomes into such communities has increased but at the expense of traditional mutual aid systems and the stronger implantation of social hierarchies within the communities themselves. The flow of value out of such communities has also increased substantially. This has led many to look with surprise at the local dynamics of urban development and to argue for the toleration, acceptance and even encouragement of informalization, thus lending credence to the neo-conservative argument that private entrepreneurial activity is always the path to economic growth and success – as if that could solve the problems of all the poor rather than those of just a select few. Nevertheless, the growth of informalization – and the emergence of unregulated urban spaces within which such practices are tolerated – is a phenomenon thoroughly consistent with the new regime of flexible accumulation.

The production of symbolic capital

The frenetic pursuit of the consumption dollars of the affluent has led to a much stronger emphasis upon product differentiation under the regime of flexible accumulation. Producers have, as a consequence, begun to explore the realms of differentiated tastes and aesthetic preferences in ways that were not so necessary under a Fordist regime of standardized accumulation through mass production. In so doing they have re-emphasized a powerful aspect of capital accumulation: the production and consumption of what Bourdieu (1977: 171–97; 1984) calls 'symbolic capital'. This has had important implications for the production and transformation of the urban spaces in which upper income groups live.

'Symbolic capital' is defined by Bourdieu as 'the collection of luxury goods attesting the taste and distinction of the owner'. Such capital is, of course, a transformed kind of money capital, but 'produces its proper effect inasmuch, and only inasmuch, as it conceals the fact that it originates in "material" forms of capital which are also, in the last analysis, the source of its effects.' The fetishism involved is obvious, but it is here deliberately deployed to conceal, through the realms of culture and taste, the real bases of economic distinctions. Since 'the most successful ideological effects are those which have no words, and ask no more than complicitous silence', so the production of symbolic capital serves ideological functions, because the mechanisms through which it contributes 'to the reproduction of the established order and to the perpetuation of domination remain hidden' (Bourdieu, 1977: 188).

It is instructive to bring Bourdieu's theorizations to bear upon the production of upper class communities and their built environments. It has a lot to tell us about the material processes of gentrification, the recuperation of 'history' (real, imagined or simply re-created as pastiche) and of 'community' (again, real, imagined or simply packaged for sale by producers), and the need for embellishment, decoration and ornamentation that could function as so many codes and symbols of social distinction (cf. Simmel, 1978; Firey, 1945; Jager, 1986). I do not mean to argue that such phenomena are in any way new – they have been a vital feature to capitalist urbanization from the very beginning and, of course, bear more than a few echoes of distinctions passed on from older social orders. But they have become of much greater significance since 1972, in part through their proliferation into layers of the population that were hitherto denied them. Flexible accumulation permits a profitable response to the cultural discontents of the 1960s, which implied rejection of standardized accumulation and a mass culture that provided too few opportunities to capture symbolic capital. To the degree that political economic crisis encouraged the exploration of product differentiation, so the repressed market desire to acquire symbolic capital could be captured through the production of built environments (Smith and Lefaivre, 1984). And it was, of course, exactly this kind of desire that post-modernist architecture set out to satisfy. 'For the middle class suburbanite', Venturi et al. (1972: 154) observe, 'living, not in an antebellum mansion, but in a smaller version lost in a large space, identity must come through symbolic treatment of the form of the house, either through styling provided by the developer (for instance, split-level Colonial) or through a variety of symbolic ornaments applied thereafter by the owner.'

Symbolic capital is, however, open to devaluation or enhancement through changes in taste. If symbolic capital contains a hidden power of domination, then power relations are themselves vulnerable to mutations in taste. Since competition between producers and the machinations of consumers render taste insecure, struggles over fashion acquire a certain significance within the urban scene (see, e.g. Zukin's (1982) study of loft living). The power to dominate as well as the ability to convert symbolic into money capital becomes embedded in the cultural politics of the urban process. But that also implies that domination of space within the urban process has an even more vital cultural edge to it under a regime of flexible accumulation. To the degree that domination of whatever sort contains the potentiality of violent response on the part of the dominated, so here, too, a latent domain of conflict has been opened up for explicit articulation.

The mobilization of the spectacle

'Bread and Festivals' was the ancient Roman formula for social pacification of the restless plebs. The formula has been passed on into capitalist culture through, for example, Second Empire Paris, where festival and the urban spectacle became instruments of social control in a society riven by class conflict (Clark, 1985).

Since 1972, the urban spectacle has been transformed from counter-cultural events, anti-war demonstrations, street riots and the inner-city revolutions of the 1960s. It has been captured as both a symbol and instrument of community unification under bourgeois control in conditions where unemployment and impoverishment have been on the rise and objective conditions of class polarization have been increasing. As part of this process, the modernist penchant for monumentality – the communication of the permanence, authority and power of the established capitalist order – has been challenged by an 'official' post-modernist style that explores the architecture of festival and spectacle, with its sense of the ephemeral, of display and of transitory but participatory pleasure. The display of the commodity became a central part of the spectacle, as crowds flocked to gaze at them and at each other in intimate and secure spaces like Baltimore's Harbor Place, Boston's Faneuil Hall and a host of enclosed shopping malls that sprung up all over America. Even whole built environments became centrepieces of urban spectacle and display.

The phenomenon deserves more detailed scrutiny than I here can give. It fits, of course, with urban strategies to capture consumer dollars to compensate for de-industrialization. Its undoubted commercial success rests in part on the way in which the act of buying connects to the pleasure of the spectacle in secured spaces, safe from violence or political agitation. Baltimore's Harbor Place combines all the bourgeois virtues that Benjamin (1973: 158–65) attributed to the arcades of nineteenth century Paris with the sense of the festival that attached to world expositions, 'places of pilgrimage to the fetish Commodity'. Debord (1983) would take it further: 'the spectacle is the developed modern complement of money where the totality of the commodity world appears as a whole, as a general equivalence for what the entire society can be and can do'. To the degree that the spectacle becomes 'the common ground of deceived gaze and of false consciousness', so it can also present itself as 'an instrument of unification' (Debord, 1983). Mayor Schaefer and the urban class alliance ranged behind him in Baltimore consciously used the spectacle of Harbor Place precisely in that way, as a symbol of the supposed unity of a class-divided and racially segregated city. Professional sports activities and events like the Los Angeles Olympic Games perform a similar function in an otherwise fragmented urban society.

Urban life, under a regime of flexible accumulation, has thus increasingly come to present itself as an 'immense accumulation of spectacles'. American downtowns no longer communicate exclusively a monumental sense of power, authority and corporate domination. They instead express the idea of spectacle and play. It is on this terrain of the spectacle that the break into the post-modern urban culture that has accompanied flexible accumulation has partially been fashioned, and it is in the context of such mediating images that the oppositions of class consciousness and class practices have to unfold.[3] But, as Debord (1983) observes, the spectacle 'is never an image mounted securely and finally in place; it is always an account of the world competing with others, and meeting the resistance of different, sometimes tenacious forms of social practice'.

URBAN STRESS UNDER FLEXIBLE ACCUMULATION

Flexible accumulation has had a serious impact upon all urban economies. The increasing entrepreneurialism of many urban governments (particularly those that emphasized 'public–private partnership') tended to reinforce it and the neo-conservativism and post-modernist cultural trends that went with it. The use of increasingly scarce resources to capture development meant that the social consumption of the poor was neglected in order to provide benefits to keep the rich and powerful in town. This was the switch in direction that President Nixon signalled when he declared the urban crisis over in 1973. What that meant, of course, was the transmutation of urban stresses into new forms.

The internal adaptations within the city likewise played their part in facilitating and fomenting flexible accumulation. Poor populations had to become much more entrepreneurial, adopting, for example, 'informal' economic means to survive. Increasing competition for survival under conditions of increasing impoverishment meant serious erosion of traditional mutual aid mechanisms in urban communities that had little capacity to dominate space and were often disempowered with respect to normal processes of political integration. The ability to dominate space through communal solidarity and mutually supportive patterns of appropriation weakened at the very moment that many spaces became vulnerable to invasion and occupation by others. A tension arose between increasing unemployment of workers in traditional occupations and the employment growth triggered by downtown revivals based on financial services and the organization of spectacle. A new and relatively affluent generation of professional and managerial workers, raised on the cultural discontents with modernism in the 1960s, came to dominate whole zones of inner city urban space seeking product differentiation in built environments, quality of life and command of symbolic capital. The recuperation of 'history' and 'community' became essential selling gimmicks to the producers of built environments. Thus was the turn to post-modernist styles institutionalized.

There are serious social and spatial stresses inherent in such a situation. To begin with, increasing class polarization (symbolized by the incredible surge in urban poverty surrounding islands of startling and conspicuous wealth) is inherently dangerous, and given the processes of community construction available to the poor, it also sets the stage for increasing racial, ethnic, religious or simply 'turf' tensions. Fundamentally different class mechanisms for defining the spatiality of community come into conflict, thus sparking running guerilla warfare over who appropriates and controls various spaces of the city. The threat of urban violence, though not of the massive sort experienced in the 1960s, looms large. The breakdown of the processes that allow the poor to construct any sort of community of mutual aid is equally dangerous since it entails an increase in individual anomie, alienation, and all of the antagonisms that derive therefrom. The few who 'make it' through informal sector activity cannot compensate for the multitude who won't. At the other end of the social scale, the search for symbolic capital introduces a cultural dimension to political economic tensions. The latter feed inter-class hostilities and prompt state interventions that further alienate low income populations (I am thinking, for example, of the way street-corner youths get harassed in gentrifying neighbourhoods). The mobilization of the spectacle has its unifying effects, but it is a fragile and uncertain tool for unification, and to the degree that it forces the consumer to become 'a consumer of illusion' contains its own specific alienations. Controlled spectacles and festivals are one thing but riots and revolutions can also become 'festivals of the people'.

But there is a further contradiction. Heightened inter-urban competition produces socially wasteful investments that contribute to rather than ameliorate the over-accumulation problem that lay behind the transition to flexible accumulation in the first place (see Harvey and Scott, 1989). Put simply, how many successful convention centres, sports stadia, Disney Worlds and harbour places can there be? Success is often short-lived or rendered moot by competing or alternative innovations arising elsewhere. Over-investment in everything from shopping malls to cultural facilities makes the values embedded in urban space highly vulnerable to devaluation. Downtown revivals built upon burgeoning employment in financial and real estate services where people daily process loans and real estate deals for other people employed in financial services and real estate, depends upon a huge expansion of personal, corporate and governmental debt. If that turns sour, the effects will be far more devastating than the dynamiting of Pruitt-Igoe ever could symbolize. The rash of bank failures in Texas, Colorado and even California (many of them attributable to over-investment in real estate) suggests that there has been serious over-investment in urban redevelopment.

Flexible accumulation, in short, is associated with a highly fragile patterning of urban investment as well as increasing social and spatial polarization of urban class antagonisms.

POLITICAL RESPONSES

'Every established order tends to produce', Bourdieu (1977: 164) writes, 'the naturalization of its own arbitrariness.' The 'most important and best concealed' mechanism for so doing is 'the dialectic of the objective chances and the agent's aspirations, out of which arises the *sense of limits*, commonly called the *sense of reality*' which is 'the basis of the most ineradicable adherence to the established order.' Knowledge (perceived and imagined) thereby 'becomes an integral part of the power of society to reproduce itself'. The 'symbolic power to impose the principles of construction of reality – in particular, social reality – is a major dimension of political power.'

This is a key insight. It helps explain how even the most critical theorist can so easily end up reproducing 'adherence to the established order'. It explains Tafuri's (1976) conclusion (based on the history of avant-gardism and modernity in architecture) of the impossibility of any radical transformation of culture and therefore of any radical and transforming architectural practice in advance of any radical transformation in social relations. The insight compels scepticism towards those who have recently embraced post-modernism (or radical individualism or some other aspect of contemporary practice) as a radical and liberating break with the past. There is strong evidence that post-modernity is nothing more than the cultural clothing of flexible accumulation. 'Creative destruction' – that centrepiece of capitalist modernity – is just as central in daily life as it ever was. The difficulty, therefore, is to find a political response to the invariant and immutable truths of capitalism in general while responding to the particular forms of appearance that capitalism now exhibits under conditions of flexible accumulation. From that standpoint, therefore, let me explore some modest proposals.

Consider, first, exploring the interstices of present processes for points of resistance and empowerment. Decentralization and deconcentration taken together with the cultural concern with the qualities of place and space creates a political climate in which the politics of community, place and region can unfold in new ways, at the very moment when the cultural continuity of all places is seriously threatened by flexible accumulation. It is out of that sort of tension that Frampton (1985) advocates a regional architecture of resistance to the homogenizing forces of global capitalism and Rossi (1984) pursues an architecture expressive of the continuity of neighbourhood tradition and collective memory.[4] The cultural theses of post-modernity are, evidently, open to radical interpretation in the cause of greater empowerment of the poor and underprivileged. But that is small beer compared to the 'creative destruction' with which flexible accumulation typically scars the fabric of the city.

Flexible accumulation also opens up new paths of social change. Spatial dispersal means much greater geographical equality of opportunity to lure in new activities to even the smallest towns in the remotest region. Position within the urban hierarchy becomes less significant and large cities have lost their inherent political–economic power to dominate. Small towns that have managed to lure in new activities have often improved their position remarkably. But the chill winds of competition blow hard here too. It proves hard to hang on to activities even recently acquired. As many cities lose as gain by this. The ferment in labour markets has also undermined traditional union powers and opened up opportunities for migration, employment and self-employment for layers in the population once denied them (though under much more competitive circumstances leading to low wages and deteriorated work conditions for women, new migrants and ghettoized minorities). Flexible production opens up the possibility of cooperative forms of labour organization under a modicum of worker control. Piore and Sabel (1984) emphasize this argument and see this as a decisive moment in the history of capitalism when totally new and much more democratic forms of industrial organization can be implanted. This style of organization can also arise through the social consolidation of 'informal sector' activities as cooperative and worker controlled endeavours.

Conditions of flexible accumulation, in short, make worker and community control appear as a feasible alternative to capitalism. The emphasis of political ideology on the left has therefore shifted towards a 'feasible' decentralized socialism, thus drawing much more inspiration from social democracy and anarchism than from traditional Marxism. This corresponds with the vigorous external attack and internal critique of centralized planning mechanisms in the socialist countries (e.g. Nove, 1983).

Political practices on the left have evolved in much the same direction. Municipal socialism in Britain, economic democracy and community control in the United States and community mobilization by the 'Greens' in West Germany illustrate the trend. There is plainly much that can be done, at both local and regional levels, to defend and empower local interests. Community and religious organizations actively support plant buy-outs, fight plant closure and otherwise support the mutual aid mechanisms of traditional low income community solidarity. Institutions can also be persuaded to support the thrust for greater empowerment of the populations that surround them. A sympathetic state apparatus can find ways to support cooperatives (in service provision, housing provision and production) and perhaps find ways to encourage the formation of skills through the tapping of local talent. Financial institutions can be pressured into supporting community reinvestment, cooperative endeavours and neighbourhood development corporations. Even spectacles can be organized in a political cause. Planners can try to ensure that the transformations of neighbourhood will preserve rather than destroy collective memory. Far better that a deserted factory be turned into a community centre where the collective memory of those who lived and worked there is preserved rather than being turned into boutiques and condos that permit the appropriation of one people's history by another.

But there are acute dangers. Both the theory and the practices have the effect of reinforcing the fragmentations and reifications. It is invidious to regard places, communities, cities, regions or even nations as 'things in themselves' at a time when the global flexibility of capitalism is greater than ever. To follow that line of thinking is to be increasingly rather than less vulnerable in aggregate to the extraordinary centralized power of flexible accumulation. For it is just as geographically unprincipled and naive to ignore the qualities of a global process as it is to ignore the distinctive qualities of place and community. Practices fashioned only in the latter terms define a politics

of adaptation and submission, rather than of active resistance and of
socialist transformation.

Yet a global strategy of resistance and transformation has to begin
with the realities of place and community. The problem is to discover
a centralized politics that matches the increasingly centralized power
of flexible accumulation while remaining faithful to the grass-roots of
local resistances. The 'Greens' in West Germany and the Rainbow
Coalition in the United States appear to be taking up such questions.
The difficulty is to merge these freshly minted ideologies with a more
traditional oppositional politics shaped in response to a previous regime
of accumulation (without, however, embracing radical individualism,
neo-conservativism or post-modernism as signs of liberation). There is
plenty of scope here for progressive forces, at local, regional and
national levels, to do the hard practical and intellectual work of creating
a more unified oppositional force out of the maelstrom of social change
that flexible accumulation has unleashed.

This is mainly to speak, however, of the politics of resistance. What
of the politics of some more radical transformation? While capitalism is
always in a state of pre-socialism, it is scarcely on anyone's agenda these
days to think about something as daring as the transition to socialism.
Bourdieu (1977: 168), perhaps, provides a clue as to why: 'The critique
which brings the undiscussed into discussion, the unformulated into formulation, has as the condition of its possibility objective crisis, which in
breaking the immediate fit between subjective structures and the objective structures, destroys self-evidence practically.' Only under conditions of crisis do we have the power to think radically new thoughts
because it then becomes impossible to reproduce 'the naturalization of
our own arbitrariness'. All major social revolutions have been wrought
in the midst of breakdown in the bourgeois ability to govern.

There are abundant cracks in the shaky edifice of modern capitalism,
not a few of them generated by the stresses inherent in flexible
accumulation. The world's financial system – the central power in the
present regime of accumulation – is in turmoil and weighed down with
an excess of debt that puts such huge claims on future labour that it
is hard to see any way to work out of it except through massive defaults,
rampant inflation or repressive deflation. The insecurity and power of
creative destruction unleashed by flexible accumulation takes a terrible
toll, often on many segments of a population, thus generating acute
geopolitical rivalries. These could easily spin out of control (as they did
in the 1930s) and break up the West as a coherent political–economic
unit (protectionist and financial 'wars' have been part of our daily
diet of news for some time now). Though crisis prone, however, the
capitalist system is not *in* crisis and few of us care to consider how life

would be if it were. Indeed, the system is so shaky that even to talk about its shakiness is to be seen to rock it in unseemly ways.

This brings me to my second major point. Objective crisis may be a necessary but it is never a sufficient condition for major social transformations. The latter depend upon the rise of some political force capable of stepping into the vacuum of power and doing something truly creative with it. The nature of that political force does indeed make a difference; between, to use Marx's own polarities, a transition to barbarism or socialism. If the presently disempowered are to have a voice in that then they must first possess 'the material and symbolic means of rejecting the definition of the real that is imposed on them' (Bourdieu, 1977: 169). As Willis (1977) shows, however, the disempowered evolve their own means of symbolic representation that in many respects represent their social world more accurately than that which educators would impose upon them. 'Drop out' and oppositional inner-city subcultures, with their distinctive languages, are as widespread and vibrant as they have ever been. But that language, if only because it is the language of those trapped in space, is adaptive rather than transformative with respect to global processes that preclude empowerment for the mass of the population.

Critical theory here has a role. But only if it, too, is self-critical. To begin with, all critical theory emerges as the practice of a group of 'organic intellectuals' (to use Gramsci's phrase) and its qualities therefore depend upon the class and territory in which the practitioners have their being. Academics and professionals are not exempt. Our critical theory therefore has certain qualities that differentiate it from the critical theory expressed in working class cultural and political practices. True empowerment for the presently disempowered must be won by struggle from below and not given out of largesse from above. The modes of class and under-class opposition to flexible accumulation must therefore be taken seriously. The problem, on all sides, is to find practices that define a language of class and territorial alliances from which more global oppositional strategies to flexible accumulation can arise.

Even that kind of critical theory cannot contain the answers. But it can at least pose the questions and in so doing reveal something of the material realities with which any transition has to cope. That is, to be sure, a small contribution. But it is out of the assemblage of such small contributions that meaningful transformations must be wrought. A critical appraisal of the current regime of flexible accumulation, of the cultural practices of post-modernity, and of the re-shaping of physical and social space through urbanization, together with reflection on the ideologies through which we understand such processes, appears as one small but necessary preparatory step towards the reconstitution of a movement of global opposition to a plainly sick and troubled capitalist hegemony.

NOTES

1   The gender, racial, ethnic and religious contents of spatial practices also need to be considered in any full account of community formation and the production of social spaces in urban settings. A beginning has been made on the gender aspect in works by Stimpson (1981), Rose (1984); Shlay and Di Gregorio (1985) and Smith (1987).

2   I am here deeply indebted to the research work of Phillip Schmandt.

3   I cannot resist drawing attention to the way in which Barthes (1975) brought the concept of *jouissance* into philosophical respectability at the same time as the exploration of the city as a theatre, as a spectacle, full of play spaces, became more prominent in both the theory and practice of urban design. I also suspect that the appreciation of the urban fabric as a 'text' to be read and interpreted with pleasure had something to do with the tax advantages that derived to the real estate industry of declaring whole segments of the city 'historic preservation districts'.

4   Rossi (1984), it is interesting to note, bases his theory of architectural practice on the ideas of several geographers, notably Vidal de la Blache, regarding the importance of neighbourhoods as settings for the continuity of *'genres de vie'* and sites of collective memory. From my standpoint, Rossi chose the wrong geographer because Vidal was notoriously reluctant, at least until the very end of his life and his seminal but much neglected *Geographie de l'Est*, to explore the dynamic transformations of social and physical landscapes wrought under capitalist social relations.

REFERENCES

Aglietta, M. (1974) *A Theory of Regulation*. London: New Left Books.

Armstrong, P., Glyn, A., and Harrison, J. (1984) *Capitalism since World War II*. London: Fontana.

Barthes, R. (1975) *The Pleasure of the Text*. New York: Hill and Wang.

Benjamin, W. (1973) *Charles Baudelaire: a Lyric Poet in the Era of High Capitalism*. London: NLB.

Berman, M. (1982) *All That Is Solid Melts into Air*. New York: Simon and Schuster.

Bouinot, J. (Ed.) (1987) *L'Action Economique des Grandes Villes en France et à l'Etranger*. Paris: Economica.

Bourdieu, P. (1977) *Outline of a Theory of Practice*. Cambridge: Cambridge University Press.

Bourdieu, P. (1984) *Distinction: a Social Critique of the Judgement of Taste*. London: Routledge and Kegan Paul.

Bradbury, M., and McFarlane, J. (1976) *Modernism*. Harmondsworth: Pelican.

Castells, M., and Portes, A. (1986) World underneath: the origins, dynamics, and effects of the informal economy. *Conference on the Comparative Study of the Informal Sector.* Baltimore: Johns Hopkins University.

Clark, T. J. (1985) *The Painting of Modern Life: Paris in the Art of Manet and His Followers.* New York: Knopf.

Clavel, P., Forester, J., and Goldsmith, W. (1980) *Urban and Regional Planning in an Age of Austerity.* New York: Pergamon.

Crenson, M. (1983) *Neighborhood Politics.* Cambridge, Mass: Harvard University Press.

Debord, G. (1983) *Society of the Spectacle.* Detroit: Black and Red Books.

Eagleton, T. (1987) Awakening from Modernity. *Times Literary Supplement,* 20 February.

Fainstein, S., Fainstein, N., Hill, R., Judd, D., and Smith, M. (1986) *Restructuring the City.* New York: Longman.

Firey, W. (1945) Sentiment and symbolism as ecological variables. *American Sociological Review,* 10: 145–60.

Frampton, K. (1985) Critical regionalism: speculations on an architecture of resistance. In C. Johnson (Ed.) *The City in Conflict.* London: Mansell.

Frisby, D. (1986) *Fragments of Modernity.* Oxford: Polity Press.

Giddens, A. (1984) *The Constitution of Society.* Oxford: Polity Press.

Hanson, R. (Ed.) (1983) *Re-thinking Urban Policy: Urban Development in an Advanced Economy.* Washington, DC: National Academy of Sciences.

Harvey, D. (1985a) *The Urbanization of Capital.* Oxford: Basil Blackwell.

Harvey, D. (1985b) *Consciousness and the Urban Experience.* Oxford: Basil Blackwell.

Harvey, D. (1987) 'The geographical and geopolitical consequences of the transition from fordist to flexible accumulation'. Presented at Conference on America's New Economic Geography. Washington, DC 29–30 April.

Harvey, D., and Scott, A. (1989) The practice of human geography, theory and specificity in the transition from fordism to flexible accumulation. In B. Macmillan, (Ed.) *Remodelling Geography.* Oxford: Basil Blackwell.

Huyssen, A. (1984) Mapping the Post-modern. *New German Critique,* 33: 5–52.

Jacobs, J. (1961) *The Life and Death Great American Cities.* New York: Vintage.

Jager, M. (1986) Class definition and the esthetics of gentrification. In N. Smith and P. Williams (Eds) *The Gentrification of the City.* London: Allen and Unwin.

Jameson, F. (1984a) The politics of theory: ideological positions in the post-modernism debate. *New German Critique,* 33: 53–65.

Jameson, F. (1984b) Post-modernism, or, the cultural logic of late capitalism. *New Left Review,* 146: 53–92.

Jencks, C. (1984) *The Language of Post-Modern Architecture.* London: Academy Editions (fourth edition).

Lefebvre, H. (1974) *La Production de l'Espace.* Paris: Anthropos. (1991 in English as *The Production of Space.* Oxford: Basil Blackwell).

Markusen, A. (1986) Defense spending: a successful industrial policy. *International Journal of Urban and Regional Research,* 10: 105–22.

Marx, K. (1967) *Capital (volume 1).* New York: International Publishers.

Marx, K. (1973) *Grundrisse*. Harmondsworth: Penguin.

Nove, A. (1983) *The Economics of Feasible Socialism*. London: Allen and Unwin.

Piore, M., and Sabel, C. (1984) *The Second Industrial Divide*. New York: Basic Books.

Redclift, N., and Mingione, E. (Eds.) (1985) *Beyond Unemployment: Household, Gender, and Subsistence*. Oxford: Basil Blackwell.

Rose, D. (1984) Rethinking gentrification; beyond the uneven development of marxist urban theory. *Society and Space*, 2: 47–74.

Rossi, A. (1984) *Architecture and the City*. Cambridge, Mass: MIT Press.

Shlay, A., and Di Gregorio, D. (1985) Same city, different worlds: examining gender and work-based differences in perceptions of neighborhood desirability. *Urban Affairs Quarterly*, 21: 66–86.

Simmel, G. (1978) *The Philosophy of Money*. London: Routledge and Kegan Paul.

Scott, A., and Storper, M. (Eds) (1986) *Production, Work, Territory: the Geographical Anatomy of Industrial Capitalism*. London: Allen and Unwin.

Smith, N. (1984) *Uneven Development: Nature, Capital, and the Production of Space*. Oxford: Basil Blackwell.

Smith, N. (1987) Of Yuppies and housing; gentrification, social restructuring, and the urban dream. *Society and Space*, 5(2): 151–172.

Smith, N., and Lefaivre, M. (1984) A class analysis of gentrification. In J. Palen and B. London (Eds) *Gentrification, Displacement and Neighborhood Revitalization*. Albany: State University of New York Press.

Stimpson, C. (Ed.) (1981) *Women and the City*. Chicago: Chicago University Press.

Szelenyi, I. (Ed.) (1984) *Cities in Recession: Critical Responses to the Urban Policies of the New Right*. Beverly Hills: Sage.

Tabb, W. (1982) *The Long Default*. New York: Monthly Review Press.

Tafuri, M. (1976) *Architecture and Utopia*. Cambridge, Mass: MIT Press.

Venturi, R., Scott-Brown, D., and Izenour, S. (1972) *Learning from Las Vegas*. Cambridge, Mass: MIT Press.

Willis, P. (1977) *Learning to Labor*. Farnborough: Saxon House.

Zukin, S. (1982) *Loft Living: Culture and Capital in Urban Change*. Baltimore: Johns Hopkins University Press.

13

City Cultures and Post-modern Lifestyles

Mike Featherstone

How are we to understand the recent growth of interest in city cultures and urban lifestyles? On one level we can rightfully argue that cities have always had cultures in the sense that they have produced distinctive cultural products, artefacts, buildings and distinctive ways of life. It is possible to be even more 'culturalist' and assert that the very organization of space, the layout of buildings, is itself a manifestation of particular cultural codes. In this case particular 'deep' culture codes may dispose us to see cities as, for example, primarily economic, functional or aesthetic entities. If there is a switch from say a more economic and functional emphasis to a more cultural and aesthetic emphasis does it help to try to relate this to the asserted shifts from modernity and modernism towards post-modernity and post-modernism? If we set aside this question for the moment and focus in the first level, the notion that cities have always had cultures, we can take this to imply two senses of the term culture: culture as a way of life (the anthropological sense); and culture as the arts, spiritually elevating cultural products and experiences (high culture). One of the central themes which I will address in this chapter is that there has been a blurring of the boundaries between these two senses of culture which has broadened the range of phenomena designated as culture from the

This chapter is reprinted from M. Featherstone (1991) *Consumer Culture and Postmodernism*, chapter 7. London: Sage.

arts (high culture) to take in a wide spectrum of popular and everyday cultures in which practically any object or experience can be deemed to be of cultural interest. This has been accompanied by a shift in attention from lifestyles conceived as a relatively fixed set of dispositions, cultural tastes and leisure practices which demarcate groups from each other to the assumption that in the contemporary city lifestyles are more actively formed. Hence the focus turns away from lifestyle as class- or neighbourhood-based to lifestyle as the active stylization of life in which coherence and unity give way to the playful exploration of transitory experiences and surface aesthetic effects. It is the compound effects of these shifts which prove to be a source of fascination for a number of cultural commentators who are disposed to regard them as indicators of a more fundamental social and cultural displacement which is increasingly referred to as post-modernism.

This chapter will seek to understand these changes via a dual focus: firstly, on the transformations in lifestyles and city cultures which are taking place and alleged to amount to a post-modern shift; and, secondly, to raise the question of the changes in social structures and relationships which dispose particular sets of cultural specialists and intermediaries to exploit and develop new markets for cultural goods and experiences. In short, attention needs to be given to the role of the interpreters, carriers and promoters of both a range of new cultural goods and experiences and the perception of those goods and experiences as significant, meaningful and worthy of investment.

Before going into these questions in more detail we can briefly refer to a number of factors which point to the ways in which the culture of cities and urban lifestyles have become thematized. Firstly, there is the assumption that particular cities (for example, Florence, Venice) are cultural centres containing the art treasures and cultural heritage of the past which are housed both in museums and galleries and in the fabric of the buildings and layout which represents the prime source of their cultural capital. Alongside the notion that the city can be regarded as 'work of art' (Olsen, 1986) as in the above cases, or in the case of the outstanding natural beauty of the site (for example, Rio de Janeiro, San Francisco) which can be regarded as an alternative source of prestige, or cultural capital, we have the view that cities can also be cultural centres to the extent to which they house leisure and entertainment industries. Particular metropolises (such as New York, Paris, Los Angeles, London) may be strong in cultural capital in terms of the extent to which they are centres of cultural production, housing not only the arts (still an expanding sector), but also the mass culture industries of fashion, television, cinema, publishing, popular music, tourism and leisure. The employment of the notion of cultural capital (Bourdieu, 1984) in this context is to point to alternative sources of wealth than economic (financial and industrial) capital whose value may nevertheless be redeemable and reconvertible back into economic value, through a whole series of direct and indirect routes. Hence the willingness of national policy-makers, city administrations and private capitalists to encourage and seek investment in culture (Fisher et al., 1987) and their sensitivity to the importance of the city's image under conditions of intensified competition.

Secondly, the general expansion of the cultural sphere within contemporary Western societies not only points to the enlarged market for cultural goods and information, but also to the ways in which the purchase and consumption of commodities, an allegedly material act, is increasingly mediated by diffuse cultural images (via advertising, display and promotion) in which the consumption of signs or the symbolic aspect of goods become the major source of the satisfaction derived (Baudrillard, 1981). Here one can point to the increasing salience of forms of leisure consumption in which the emphasis is placed upon the consumption of experiences and pleasure (such as theme parks, tourist and recreational centres) and the ways in which more traditional forms of high cultural consumption (such as museums, galleries) become revamped to cater for wider audiences through trading-in the canonical, auratic art and educative–formative pretensions for an emphasis upon the spectacular, the popular, the pleasurable and the immediately accessible. In addition it can be argued that there are further convergences between these two cultural forms and a third, the development of malls and shopping centres.

Thirdly, the extension of the range of cultural and leisure pursuits available has not only extended the range of leisure lifestyles available but has resulted in some qualitative shifts too. As I mentioned earlier, there is a tendency on the part of some groups (especially the young, highly educated, sectors of the middle classes) to take a more active stance towards lifestyle and pursue the stylization of life. Here we can point not only to the imitation and popularity of the lifestyles of artistic subcultures (bohemias, avant-gardes) in contemporary metropolises, but also to what has been referred to as 'artist of life', the painters who do not paint but adopt the artistic sensibilities in order to turn their lives into a work of art. The concern with fashion, presentation of self, 'the look' on the part of the new wave of urban *flâneurs* points to a process of cultural differentiation which in many ways is the obverse of the stereotypical images of mass societies in which serried ranks of similarly dressed people are massed together. If the contemporary age can be characterized as an era of 'no style', to borrow a phrase of Simmel's, then it points to the rapid circulation of new styles (fashion, appearance, design, consumer goods) and the nostalgic invocation of past ones.

Here we can point to a further convergence in the process of the stylization and aestheticization of everyday life between the popularity of artistic lifestyles and stylistic presentation and display and the development of a differentiated and sophisticated range of consumer goods, leisure-time pursuits and experiences which incorporate a high input of design, style, and artistic and fashionable cultural imagery. It can also be argued that certain modernist artistic currents (such as Dada and surrealism) which became central to post-modernism in the 1960s themselves sought to collapse the boundary between art and everyday life to show that the most banal consumer cultural objects and the kitsch and detritus of mass culture could themselves be aestheticized and introduced as the subject of, or incorporated into, the formal structure of artworks. Post-modern art also focused upon the body, living art and the happening. Hence we have an interchange between a number of currents: a higher input of style, design and cultural imagery into consumer goods, sites of leisure and consumption and the fabric of the city; an expansion of artistic professions, intermediaries and ancillary workers with the growth of specific artistic enclaves and neighbourhoods (e.g. SoHo in New York); the move towards post-modern art with its aestheticization of everyday life and mass consumer cultures; the growing prominence of social agglomerates which show a concern with stylistic display, fashionable clothing and presentation of self (which often entails a playful or parodic emphasis which allegedly seeks to transcend traditional status games), its people move through city spaces and consumption, leisure and entertainment sites. We will now turn to a more detailed examination of these strands.

POST-MODERN CITY CULTURES

Some commentators have referred to some of the tendencies we have just mentioned as post-modern (Cooke, 1988; Zukin, 1988a; Chambers, 1987). While the term 'post-modern' and its most common derivatives 'post-modernism' and 'post-modernity' are generally used in a confusing range of ways (see Featherstone, 1991: chapters 1 and 3), they do sensitize us to a series of cultural changes which may presage a more fundamental set of transformations of social structures and relationships. Amongst the most frequently cited characteristics associated with post-modernism are (1) an antifoundational stance in philosophy and social and cultural theory which suggests that the foundational meta-narratives which ground Western modernity's claims for privileged universality in its notions of science, humanism, socialism, etc. are flawed and that we should seek to produce less pretentious modes of knowledge which are more sensitive to local differences as intellectuals swap their role as confident legislators to that of interpreters (see Lyotard, 1984; Kellner, 1988; Bauman, 1988); (2) this privileging of the local and the vernacular is translated into a democratic and populist collapsing of symbolic hierarchies within the academy and intellectual and artistic circles in which, for example, the distinctions between high culture and popular or mass cultures, art and everyday, are contested – put simply we should 'learn from Las Vegas' (Venturi et al., 1977); (3) there is a shift from discursive to figural forms of culture manifest in an emphasis upon visual images over words, primary processes of the ego over secondary and immersion rather than the distanced appreciation of the detached spectator (Lash, 1988); and (4) these aspects are captured in the phrase 'post-modern depthless culture' (Jameson, 1984a) and the notion that ordered historical development should give way to the perception of the past as a conglomerate of images, fragments and spectacles which are endlessly reduplicated and simulated without the possibility of discovering an essential order or point of value judgement. These features have been noted by commentators within a wide range of academic fields, and however suitable the emphasis on the move beyond the modern implied by the term 'post-modernism', the use of the term has the merit of directing us towards what are perceived to be significant changes in artistic and popular cultural practices, regimes of signification and modes of orientation within everyday life. The populist and de-hierarchizing spirit of post-modernism directs our attention to the way in which culture has surfaced as an issue, as something to be theorized and explored alongside the de-monopolization of long-established symbolic hierarchies whose former dominance meant that particular notions of culture were taken for granted and unthematized. Hence it is possible to follow DiMaggio (1987) and regard the Western world as entering a phase of 'cultural de-classification' in which there will be heightened competition between a wide variety of notions of culture and a reduced ability to impose a value-hierarchy.

For our particular purposes it is interesting to note that commentators have adopted the rhetoric of post-modernism to understand the changes to the culture of cities and urban lifestyles we have alluded to. Particularly influential has been the work of Baudrillard (1983a, b) with his notion of a simulational culture. Arguing that consumer commodities in late capitalism have developed the capacity to take up a wide range of imagistic and symbolic associations which overlay their initial use-value and hence become commodity-signs, he detects a qualitative shift in the intensification of this process which leads to the loss of a sense of concrete reality as the consumer–television culture with its floating mass of signs and images produces an endless series of simulations which play off each other. Baudrillard refers to this as a 'hyperreality', a world in which the piling up of signs, images and simulations through consumerism and television results in a destabilized, aestheticized hallucination of reality. For Baudrillard, culture has effectively become free-floating to the extent that culture is everywhere, actively mediating and aestheticizing the social fabric and social relationships. A move beyond the discursive reflexive primacy of language towards figural cultural forms, which emphasize the immediacy and intensity of aural and visual sensations which provide inchoate and dispersed pleasures for de-centred subjects.

If these perceptions are translated into an urban context it is apparent that the old notion of premodern city cultures, which implies that certain cities are sedimented in tradition, history and the arts, housing famous buildings and landmarks which provide a strong sense of place and collective identity – or the 'de-cultured' city, the modernist functional economic city whose spatial form is dominated by the grid-iron layout and high-rise modernist architecture – both give way to the post-modern city which marks a return to culture, style and decoration, but within the confines of a 'no-place space' in which traditional senses of culture are decontextualized, simulated, reduplicated and continually renewed and restyled. The post-modern city is therefore much more image and culturally self-conscious; it is a centre of both cultural consumption and general consumption, and the latter, as has been emphasized, cannot be detached from cultural signs and imagery, so that urban lifestyles, everyday life and leisure activities themselves in varying degrees are influenced by the post-modern simulational tendencies.

To take some examples: post-modern tendencies in architecture can be seen as a revolt against architectural modernism with its austere Miesian functionalism and abstract formalism (Jencks, 1984; Davis, 1985) by the reintroduction of decoration, the mixing of styles and a playful pop art simulation of commodities (such as Philip Johnson's Chippendale ATT Building in New York). It also introduces what Venturi and associates (1977) in *Learning from Las Vegas* refer to as 'Roadside Eclecticism': the eclectic stylistic hotchpotch of big signs and little buildings which run along the highway. Words, pictures, sculpture and neon are mixed together and, in contrast to modernism's austerity, symbolism is reintroduced to produce a hedonistic consumer culture landscape. Here pop art's parodic duplication of mass consumer cultural objects is fed back into the urban landscape and culture industries. Not only the billboard but especially electronic media images provide sources of inspiration. There is a plethora of ornamental, overcoded multicoloured facades whose impact is immediate with no opportunity for distanciation (Cooke and Onufrijchuk, 1987).

If architecture and art take quotations from everyday consumer culture and play them back to produce post-modern cities 'where everything is "larger than life", where the referents are swept away by the signs, where the artificial is more "real" than the real' (Chambers, 1987: 1), then what of the people who move through these urban spaces? In many ways the people are regarded as engaging in a complex sign play which mimics or resonates with the surfeit of signs in the built environment. Contemporary popular culture (fashion, music, television, videos, drinking, dancing, clubbing) is regarded as dominated by the 'as if . . .' world of advertising. Clothes, bodies, faces become 'quotations drawn from the other, imaginary side of life: from fashion, the cinema, advertising and the infinite suggestibility of urban iconography' (Chambers, 1987: 7). These signs, which are de-contextualized from tradition or subcultural ordering, are played with in a superficial way, with people revelling in the fact that they are artificial, opaque and 'depthless' in the sense that they cannot be de-coded to offer access to some revelatory meaning or fundamental sense of truth. Everyday life becomes a 'fantastic *mélange* of fiction and strange values' which captures the sense of the surreal as an everyday presence, both as excess, style and experimentation and as randomness, banality and the repetition of street images (Calefato, 1988: 225). The contemporary is a 'dandy of a new and more democratic bohemia', a new metropolitan figure who 'explores routes already travelled by avant-garde art, crossing the boundary between the museum and mass culture, but transfers the game from the art gallery to the fashion catwalk of the street' (Del Sapio, 1988: 206–7).

It should be apparent that this group of people who seek to cross, re-cross and transgress the boundaries between art and everyday life are predominantly the young and are the inheritors of the tradition of youth subcultures. The latter operated as fixed symbolic structures which are now rejected or ironically parodied and collaged. Yet there is the assumption on the part of commentators that these new tendencies are indications of the processes which are breaking up traditional patterns of social regulation which link lifestyles closely to class, age and normativity (Baudrillard 1983a; Chambers, 1987: 7). Hence Chambers (1987: 2) quotes Robert Elms, a writer for the fashionable youth magazine *The Face*, as remarking 'nobody is a teenager any more because everybody is'. Certainly there is some evidence that youth styles and lifestyles are migrating up the age scale and that as the 1960s generation ages they are taking some of their youth-orientated disposi- tions with them, and that adults are being granted greater licence for childlike behaviour and vice versa. This relationship between lifestyle, habitus and class will be discussed towards the end of this chapter.

One interesting aspect of the new urban lifestyles and depthless stylistic eclecticism commentators label as post-modern is that they are linked to the notion of a movement beyond individualism, to a de-centring of the subject. The de-centred subject has a greater capacity to engage in a controlled de-control of the emotions and explore figural tendencies, immediate sensations and affective experi- ences formerly regarded as threatening, as something which needs to be kept at bay or strictly controlled. It has been argued by Maffesoli (1988) that in the post-modern city we have a move beyond individualism with a sense of communal feeling being generated, a new 'aesthetic paradigm' in which masses of people come together in temporary emotional communities. These are to be regarded as fluid 'post-modern tribes' in which intense moments of ecstasy, empathy and affectual immediacy are experienced. Of course it should be emphasized that these tendencies are not in themselves historically new. One can find examples of the disorientating mêlée of signs and the aestheticization of everyday life in the carnivals and fairs of the Middle Ages and mid-nineteenth-century Paris with its *flâneurs*, or the great world exhibitions in metropolises like Berlin and Paris (see Featherstone, 1991: chapter 5). What is new is not only the capacity to reduplicate and simulate these previously enclaved examples of the aestheticization of everyday life – and indeed any other cultural experience – on a hitherto unexperienced level of intensity and vividness of reproduction. Also new is the attitude of intellectuals and theorists towards the process. Whereas Simmel was troubled by the threat to art posed by the de-auratization of art and the ways in which the stylization of everyday objects lead to an interference with the distanced appreciation demanded by the artwork, Benjamin, especially in his *Passagen-Werk*, celebrated the fragmented images of mass culture and the shocks and jolts of the perceptions in everyday city life from a theoretical perspective clearly influenced by surrealism, Dadaism and montage (see Wolin, 1982), which resonates well with post-modernism.

If post-modern cities have become centres of consumption, play and entertainment, saturated with signs and images to the extent that anything can become represented, thematized and made an object of interest, an object of the 'tourist gaze', then it is to be expected that leisure activities such as visiting theme parks, shopping centres, malls, museums and galleries should show some convergence here.

To take some examples, Disneyworld is often taken as the prototype for post-modern simulational experiences (Baudrillard, 1983a) and it is interesting to see that the format of moving between spectacular experiences (white-knuckle rides, hologram illusions etc.) and the simulation of historical national-founder or childhood worlds (the Magic Kingdom) or wandering through simulations of buildings, which are chosen to symbolize selected national cultures (such as the Merry England pub) or futuristic scenarios (EPCOT) in sanitized, highly controlled surroundings, has not only been imitated by theme parks around the world, but has also been merged with other formats such as museums. The growth of open-air museums directed at a wider spectrum of people has broadened the range of objects worthy of preservation (such as working coal mines, miners' terraced houses, trams, metal advertising signs dubbed 'street jewellery', as at the Beamish Open Air Museum in Tyne and Wear in north-east England). It has also encouraged a new attitude on the part of spectators with actors (often the unemployed on government schemes) trained to play historical roles to enliven the recreated physical settings, so that the mood of walking through a film set is extended as spectators are encouraged to participate and bring the simulation to life (Urry, 1988). The range of sites worthy of the tourist gaze and exploration is extended. One increasingly lives in a 'heritage country' in which the sense of historical past gives way to myths. Hence if one crosses the north of England one moves rapidly from Wordsworth country, to Brontë country, to Herriot country, to Captain Cook country – and to show that working-class popular culture is respectable too – to Catherine Cookson country, each with tour guides, itineraries, museums and souvenirs. Even former non-attractive locations are clamouring to join the queue with towns like Bradford capitalizing on its 'Northern Grit' industrial past and current large Asian community to become the site for 'getaway break weekends'. Here we have typical sites for what have been referred to as 'post-tourists' (Feifer, 1985: Urry, 1988), people who adopt a post-modern de-centred orientation towards tourist experiences. Post-tourists have no time for authenticity and revel in the constructed simulational nature of contemporary tourism which they know is only a game. They welcome the opportunity to explore back-stage regions and tackle the experience from many points of view.

Similar orientations are also to be found in contemporary museums, many of which are abandoning their commitment to the cultural canon and education project, in which the old and the new were organized in terms of a hierarchy of progress developed in the nineteenth century to reflect the values of ascendent Western modernity (Bann, 1984;

Bennett, 1988), in favour of a more populist ethos. From this perspective, museums should cease to be dull places of education; rather, they should incorporate the features of post-modernism and become 'amazing spaces' which present spectacular imagery and simulations. This encourages a different, more playful, orientation from much broader based crowds whose mass media influenced perceptions are at home with the abandonment of symbolic hierarchies and a more playful approach to montaged exhibits that offer experiences organized in terms of the equality of a plurality of styles, which shows the abandonment of a civilizing mission and hierarchized vision of a unitary culture (Roberts, 1988; Horne, 1984). This is captured in Baudrillard's (1982) description of the Beaubourg Museum in Paris, which draws in the masses to what he calls this 'hypermarket of culture'. He states:

> The people want to accept everything, eat everything, touch everything. Looking, deciphering, studying doesn't move them. The one mass effect is that of touching or manipulating. The organizers (and the artists, and the intellectuals) are alarmed by this uncontrollable impulse, for they reckoned only with the apprenticeship of the masses to the *spectacle* of culture. They never anticipated this active, destructive fascination – this original and brutal response to the gift of an incomprehensible culture, this attraction which has all the semblance of housebreaking or the sacking of a shrine. *(Baudrillard, 1982: 10)*

It can be argued that the conflict between populism and elitism is a perennial feature of museums (Zolberg, 1984), yet the populist tendencies certainly have come to the fore in the 1980s.

This populism is hardly an unexpected feature of shopping centres, malls and department stores. Within these sites it is apparent that shopping is rarely a purely calculative rational economic transaction to maximize utility, but is primarily a leisure-time cultural activity in which people become audiences who move through the spectacular imagery designed to connote sumptuousness and luxury, or to summon up connotations of desirable exotic far-away places, and nostalgia for past emotional harmonies. In short shopping has become an experience. As cities de-industrialize and become centres of consumption one of the tendencies in the 1970s and 1980s has been the redesigning and expansion of shopping centres which incorporate many of the features of post-modernism in their architectural design of interior space and simulated environments: use of dream-like illusions and spectacles, eclecticism and mixed codes, which induce the public to flow past a multiplicity of cultural vocabularies which provide no opportunity for distanciation (de-distanciation) and encourage a sense of immediacy, instantiation, emotional de-control and childlike wonder. One of the major North American examples is the West Edmonton Mall – or more appropriately 'mega-mall' – which has a supplementary 64 acre entertainment centre with a 'Fantasyland' fun fair and water park which includes an indoor saltwater lake containing dolphins, mini-submarines and Spanish galleons (Shields, 1987: 9). Europe's largest shopping centre is the Metrocentre in Gateshead, in north-east England. The Metrocentre is a good example of the de-industrialization process and switch of cities to become centres of consumption, being built upon derelict industrial land in an economically depressed metropolitan region. The Metrocentre has promoted itself as a tourist attraction with its 'Antiques Village', fantasy fairytale 'Kingdom of King Wiz', Ancient Roman Forum gallery and general eclectic smattering of symbolism to evoke the myths of a communal past via Christmas card and chocolate-box iconography (Chaney, 1990).

There are therefore common features emerging between shopping centres, malls, museums, theme parks and tourist experiences in the contemporary city in which cultural disorder and stylistic eclecticism become common features of spaces in which consumption and leisure are meant to be constructed as 'experiences'. As Lefebvre (1971: 114) remarks, in the contemporary city we have 'consuming displays, displays of consuming, consuming of signs, signs of consuming'. This convergence takes place not only on the level of the common form to the sets of experiences which are sought to be generated by advertisers, designers, architects and other cultural intermediaries, but also in terms of the alliances forged between the proprietors, patrons, trustees and financiers of these institutions. For example, a New York department store promoted a China Week in which art works and museum treasures were exhibited in the store. The Metropolitan Opera in New York hosts fashion shows (Silverman, 1986). Japanese department stores regularly display art treasures and hold exhibitions of paintings. Such promotion phases and exhibitions blur the distinctions between high culture and low culture and the distinctions between commerce and culture.

These convergences are not without forerunners, although they are new to the extent that the mixing of codes and the deconstruction of the symbolic hierarchies involving discriminations between high and mass culture now take place across a wider range of cultural forms and within what were almost exclusively regarded as places of inculcation of high cultural values and a coherent education formative process (such as museums). With regard to forerunners, the department stores which developed first in Paris and then in other cities in the second half of the nineteenth century were essentially conceived as 'palaces of consumption', 'dream-worlds' and 'temples' in which goods were worshipped by new consumers (largely female) who were able to wander through display areas which introduced simulations and an evocative, exotic imagery (R. H. Williams, 1982; Chaney, 1983). Similar experiences were also generated by the world exhibitions and expositions which became regular events until the early years of the twentieth century, in the wake of the Crystal Palace Great Exhibition of 1851. These presented simulation involving stuffed animals and ethnographic scenarios, stands for various nations involving replicas of cultural treasures and everyday life (for example, a Moorish palace, a Chinese house) and even simulations of experiences (for example, a Trans-Siberian Railway journey) (see R. H. Williams, 1982). In addition the phantasmagorical distractive overload of signs and impressions which Simmel (1978) refers to in *The Philosophy of Money* produced many similar experiences to those which have been labelled post-modern (Frisby, 1985). We have a similar emphasis upon play and display. As the 'Short Sermon to Sightseers' at the 1901 Pan-American Exposition instructed, 'Please remember when you get inside the gates you are part of the show' (cited in Bennett, 1988: 81). In effect the crowd itself became part of the spectacle and the reason for going just as much in the Great Exhibition of 1851 and the Berlin Trade Exhibition of 1896 its in the Parisian Beaubourg Museum described by Baudrillard in the 1980s. Yet to be a *flâneur*, a stroller, who watches others and displays him or herself, necessitates an ordered space as much in the Parisian Arcades so dear to Baudelaire in the 1840s and 1850s, which became central to Benjamin's *Passagen-Werk* (Berman, 1982), as in the exhibitions and department stores of the late nineteenth century and as much in the theme parks, shopping centres and museums of today. In short, to wander through goods or art treasures on display demanded discipline. The imagery may summon up pleasure, the carnivalesque and disorder, yet the emotional de-control these encouraged must itself take place within a framework of self-control. And for those who lacked it or were in danger of losing it there existed a battery of external controls designed along the principles of panopticism (Foucault, 1977). These entail surveillance and exclusion. It is a central principle of theme parks and shopping centres that these are privately owned public spaces in which the public are under the watchful eye of video-cameras, and rowdy, troublesome elements are excluded before the disorder might disturb others.

This suggests that before going along with the thesis that de-industrialization and the shift to cities as centres of consumption have entailed the accumulation of spectacles, mixing of codes and merging of high and low cultures, a shift towards post-modern lifestyles, we need to ask specific questions about (1) the extent of forerunners and (2) the extent to which such lifestyles represent minor enclaved experiences in the lives of specific groups of people in specific urban locations. In short, we need to ask the stark sociological questions about not only where the post-modern lifestyles take place; but how many people from which range of groups participate and for how long. We need also to attempt to understand the forces which are propelling culture to greater importance within the contemporary city and investigate the interdependencies and conflicts between specific groups (such as cultural specialists, economic specialists, policy makers) which are bringing this about.

CULTURAL CAPITAL, GENTRIFICATION AND THE STYLIZATION OF LIFE

In recent years there has been increasing recognition of the value of culture industries to the economy of cities and the many direct and indirect ways in which the presence of cultural institutions, activities and a general sensitivity to the enhancement, renovation and redevelopment of the cultural facades, fabric and lived space of cities carries benefits. The awareness that culture industries such as publishing, recorded music, broadcasting and tourism generated by arts and cultural institutions can play a growing role in national and local economies has grown alongside the general expansion in the production and consumption of symbolic goods in contemporary Western societies. Here we might usefully refer to the concept of *cultural capital* which has been developed by Pierre Bourdieu (1984, 1987) and others (see Lamont and Lareau, 1988). The concept points to the way in which in parallel to economic capital, which is immediately calculable, exchangeable and realizable, there also exist modes of power and processes of accumulation based upon culture in which the value of the latter, the fact that culture can be capital, is often hidden and misrecognized. Bourdieu (1987: 243) points to three forms of cultural capital: it can exist in the *embodied* state (style of presentation, mode of speech, beauty, etc.), *objectified* state (cultural goods like pictures, books, machines, buildings, etc.) and *institutionalized* state (such as educational qualifications). It is the objectified state which is of particular interest with respect to cities and I have already mentioned the ways in which specific cities may have accumulated cultural capital because of their exemplary preservation of buildings, artefacts and goods which have become defined as 'art treasures'

(Olsen, 1986). From this perspective one could construct a symbolic hierarchy of cities according to their accumulated prestige in terms of culture capital, with Florence, Paris and Rome near the top. Conventionally the culture industries are defined as producing mass cultural goods (Horkheimer and Adorno, 1972; Garnham, 1987) which traditionally have featured low on the scale of cultural capital. Yet one can argue that the legitimacy of particular forms of cultural capital and the legitimacy of the existing symbolic hierarchy and structural features of the field of cultural capital should not be eternalized. Rather, they should themselves be conceived as a process which is the result of the intentional and unintentional outcome of particular groups who are bound together in interdependencies and struggles (often misrecognized or masked by claims to disinterestedness) to maximize their own particular form of cultural capital. Hence it is possible that particular forms of cultural capital, such as popular and mass culture (jazz, rock music, cinema, theme parks), may themselves become regarded as more legitimate, as the source of prestige and as further up the symbolic hierarchy. Hence New Orleans and districts of large cities may gain attraction and cultural capital as sites of formerly defined 'low' life, now elevated to respectability and worthy objects of the tourist gaze.

There are therefore an expanding range of criteria on which cities may be ranked in terms of cultural capital. What the shift towards post-modern culture is held to introduce is a movement away from agreed universal criteria of judgement of cultural taste towards a more relativistic and pluralistic situation in which the strange, the other, the vulgar, which were previously excluded can now be allowed in. In this sense the tendency is for the long-held Western universally based symbolic hierarchy to become spatialized out with a greater tolerance of difference and diversity. From the perspective of the economic utility of cultural capital this means that while traditional smokestack indus-trial towns of the 'rust belt' are to be regarded as low in cultural capital (with the exception of those who are able to repackage and museumify these elements as assets), the range is extended from traditional historic value and treasures to include newly created and simulated environ-ments that take in some of the post-modern and more popular cultural forms we have mentioned (theme parks, malls, shopping centres, museums as well as popular cultural venues), which are perceived as attractive and saleable. In short, those who seek to invest in new service, information and high-tech industries may be swayed by the ambience and cultural capital of cities and may have helped to speed up the reconversion strategies such as the redevelopment and gentrification of docklands and inner city areas. Under global conditions of intensified competition and the freeing of market forces for investment and capital flows, cities have become more entre-preneurial and aware of their image and the ways in which image translates into jobs for the local economy. As Harvey (1988) puts it, cities have to mobilize culture to become 'lures for capital'. Hence in the early 1970s Seattle attempted to remove mass unemployment by bringing together business leaders and planners who lobbied for investment to expand the arts infrastructure, and gained much favourable publicity as a self-proclaimed 'quality of life capital'. Baltimore develops its Harbor Place, Hamburg becomes a 'media city', Gateshead has its Metrocentre and so on.

This is the process which has been referred to as *post-modernization* (Cooke, 1988; Zukin, 1988b) to point to the global restructuring of socio-spatial relations by new patterns of investment which lead to some counter-tendencies to urban decentralization through the redevelopment of inner city areas. This process entails the deindus-trialization of inner city areas and docklands, which become gentrified by members of the new middle class and developed as sites of tourism and cultural consumption. At the same time the working class and poor who previously resided in these areas are moved out or driven into other enclaves. A good example of this is Battersea in London, where large blocks of working-class council housing were sold and redeveloped for the yuppie market. In this case the new inhabitants were made to feel secure from the neighbouring lower orders by security fences and guards. This process of increased segrega-tion as the middle classes move back into the central areas is also symbolized in the post-modern architecture, with towers, moats and drawbridges which create defensible privatized spaces free from the unemployed, the poor, rebellious youth and other residues of the 'dangerous classes'. It creates what David Harvey (1988) has called 'voodoo cities' in which the post-modern facade of cultural redevelop-ment can be seen as a carnival mask which covers the decline of everything else. In Los Angeles, for example, side-by-side but segre-gated from the financial node of the Pacific Rim economy and gentrified area, we have a Hispanic–Asian enclave of one million people fuelled by Third World migration and the demand for labour which results in undocumented homeworkers and child labour (Davis, 1985). It is those processes which have helped to destroy the former fragile consensus within the middle classes that supported high culture and the culture industries, and which raise the questions of the political uses of the arts and other forms of cultural capital within the city, and whether there can be a more democratic cultural policy (Garnham, 1987). It also entails, in a wider sense, the question of resistance to redevelopment, to what some refer to as 'urbicide' (Berman, 1982).

The process of gentrification is of interest because it not only points to the redevelopment of the cultural fabric of inner city areas, it also provides a higher profile for groups within the new middle class who are in many guises the producers, carriers, consumers of lifestyles which entail the culturally sensitive 'stylization of life' and have developed dispositions which make them receptive to postmodern cultural goods and experiences. They therefore have direct and indirect interests in the accumulation of cultural capital, both on a personal basis and in terms of that of their neighbourhood and the wider city.

The location which has been widely studied and can best illustrate this process is SoHo in New York City (Zukin, 1987, 1988a; Simpson, 1981; Jackson, 1995). As Zukin (1988a) points out, the regeneration of SoHo into an artist's colony and then a gentrified new-middle-class neighbourhood with incomers attracted by the ambience of the artist's lifestyle is a complex story. It is based upon the rise in the investment value of art in the post-war era which has seen art become a strong international market in its own right. It also entails an elevation in the status of artists and ancillary occupations to the extent that other groups become more favourably disposed to associate themselves with artistic lifestyles. It is further based on the fact that city governments begin to realize the potential for redevelopment and reversal of the negative side of deindustrialization and general enhancement of the city's image by granting such enclaves a protected status. New York replaced Paris as the centre for Modern Art in the post-war era and a dramatic increase in the numbers of artists, galleries, museums and exhibiting outlets occurred (see Crane, 1987; Zukin 1988b; DiMaggio, 1986). There was also a more general change on the part of national and local governments, foundations and corporations who began to perceive the arts as socially useful. In short, the economic value of cultural capital increased and from the 1960s the artistic avant-garde ceased to be seen as a troublesome and transgressive bohemian counterculture and were regarded by city politicians, speculators and developers as a different avant-garde, as those who beat the trail to large-scale low-rent rundown areas ripe for redevelopment through gentrification.

This was coupled with a more general re-evaluation of the status of the artist in American society which made art less high-culture and elitist and more democratic. Artists now made money; some of them made a good living from art. With the transition from artistic modernism to post-modernism their oppositional pretensions and austere indecipherability of artworks were displaced and celebrity artists such as Andy Warhol gained much media attention and coverage. The artist became perceived as an attractive persona and his studio – the loft – an interesting place to be and live. The new middle classes (Burris, 1986), and in particular those sectors which Bourdieu (1984) has referred to as 'new cultural intermediaries', have a fascination for artists' and intellectuals' lifestyles and a general interest in the stylization of their lives. Theirs is a lifestyle which focuses very much on identity, appearance, presentation of self, fashion design, decor; and considerable time and effort have to be expended in cultivating a sense of taste which is flexible, distinctive and capable of keeping abreast of the plethora of new styles, experiences and symbolic goods which consumer culture and the culture industries continue to generate.

The habitus of the cultural specialists within the new middle class points to a flexible, learning mode towards life. Here it may be that the new cultural intermediaries have an important role in the transmission of new style. Their interest may be less in the attempt to impose a particular style on consumer audiences and more in terms of a general interest in the full range of styles from different cultures, civilizations and traditions which they can play and replay. Hence there is an interest in the stylization and aestheticization of life on the part of particular factions within the new middle classes who have been referred to as 'para-intellectuals' in their role of admiring intellectual and artistic pursuits and lifestyles. They, therefore, are able to transmit the latest styles such as post-modernism to wider audiences and themselves form part of the reception class for post-modern goods and experiences.

CONCLUSION

The proponents of post-modernism detect a major shift in culture taking place in which existing symbolic hierarchies are deconstructed and a more playful, popular democratic impulse becomes manifest. Here we have spatialization out of the previous more firmly structured symbolic hierarchies which became dominant motifs within Western modernity and established particular notions of universal history, progress, the cultivated person, state political structures and aesthetic ideals. With respect to the contemporary Western city it has been argued that post-modern and post-modernizing tendencies can be observed in the new urban spaces which point to a greater aestheticization of the urban fabric and the daily lives of people, the development of new consumption and leisure enclaves (such as shopping centres, theme parks, museums) and the drawing back of new middle-class gentrifying populations into the inner city. These post-modern impulses suggest less strong neighbourhood identifications and a less fixed habitus or rigid set of dispositions and classifications into which encounters are framed. Some of the new urban lifestyles point to a de-centring of identity and a greater capacity to engage in a de-control of the emotions and aestheticized play. It can also be argued that on the global level we are witnessing the end of the dominance of a few metropolitan centres over artistic and intellectual life (R. Williams, 1983). Paris and New York as centres of culture, the arts, fashion, culture and entertainment industries, television, publishing and music, now face greater competition from a variety of directions. New forms of cultural capital and a wider range of symbolic experiences are on offer within an increasingly globalized – that is, more easily accessible via financial (money) communications (travel) and information (broadcasting, publishing, media) – field of world cities.

Hence it could be argued by those who emphasize the novelty and historical events which post-modernism is purported to bring, that we are entering a phase in which the old cultural hierarchies are becoming obsolete. The de-hierarchizing impulse suggests that high/low, elite/ popular, minority/mass, taste/tasteless, art/life, vertical classificational hierarchies (Goudsblom, 1987; Schwartz, 1983) which are held to be endemic features of social life, no longer apply.

Against this seductively oversimplified post-modern story of the end of history we have to point to the persistence of classification, hierarchy and segregation within the city. As we mentioned, the new middle class and new rich live in enclaved areas of gentrification and redevelopment which are designed to exclude outsiders. These enclaves are areas of high investment in designed environments, stylized form and the aestheticization of everyday life. Such groups expect to be entertained while they shop and shop at places of entertainment. They seek to cultivate a style of life and have an interest in the arts and a pleasurable aestheticized living environment (Boyer, 1988). For certain fractions of the new middle class this style of life certainly has affinities with the range of characteristics and experience designated post-modern. There are tendencies which point to an overload of information and signs, which make the ordered reading of bodily presentation, fashion, lifestyle and leisure pursuits much more difficult. People are able to draw from a much wider repertoire of instantly accessible symbolic goods and styles from the 'global showcase' and it is more difficult to make a judgement of class from taste and lifestyle. Since the 1960s there has been a more general informalization and elaboration of previously restricted codes of behaviour. Notions of beauty prominent in consumer culture, for example, widened beyond the classic Western one in the 1960s to take into account standards of other cultures (Marwick, 1988). Yet for all the democratizing tendencies there are status differences. As Douglas and Isherwood (1980) point out, the informational component of consumer goods rises as one moves up the class scale. Those in the middle and upper reaches continue to use information about consumption goods to build bridges with like-minded people and close doors to exclude outsiders. This is very much the case with knowledge of the arts.

If, then, we are arguing that it is still possible to read bodily presentation and lifestyles as indicators of social status it is clear that the game is much more complex now. If post-modern points to something it is the eclipse of a particular coherent sense of culture and associated way of life which was dominant in the Western upper and middle classes which set the tone for the culture as a whole. This happens as the historical generations which carried them slowly recede in numbers and influence. Here one thinks of the notion of a common culture as a goal; as based on an educational formative project, as something unified, a totality of knowledge (the classics in literature, music and the arts), which had to be struggled through to improve the person. Along with it went the notion of a cultured or cultivated person, the ideal of a gentleman, the product of a civilizing process (Elias, 1978, 1982). The middle and upper classes in the second half of the nineteenth century were prime carriers of this cultural ideal and sought to extend it through museums and educational institutions.

Since the 1960s the process of cultural de-classification has seen the decline and relativization of this ideal. The question is whether these tendencies, which have been labelled post-modern, merely point to a collapse of an established hierarchy, a temporary phase, a cultural intermezzo of intensified competition, varied standards and value complexes, before a re-monopolization by a new establishment. Or should we see the extension of the current tendencies *ad infinitum* – the end of history? In this context it is salutary to refer to similar historical ages of cultural turmoil and incoherence. If it is proclaimed today that there is no fashion, only fashions, then we should bear in mind that Simmel discovered similar tendencies in Florence around 1390 when the styles of the social elite were not met with imitation and each individual sought to create his own style. Fashion and other lifestyle pursuits, to use Simmel's metaphor, are used as 'bridges and doors' to unite and exclude. If these functions appear to decline does it mean that we are merely in a temporary intermezzo? Or does the extension of the game to draw more groups, cultures and nations into a widened global system mean that the conditions for particular dominant elites to exercise global hegemony over taste and culture are destroyed with the unlikelihood of foreseeable re-monopolization, thus pointing us towards a historical development in which some of the impulses detected and labelled post-modern may become more widespread?

REFERENCES

Bann, S. (1984) *The Clothing of Clio: a Study of Representations of History in Nineteenth Century Britain and France*. Cambridge: Cambridge University Press.

Baudrillard, J. (1981) *For a Critique of the Political Economy of the Sign*. St Louis: Telos Press.

Baudrillard, J. (1982) The Beaubourg effect: implosion and deterrence. *October*, 20.

Baudrillard, J. (1983a) *Simulations*. New York: Semiotext(e).

Baudrillard, J. (1983b) *In the Shadow of the Silent Majorities*. New York: Semiotext(e).

Bauman, Z. (1988) Is there a postmodern sociology? *Theory, Culture and Society*, 5(2-3).

Bennett, T. (1988) The exhibitionary complex. *New Formations*, 4.

Berman, M. (1982) *All that Is Solid Melts into Air*. New York: Simon and Schuster.

Bourdieu, P. (1984) *Distinction: a Social Critique of the Judgement of Taste*. London: Routledge and Kegan Paul.

Bourdieu, P. (1987) The forms of capital. In J. G. Richardson (ed.), *Handbook of Theory and Research for the Sociology of Education*. New York: Greenwood Press.

Boyer, M. C. (1988) The return of aesthetics to city planning. *Society*, 25(4).

Burris, V. (1986) The discovery of the new middle class. *Theory and Society*, 15.

Calefato, P. (1988) Fashion, the passage, the body. *Cultural Studies*, 2(2).

Chambers, I. (1987) Maps for the metropolis: a possible guide to the postmodern. *Cultural Studies*, 1(1).

Chaney, D. (1983) The department store as a cultural form. *Theory, Culture and Society*, 1(3).

Chaney, D. (1990) Dystopia in Gateshead: the Metrocentre as a cultural form. *Theory, Culture and Society*, 7(4).

Cooke, P. (1988) Modernity, postmodernity and the city. *Theory, Culture and Society*, 5(2-3).

Cooke, P. and Onufrijchuk, I. (1987) Space, the final frontier . . . Unpublished paper.

Crane, D. (1987) *The Transformation of the Avant-garde*. Chicago: Chicago University Press.

Davis, M. (1985) Urban renaissance and spatial postmodernism. *New Left Review*, 151.

Del Sapio, M. (1988) The question is whether you make words mean so many different things: notes on art and metropolitan languages. *Cultural Studies*, 2(2).

DiMaggio, P. (1986) Can culture survive the marketplace? In *Non-profit Enterprise in the Arts*. Oxford: Oxford University Press.

DiMaggio, P. (1987) Classification in art. *American Sociological Review*, 52(4).

Douglas, M. and Isherwood, B. (1980) *The World of Goods*. Harmondsworth: Penguin.

Elias, N. (1978) *The Civilizing Process. Volume I: The History of Manners*. Oxford: Blackwell.

Elias, N. (1982) *The Civilizing Process. Volume II: State Formation and Civilization*. Oxford: Blackwell.

Featherstone, M. (1991) *Consumer Culture and Postmodernism*. London: Sage.

Feifer, M. (1985) *Going Places*. London: Macmillan.

Fisher, M., Bianchini, F., Montgomery, J. and Warpole, K. (1987) *Cities and City Cultures*. Birmingham: Birmingham Film and Television Festival.

Foucault, M. (1977) *Discipline and Punish*. Harmondsworth: Penguin.

Frisby, D. (1985) *Fragments of Modernity*. Cambridge: Polity Press.

Garnham, N. (1987) Concepts of culture, public policy and the culture industries. *Cultural Studies*, 1(1).

Goudsblom, J. (1987) On high and low in society and sociology. *Sociologisch Tijdschrift*, 13(1).

Harvey, D. (1988) Voodoo cities. *New Statesman and Society*, 30 September.

Horkheimer, M. and Adorno, T. (1972) *Dialectic of Enlightenment*. New York: Herder and Herder.

Horne, D. (1984) *The Great Museum*. London: Pluto Press.

Jackson, P. (1985) Neighbourhood change in New York: the loft conversion process. *Tijdschrift voor economische en sociale geografie*, 74(3).

Jameson, F. (1984) Postmodernism: or the cultural logic of late capitalism. *New Left Review*, 146.

Jencks, C. (1984) *The Language of Postmodern Architecture*. London: Academy.

Kellner, D. (1988) Postmodernism as social theory: some challenges and problems. *Theory, Culture and Society*, 5(2-3).

Lamont, M. and Lareau, A. (1988) Culture capital. *Sociological Theory*, 6(2).

Lash, S. (1988) Discourse or figure? Postmodernism as a regime of signification. *Theory, Culture and Society*, 5(2-3).

Lefebvre, H. (1971) *Everyday Life in the Modern World*. London: Allen Lane.

Lyotard, J. F. (1984) *The Postmodern Condition*. Manchester: Manchester University Press.

Maffesoli, M. (1988) Jeux de masques: postmoderne tribalisme. *Design Issues*, 4(1-2).

Marwick, A. (1988) *Beauty*. London.

Olsen, D. (1986) *The City as a Work of Art*. New Haven, CT: Yale University Press.

Roberts, D. (1988) Beyond progress: the museum and montage. *Theory, Culture and Society*, 5(2-3).

Schwartz, B. (1983) *Vertical Classification*. Chicago: University of Chicago Press.

Shields, R. (1987) Social spatialization and the built environment: the West Edmonton mall. Mimeo, Sussex University.

Silverman, D. (1986) *Selling Culture*. New York.

Simmel, G. (1978) *The Philosophy of Money*. London: Routledge and Kegan Paul.

Simpson, C. (1981) *SoHo: the Artist in the City*. Chicago: Chicago University Press.

Urry, J. (1988) Cultural change and contemporary holiday-making. *Theory, Culture and Society*, 5(1).

Venturi, R., Scott Brown, D. and Izenour, D. (1977) *Learning from Las Vegas: the Forgotten Symbolism of Architecture Form*. Cambridge, MA: MIT Press.

Williams, R (1983) *Towards 2000*. London: Chatto and Windus.

Williams, R. H. (1982) *Dream Worlds: Mass Consumption in Late Nineteenth Century France*. Berkeley: University of California Press.

Wolin, R. (1982) *Walter Benjamin: an Aesthetic of Redemption*. New York: Columbia University Press.

Zolberg, V. (1984) American art museums: sanctuary or free-for-all? *Social Forces*, 63 (December).

Zukin, S. (1987) Gentrification. *Annual Review of Sociology*.

Zukin, S. (1988a) The postmodern debate over urban form. *Theory, Culture and Society*, 5(2-3).

Zukin, S. (1988b) *Loft Living*, 2nd edn. London: Hutchinson/Radius.

14

The Fortress City: Privatized Spaces, Consumer Citizenship

Susan Christopherson

INTRODUCTION

In one view of the contemporary city, urban space is playful space – a realm of spontaneity where the restrictions of locale and time have been lifted to allow the free play of individual creativity. It is also an international mosaic in which diverse communities remind us of the 'global-ness' of contemporary life.[1] This depiction of the urban experience is seductive and at moments even resonates with our experience, but it is also ironic. Beneath the surface, the signal qualities of the contemporary urban landscape are not playfulness but control, not spontaneity but manipulation, not interaction but separation. The need to manage urban space and particularly to separate different kinds of people in space is a pre-eminent consideration in contemporary urban design, matched only by the ever-present requirement to gratify the egos of developers. The soft images of spontaneity are used to disguise the hard reality of administered space.

Because the problems urban developers seek to solve are administrative as well as aesthetic, the design solutions they favour are those tested and proven in other places. Their very appeal lies in their effectiveness regardless of the particularities of place. This central concern for the administration of space is reflected in the replacement of streets by secured skyway systems, in the private airport quarters for business travellers, in the prominence of fences as design elements and in the emergence of 'gated' housing developments as the fastest growing mode of community living.

The expanding documentation of these developments contradicts the notion that the contemporary city is apart from space and time – global and beyond history. The homogeneity of solutions to the problem of spatial 'management' gives the impression of suspension from the particularities of place and time. As responses to contemporary capitalism, however, these solutions are deeply embedded in their age, vivid contemporary demonstrations of 'the spatial consequences of combined social and economic power' (Zukin, 1991). The strong tendencies in contemporary design to 'loosen ties to any specific space' and to paper over 'the intimate undisciplined differentiation of traditional cities . . . with a generic urbanism' (Sorkin, 1992) directly express contemporary political and economic imperatives rather than negating them.

The experience of the contemporary city, with its highly manipulated islands in the midst of anarchistic non-space, cannot be reduced, however, to an impoverished aesthetic or to the oppression of economic forces. The contemporary city reflects choices regarding how to live (however constrained) and thus a particular normative vision of urban life. It also reflects unresolvable conflicts concerning rights and responsibilities. And there are justifiable questions concerning whether new forms of urban development, in fact, create a different urban experience. It would be disingenuous, for example, to suggest that US cities ever functioned in such a way as genuinely to foster interaction and mutuality among people of different races and classes. From the earliest history of US urban settlement, the private realm has taken precedence over the public and separation over interaction.[2] This said, it is still possible to argue that the contemporary city is different from the city of the 1950s and 1960s. One prominent manifestation of this difference is the fortress character of urban development and the intensive administration of urban space. As social disintegration and increasing economic inequality have made the city more dangerous, designs in response to danger, particularly those to secure property, have altered the spatial relationship between public and private, a relationship built around a sense of common ownership and control of the street.

Another major difference derives from dependence on consumption as the primary urban function and source of profit and tax revenues. The centrality of consumption to the contemporary urban experience and the neglect of the city as a home, a place of cultural expression and a political venue have arguably limited our notions of the broader purposes served by urban life. The practice of citizenship, originating in urban experience, is gradually being transformed to emulate consumer behaviour. Also emulating the consumer's world and its increasing emphasis on market segmentation is the fragmentation of political interests into ever more narrowly defined 'communities'. Just as market segmentation makes mass production less feasible, so the emergence of communities of identity undermines the possibility of constructing a coherent 'social rationality'. Although one might recognize and, indeed, celebrate the multiple voices of the city, there have been few attempts to construct a common voice out of multiple communities. In the absence of the will to define and articulate broader common purposes a political vacuum has emerged, a vacuum that has been filled by raw economic power. This is no more apparent than in the built environment.

In this chapter I examine evidence that suggests how the contemporary private and segregated city is different from its predecessors. I also explore the possibility of addressing the problems associated with the segmented, privatized city through the politics of community.

THE POST-FORDIST CITY: CONTINUITY AND INNOVATION

Both the practice and products of urban development in the 1980s were transformed in ways that have reshaped the physical fabric of cities and the urban experience. As has already been suggested, this transformation was the product of political and economic struggles particular to this historical period. The origins of contemporary development schemes can be traced to several widely acknowledged processes, most prominently a changing international spatial division of labour. Business and financial service activities have become concentrated in a small number of countries and urban centres while manufacturing has been redistributed from already industrialized countries to a wide range of international locations. In the UK and USA the new division of labour constructed economies focused on the manipulation of what David Harvey refers to as 'ficticious capital' (debt, speculation, rent) (Harvey, 1982) and contributed to widening income dispersion. The expanding income gap is at the heart of the market segmentation associated with 'post-Fordist' economies.

Concentration on financial transactions and the loss of direct productive activities in the USA and UK was accompanied by a wave of state-sponsored deregulatory measures aimed at freeing up the financial sector. This political policy produced an explosion of financial product innovations and investments in the 1980s, including real estate investment deals (Fainstein, 1994). The character of these urban and suburban development projects is notable for the dominant role played by the private sector in the planning and development process, through, for example, public–private partnerships (Barnekov et al., 1989). Since urban real estate development requires public sector intervention in areas such as infrastructure, regulation and taxation, the development schemes of the 1980s frequently involved innovations in public sector and private sector relations and a blurring of the boundaries between the two spheres.[3] Finally, urban property development in the 1980s was influenced by increasing social divisions and their expression in poverty, homelessness and crime.

Several distinctive types of urban and suburban property development became prominent in response to this new political, social and economic environment. The first was oriented around the needs of the financial and business community, the travelling transactors who manage dispersed business enterprises. The second type of development aimed to capture profits via the now central consumption sphere – catering to differently situated consumer segments. The third was the 'common interest' or 'gated' housing development, the purpose of which is to protect property values by maintaining the social homogeneity of the development, by restricting individual property rights and by providing extensive security and services to commonly held property.

The character of these developments has evoked a strong response from urbanists who see in the contemporary city, including its suburbs, a symbolic and actual loss of the urban sphere as a place which fosters interaction, diversity and social justice (Davis, 1990; Zukin, 1991; Harvey, 1992; Sorkin, 1992; Judd, 1994). From the viewpoint of at least one sceptical observer, however, these critiques are naive and short-sighted. They fail to recognize the enduring private character of US cities and the way in which contemporary urban development reflects genuine preferences. The inauthenticity which many of the critics abhor in these developments is, in fact, a matter of taste rather than moral values (Fainstein, 1994). What looks like an inauthentic 'Disneyland-like' environment to one person may look like fun to another.

It is true that none of the development forms of the 1980s represent a dramatic break with the past. Shopping centres have been around since the 1950s and US housing has historically been segregated through conditions, restrictions and covenants. Still, contemporary developments appear to differ in some important respects. At every design scale, from building to business improvement district, there is emphasis on the control and regulation of human behaviour. In contrast to the personal control exercised in previous periods, for example by police power, this regulation is impersonal and obscured in design and unobtrusive techniques. The geographic scale at which regulation and surveillance occur has expanded from the building to a larger environment (business improvement district, commercial development or shopping mall). To some extent, what is 'new' about these environments has been made possible by technological advances that have allowed more sophisticated and unobtrusive surveillance over larger areas, and design innovations that have perfected the creation of total consumption environments. Even these innovations are the consequence of trial and error over time. That is what makes these environments so remarkably similar to one another.

What is implied in much of the new critical analysis of contemporary urban development, however, is that people's experience of the city and of the relation between city and suburb has been altered. Urbanity has been narrowed and redefined as a consumption experience; the suburban 'gated community' is perceived as a haven in a highly dangerous environment. And, because of the enclosed and guarded nature of much contemporary development, people are hesitant to step outside, to explore other alternatives. The critics raise questions about whether these narrower experiences are reflected in people's values and expectations and in their political behaviour. Thus, the interesting question stimulated by their work is not whether Battery Park is authentic or inauthentic but how its material form and our experience in it influence our ideas of, say, what it means to be a citizen. The interesting question is not about diversity or the lack of it but how diversity is understood. The question is not whether people choose a quiet, safe environment in which to live, work and play but what rules and interventions they are willing to accept in order to ensure that security. What do they understand as the source of the rules that govern their lives if they grow up in the arms of the parent corporation? These questions are, some would say, unanswerable. They are worth probing, however, because they focus our attention on the relationship between material conditions and changes in values and meaning. If nothing else, they help us to become more observant. They help us look closely to see the particular ways in which the old is being made new.

THE CITY AS (INTERNATIONAL) CONSUMERS' WORLD

Diversity, choice and consumer citizenship

Urban development is not a sufficient explanation for the consumer culture but it plays a critical role. Given the concentration of retail facilities in regional and city 'malls' and the loss of locally based retail outlets in cities as well as small towns and villages, the shopping experience has become the urban experience for many people.

One of the interesting twists in the production of contemporary consumption spaces is their relationship to the emergence of multicultural 'communities' and the elevation of cultural 'diversity' to almost religious significance in the USA.[4] At the most primitive level, the selling of diversity and multicultural experience is reflected in the international food courts that now dominate US shopping malls. In gentrified urban neighbourhoods, the conflation of a multicultural experience and consumption is more complex, reflecting a struggle between genuine ethnic culture and that which is manufactured for sale. This commodified version of diversity is not about traditions and needs but about surfaces – colours, styles, tastes, all packaged in easily consumable forms.

The cultivation of a taste for diversity and the market segmentation that accompanies it are most apparent in the food industry, where new food products – arugula, shitake mushrooms, ugli fruit (the list goes on and on) – have been introduced constantly since the early 1980s. These food items can provide the appearance of differentiation and add value to fairly standard preparations. (A salad is a salad, whatever its exotic ingredients.) Some of the most successful chef-entrepreneurs of the 1980s have used the increasing diversity of products to develop high value-added food preparation systems for expensive restaurants. These systems combine forms of food preparation (such as grilling) which require few culinary skills and can use a less skilled kitchen staff with exotic decorative ingredients to create the impression of haute cuisine. These flexible food systems often depend on the 'appropriation and subversion of . . . vernacular traditions' (Zukin, 1991, p. 212). They provide the illusion of skill and create tastes for particular food 'inputs' which can be recombined in various ways.

A consumption-driven definition of diversity is also apparent in the transformation of some urban neighbourhoods, such as Adams Morgan in Washington, DC, which before the 1980s supported a variety of small businesses catering to the local African-American, Ethiopian, Guatemalan and Salvadoran population. In the 1980s, the commercial strip in Adams Morgan evolved to reflect the international 'multicultural' tastes of the new residents, primarily government employees. The conception of cultural diversity in the minds of the new residents is aptly demonstrated by their views on consumables. 'One can purchase banana leaves, cockles in brine, pickled octopus, mangoes, Salvadoran cheese and every conceivable part of a pig in just one grocery store. All I want is a place where I can buy twelve kinds of mustard' (Williams, 1988). In the course of the creation of this sophisticated consumption environment, small locally oriented businesses have been replaced by ethnic restaurants in which the ethnically 'diverse' work but cannot afford to eat and by boutiques whose products they do not need (Weber, 1992).

The underlying notion behind the construction of diversity in market goods is that people crave innovation and want to feel that they are making an individual choice. But people are conservative and will only choose what they already know. In the contemporary consumption space, the range of choices and of real innovation or expression of differentiated skill is actually quite limited. One need only visit the standardized consumption places of the UK (Boots, Mothercare, The Body Shop, Tesco etc.) or the USA (The Gap, CVS Pharmacy, B. Dalton, Sears etc.) to recognize that product innovation and product differentiation occur only within severe limits. Why, then, is the illusion of diversity so powerful? Perhaps it is because feelings of efficacy, of choice, have become concentrated in the consumption sphere as the possibility for other choices has narrowed. The consumer identity has become all-encompassing. That this might be the case is suggested by the widespread use of consumer terminology to describe other types of relationships in society which have been rooted in values that are not exclusively market driven, such as those between student and teacher or between citizen and government.

The conceptualization of politics as analogous to consumption is expressed in both direct and subtle ways. Government officials speak of providing effective services to their 'customers' and of 'consumer choice' in the decisions concerning which policies the government will undertake. Politicians must pretend to divergent opinions, even when they don't hold them, in order to provide the perception of a 'real' choice. To the consumer-citizen, politics is the practice of selecting from a given array of goods, not questioning and compromising to create a good. It is a private, individual process in which pre-existing individual preferences are expressed through votes of various kinds, including through telephone call-ins.

Another effect of consumerist conceptions of politics is the obliteration of the idea of the public good. Issues such as environmental quality, safety and freedom from urban congestion are not conceived of as urban qualities that citizens create but as commodities. Access to these commodities is to be obtained not through citizen action but through consumer rights (Mayer, 1991). The flaw in the application of consumerist thinking to quality of life issues is that environmental quality and safety are public goods that should be accessible to everyone, not commodities that a select group purchases. Public goods constitute one source of a sense of membership in a wider community and so the loss of publicly controlled public goods contributes to a fragmented polity, a kind of political market segmentation.

The redefinition of citizenship as a consumption activity is also a major instrument for effecting change in the perception of values behind social institutions. So school vouchers are not just about efficiency but about the privileging of individual 'consumer' values over those of 'the common good'. When the celebration of consumer values is combined with a limited domain of discussion in the public sphere the result is a limited sphere of public action for larger social purposes. This is particularly pernicious with respect to claims to social justice. Normative claims to social justice such as those for universal health care or for the homeless are equated with particularistic claims (for the insurance industry or the American Medical Association). They are all 'special interests'. According to Young (1990, p. 72), this is a 'process that collapses normative claims to justice into selfish claims to desire [and] lacks the element of public deliberation that is a hallmark of the political.'

In addition to these admittedly elusive connections between the urban experience and social and economic roles, there are other, material, alterations in cities manifested in the 'real space' of urban development that are altering our vision of the city and our place in it.

THE CITY AS A MANAGED ENVIRONMENT

The transformation of ethnic neighbourhoods into shopping areas and the rise of an international consumerist 'style' of multiculturalism present one face of the reconstruction of the urban experience. The control and construction of urban experience is even more apparent in the spaces designed originally and specifically around consumption and commerce. Two processes are apparent in the design and management of these spaces. The first is a reconstruction of scale (Herod, 1993; Smith, 1990). The second is the loss of the tension and interest of the street which has always been central to a conception of a lively urban life. In Jane Jacobs's urban world, for example, the street is 'the medium in which the totality of modern material and spiritual forces could meet, clash, interfuse and work out their ultimate meanings and fates' (Berman, 1982). The street is neither public nor private but at the intersection of both.

Streets such as those in the East Village in New York City or Melrose Avenue in Los Angeles are highly functionally differentiated building to building. They are disturbing and provocative, effects produced by the juxtaposition of apparently contradictory uses: nursing homes with disapproving old people sitting on the porch, adjacent to sleazy boutiques, adjacent to chic boutiques, adjacent to Hasidic Jewish temples, adjacent to public high schools. While these streetscapes continue to exist as sideshows, the dominant design tendency is to construct larger, highly managed commercial and consumption environments. These mesoscale urban environments are designed to insulate and isolate, to buffer and protect so-called 'normal users' in the space. The highly managed character of these spaces is reflected in regulations which govern tenancy, permissable activities and environmental design. Thus, the character of these spaces is as much defined by what is excluded as by what is included.

There are many examples of buffered and isolated mesoscale urban spaces organized around a set of functions oriented to the business traveller or commercial tenant and intended to separate this 'person as profit centre' from the urban environment. These places include Bunker Hill in Los Angeles, the Renaissance Center in Detroit, Harbor Place in Baltimore, Battery Park in Manhattan and Peach Tree Center in Atlanta. Although similar types of developments exist in the UK, the city is not as threatening and so the designs are not as distinctive in their inaccessibility. It has not been necessary to take Draconian measures to separate the commercial traveller from the street.

The quintessential features of these environments are separation from the larger urban environment, limited pedestrian access, multilevel functionally integrated spaces through which users are channelled via walkways and high levels of security. Although these spaces may provide spectacle – puppet shows, musical performance, fashion shows – all activities are programmed and intended to enhance the central uses of the space.

The predecessor of these spaces is, of course, the shopping centre or mall, whose influence on every aspect of American experience has only begun to be documented (Kowinski, 1985). The success of the shopping centre as a model for American urban space reflects the continuing preference for private, segregated space that has always animated US urban design. It has not been without tensions, however. There is always an undercurrent celebrating the disorderly city, and the uses of a non-commodified public sphere. In many cases, the rejection of contemporary consumer urbanism takes negative forms: the glazed eye expressions of boredom in response to highly controlled and managed urban spaces. There is always, too, a sense that these single-minded urban places are not really urban even when they are located in the city proper. They do not offer the kinds of spontaneous, unexpected, various expressions of life that were associated with 'the urban'. The mall, instead, emulates the suburban house. 'It looks inward, turning its back on the public street . . . and reflecting a profound mistrust of the street as a public arena' (Crawford, 1992, p. 21).

The pervasiveness of the mall as the urban environmental model has been extended to more conventional urban spaces through such mechanisms as business improvement districts.[5] Downtown business owners who must compete with the safe and managed shopping experience of the malls devised the business improvement district as a way to emulate the controlled conditions and comprehensive management of the mall. They define a significant portion of the central city, typically fifty to a hundred blocks, in order to create 'downtown as mall' (Mallett, 1993).

Because business improvement districts are not wholly private, that is they incorporate and make use of public facilities and services, such as streets, sewers and police, they are a stronger manifestation of the reworking of public and private space than the private mall itself. They are a creative and selective response to the inability of local government to maintain the urban environment and demonstrate the possibilities of transforming and managing 'public space' for private ends. In the 1990s, this management of urban space has replaced redevelopment as a primary objective of business. For most business improvement districts, actual physical improvements compose a minuscule portion of their budget. Emphasis is instead placed on services, such as cleaning and policing. One important aspect of emulating the mall experience is to rid the business improvement district of the homeless and deinstitutionalized mentally ill through design, daily regulation and longer-term solutions such as displacement to the urban fringe (Mair, 1986).

Another manifestation of the reworking of public and private spaces in the contemporary American city is the creation of spaces which are designated as public but privately controlled and managed for private purposes: again, the stimulation of consumption. As in the case of business improvement districts, the development of privately developed and held 'public' space reflects, in part, the inability of local governments to maintain public spaces, including parks. The increasing poverty and social pathology evident in publicly controlled urban public spaces has also driven a demand for open spaces which are regulated to exclude threatening people. Approximately 40 per cent of all office space ever constructed in the USA was built during the 1980s, a substantial portion in central cities. There were, therefore, many opportunities to take advantage of incentives to provide 'public space' in conjunction with commercial space. Developers welcomed this opportunity, realizing that 'open space reinforces retail activity. Food brings people. Open space contributes to tenant retention and a slightly higher rental rate' (Loukaitou-Sideris, 1993a).

A study of privately controlled public space in Los Angeles suggests many features in common with private shopping mall space (Loukaitou-Sideris, 1993b) . Designs are inwardly oriented, with high enclosing walls, blank facades, distancing from the street and obscured street level access. These 'public open spaces' are effectively disconnected from the surrounding city. The activities that can take place in these spaces are severely restricted. There is no provision for children to play, for example. All the spaces are oriented to a specific clientele: workers in the vicinity and shoppers. This allows the owners of adjacent commercial space, in effect, to capture a particular segment of the market and orient other marketing strategies to that segment.

That it is not simply the privatization of space that is responsible for single-minded useage is demonstrated by such older privately provided public places as the Rockefeller Plaza in New York City, developed in the 1930s. This space has attracted people for decades, especially to watch skaters on the ice rink in the winter. Unlike the contemporary consumption-oriented privately provided public spaces, the Plaza is closely integrated into the urban fabric.

The management of private space for private purposes would not be as debilitating if there continued to be places and opportunities for a wide range of human activities. The most obvious of these types of places – parks where children can play safely and where neighbours can meet and talk – are, in the contemporary city, dangerous or neglected. In California, 41 per cent of park districts have eliminated facilities or reduced hours since the late 1970s. These cutbacks have particularly impacted upon urban areas where the need for public open space is most severe (Loukaitou-Sideris, 1993b). Both security and other risks and the maximization of property values create strong incentives to limit the clientele for such public and quasi-public facilities, such as libraries or churches, to 'normal users' or those willing to pay to use the space for a 'reasonable' time. These restrictions contribute to the diminution of diverse options for urban life. The conception of 'free spaces', for example, depends on the maintenance of a sense of urban life that, while it may take place in profit-making establishments, somehow enlarges the purposes of those establishments beyond monetary transactions.

While intensified commodification plays a central role in the reconfiguration of urban space, the ability to maintain property values and derive profits in the contemporary city is equally related to security. Here again, the need for control leads to a homogenized and administratively segregated urban environment.

THE DESIGN OF AVOIDANCE

Like the intensified commodification of the urban environment, the concern for security demonstrates the extent to which contemporary US cities reflect rather than deny a specific historical context. The work of architect Frank Gehry exemplifies the way in which high style architectual design has an underlying message about the fortress mentality in cities like Los Angeles, his home base. The recently constructed Hollywood branch library, designed by Gehry, reflects these design principles. The building, constructed of concrete block, is surrounded by a ten-foot iron fence and concrete berm. Tiled sculptures along the walls prevent people from having direct access to the exterior surface of the building. There are no street level windows to provide a clue to the building's use or visual accessability to library users; no benches or steps on the building exterior to provide a place to rest or talk. While his design fulfils the commission for a vandal-proof structure, it also alters the meaning of a 'public' building, a staging place for social interaction.

Contemporary defensive design responds to the connection between profit and safety. It also reflects an awareness that property values are significantly affected by security. In contemporary cities the security of property is of more concern than the safety of people. For example, since the Los Angeles riots in spring 1992, dozens of neighbourhoods in Los Angeles have demanded the right to fence themselves off from the rest of the city, to become gated communities. The reason is not primarily personal safety but the protection of equity. Realtors in Southern California estimate that 'gatedness' can raise home values by as much as 40 per cent over ten years (Davis, 1993).

There is no doubt that the new fortress-like environments respond to some version of consumer preferences. The commercial traveller, for example, is not interested in sociability or the experience of ethnic diversity but in a predictable, secure place in which to purchase goods or services and to transact business. And since, in many cities, newly created environments, such as Harbor Place in Baltimore, cater to this market segment, their design strongly emphasizes separation from the larger urban environment and the prevention of customer 'leakage' to the outside world. These developments follow the precepts of 'crime prevention through environmental design' (CPTED), which specifically advocates the design of buildings and larger environments to limit access to 'normal' users of the space and to buffer and protect those users once they are in the space. In contrast with earlier ideas of defensible space, such as those derived from Jane Jacobs's 'eyes on the street', which associated safety with residence, CPTED is oriented towards 'users' of a space, particularly customers. So CPTED differentiates 'the values of various users' in determining whether they should be given access to the space or excluded (Crowe, 1992).[6]

The street – the venue for interaction – has been abandoned to the unhoused, the poor and the undesirable, the unprofitable. In the course of this change the boundaries between public and private space have been reworked. The street is no longer perceived as public in the sense that it is owned by all people who use it. Its role as an in-between, liminal space – a place for conversation, cafes and casual interaction (people-watching) – has been stripped away. The street has become a gauntlet to run between safe places. Activities that once took place on the street are displaced to privately maintained spaces such as business complex atria. In these territories, the responsibility for the safety and security of all who use the space lies with the property owner, not with the user.

By extension, it is the property owner who must extend the concept of territoriality to that liminal space outside his door, thereby protecting his clientele. In its mildest form, this function is served by symbolic barriers: plantings, paving, signage. In many areas of contemporary US cities, these subtle reminders are not sufficient, perhaps because of the inability or unwillingness of passers-by to interpret their meaning. The next two levels employed are organized security, through personnel, and mechanical control – locks and mechanical visual surveillance. The purpose of these measures is to establish a hierarchy of public to private space under the control of the property owner. In cities such as Newark, New Jersey, the scale of surveillance has been extended to the entire portion of the city traversed by the commercial user and consumer. Grants from the federal government have allowed a selected number of cities to set up video surveillance posts throughout a 'protected' downtown area. Swivelling video cameras high above the street capture every human move for a police surveillance team located at a central command post. This surveillance is an aspect of city government participation in public–private partnerships with developers. In contrast, those spaces where property values are not dependent on safety, such as parking lots, are increasingly 'owned' by no one. They have become the no man's, and even more so the no woman's, lands of the city.

In the process of creating this piecemeal spatial mosaic of the safe and the unsafe, the larger hierarchy of public and private, in which the street played a central role, has been all but destroyed. The city has, instead, come to be dominated by security cages and a honeycomb of residential and business fortresses. This urban environment, which

Fainstein (1994, p. 226) describes as 'paradoxically neither coherent nor diverse', is, in some part, the result of an urban politics which is diverse but incoherent. The reason for this loss of coherence, of common purpose, can be traced to political market segmentation and to a sense of the city as a place composed of multiple communities.

BEYOND THE COMMUNITY AND BACK TO THE CITY

One important reflection of change in the way the city is perceived is the redefinition of 'the local'. Community – ethnic, identity or like-minded – has replaced city as 'the local' in the policy lexicon. The change is not simply semantic. The celebration of community, difference and multiplicity has replaced old ideas of urban politics. The elevation of community, however, like much else in politics, is double-edged. On the one hand, the recognition of multiple perspectives and values represents a striving for more authentic representation. It also represents a revaluation of the particular over the universal and a consciousness of multiple rationalities – good ideas. On the other hand, the idea of community poses some paradoxes for those who strive for an inclusive sense of social justice. As Harvey suggests, 'if we accept that fragmented discourses are the only authentic discourses and that no unified discourse is possible, then there is no way to challenge the overall qualities of a social system' (Harvey, 1992, p. 594).[7]

In addition, the notion of community identity and autonomy can be used in regressive ways. Within the new localist idiom, communities are self-sustaining and depend on private rather than public action. While communities can be portrayed as nurturing and an antidote to an interventionist state, they can also be held responsible for the violence with which they are afflicted and for their own safety and security. The walled-in neighbourhoods of Los Angeles, protected by private 'armed response', are one contemporary expression of how community action can ultimately work to the detriment of a wider public good.

Given the difficulties in overcoming barriers to building an enlarged sense of community in the contemporary city it is useful to look at some examples in which groups of citizens have managed to do just that. These examples demonstrate that it is possible to move towards common social purpose through normative ideals of participation and interaction across the boundaries of narrowly defined communities. The possibilities for this move back to the city from the community lie in the ability of communities and identity groups to define their agendas and the 'good' for which they strive to encompass a wider public good. In this process, traditional political institutions such as coalitions are used but their purpose is altered. A key to the appeal of these efforts is that they have addressed concrete problems in real urban space, problems of accessibility and safety, housing and transportation.

The ability to transcend narrow community boundaries can even extend to groups which primarily identify their agendas in terms of rights. This ability is exemplified by planning and urban design projects sponsored and promoted by disabled groups in many US cities. The Americans with Disabilities Act establishes the rights of disabled people to access to facilities and services. This political achievement is a classic example of rights assertion by an identity group. Some members of the disabled 'community', however, have effectively extended their fight for specific rights to a more general discussion of how accessible environmental design serves the public good. They point out that all people are 'disabled' at one point or another in their lives because of child transport responsibilities, injury and age. Arguments for access-sensitive design by groups such as Whole Access in California have broadened support for their initiatives to a much broader community of citizens (Woodbridge, 1989).

Another example which demonstrates how an enlarged community can be created out of a rights-based movement has been documented in Toronto (Wekerle, 1993). The ability of Toronto feminists to construct a wider community and a public sphere reflects an understanding of the city as a whole, one which extends beyond the interests of the feminist community to a wider public. Although Toronto feminists began with an agenda that defined a safe city as a feminist issue, they soon found themselves with unexpected allies from outside their 'community'. The extension of their political interaction led to an increase in their political strength relative to feminist issues but also to an expansion of their agenda, incorporating concerns that extended across the city, such as housing and public transport. In the course of this effort the feminist participants not only questioned conventional sources of expertise but also learned the skills of political interaction across community boundaries. Political concerns were redefined beyond the communities to include the wider urban citizenry and the city was redefined as a political space.

Along with recognizing how interest-based communities can redefine their goals to construct a genuine urban agenda, we also need to recognize more clearly the limits of identity politics in achieving social justice in the city. Attempts, for example, to 'humanize' homeless people depend on appeals to a sense of connection, a sense that 'these people are like me'. Or, if the poor and homeless are different, my ethnical survival depends on their well-being. Ironically, to humanize is to appeal to the common sense of humanity rather than to the particular. We don't see any T-shirts printed with 'It's a homeless thing. You wouldn't understand.'

Ultimately, cities serve a different purpose in society from like-minded 'communities'. Our experiences of the city and in the city shape our ability to understand and resolve differences across the fault lines of widely variant life experiences and values, to create a larger community. This critical political role has been neglected in analyses of the urban condition which reduce urban functions to economic functions and disguise the political content of economic policies at all levels of government.

To recover the city as the first place of politics we need to recover a sense of how economics and politics are interrelated in real space and time. We also need to understand, in a dialectical way, how politics has shaped the contemporary city and affected our willingness and ability to construct consensus and take collective action. To the extent that the spaces within which we interact limit our experience they also limit our potential to develop a politics that supports social citizenship. According to Iris Young (1990, p. 240),

> Politics, the critical activity of raising issues and deciding how institutional and social relations should be organized, crucially depends on the existence of spaces and forums to which everyone has access. In such public spaces people encounter other people, meanings, expressions, issues, which they may not understand or with which they do not identify.

The city has historically provided the context within which we interact with strangers, and encounter the unknown other. Cities are the places in which we construct a wider social identity and shared meanings beyond those of family and tribe. They provide the avenues through which we come to understand 'the needs of strangers' and the nature of our obligations to them (Ignatieff, 1985). To the extent that the city mirrors social life the nature of our encounters and the meaning we attach to them will differ over time. This will, in turn, be reflected in how we define citizenship, its practices and responsibilities.

NOTES

I am much indebted to Todd Swanstrom for helpful discussions and advice.

1   This depiction of the urban condition is specific to the United States but aspects of it apply to Anglo-American countries.

2 'Each of them, living apart, is as a stranger to the fate of all the rest; his children and his private friends constitute to him the whole of mankind. As for the rest of his fellow citizens, he is close to them, but does not see them; he touches them but does not feel them; he exists only in himself and for himself alone; and if his kindred still remain to him, he may be said at any rate to have lost his country' (de Tocqueville, 1973).

3 This process in and of itself had implications for the democratic decision-making process, compromising the ability of the public sector to represent the public interest in the development process and forcing conflicts of interests into the court system. Public oversight of development alternatives, including opportunity costs, was narrowed.

4 The sacredness of cultural diversity is one of a set of secular religious ideas – including the politics of meaning and the search for 'quality' through total quality management – which have become pervasive in contemporary American culture as ways to obscure economic change and the inequalities and hardships it has wrought. For versions of the same ideas in an earlier period, see (Lears, 1981).

5 Business improvement districts are areas where some form of revenue generation is enforced to provide services not supplied by the municipality (Mallett, 1993).

6 See Jeffrey (1971) for a discussion of the relationship between crime and environmental design. For a recent perspective, see Atlas (1991).

7 I was reminded of this paradox when working on the US–Mexican border. I was told by many Americans that Mexicans were poor because 'they are different from us. Besides, they have their community to rely on.'

REFERENCES

Atlas, R. (1991) The other side of CPTED. *Architecture and Security*, 35, 63–6.

Barnekov, T., Boyle, R. and Rich, D. (1989) *Privatism and Urban Policy in Britain and the United States*. Oxford: Oxford University Press.

Berman, M. (1982) *All That Is Solid Melts into Air: the Experience of Modernity*. New York: Simon and Schuster.

Boddy, T. (1992) Underground and overhead: building the analogous city. In M. Sorkin (ed.), *Variations on a Theme Park: the New American City and the End of Public Space*. New York: Noonday Press.

Crawford, M. (1992) The world in a shopping mall. In M. Sorkin (ed.), *Variations on a Theme Park: the New American City and the End of Public Space*. New York: Noonday Press.

Crowe, T. (1992) The secure store: a clean, well-lighted place. *Security Management*, March, 22–4.

Davis, M. (1990) *City of Quartz*. London: Verso.

Davis, M. (1993) Beyond Blade Runner: urban control, the ecology of fear. *Open Magazine*, no. 23.

Fainstein, S. S. (1994) *The City Builders*. Oxford: Blackwell.

Harvey, D. (1982) *The Limits to Capital*. Chicago: University of Chicago Press.

Harvey, D. (1989) *The Condition of Postmodernity*. Oxford: Blackwell.

Harvey, D. (1992) Social justice, postmodernism and the city. *International Journal of Urban and Regional Research*, 16, 588–601.

Herod, A. (1993) Towards a labor geography: the production of space and the politics of scale in the east coast longshore industry, 1953–1990. Unpublished PhD dissertation, Rutgers University, New Brunswick, NJ.

Ignatieff, M. (1985) *The Needs of Strangers*. New York: Viking.

Jeffrey, R. (1971) *Crime Prevention through Environmental Design*. Beverly Hills, CA: Sage.

Judd, D. (1994) The rise of the new walled cities. In H. Liggett and D. Perry (eds), *Representing the City*. Newbury Park, CA: Sage.

Kowinski, A. (1985) *The Malling of America*.

Knox, P. (1991) The restless urban landscape: economic and socio-cultural change and the transformation of metropolitan Washington, DC. Mimeo.

Lears, T. J. (1981) *No Place of Grace: Antimodernism and the Transformation of American Culture, 1880–1920*. New York: Pantheon Books.

Logan, J. and Molotch, H. (1987) *Urban Fortunes: the Political Economy of Place*. Berkeley and Los Angeles: University of California Press.

Loukaitou-Sideris, A. (1993a) The negotiated plaza: design and development of corporate open space in downtown Los Angeles and San Francisco. *Journal of Planning Education and Research*, 13(1), 1–12.

Loukaitou-Sideris, A. (1993a) Privatization of public open space. *Town Planning Review*, 64(2), 139–67.

Mair, A. (1986) The homeless and the post-industrial city. *Political Geography Quarterly*, 5(4), 351–68.

Mallett, W. (1993) Managing the post-industrial city. *Area*

Mayer, M. (1991) Politics in the post-Fordist city. *Socialist Review*, 21(1), 105–24.

Sennett, R. (1974) *The Fall of Public Man*. New York: Random House.

Smith, N. (1990) *Uneven Development: Nature, Capital and the Production of Space*, 2nd edn. Oxford: Blackwell.

Soja, E. W. (1990) *Postmodern Geographies: the Reassertion of Space in Critical Social Theory*. New York: Verso.

Sorkin, M. (1992) *Variations on a Theme Park: the New American City and the End of Public Space*. New York: Noonday Press.

Tocqueville, A. de (1973) *Democracy in America, Volume 1*, trans. H. Reeve. New York: Alfred A. Knopf.

Wekerle, G. (1993) Feminist movement groups as agents of change in the local state. Mimeo, Faculty of Environmental Studies, York University, Ontario.

Weber, R. (1992) Retailing ethnicity: gentrification and the quest for diversity in Adams-Morgan. Unpublished manuscript, Department of City and Regional Planning, Cornell University, Ithaca, NY.

Williams, B. (1988) *Upscaling Downtown: Stalled Gentrification in Washington, DC*. Ithaca, NY: Cornell University Press.

Wilson, E. (1990) *The Sphinx in the City: Urban Life, the Control of Disorder, and Women*.

Woodbridge, S. (1989) Design by community. *Landscape Architecture*, October.

Young, I. (1990) *Justice and the Politics of Difference*. Princeton, NJ: Princeton University Press.

Zukin, S. (1991) *Landscapes of Power: from Detroit to Disneyworld*. Berkeley: University of California Press.

Index